DATE DUE

DEMCO 38-296

World Economic Primacy: 1500 to 1990

World Economic Primacy: 1500 to 1990

Charles P. Kindleberger

Ford International Professor of Economics, Emeritus
Massachusetts Institute of Technology

New York   Oxford
OXFORD UNIVERSITY PRESS
1996

Oxford University Press

Oxford   New York
Athens   Auckland   Bangkok   Bombay
Calcutta   Cape Town   Dar es Salaam   Delhi
Florence   Hong Kong   Istanbul   Karachi
Kuala Lumpur   Madras   Madrid   Melbourne
Mexico City   Nairobi   Paris   Singapore
Taipei   Tokyo   Toronto

and associated companies in
Berlin   Ibadan

Copyright © 1996 by Oxford University Press, Inc.

Published by Oxford University Press, Inc.,
198 Madison Avenue, New York, New York 10016

Oxford is a registered trademark of Oxford University Press

Library of Congress Cataloging-in-Publication Data
Kindleberger, Charles Poor, 1910–
World economic primacy : 1500–1990 / by Charles P. Kindleberger.
p. cm.   Includes bibliographical references and index.
ISBN 0–19–509902–8 (cloth)
1. Economic history.   I. Title.
HC51.K49   1996
330.9—dc20   95-10091

3 5 7 9 8 6 4 2

Printed in the United States of America
on acid-free paper

In Memory of the Pantheon of Greats
(far) under whom I served:
Omar N. Bradley
William L. Clayton
George C. Marshall
Allan Sproul

Foreword

This book by Professor Charles Kindleberger on world economic primacy grew out of a larger, long-term project launched by the Luxembourg Institute for European and International Studies (I. E. I. S.) in 1990 on "The Vitality of Nations." The purpose of this project is to look, using a multidisciplinary and multinational approach, at the issue of the rise and decline of countries. The project distinguishes among four analytical stages: assessing, explaining, forecasting, and prescribing.

Within this project there have been eight major conferences on countries, regions, or specific issues. After two conferences in Luxembourg and at Harvard University of a more general character, there have been meetings on specific topics: "The Vitality of Central and Eastern Europe," "The Vitality of Japan," "The Vitality of Britain," and "The Vitality of the Netherlands." Finally there have been two conferences on the topic of books to be prepared in the framework of the project, the first at Harvard, which concerned Professor Kindleberger's book, and which brought together some 40 eminent scholars, above all, economic historians, and a workshop in London prepared by Christopher Coker on "The Decline of the Western Alliance: A Cultural Perspective."

In mid-May 1995 there will be a further conference to discuss the work of David Landes, "The Wealth and Poverty of Nations: Why Some Are Rich and Some Poor," to be followed by workshops on "The Vitality of Russia"; "The Vitality of City-States"; "The Significance of Chinese Immigrants in the Vitality of Some Asian Countries"; "The Importance of Nurturing in the Vitality of Nations"; "The Vitality of Spain"; and "The Vitality of Asia: A Cultural Perspective."

Professor Kindleberger is the first to write a major study in the context of this project. His book ranges from the Italian city-states through the Low Countries and Britain to the United States and Japan. During these centuries, there have been times when there was a clear economic leader, and times of uncertainty about world economic primacy. His study focuses not just on individual countries, but also on important general and theoretical considerations, e.g., national cycles and successive primacies. It addresses important questions about the external as well as the internal causes of decline.

This book comes out at a time when many people are questioning the future economic leadership, at a moment when the United States remains the only superpower, yet is increasingly less able to impose its political and economic rules; a time when Japan remains an important challenger but seems to be unable to assume the role of world economic leader; when Germany continues to rise yet also remains vulnerable and limited in its global reach; when the European Union appears, despite its plan for an EMU and a CFSP, to be unable to become a decisive player in world politics; and when nobody can say with any certainty where China will stand politically and economically in 15 or 20 years.

Charles Kindleberger's book provides a brilliant overview of the position of nations in the world economy of the past centuries and also conveys profound insights into the cause for the economic rise and decline of countries.

A. Clesse
Director of the I. E. I. S.
Luxembourg

Acknowledgments

As always, I have benefited in high degree from scholarly cooperation. A number of friends have sent me copies of books they have written or edited: Moses Abramovitz, Rondo Cameron, Rudiger Dornbusch, Barry Eichengreen, Gerald Feldman, Ryutaro Komiya, Henry Nau, Henry Rosovsky, Peter Temin, and Shigeto Tsuru. Reprints, draft papers, references, and information have come from Christos Athanas, Carolyn Shaw Bell, Daniel Bell, Paul David, Robert Forster, Robert Gordon, Koichi Hamada, Peter W. Klein, Dr. Philip LeCompte, Joel Mokyr, Patrick O'Brien, William Parker, Jack Powelson, and Va Nee L. van Vleeck.

A considerably heavier hand was laid on Martin Bronfenbrenner, who read chapter 11 on Japan in draft, but cannot be blamed for my inability to come close to his matchless understanding of the issues in that country. Paul Hohenberg read the entire manuscript with a critical eye and encouraged me enormously, especially in failing to criticize some stretches of the early text. Karen Smith, a graduate student in history at Harvard, tracked down a slew of elusive references, along with Keith Morgan, the reference librarian of MIT's Dewey Library. The conversion of my two-finger typing, replete with strikeovers and illegible insertions, to flawless processed hard copy (if I properly understand the argot) was undertaken at MIT by David Futato, with important help from Emily Gallagher.

The idea for research on "the vitality of nations" comes from Dr. Armand Clesse of the Institute of European and International Studies, Luxembourg. The Institute also provided financial support. A conference on the notion of the changing economic primacy among nations but not on this book was sponsored at Harvard in May 1994. Each participant, I am sure, knew far more than I about some aspects of what I set forth. I hope, perhaps vainly, that not all knew more about all.

I am most grateful for all this assistance, and hope I have not abused it.

Contents

World Economic Primacy: 1500 to 1990

Entrepreneurial activity [in addition to land, labor, and capital] is a necessary ingredient, but not a sufficient one. It is the human vitality of a whole society which, given the opportunity, comes into play and sets loose the "creative response of history."

CARLO M. CIPOLLA, 1986, p. 113

1

Introduction

This book is written as the United States is going through a debate over its world role, both political and economic. Some in political science claim the United States is "bound to lead" (Nye, 1990; Rosencrance, 1990; Nau, 1990). Others, with perhaps more of an eye to history, think nations can and do fall from positions of leadership for one or another reason: foreign policy overstretch (Paul Kennedy, 1987); consolidation of groups looking after narrow parochial interests rather than the public interest (Olson, 1982); slowdown in investment, savings, innovation, overall productivity; a shift of national focus from industry to finance, and in particular financial manipulation. The point is repeatedly made that national decline is relative to other national economies, not absolute, that the country in the lead at a given time gets overtaken by others in a "catching-up" process that is inevitable as knowledge of new goods and new processes spreads from one country to another (Abramovitz, 1990). The process is thought not to apply to less developed or developing countries, but mainly to the developed ones that have what is called, for want of a better term, *social capability*. Thus sociological considerations come into the question along with more purely economic and political ones. The catching-up model explains how, among the leading countries with social capability, differences in national income per capita may narrow, reducing the variance among them. Such has been the case especially since World War II in North America, Europe, and the Pacific Rim, but was not noticeable earlier, partly for lack of reliable data. The model does not explain why individual countries overtake and surpass others in economic primacy, or that the country being caught up with may in some

3

instances decline absolutely. It has not escaped notice that after World War II, first Germany, then France, and most recently Italy overtook Britain in income per capita.

The distinguished historian, Fernand Braudel, asserts that there surely is no such thing as a model of decadence. He objects especially to economists with simple theories of the collapse of vital functions such as public finance, investment, industry, and shipping. "A new model has to be built from the structure of every case" (Braudel, 1966 [1975], p. 1240). I am not so certain, and readers are invited to judge for themselves. I do agree about the simplicity. The model cannot be exclusively economic, and I applaud the statement of Simon Schama, another historian, who would "free the description of early modern culture from its imprisonment in nineteenth-century terminology, especially that which planes down social paradox, contradiction and asymmetry to the smooth surface of an economic model" (1988, p. 568).

My interest is not in who is now "number one," a juvenile question perhaps tolerable in team sport but hardly appropriate for serious discourse. Rather the concern is with long-run economic growth and whether the world economy inevitably gravitates to a hierarchical structure, or whether it maintains the politically more attractive form of pluralism among a number of equals. There is of course a range of compromises with a "first among equals," which shades off into leadership, or economic hegemony as some call it, as the gaps between *primus* and *secundus, tertius,* and so on widen.

Some years ago in a book on the world depression in the 1930s, I suggested that economic leadership imposes burdens on the leader in maintaining international markets for goods, capital, and foreign exchange; in working to coordinate macroeconomic policies; and in acting in crisis as a lender of last resort (Kindleberger, 1973 [1986], chap. 14). My old notebooks reveal an interest in economic decline of earlier vintage, going back to the 1950s and Spain of the Civil War era and earlier. A paper, "An American Climacteric?," appeared as the Golden Age was coming to an end (Kindleberger, 1974), and a lecture on "The Aging Economy" appeared in July 1978 (Kindleberger, 1978 [1990]). The concerns in this book are thus not new to me.

Economic growth has been a subject of intense but largely frustrated interest among economists and economic historians. Decline, whether absolute or relative, has received less attention until the last several decades. Attention started largely with the debate over whether British entrepreneurship had failed and been responsible for the country slipping from its nineteenth-century economic world primacy, or whether the entrepreneurs had encountered unforeseeable obstacles, such as the wrong kind of iron ore for modern technology, or shrinking markets for cotton goods, and therefore should not be faulted. The literature, some of which will be encountered in this book, is voluminous and confused, in that it involved the early application of mathematical economic theory and econometrics to an historical problem. The pioneers were for the most part revisionists, taking a widely accepted historical conclusion and standing it on its head. Revision of an accepted doctrine is a fairly reliable way to make a fast start in academic life. Most of the literature, however, fails to distinguish between static economic theory in which economic actors maximize output for a given cost, minimize cost for a given output, or some of both, and situations calling for dynamic analysis, such as those in which entrepreneurs who encounter obstacles in their profit-making break through them, innovating by developing new processes, new institutions, or new goods. This is more readily done, to be sure, when a company, industry, town, region, or country is starting on the path to economic development, less so when it has traveled a considerable distance along that route and become, if you will, mature, aging, or even sclerotic.

This study is supported by the Institute for European and International Studies of Luxembourg, which is engaged in a wide-ranging investigation of "national vitality." At a conference on the subject in September 1990 there was considerable question among social scientists and historians whether any precise meaning could be given to that term. The hesitation is understandable. Yet as I have read economic, political, and social history after having been sensitized to the term, I have been struck by the number of times one encounters its synonyms and antonyms, equally difficult to define rigorously: as synonyms, adaptive capacity, capacity to transform (i.e., to reallocate resources), creativity, determined responses, dynamism, élan vital, energy, ingenuity, initiative, intelligence, momentum, resilience, responsiveness, suppleness, verve, vigor; and among the opposites: apathy, indolence, languor, lassitude, lethargy, passivity, sloth, torpor. Writing in *The American Challenge*, Jean-Jacques Servan-Schreiber urged his compatriots to avoid "the path of Arab civilization to fatalism and impotence" (1968). Economics uses precise definitions of such concepts as elasticity and inelasticity, dealing with demand and supply responses to price changes, but behind the numbers, which may range from very high to zero and even negative, lie more elusive characteristics of consumers and producers connected with the alacrity and speed with which they respond to economic change. National vitality, it will be claimed, moves in a cycle.

As noted, economic growth is elusive. Many economists and economic historians focus on one or more of its aspects: population, discoveries, investment, technology, institutions, property rights, fiscal policy including taxation and debt, education (investment in human capital), public goods, attitudes toward risk, monopolies with the newly developed branch of "rent-seeking" in which economic actors spend money and effort to gain monopolies from government favors. Studies of the economic growth of particular countries sometimes attempt to cover a range of such aspects in a given country in a given period. Ambitious economic historians such as W. W. Rostow (1960), Alexander Gerschenkron (1962, 1968), and E. L. Jones (1981 [1987], 1988) trace the trajectory of country growth in general and in particular, with "stages," "spurts," or "recurring growth." The present exercise perhaps differs little from their work in ambition and scope, except that it attempts to allow for decline and for relations among growing and declining states in a world hierarchical economic order.

Analogies are as dangerous as in some cases they are beguiling. I suggest that a country's economic vitality goes through a cycle like that of the human individual. Shakespeare's seven stages of man, from "infant, mewling and puking in its nurse's arms" to "old age, sans eyes, sans teeth, sans everything," puts it too strongly, because countries are not exactly born and do not die. The economic trajectory of a country will vary widely from case to case. As a rule it starts slowly, then picks up speed, rockets along for a period, and ultimately slows down, following an S-curve. Other names for this growth pattern are the *logistic curve*, the *curve of material transformation*, the *five-phase product cycle* (Berry, 1991, p. 47), and the *curve of technological maturity*, describing the movement from knowledge-oriented basic research through mission-oriented basic research, applied research, development, and application (Shell Briefing Service, 1991, p. 1). (This last, however, fails to allow for technologies that fall into obsolescence and disuse.)

Like human beings, the growth of a state can be cut off by accident or catastrophe short of old age, that is, it may be stunted by external forces. Unlike human beings, however, economies can have a second birth. New S-curves may grow out of old, as I suggested some years ago in fitting a notional S-curve to the Rostovian stages (Kindleberger, 1958 [1965], p. 56).

To complete the dangerous analogy, modern doctors as a rule specialize in a particular organ system of the human body or type of medicine—heart, lungs, glands, viral disease, pediatrics, geriatrics, but few specialize in the essence of the complete life. Few doctors, apart possibly from psychiatrists, go beyond their specialties into sociology, that is, the relations of their patients to the outside world. In the same fashion, apart from those economists dealing with growth in the large—and some of them describe rather than explain—economists tend to specialize in markets, industry, institutions, and technology.

Many economic historians embrace both economic and social history and seek causes of economic history in elusive aspects of a society such as national character, itself determined by historical, geographic, social and economic conditions. These become especially important when the quest goes beyond a single city, region, or nation into the relations among them, including the question of economic primacy.

I approach economic primacy and its ending for particular countries historically, beginning with the Italian city-states from some uncertain time around 1350, coming to Portugal and Spain to the Low Countries—first Bruges in Flanders, Antwerp in the Brabant, finally the United Provinces with Amsterdam in Holland—to Great Britain, the United States, and finally to the question of the United States' alleged (reputed? actual?) decline. Additional chapters treat France as a perennial challenger; Germany, which twice has aggressively sought its place in the sun; and Japan, which may or

Figure 1-1   "In the race to progress, France is held back by prices." *Source*: Comité pour l'Histoire Économique et Financière de la France, 1989, p. 505.

may not now be a candidate for the role of "number one." As an introduction to the country studies there is first a generalized description of the national cycle or S-curve, including some negative observations on the claim of some analysts that there are long cycles—the Braudel cycle of 150 years, the Kondratieff cycle of 50 to 60 years—and then discussion of the question whether at all or most times a single country stands out as an economic leader or hegemon.

Fernand Braudel and his follower, Immanuel Wallerstein, write in terms of a world center or core, and within Wallerstein's pattern, a periphery and a semiperiphery. Braudel asserts that world economic history is a series of centerings and recenterings, with presumably a decentering between them (1977, p. 185). The view does not go unchallenged: it is claimed that the great deal made in the literature about switches in economic leadership masks how coherent and widespread progress already was in late preindustrial Europe (E. L. Jones, 1981 [1987], p. 236). In a similar view, it is said that this approach to history turns it into a mechanical dog race (W. N. Parker, 1984, p. 226 note). On the other hand, a succession of single national economic leaders has been said to be "a commonplace of history," a statement that fails to signify whether it is true or false (Braudel, 1979 [1984], p. 169). But a race is not a bad metaphor for a social science that rests in great degree on the hypothesis of competition.[1] Writing on the Middle Ages, an historian observed that the European economy at the time of the fairs of Champagne, Geneva, Lyons, and Piacenza in Italy represented "a relay race as one town overtook another and was itself overtaken" (Bautier, 1971, p. 176). As is already apparent, I rely to a great extent on Fernand Braudel, whose masterly studies *The Mediterranean* (1966 [1972]), *Civilization and Capitalism* (1979 [1984]), and *The Identity of France* (1986 [1990]) I use without sufficient historical expertise to judge reliably

[1]The metaphor of a race was evoked by Alfred Sauvy in a comment on the program of Pierre Mendès-France on August 5, 1954, in a pamphlet reproduced as a document in *Etudes et documents* (Studies and documents) (1989), no. 1, pp. 493–524. It is encapsulated in one of many cartoons, showing France handicapped by past inflation in the race against the United States, Germany, and the United Kingdom (p. 505):

the many controversies referred to. Braudel uses the metaphor that "France was out of the race for years to come in the age of Venetian supremacy" (1986 [1990], vol. 2, p. 165) and that England in 1688 was "one jump ahead of the Continent" (ibid., p. 640).

The races described will not be timed with stopwatches. Close dating as to what state was ahead or behind at a particular time is unpersuasive. Historians tend to devote time to isolating "turning points," sometimes sniping at those of others. The essence of history, it seems to me, is its complexity. Monocausal explanations are largely suspect. It is true that social science prefers explanations that are parsimonious, that is, reduced to the fewest and simplest causes. At the same time it recognizes that many effects arise from a long series of "necessary" causes, without any one of which the result would not have occurred, rather than from one or two "sufficient" causes. Aging in a person, and in my judgment in a country, is an endogenous process, but outcomes can be affected by chance, shocks, accident—all exogenous or outside events. History is less social physics, in which cause and effect are tightly linked, than biology, and especially Darwinian evolutionary biology, with chance mutations that wilt or develop depending on random or nearly random circumstances. Chaos theory now recognizes the stochastic element in social (and physical) processes; the nuclei of what later become wide-ranging changes are often difficult or impossible to detect at early stages (C. S. Smith, 1975, p. 605).

For the most part, economic history is preoccupied with the pursuit of wealth. Wealth is not the only motive for economic activity. Henri Pirenne notes that small monetary transactions in the Middle Ages were driven by the desire to satisfy human needs, "and also, no doubt . . . to satisfy that instinct of sociability which is inherent in all men" (1933 [1936], p. 10). Commerce he ascribed to the love of gain and the craving for adventure (ibid., p. 26). The dark side of human nature is stressed by John Nef, who asserts that warlike impulses—fear, hatred, cruelty, revenge, pleasure in destruction and human suffering, together with religious convictions, courage, and the sense of honor aroused by the obligation to fight—are not peculiar to Western people (1952, p. 115). At the same time, a positive force for industrial innovation has been the quest for beauty (C. S. Smith, 1970). Alongside the desire for material gain is the drive for power and prestige, especially noticeable in the French preoccupation with glory. Efficiency and beauty, wealth and prestige are sometimes complements, sometimes substitutes, between which people and countries must choose.

The quest for gain cannot have been said to be general. In the Middle Ages, "the object of labor was not to grow wealthy," for avarice was a sin, but "to maintain oneself in the position to which one was born until life eternal" (Pirenne, 1933 [1936], p. 13). If one insists on looking for a general attribute of human nature, apart from the evil mentioned earlier, it is the spirit of emulation. "Monkey see, monkey do." In *The Theory of Moral Sentiments* Adam Smith states that emulation runs through all ranks of men and has its origin in admiration of the excellence of others (1759 [1808], vol. 1, pp. 113, 270). In *The Wealth of Nations* he goes on: "Rivalship and emulation render excellence, even in mean professions, an object of ambition and frequently occasion the very greatest exertions" (1776 [1937], p. 717). In a statement somewhat limited to technology, Nef connects imitation to "intellectual vitality" (1952, p. 152). An eminent American historian puts it that "personal identification with a group of fellows is the whole basic guide for most behavior" (McNeill, 1992, p. 15). To identify with the rich is one widespread motive, but there are other groups to emulate: poets, painters, musicians, scholars, soldiers, athletes, some of whom are rich as well. Writing on Germany, Thorstein Veblen thought borrowing the achievements of others for their own purposes was a notable characteristic of Baltic peoples, among them Germans (quoted in Dahrendorf, 1965 [1969], p. 41). By way of contrast, Braudel in *The Mediterranean* asserted that "a great civilization can be recognized by its resistance to certain alignments, by its resolute selection among influences offered to it" (1966 [1972], p. 766).

War is an important element in economic growth and decline, and in leadership. Economic conflict is a cause of war, one cause among a number, including religious belief, competition among dynasties, imperialism, and accidents. It is evident that war has impacts on economic growth, and a number of analysts believe that economic growth leads to war by various paths. The question arises in chapter 3 and in particular in the country studies that follow. The relations between war and economic growth are complex and do not permit of simple generation.

War may be the result of "overstretch," ambition that exceeds the capacity of the actor to carry through to his or its goals. Overstretch evokes other apothegms from Adam Smith:

> Examine the record of history, recollect what has happened within the circle of your own experience, consider with attention what has been the conduct of almost all the great unfortunate, either in private or in public life, whom you may have read of, or heard of, or remember; and you will find that the misfortunes of by far the greater part of them have arisen from their not knowing when they were well, when it was proper for them to sit still and be contented. (1759 [1808], p. 351)

> A great source of misery and disorder seems to arise from overrating the difference between poverty and riches; ambition that between a public and private station; vainglory between obscurity and an extensive reputation. (ibid., p. 347)

In his book *Lucien Leuwen*, Stendhal asks "Has any one ever seen a man born rich who did not wish to double his fortune?" (1835 [1960], p. 612). In an earlier work I have applied the concept of overstretch to speculative manias that often ended in financial crises (1978 [1989]). It is difficult not to see its application to individuals such as Philip II of Spain, Louis XIV of France, Napoleon Bonaparte, and Adolph Hitler.

Economic analysis and economic history have lately been concerned with *path dependency*, the impact on economic processes and institutions of events that unfold in particular ways and render the processes and institutions rigid and unalterable. When external conditions change it is frequently difficult, to the point of impossibility, to reshape some institutions that have evolved to accommodate earlier forces. The Coase theorem holds in part that institutions adapt readily to economic needs except when transaction costs—the cost of making the change from one set of institutions to another—are so high as to frustrate a desirable transformation. Old technologies frequently survive alongside new because the marginal cost of using the old—viewing past investment as a sunk cost—must be compared with the average cost of the new, to the advantage in many cases of the former (Salter, 1960). The same holds true in pressures and decisions to scrap or retain old institutions. In consequence, there is danger in forming an opinion on the value of a given institution in any and all circumstances. Monopolies, as Schumpeter insisted, can be efficient, provided that the higher-than-normal profits are reinvested in improved technology and greater capital equipment; the profits, however, may merely go into conspicuous consumption. Again, tariffs may stimulate growth in an economy with substantial vitality, or hasten decline in geriatric rather than pediatric circumstances. Well-defined private property rights, which constitute the driving economic force for economic growth in the analysis of Douglass North and Robert Paul Thomas (1973), and have been given a central role in the privatization movement in Western Europe and the movement from socialism to the market economies in the East, do not constitute a universal solvent. Both tax-farming—private financiers bidding for the right to collect princely taxes—and irrigation schemes that allocate scarce water among thirsty properties, among other examples, require exceptions from the virtually unanimous applause for property rights.

To conclude these broad introductory thoughts, notions, and "animadversions," return for a moment to chaos theory and consider the role of public policy. In the first place are unintended consequences, typically the result of some force or forces that were not considered when a policy decision was taken. Ferdinand and Isabella's financing of Columbus's voyage is perhaps the outstanding example of such a policy decision, but the number of unintended consequences is legion. Second is the question of the efficacy in halting decline of even the most adroit and informed public policy. To return to the human aging analogy, there is little doubt that the aging process can differ widely among persons, depending on good medicine or bad medicine, or even on medicine or no medicine. Economic optimists will favor governmental policies through appropriate spending, spending cuts, taxes, economic credits, subsidies, perhaps even prohibitions and controls; skeptics will be reminded of the post-1973 disappointments in the United States with monetary policy, fiscal policy, the inconclusive debates over industrial and incomes policy, and most recently the failure of the 1981 tax reduction to stimulate personal savings and business investment. In Europe imperative and indicative planning have equally failed to score unalloyed success. Since the Enlightenment, the world has believed less in magic, superstition, and heavenly ordinances and more in cause and effect, but the links in social science are not always tight.

Chaos theory and unforeseen consequences can be joined with loose linkages to yield a wide variety of results from a single cause. One such cause is population pressure. In a society with limited social capability, such pressure results in hunger and high land rents as population grows faster than the food supply—the Malthusian model. In Europe in the Middle Ages, the rise of numbers resulted first in extension of the margin of cultivation into heath, which was plowed; into forests, which were cut down; and into marshes, which were drained, and polders reclaimed from the sea. In modern times in areas with limited land and diminishing returns, continued increases in population have led to cottage industry, as the family tried to keep itself together with the help of traveling merchants who brought raw materials to the home for spinning and weaving and took away and sold cloth. In other situations, young women left the farm for the city to work as servants, youth joined the church as celibate nuns and monks, and young men were recruited for mercenary armies, perhaps Swiss peasants from the mountainside near Berne, first migrating to the Palatinate in Germany as did my patronymic forebear (Braun, 1960 [1965]).

Still other outcomes of population pressure can be found. The standard explanation of the industrial revolution in Britain (about which there is now considerable question) was the rise in population from a succession of good harvests in the 1740s and 1750s that reduced levels of infant mortality because of better nutrition and some decades later drove young people into the cities in search of work (Deane, 1965 [1979], chap. 2). Observing that similar population surges occurred elsewhere in Europe at the same time without the precedent bumper crops, William McNeill has hypothesized that the increases in population came less from the accidents of good weather and rich harvests than from the fact that after long years of intermingling of populations, Europeans had built up immunities to the diseases that had formerly been transmitted by early contact from one continent to another, which led to a fall in the death rate (1976; 1983, pp. 33–38). The rise in numbers broke down the monopolies held by the guilds, and touched off the industrial revolution in Britain and the political revolution in France (McNeill, 1983, pp. 37–38). In another passage McNeill holds that population pressure led England to export goods and France to export armed men (1982 [1984], p. 186).

Other unintended or unanticipated consequences have been adduced by various analysts. In one view, the price revolution of the sixteenth century, with its debated causes of imported silver from Spanish America versus the rise in population at a rate faster than the rate of recovery of agriculture from earlier setbacks, led to the Thirty Years' War (1618–1648) in the Holy Roman Empire; the religious wars in France, starting about 1562; and the Puritan rebellion of the 1640s in England (Reddy, 1987, pp. 25, 53, 82).

This book is more or less organized by countries. Organization poses several questions. First is whether one ought to deal with the various units by "coal" or by "culture," that is, by natural resources on the one hand or by national institutions as shaped by culture on the other. I attempt to do both. Second is the continuous question whether to disaggregate or aggregate, for example to deal with Great Britain and Northern Ireland as a whole, or with England, Scotland, and Wales separately, and even with northwest England (textiles and the Black Country) separately from the rich agricultural southeast. For the most part I aggregate, except that the northern Italian city-states—Venice, Florence, Genoa, and Milan—are dealt with separately, with most attention given to Venice. Third comes a cultural, institutional, historical issue—whether a given country is a unit, with central direction, or pluralistic, perhaps federal, with many centers of initiative and energy. Still a fourth issue turns on class structure and income distribution and what they mean for economic growth and development, including social capability. Over a period of half a millennium, moreover, things change. City-states come to dominate their surroundings and grow into provinces, which in due course join others to form nations. Nations on occasion grow into empires. No doubt I should treat regions, city-states, nations, and empires separately, rather than, as below, handling the subject of growth and decline in all at the "country" level. These social and political evolutionary and revolutionary changes have impacts on economic processes of growth and slowdown. To cram them all into the black box of social capability may be inescapable in the absence of understanding. It explains little.

Readers may find it useful to have a road map and some description of the scenery to be encountered on their journey. First come two chapters of generalizations, chapter 2 on the rise and decline of the single country, chapter 3 on the change from one "country" as world-leading economic center to another, from the declining leader or hegemon to the rising one. There follow eight chapters discussing the rise to economic eminence of the Italian city-states, Spain, the Low Countries, France, Britain, Germany, the United States, and Japan, and their decline. In a few cases the causes of decline are external, such as defeat in war. For the most part the causes pointed to by historians, economic historians, and economists—overstretch, loss of creative capacity, lower savings and investment, foreign competition, and the like—are symptoms of an aging process rather than independent, isolated factors. Resistance to change, rigidity, avoidance of risk, and a redirection of interest from production to consumption and wealth indicate economic aging. It is not readily reversed by even the wisest of policies.

The term *economic primacy* probably deserves a little elucidation. The idea has no simple scalar, such as exists in deciding who or what team is number one in a given sport. Moreover, it can be, but is not necessarily, congruent with political or military or cultural primacy. The United States today can perhaps claim military and even cultural superiority (the latter in the sense of dominance, defined below) but its earlier economic primacy, in my view, is slipping. At times economic power leads to political preeminence, at times the other way round when a country amasses and exploits an empire. But the connections are not linear or simple.

Economic primacy is not measured solely by national income (overall or per capita); rate of growth; the number of innovations and their seminal importance; productivity growth; the level of investment, domestic and/or foreign; control of raw materials, foodstuffs, or fuel; shares in various export markets; holdings of gold and foreign exchange; the use by other countries of its currency as a medium of exchange, unit of account, and store of value. Rather, economic primacy arises from a combination of these and other economic measures, with weights that change with time and place. In particular, the weight of finance has increased in the late twentieth century as countries, especially the United States, have become more fascinated with wealth, the buying and selling of assets rather than goods and services, and capital gains. And relative decline proceeds at different paces in different functions, faster in savings, productivity, and innovation in the United States of late than in the world use of the dollar, for which no adequate substitute has yet been found.

François Perroux, late professor at the Collège de France and director of the Institut Scientifique d'Economie Appliquée, introduced into the discussion the concept of *dominance*. A country, company, or person dominated others when the others had to take account of what the first did, but the first could ignore the others. *Hegemon*, a term used widely by political scientists, comes close to this notion. Economic primacy, at its best, involves less dominance or hegemony than the public good of leadership of the world economy, not ordering others to behave as the leader directs, but pointing the way and convincing others of the desirability of following. This was more true of Britain in the last half of the nineteenth century, and of the United States in the third quarter of the twentieth, than of, say, Spain in the sixteenth century. The United Provinces of the Netherlands in the seventeenth century, though small in comparison with the great powers, led by example, not by military or political power.

There are many concepts like economic primacy—a moral man, good health, a good idea—that cannot be defined rigorously, but most people know what is meant by them. Economic primacy cannot be measured exactly, and, as Lord Elgin said, in such circumstances our knowledge is not completely satisfactory. Despite this, I assert that the idea has meaning, and that in the past, from time to time, perhaps a great deal of the time, economic primacy has had reality.

2

The National Cycle

If it be agreed that there is a life cycle of the human individual, one may ask whether there is a life cycle of a nation. Individuals are born, grow, mature, and die, but new generations follow in their train and may keep the city-state or nation-state on a steady track. Nations may not die, though Fernand Braudel claims that civilizations are mortal (1966 [1975], p. 775). The cyclical idea of history was broached by Spain as early as 1600 (Elliot, 1961 [1970], p. 170). With national economies, economists have pointed to business cycles, and within them the cycle of invention, followed by improvement and stasis (Wijnberg, 1992); a corporate cycle (Mueller, 1988), well illustrated in 1993 by the problems of General Motors, IBM, General Electric, and Sears Roebuck; and, with particular application to manufactured products innovated in one country and then spread abroad, the product cycle (Vernon, 1966). A Spanish historian has even noted a cycle in the guild, an organizational structure encouraged by Ferdinand and Isabella and useful at the start of industrial growth because it helped maintain standards of quality, but ending as "obstruction, oppression and fraud" (Vicens Vives, 1970, p. 142). One modern political scientist refers to a national power cycle (Doran, 1985), another to cycles in war (Bergesen, 1985). Even a literary critic, reviewing Spengler's *Decline of the West*, comments:

> Everything shows an organic rhythm, moving through stages of birth, growth, decline and eventual death. If this happens to all men without exception, there is surely no inherent improbability supposing that the same organic rhythm extends to larger units of life. (Frye, 1974, p. 2)

14

The double negative—no improbability—may not be persuasive, but folk wisdom emphasizes a life cycle in families with a specific time frame—three generations from shirtsleeves to shirtsleeves (in England, from clogs to clogs), a theme that Cipolla extends to countries as well as business: one generation to make a fortune, one to hold it, and the third to dissipate it (1970, p. 12).[1]

Penultimately, before getting down to business, note that the classic economic theorist of the turn of this century, with a wide and deep knowledge of economic history and a biological orientation to economic development, has written, to be sure an aside: "German industry and trade, being younger than British, naturally grew faster: a young boy grows very fast" (Marshall, 1920, p. 139). Over a longer time frame, the idea was expressed by a Spanish professor of jurisprudence in a mock "oration" of 1799:

> All nations of the world, following the steps of nature, have been weak in their infancy, ignorant in their puberty, warlike in their youth, philosophic in their manhood, legists in their old age and superstitious and tyrannical in their decrepitude. (Herr, 1958, p. 333)[2]

And finally, an economic historian a full generation younger than I, Richard Sutch, argued in his presidential address to the Economic History Association in the United States for incorporating a life-cycle perspective into all economic history (1991).

The S-Curve

The S- or Gompertz or logistic curve in Figure 2–1 is taken from the cover of a report on youth in Austin, Texas, and is divided into three stages: children from birth to 8 years of age (mostly off the chart), 8- to 16-year-olds in the middle, and 17- to 25-year-olds at the right. It is not clear what is measured on the vertical axis: perhaps height, although that shoots up in adolescence, and not smoothly; weight, which doubles from birth to 5 months and triples from birth to a year; or some more elusive quality such as capacity to function in society. In the normal life expectancy of, say, 75 years, this leaves a period of a generation peaking in the late forties, with menopause ("climacteric" in British parlance) for women, and in some cases mid-life crisis for men, before maturity, aging, and decline set in. The diagram should on this account be extended far to the right, and turn first flat

---

[1]Cipolla's brilliant fifteen-page introduction to the book he edited, *The Economic Decline of Empires* (1970), makes many of the points in this book. When I reread it late in assembling material, I was tempted to abandon the enterprise. His essayists, however, go lightly on the rise of empires, do not cover a number of the countries I do, and go well beyond Europe, the United States, and Japan. There may be room left.

[2]Spain, as the modern historian records Professor Salas of the University of Salamanca orating, exhibited all these stages at once. Salas went on sarcastically: "Spain has what no other nation has: its bull fights are the ties of its society, the forges of its political habits. From them Spain derives its martial spirit, in them it learns the wisdom of government" (Herr, 1958, p. 334).

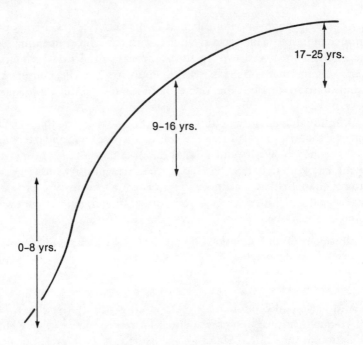

17–25 yrs.

9–16 yrs.

0–8 yrs.

Figure 2–1   The S-curve. An Investment Plan for the Young: The Austin Project, First Phase.

and then down, as in the portrayal of the logistic curve in Rondo Cameron's world history (1989, p. 16, fig. I-1). Somewhat different S-curves are shown in Brian Berry's book on the Kondratieff (long-wave) economic cycle for separate industries. Measured in percent of peak development, these turn down a considerable distance as separate industries pass through "introduction, growth, maturity, saturation and decline" (1991, pp. 46–47, figs. 26, 27). All are idealized or smooth S-curves. In the real world there are many wiggles, speedups, and setbacks, new S-curves growing out of old, separate curves for different sectors and regions of a national economy, all of which present difficulties when an attempt is made to aggregate them on a weighted basis. The essence is slow start, speedup, slowdown in the rate of growth, steady growth, and then decline, usually relative to other industries, sectors, regions, or economies, sometimes in absolute terms.

The S-curve follows fairly closely the stages of economic growth of W. W. Rostow (1960), and Alexander Gerschenkron's "big spurt" (1977), except that these authors start with the eighteenth-century industrial revolution in Britain, rather than with the commercial revolution in Italy half a millennium earlier, and are less interested than I in slowdown and aging, or in the succession of one country after another in world economic primacy, or in the occasional awkward transition from a falling to a rising leader. A variety of other minor differences will also appear. The main difference, however, is that Rostow's series of stages, for example, ends with high-level consumption,[3] and I emphasize decline. I also allow for more variance around the idealized pattern: growth starts that abort, interruptions, rigidity that renders an economy unable to respond to shocks, chaos theory, path dependency, and collective memory, which may frustrate opportunities that would otherwise have been followed up.

Most theoretical work on economic growth deals with labor, capital, and a "residual" that incorporates exogenous (introduced from outside) technological change, investment in human capital (education), and sometimes "land" (or resources). Economic historians are rarely so parsimonious, and incline to extend the list to noneconomic, including sociological, factors. The French, especially, make room for *mentalités*, the Germans for *Zeitgeist*, or social values. Some would emphasize economic or other policy, mostly of government. A major purpose of this book, however, is to question whether good policy can do much to stretch out growth of a national economy, just as good medicine is limited in its ability to prolong human life much beyond the limits set by genetic endowments. Distinction must be made, of course, between short-run policy responses to shocks, and measures to continue long-run growth, just as good medicine can succeed in treating particular diseases and afflictions, but is notionally distinct from that designed to extend the human life span.

Scanning the Future

A recent study by the Central Planning Bureau of the Netherlands tackles the issue of economic growth in a complex way that departs drastically from the Bureau's economic tradition (1992). The study offers three idealized models of economic growth: (1) the "equilibrium model," associated with the name of Adam Smith, in which rational human beings with full information, using natural resources, savings, education, and a well-functioning system of prices for labor, capital, goods, and services, optimize output in the light of demand conditions, including standing ready to invent new

---

[3]In his later work, particularly in dealing with the history of thought on economic growth, Rostow indicates more interest in slackening and retardation. He observes that Joseph Schumpeter in 1939 thought capitalism was threatened not by a shrinkage of investment opportunities but a hostile political, social and intellectual environment plus self-generated degenerative forces (Rostow, 1990, p. 242, quoting Schumpeter, vol. 2, 1939, p. 1050), while Simon Kuznets explained slackening of economic growth and retardation in terms of the "slowing down of technological progress, dependence of the innovational sectors on slower-growing sectors supplying raw material inputs, a relative decline of funds available for expansion of the innovational sectors and competition from the same industry in a younger country" (ibid., pp. 243–44, with the quotation from p. 244). This last assumes, it seems, that there are always innovational sectors at hand. In a later paper, Rostow quotes Kuznets again in a statement close to my view: "If we single out the various nations or the separate branches of industry, the picture becomes less uniform, some nations seem to have led the world at one time, others at another" (Rostow, 1991, p. 410, quoting Kuznets, 1930, p. 1). But Kuznets does not explain economic retardation in any detail, ascribing it to "factors discussed by economic historians."

products and innovate in their production; (2) a "free-market" model, with uncertainty, strong property rights, individual adaptability, high autonomy in economic activity, vigorous innovation and consequently a high rate of creative destruction—the Schumpeterian model; (3) a "coordination" model, called rather opaquely the "Keynesian model," with collective rather than individual adaptability, good government instead of the self-serving bureaucrats postulated by public-choice theory, attention to public goods such as infrastructure, and policy coordination between as well as within countries. The three models are by no means mutually exclusive, and different countries at different times pursue different mixes of the three, which can be thought of as rational human, competitive human, and cooperative human. Figure 2–2, taken from the Netherlands study, shows the models arranged in a circle at the center of which is "social innovation," representing the "capability and will of individuals, companies and governments to break free of existing habits, perceptions, institutions and task allocations, revise them in light of constantly changing circumstances and new development" (ibid., p. 47). The discussion continues:

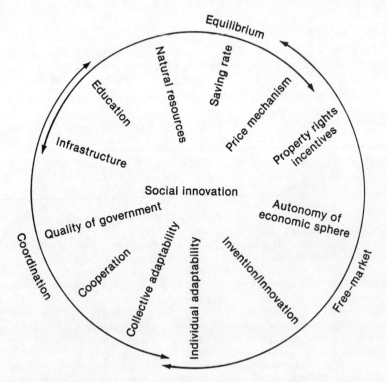

Figure 2–2 The prosperity circle. *Source: Scanning the Future: A Long-Term Scenario of the World Economy, 1990–2015.* The Hague: Central Planning Bureau of the Netherlands, 1992, p. 47.

. . . History also teaches that time after time, individuals, firms, sectors and entire economies often push their success formulas too far, for too long. Even when clear signals are sent that the limits are being reached, the inability to adjust to new circumstances is often striking. It explains why social innovation has been placed at the heart of the prosperity circle. Especially for developed countries which are striving for continued economic growth and development, social innovation is extremely important and, as history has shown time and time again, very difficult. Failure to achieve it opens the door to institutional sclerosis and ultimately relative economic decline. (Ibid., p. 51)

Resources

In the S-curve model of economic growth, I pay little attention to agriculture, population or cities except as they establish the initial conditions out of which accelerating growth starts. The resource "coal" in the choice of emphasis between "coal" and "culture" was not involved in real terms until the eighteenth century, apart primarily from its use in space heating in London, but other sources of energy were: humans, animals, timber, wind, peat, and many others. Feudalism developed on rich bottomland. The lord exchanged protection against part of the production of his serfs. In mountains there was little output to protect from roving bands or for the lord to extort, and thus mountain settlements developed along republican lines (Rappard, 1914, chap. 1). Cities in harbors on the sea were populated by mobile merchants and seamen, and they—Venice, Genoa, Amsterdam, and Hamburg—also evolved republican rather than princely governments, governments that gradually evolved into self-perpetuating oligarchies, run by the wealthiest merchants. Nobility was equally weak or nonexistent in large parts of Scandinavia and the Baltic and North Sea coasts. In Norway, for example, sufficient land to support the number of families needed to work the lord's domain would have been widely spread and difficult for a steward to keep under surveillance. Along the European north coast, dikes needed to prevent flooding required cooperative maintenance, leaving little time to produce a seigneur's share (Kellenbenz, 1963, pp. xxi, xxii).

Location was a critical resource. Venice, at the head of the Adriatic and hence fairly easily defended against marauders, accessible to the Levant by sea and to southern Germany by means of Alpine passes, enjoyed a superior location for intermediary trade. So did Genoa, linked to the western Mediterranean, and through Gibraltar and the Bay of Biscay to the Low Countries, England, and northern Europe, as well as by pack train through the western Alpine passes. Surrounded by mountains, Genoa lacked a hinterland. It fashioned the equivalent abroad in south Italy and the Mediterranean islands. Seville lay at the gateway of the Atlantic trade winds, with its back to the farmland of Andalusia producing citrus fruit, olive oil, and wine. Bruges, Antwerp, and Amsterdam had access to the Atlantic in one direction, to England to the north, and to the North Sea and Baltic to the east, with a vast plain drained by the Rhine and the Meuse landward. Many cities—Paris, Lyons, Frankfurt, Geneva, Ulm, Augsburg—were built on river crossings of east-west routes. Each of the great centers in turn tried to establish trade monopolies with initial economies of scale and advantageous costs. Direct trading between outside suppliers and demanders finally left them in the lurch. Not all ports went in for shipbuilding or their own fleets. In some instances, the reasons are fairly obvious. Rome, for example, was not a nation of mariners. It had to improvise naval forces by borrowing ships and imitating the techniques of others, largely those of the Greek city-states (Mollat du Jourdain, 1993, p. 31). Florence and Milan were located inland; Genoa crushed rivals Amalfi and Pisa, and competed vigorously with Leghorn. There are questions about Bruges and Antwerp, despite the building of a fleet in Genoa by Philip the Fair and the appointment of the Genoan Zaccaria as its admiral, and later efforts of Philip the Good to build ships in Bruges with Portuguese engineer specialists. These efforts seem not to have gone much distance to make Flanders into a maritime nation except for the privateers of all nations concentrated in Dunkirk (ibid., pp. 62, 66, 68). Various reasons have been given for this failure: Bruges and Antwerp were both long served by the Hanseatic League; Spain had insufficient naval capacity to protect commercial fleets other than her own; labor and capital were divided between industry in Flanders and the Brabant and shipping in the United Provinces (van Houtte, 1972, pp. 104–5). Mentalities also may have had something to do with it: Henri Pirenne stated that throughout history maritime countries have been individualist and liberal whereas continental countries have been social and authoritarian with a taste for hierarchical organization (quoted in Mollat du Jourdain, 1993, p. 231). It is not apparent from the reference which way the causation ran, or whether such countries as Spain and France were "maritime" or sufficiently maritime. Still another possibility is that there were not enough men of vitality in Bruges and Antwerp beyond the numerous largely Italian merchants and bankers to develop a vigorous shipping industry that could match the Italian galleys and Hanseatic cogs.

A vivid illustration is furnished by a symposium discussion of the Finnish failure to make the transition from sailing ships to steam:

> . . . there are "peasant" shipowners in all countries . . . what we are looking for is SHIPOWNERS [capitals in the original]: men who are rich and ruthless, energetic and enterprising . . . tomorrow's men do not invest in today's technology, and even less in yesterday's technology. (Jackson, 1991, p. 152)

Another participant in the same symposium, however, declared that explaining the rate and mode of participation of individual nations in international shipping remains "one of the most difficult problems in maritime history" (Broeze, 1991, pp. 127–28).

An extension of the problem is to explain changes in that participation. Competition is involved, to be sure, but there is more. A port may be suitable for small ships but be unable to accommodate larger ones, especially if there is a bar in the river, as in the Guadalquivir at San Lucar, which required the eventual shift to Cadiz, or silting, which rendered Bruges inaccessible. Shipbuilding may decline because of depletion of accessible timber, emigration and hence higher wages for shipwrights, and especially innovation abroad, which local shipyards are unable to copy quickly and cheaply.

Distant Trade

A sharp distinction was made in early modern times in Europe between commerce, the ordinary distribution of local product in market towns, and "distant trade." Adam Smith said that they were alike except for the greater amount of capital involved in distant trade, but he overlooked a series of questions dealing with accounting, foreign exchange, foreign languages, and knowledge of where goods were available and where highly valued (Smith, 1776 [1937], p. 112). Within distant trade, moreover, there was a distinction between luxury goods and bulk commodities such as grain, timber, wool, alum, fish, and salt (Israel, 1989). The commercial revolution of the twelfth and thirteenth centuries involved initially luxury goods, brought from the eastern shore of the Mediterranean, whither many had come from India and China, and paid for in part with silver mined in central Europe and in part by fine woolens woven in Flanders and the Brabant, sold to Italian merchants at Champagne fairs. The demand for eastern goods required disposable income above subsistence levels acquired by nobles extracting income from their serfs, along with mercantile profits earned in towns and a taste for eastern goods acquired during the Crusades. Many of these goods showed their Arab origin in their names: sugar, muslin, damask, cotton, coffee (mocha). Other goods—spices, calico, and silk—came by ship from China, the islands of Southeast Asia, and India to the Persian Gulf and the Red Sea and then by caravan to Aleppo and Cairo.

In the early stages of the commercial revolution, merchants traveled with their goods both to protect them to the extent possible from pirates and from jettison in storm, and to sell them abroad. In time the merchants became sedentary, stayed home with counting house and warehouse, and depended on commission agents abroad for sales. Goods moving overland were sold for the most part at fairs, held twice or four times a year in various towns. Merchants at fairs would keep records of what they bought and sold, cancel out debits and credits to the extent they balanced, and pay or receive the difference in coin or bills of exchange on other localities or on a forthcoming fair. In due course financial institutions developed, such as banks dealing in bills of exchange, insurance, standard money, standard weights and measures, and governmental protection against piracy, privateers, and interlopers who tried to invade government-assigned monopolies.

Some nations were better at producing merchants than others. Italians pioneered in the commercial revolution, from 1100 on, and again as bankers when they moved over western and central Europe, except for the Hansa towns from which they were excluded. The Dutch and the British, and to a somewhat lesser extent the French, eager for profit and willing to take risks, followed from the late sixteenth century. The Spanish, on the other hand, allowed themselves to be outcompeted in providing goods to their settlers in the New World by foreign merchants located in Seville, until after 1713 when direct trade by foreign merchants was allowed. Apart from those in its cities of Hamburg, Lübeck, and Cologne, the Germany of the Holy Roman Empire lacked effective merchants for the marketing of Rhenish cloth, Silesian linens, and East Prussian grain and timber. In one explanation this was a consequence of the devastation of German trade in the Thirty Years' War beginning in 1618 (Braudel, 1979 [1982], p. 159).

Mediterranean shipping started with galleys propelled by oarsmen, which gave way in due course to sailing ships, patterned after cogs, a technology borrowed from the Hansa cities. Slowly but relentlessly the technology of sailing grew, with some major innovations and much borrowing. Naval and merchant galleys grew in size. Sailing ships added more masts, more sail, more displacement, a stern-post rudder to replace the steering oar, improvements in navigation and cartography. In due course in the fifteenth century this produced the Age of Discovery, led by the Portuguese, culminating in new routes to the Far East and the discovery of America.

Increases in ship size and draft altered the relative utility of ports. Silting, bars, and seasonal lack of flow meant that a number of inland, upriver ports—Aigues Mortes, Seville, Bruges, and Cologne the more prominent among them—were cut off from the standard ship. Larger vessels also required more timber, which became less accessible as forests in the west were depleted. Other limitations on shipping were seasonal—ice in the Baltic and winter storms in the Mediterranean and the Atlantic.

Heavy goods were carried not only by sea but inland on navigable rivers and later canals. Not all rivers lent themselves to goods traffic on a regular basis: some dried up in summer (the Loire), others were torrential in spring (the Rhone). Canalization, when it came in the eighteenth century, met opposition from fishermen managing weirs and from farmers needing water for irrigation or accelerated flow for drainage. Canalization varied in ease depending on the contours of land and its geology. National styles in canal building could also differ, as Michel Chevalier pointed out in the nineteenth century. England was relatively early in canal building after the Dutch, and as barges and loads grew in size England left its canals at their original size despite their increasing inefficiency. French canals came later, with construction well ahead of need, involving an inefficient use of capital. In the United States, canals were constructed to a size to meet contemporary needs, and then continuously rebuilt as demands for improvement presented themselves (Chevalier, 1836, vol. 2, pp. 40–42).

Growth of transport on land was slow. Roman roads in France and Britain failed to stand up well over the centuries. Mule pack trains through Alpine passes were expensive and suitable only for specie and high-value goods. Overland communication by horseback, pack train, oxcarts, and horse-drawn carriages, first on poor roads, then on British turnpikes, was followed in the nineteenth century by railroads and in the twentieth by automobile, truck, and airplane. In one view, innovation in transport is the most pervasive form of technological change, because it joins markets and promotes the division of labor that Adam Smith held to be the basis for the growth of the wealth of nations (Isard, 1945). In another analysis, innovation in transport is the unintended consequence, among other things, of a given mode of transport charging monopoly prices and thereby encouraging the entry of new modes (Girard, 1965).

Industry

The manor was largely self-sufficient, except perhaps for salt, fish, and iron pots for the peasants, and of course luxury goods for the lord and lady. Industry originated from three sources: import substitution with products made at home, sometimes with the help of tariffs and/or import prohibitions; cottage, sometimes called "proto," industry undertaken to keep excess youthful population in the home, young women from seeking jobs as servants, and men from wandering or serving in mercenary armies (Braun, 1965); and skilled artisans in cities. These last produced new types of goods: silver and gold jewelry, glass including mirrors, leather goods, printing, art. In the general view, necessity is the mother of invention. Cyril Stanley Smith, the metallurgist, however, pointed out that much innovation originated in a search for beauty: new alloys for sculpture, the extrusion process in the course of making channels to hold stained glass, chemicals and dyes to make cloth more pleasing—whether softer, more brightly colored, or whiter (1970).

Cottage industry was an outgrowth of traveling merchants who delivered raw materials—initially wool and flax, later cotton—to peasant cottages and returned to collect and sell the finished product. In due course industry moved into the factory. Small-scale merchants might move from putting out piece work to manufacturing, or from petty commerce to industry. Great merchants did not. Their fortunes went rather into banking, estates that included some farming, and government office. Reasons for moving from putting out to the factory included the availability successively of animal, wind, water, steam, and ultimately electric power as technology advanced; the wish to guard against worker theft; and the need to defend against competitor theft of industrial secrets. In one view, not widely shared, it occurred to hold down wages (Marglin, 1974).

Technical advance spread from country to country through travel; intellectual theft, including smuggling abroad of newly invented machines; imitation, both permitted and forbidden; enticement of entrepreneurs and artisans to migrate; subsidies to travel; technical training; and increasing numbers of technical publications. One economic historian of Finland, a late-industrializing state and an acquirer of modern technology from abroad, lists eight methods of bringing up a country technologically, with importing of foreign machinery, study and observation abroad, analysis of foreign products, and reading of foreign technical literature in the top positions

(Myllyntaus, 1990). Discussing the eighteenth century, an economic historian held that the wandering of hand workers and the travels of industrially concerned aristocrats and leading businessmen were "an important, perhaps the most important factor in the spread of early industrialization" (Redlich, 1968, pp. 344–45). New technology in both products and processes was encouraged by the patent system, which granted an inventor private intellectual property and a limited monopoly, and by prizes, subsidies, exhibitions, and honors.

As in canals, styles of invention and innovation differed from country to country. The British were largely experimental, the French more closely based on scientific principles. All firms and governments tried to maintain monopolies of technical information. It was said that Spanish pride forbade most industrialists in that country from seeking to imitate foreigners, as mentioned earlier. But pride can also work in the opposite direction. The Dutch author of a treatise on shipbuilding in 1671 felt safe in explaining national methods to alien readers, because, as he wrote, foreigners with alien workers could not imitate the thrifty and neat disposition of the Hollander (Barbour, 1930 [1954], p. 234). He was unduly optimistic.

Migration

After the rise and spread of technical change, I come to its decline and that of industrial productivity. First, however, a digression on migration, mostly in relation to technical progress. Some countries welcomed people driven out of other societies, and benefited from receiving them, notably the Burgundian Low Countries, which opened their doors to the Jews expelled from Spain in 1492, the Italian and Flemish merchants and bankers who fled Antwerp in 1585, and the Huguenots who left France at the time of the Revocation of the Edict of Nantes in 1685. Others tried to prevent their subjects from emigrating, especially with industrial secrets, among them Britain with its stringent but largely unsuccessful legislation against the export of machinery and plans and its discouragement of the movement abroad of skilled artisans (Musson, 1972). In the seventeenth century, Colbert in France tried to recruit Dutch shipwrights (Konvitz, 1978, p. 124) and fine-cloth workers, to halt the loss of Huguenots abroad, and to encourage the return of sailors who were in short supply (Scoville, 1960, p. 116). It is widely claimed that the Spanish expulsion of the Jews in 1492, and of the Moors in 1609–1614, deprived that country of talent in financial skills and in the management of irrigation, respectively. Fernand Braudel discounts both effects (1966 [1975], vol. 2, p. 825).

One final note on migration and national styles: the French are not adventurous migrants. The 1848 movement to Algiers came largely from Alsace and Lorraine, the population of which is French but with strains of German intermingled. On the other hand, the Portuguese are notorious wanderers (Brazilian sociologist Gilberto Freyre calls Portugal a nation of Ulysses), inclined to settle abroad more or less permanently, without racial discrimination, and to consort with native and even slave women (quoted by Boxer, 1969, p. 2). Still a third and middle pattern is the Italian, going abroad to work for long periods but returning to Italy once to marry, again to die (Brachtel, 1980). A question that arises with regard to migration is whether there is any general pattern in the nation cycle whereby skilled workers are attracted in the early stages of economic vitality and repelled when decline has set in.

The Industrial Revolution

To return to technological change and productivity. Much of the literature on European economic growth starts with the "industrial revolution,"
which had its intellectual origins in the eighteenth-century Enlightenment
and its economic start in the second half of the same period. A considerable effort has lately been devoted to denying the reality of an industrial
revolution in Britain, as contrasted with an industrial "evolution," a term
originally put forward by N. S. B. Gras (1930). The issue approaches scholasticism. The spurt in inventions from the 1760s can be regarded as revolutionary, or one could wait until the sharp rise of British exports in the
1780s, or until the rise in income per capita that picked up speed after the
Napoleonic wars. Nor is it necessary to pick up the Rostovian model that
sees "preconditions" for the industrial revolution in a "propensity to produce science" early in the eighteenth century, followed by a "propensity to
apply science." The spurt in economic growth in France and Britain in the
third quarter of the eighteenth century was different in the two cases, empirical in Britain, Cartesian in France. Each was more or less connected with
the Enlightenment as that movement dispelled much of the belief in the
supernatural, the evil eye, magic, and the like in favor of cause and effect.
The styles differed. We return to the issue in the country studies.

Cardwell's Law

In his brilliant book, *The Lever of Riches*, dealing with technological progress,
Joel Mokyr refers in a number of places to Cardwell's law, a crude historical regularity that no country has been on the cutting edge of technical
innovation for more than two or three generations (Mokyr, 1990, pp. 207,
241 n. 31, 261, 266, 268–69, 301, 304; D. S. L. Cardwell, 1972, p. 210).
Mokyr is somewhat mesmerized by Cardwell's law, wondering whether it
can be extrapolated in the present day to predict the United States falling
behind (ibid., p. 304). He is troubled, however, by the fact that Cardwell
himself provides no theoretical basis for such a uniformity (and, one might
add, provides at least one counterexample in stating that "between 1712
and 1850 virtually every improvement in heat engines and every name with
a few exceptions . . . were British. After 1861 the situation changed deci-
sively . . ." [1972, p. 190]). But it may be worthwhile to reproduce
Cardwell's exact words:

The proper indifference of the historian of technology to the nationality of particular inventors and technologists has tended to conceal the important fact that no nation has been very creative for more than an historically short period. Fortunately as each leader flagged, there has always been, up to now, a nation or nations to take over the torch. The diversity, inside a wider unity of European culture—for Europe is the true home of technology—has made possible the continuous growth of technology over the last 170 years. (Cardwell, 1972, p. 210)

In an earlier passage Cardwell stated that the loss of technical leadership comes generally across the board, though he cites a possible exception of Parsons's steam turbine of 1897 in Britain (ibid., p. 190).

Mokyr, as noted, is troubled by the lack of a formal model that would explain the uniformity Cardwell believed he had discerned. Biological evolution might go some distance to explain the location of a start, with mutations analogous to inventions. Mokyr finds this unpersuasive, since biological evolution is not intentional. In a later paper he discusses evolutionary biology and technology with no mention of Cardwell (1991a), but then comes back to him in a lecture published the following year, largely dealing with path dependency, a concept developed by Paul David (1985), and the likelihood that innovations may evolve in suboptimal ways through taking an early wrong turn (Mokyr, 1992, pp. 14, 19). I suggest that the notion of a national life cycle in which vitality waxes and then wanes, with one country succeeding another in economic primacy—discussed in the next chapter—may hold a clue. If succession prevails, moreover, it throws doubt on Mokyr's hopeful suggestion that two countries moving more or less simultaneously might interact to sustain technological progress, and thus fit Cardwell's law (ibid., p. 19).

Agriculture

Change in agriculture varied widely from country to country and even within countries. The Po valley in northern Italy was regarded by Arthur Young, preoccupied with agriculture, as the richest spot of all Europe when he visited Italy at the end of the eighteenth century. The rich Dutch coast and southeast England—Norfolk and Sussex—were in touch with one another and technologically forward in manuring, including green manures, crop rotation, cleaning crops, and the like. On the other hand, in most of Europe agricultural change was agonizingly slow; peasants near the subsistence line worried about the risks of new techniques, and communication among farmers was limited. The classic example is the more than a century it took to replace the sickle with the scythe in the harvest of grain in France (Chatelaine, 1956). Theodore Schultz finds economic justification for the hesitation, in the uselessness of straw before the stabling of cattle and draft animals, after which it was needed in the barn for bedding. Earlier it was more efficient to harvest the heads of grain with a sickle and leave the straw in the field (Schultz, private communication of the 1960s). An alternative explanation relies on the availability of women, children, and old people who were strong enough to handle the sickle, and the relative scarcity of strong males competent with scythes (Grantham, 1993, p. 495).

Even in the stately homes and chateaux of wealthy merchants there was a wide gap between those who were, as Adam Smith claimed, the "best of improvers" (1776 [1937], p. 384), and others in Italy, Spain, and parts of France who retired to the country with little interest in agriculture except for the noble lifestyle, ran their estates through stewards, and were constantly pushing their stewards for more cash income.

Decline in Productivity

Declines in the rate of invention, innovation, and productivity in the life cycle of individual countries came from a variety of causes: the three-generation effect without the replacement of the third generation by new men, ready to repeat the cycle in new or old industries; changes in attitudes toward risk-bearing; widening social stratification with gaps between classes in income distribution and without the reinvestment of high profits in productive capital; monopolization by guilds, unions, corporations, and government; resistance to change by workers and by entrepreneurs with investment in old techniques.

In one view, so long as old machinery and skills were still usable, why submit to the expense, trouble, and trauma of learning new? In the early stages of industry, guilds were a force for improvement because they fostered education of apprentices and journeymen and quality control. Gradually they turned monopolistic and conservative, limiting entry and opposing change, especially any reduction in quality that would reduce cost but devalue their skills. Continuous change in the industrial revolution took place outside the areas of guild strength. Skilled men in small shops divided into "honorables," who belonged to guilds and were the aristocrats of the working class, and "dungs" or dishonorables, who were ready to take nonguild jobs at lower pay (E. P. Thompson, 1963).

Finance

Finance was tied to distant trade, noble consumption, and government borrowing, but not to local commerce, and very little to industry. If Adam Smith was wide of the mark in a statement that there is little difference in the knowledge of a smart grocer in a seaport town and that of a great merchant, he was right in saying that great fortunes were seldom made in great towns by any one established and well-known branch of industry except as a consequence of a long life of industry, frugality, and attention (1776 [1937], p. 113). The greatest fortunes in Britain came from inherited land. Fortunes were also made (and lost) in speculation, trading commodities in different places. With a fortune made, a merchant might move out of business altogether and retire to the country or to public life. Or the switch might be made to finance, which was perceived to require less energy and be less risky.

The transition from trade to finance occurred early in the commercial revolution as traders at fairs began to deal first in trade bills of exchange, then in purely financial bills to settle imbalances in space and in time, and ultimately moved from lending to merchants to lending to royal and noble spenders. In due course mercantile capital was used to form banks. Maritime risks were transferred from owners to financiers and were diversified, first through primitive forms such as bottomry—a loan that need not be repaid if the ship were lost—that evolved into marine insurance.

Bills of exchange were a private form of finance providing a medium of exchange, in contradistinction to the minting of coin, which was under the authority of the state (Boyer-Xambeau, Deleplace, and Gillard, 1986). As the nation-state grew, governments tried to build standard money, readily recognizable with an image, often of royalty, with fixed designation and established weight and fineness of metal (when it was not debased by adulteration or change of denomination to capture more seignorage—the profit from issuing coins of less value than that stated). Money to facilitate market transactions was a public good, along with standard weights and measures and their enforcement by surveillance of yardsticks and scales to prevent exploitation of the innocent by the unscrupulous. Local systems of coinage and weights and measures competed with one another until one gained acceptance over others through economies of scale and the losers were abandoned. One device to render money acceptable to creditors was to weigh and assay metal coins and collect them in sacks, with the value attested on the outside and heavy governmental penalties for falsification. A private path to the same end was for banks to test coins against which they issued bank money, relieving the recipient of the necessity to test coins themselves.

Financial institutions grew from the commercial revolution at different speeds in different countries, becoming gradually less attached to trade, industry, consumption (especially lending to free-spending nobles against mortgages), and government, until various types of financial instruments took on specialized lives of their own. A witty economic historian observes that the separation of finance from production—it would have been more accurate to say trade—is like that of sex from procreation, acceptable in moderation but in excess leading to destability, disruption, and depression (William Parker, 1991, p. 235).

Government Finance

Government finance also developed slowly along different paths in different cities and states. Early in the modern age, most kings of larger states lacked bureaucracies and "farmed" their taxes to private financiers—in France *financiers* and *officiers*, who advanced funds to the monarch and, if successful, got them back, plus a profit, through collecting the tax. The switch to government taxation and direct debt in Britain after the Glorious Revolution of 1688 was called a "financial revolution" (Dickson, 1967).

In some jurisdictions such as Prussia a king had large holdings of land with attendant industrial activities such as grain mills and breweries on which he collected rent and profit, thus calling for setting up a bureaucracy at an early stage to manage the royal domain. The nature of taxes and their incidence on the different sectors of a country varied from country to country. An outstanding example of difference runs between England and France. In England, nobility paid taxes along with the rest of the country. In France (and in Spain) nobility was exempted on the ground that it discharged its obligation to the crown and to society by risking its life in battle. The difference may have arisen from the greater labor intensity of land warfare, as opposed to sea battles of island forces.

Royalty borrowed monies especially for war, as well as for ceremonial occasions such as coronations, marriages, and funerals. Since the king was above the law—though government in republics was not—financiers were leery of lending to the king unless the debt was collaterized by a precedent claim on a specific tax or monopoly, the security of the crown jewels, or the intermediation of a quasi-private body such as the City of London and its merchants, or the Hôtel de Ville of Paris. In a number of instances, a foreign lender received special privileges such as the right to export wool from England along with the Merchant Adventurers, the official English monopoly, or silver from Spain. The precautions of money men grew out of a long history of royal defaults stretching from the early years of the millennium.

Government raised money not only from farming taxes and monopolies but also from selling offices, titles, and honors and from confiscating and selling church and noble property. Government revenue fell short of expenditure especially in war, leading to borrowing in various forms. There were rare exceptions. Frederick the Great of Prussia sought to finance his wars in advance by accumulating a war chest of gold. In emergency a government might delay paying its soldiers and sailors, though at risk of mutiny; lay violent hands on the assets of goldsmiths or those of merchants transporting silver; force its citizens, especially those with whom it disagreed, as with the Protestant Huguenots in Catholic France, to billet and feed its troops; and repudiate its debt or substitute long-term currency obligations for short-term debt payable in coin of the realm.

In the twentieth century government deficits and borrowing tended to soak up savings needed for investment in industry. Before 1800 this was less of a problem. Capital was provided to industry, as distinct from trade and agriculture, largely on the local level, and was needed only in small amounts. Some large trading companies, such as the British and Dutch East India companies, sold securities in organized markets, as did insurance companies after the last quarter of the seventeenth century. Banks loaned mostly to finance trade. Government debt rose sharply in wartime, and was reduced in its weight on the national income on occasion by small peacetime surpluses, but mostly by repudiation and inflation.

Adam Smith lists three forms of public goods: national defense, the administration of justice, and construction projects too large to be undertaken privately for profit (1776 [1937], book 5, chap. 1). Each of these classes can be stretched to encompass a variety of governmental tasks. Aggressive and defensive wars and convoys to protect merchant fleets against piracy and privateering presumably come under the heading of national defense. Smith went so far as to justify the Navigation Acts restricting trade to and from Britain and her colonies to British ships, since they helped train sailors, needed in large numbers by the Royal Navy in wartime (ibid., p. 429). Administration of justice can be stretched to include the provision of sound money and honest measure. Public works include construction of roads, bridges, harbors, docks, canals; planned cities (in France) (Konvitz, 1978); perhaps palaces (which led Louis XIV on his deathbed to apologize for "too many palaces, too many wars"[4]).

Modern lists would go further and stress other public goods, in particular that of feeding the populace in periods of crop failure at a time when transport was insufficiently advanced to ensure that a local deficiency could be met by imports. Belief in the free market sufficient to think that it would care for the Irish populace at the time of the potato blight when the grain crop failed over a wide portion of western Europe came close to being a public bad (Woodham-Smith, 1962). With a limited hinterland, Venice maintained a stock of grain against shortfalls, and until the eighteenth century when shipping alleviated the pinch, most countries restricted grain exports until it became clear that there was enough to meet national need— a policy to which the Physiocrats—noble intellectual agriculturists—with their interest in higher prices for grain, objected strongly. Other public goods or bads included attention to or neglect of income distribution in the way taxation was levied, intervention in trade as part of what might be called industrial policy, and various subsidies to invention and innovation, already discussed, and quality control.

A German economist, Adolph Wagner, enunciated a "law" to the effect that the role of government constantly expanded (1879). An Australian statistician went further, to hold that when government accounted for more than 25 percent of gross national product, it broke down (Clark, 1945). The first statement has been proved to be more nearly correct than the second. In the early part of the period under discussion the line between government and private enterprise was shadowy. Merchant shipping needed naval convoys. Privateering ships differed little from men-of-war except in the distribution of booty; a government shipyard such as the Arsenale of Venice or the Royal Navy yard at Deptford on the Thames lay on the same water as shipyards of private builders. Royal soldiers on the Continent fighting for Italian city-states, for Spain, or for the Holy Roman Empire operated alongside mercenaries although they changed allegiance less frequently. Cadastres that established the ownership of private land and thus enhanced

---

[4]Such at least is the customary rendering in English. The French is less aphoristic: "*Ne m'imitez pas dans le goût que j'ai eu pour les batiments, non dans celui que je suis eu pour la guerre*" (Faure, 1977, p. 63).

incentives for agricultural improvement were undertaken better to levy government taxes. And tax and monopoly farmers worked for private profit in collecting monies for the crown until they were replaced, convulsively or in evolutionary fashion, by civil servants.

Social Capability

The crude proxy for "social capability" in modern growth is years of education of the population. The measure is crude because education in one country may differ from that in another in dimensions well beyond the average number of school years. Education may refer primarily to literacy. Beyond reading and writing there may be classical education in religion, philosophy, literature, and the like, linked before the Enlightenment especially to Aristotle and scholasticism; vocational education at the secondary level; and higher reaches of letters on the one hand and technical and scientific education on the other. The subject returns in the country studies.

For historical studies back to early modern times, social capability is more complex and involves values and vitality. The frequent comparison between Amsterdam and Venice led Peter Burke to quote a Dutch remark of 1652 "that the regents were not merchants, that they did not take risks on the seas, but derived their income from houses and securities, and so allowed the sea to be lost" (Burke, 1974). Burke went on to say that "the shift was from sea to land, from work to play, from thrift to conspicuous consumption, from entrepreneur to rentier, from bourgeois to aristocrat" (ibid., p. 104). The same evolution is not made at a similar pace in each of the countries dealt with in this book, since not all started from the same place; several were conspicuous for seafaring, work, thrift, entrepreneurship, or their permeation by bourgeoisie. Most, however, ended their period of primacy with different values from those with which they had started. The older a country becomes, the more it is interested in the past, rather than the future, and in art, scholarship, and literature rather than trade and industry. As David Riesman and his colleagues said of the United States, heroes of production are replaced by heroes of consumption (Riesman, Glazer, and Denny, 1950). Finance may occupy a prominent place in the spectrum of activities but its focus changes. Banks lend to sovereign states, foreign borrowers, and local builders of stately homes rather than finance trade and industry at home. Descendants tend to take capital out of the productive plant of progenitors and move it to trustee securities, including government debt. Government debt grows in turn, as expenditure on palaces and war or defense rises beyond the readiness of taxpayers in most countries, late in the growth process, to contribute.

The decline in vitality of one generation would be of little consequence if the new men of the next demonstrated equal energy and innovative capacity and transformed resources from mature industries and outlets to new and rising sectors. There is a need for new families to come along and elbow the old aside. Or change may occur within the family and in a given area:

in the United States, New England started in trade and shipping, moved to cotton and woolen textiles, then to investment in western copper mines and General Motors, most recently to computers and genetics. This sort of progression is rare. New men may rise to fill the vacuum of leadership left by defeat (Olson, 1982), as in Prussia in 1806, Denmark in 1864, Germany, France, and Japan in 1945. Victory solidifies the position of "distributional coalitions" (Olson's term), or vested interests. Defeat moves them aside, making room for "new men" (Postan, 1967). In one formulation there is a "Phoenix effect" from war, in which the loser recovers its economic power and international ranking ten to fifteen years after a war (Organski and Kuglar, 1981). Such an effect can be realized on a microlevel, as a rich family that has left active economic life loses its wealth and returns to work hard again, stopping, however, for the good life when it has repaired its losses (Pitts, 1964).

Despite these demonstrations of resilience, for the most part wealth bred first perhaps more wealth and then decline. A high rate of profit, said Adam Smith, has many bad effects on a country, but there is one, more fatal than all the others together: it destroys the parsimony that is normal to the merchant. "When profits are high that sober virtue seems to be super-fluous and an expensive luxury"—the eighteenth-century equivalent of Veblen's "conspicuous consumption"—seems "to suit better the affluence of his situation" (1776 [1937], p. 578). A century earlier, a Spaniard commenting on the inflation in his country from the influx of silver from Peru wrote

> . . . the possession and abundance of such wealth altered everything. Agri-culture laid down the plough, clothed herself in silk and softened her work-calloused hands. Trade put on a noble air, and exchanging the work-bench for the saddle, went out to parade up and down the street. The arts disdained mechanical tools. . . . Goods became proud. . . . As men promised more from their income than in reality they had, ostentation and royal pomp grew, pen-sions, pay and other items of Crown payments rose on the basis of this for-eign wealth, which was too badly administered and kept to meet such expense, and this gave rise to debt. (Vilar, 1969 [1976], pp. 167–68)

Ostentation is observed at the height of their wealth in most of the coun-tries dealt with in this book, less so in Britain than countries in southern Europe. It was accompanied by ambiguity and considerable embarrassment in Holland where the Calvinist doctrine of thrift warred with the worship of the golden calf (Schama, 1988). Gambling seems to flourish in economic decline, along with feasting, acquisition of many luxury articles, and dress for vain display.

Mentalités

The French historical school lays great weight on *mentalités*, or social val-ues, in steering economic development. The concept is not always treated with respect. In a conference on the "failed transitions" to industrialization of Italy and Holland, one American dissenter called it "garbage," eliciting a mildly acrimonious debate in which a Dutch historian objected to the "flat denial of the possible role of ingrained habits and customs, and of concepts of social stratification or of artisanal professional pride" (Kranz and Hohenberg, eds., 1975, pp. 34, 63, 87). *Mentalités* can be thought of as institutions, which Paul David called "the Carriers of History." An economic historian, David includes with institutions "conventions and organizations" (1994). A similar concept has been developed in political science, called "regimes," defined as "principles, norms, rules and decision-making procedures around which actor expectations converge in a given issue area" (Krasner, 1983, p. 1).

In modern economic analysis the incentive to work hard and take risks is assumed to come from the urge to maximize or optimize income and wealth. In history, a more basic drive is found in the desire to emulate, a propensity that Adam Smith speaks to in both *The Wealth of Nations* (1776 [1937], p. 717) and *The Theory of Moral Sentiments* (1759 [1808], p. 113). The two goals may converge if people choose to emulate the rich, or may run parallel to one another if one goal is wealth as such and another is "positional goods," which demonstrate to the world that one does better than others (Hirsch, 1976). The target of emulation may differ from person to person, from country to country, and from time to time depending on psychological makeup of individuals and families, on class structure and social mobility. Even in countries without feudal tradition nobility, or its equivalent in comfort and prestige, is often the goal through taking on the trappings of nobles—a chateau, stately home, public office, noble spouses for one's children through dowries, or their education in elite institutions. A wide-ranging historical debate is whether merchants in moving to country estates are making an economic decision because food prices are rising faster than those of industry, or because they fluctuate less wildly; that is, is the move to the country to better themselves economically or to escape the risks of trade and in some cases finance?

In trading cities like Hamburg and Lübeck, tradition called for keeping the business going, spurning noble status, and even not allowing one's daughters to marry Junkers (members of the Prussian aristocracy). Where class distinctions made emulation of the nobility difficult or impossible, it was safer to stay in contact with one's own milieu.

Even if the merchant moving into the country is an "improver," in Smith's terminology, there is likely to be a decline absent a surge of new men:

> A managerial elite that lives by trade and manufacture must maintain an active, inquisitive, energetic mode of life. Merchants deal mostly with equals; to prosper a man must perpetually respond to new situations, be ready to defend himself or flee, calculate margins, take risks. . . . Landlords and tax collectors who squeeze a sullen and resentful peasantry have a far less stimulating experience of life. (McNeill, 1974a, p. 227)

This says nothing about the world of finance, which may keep financiers on their toes as they deal with equals or let them approach the style of tax collectors as the unscrupulous exploit the naïve.

The notion of mentality is applied especially to the Spaniards, and to a certain extent rubs off on the Portuguese. An outstanding Spanish trait is pride. The Spanish thought themselves unique, sui generis (Brenan, 1950, p. xvii); so did the Portuguese (Rogers, 1989, p. 76). Most countries and most thoughtful people believe themselves unique. In the Spanish case uniqueness has usually been coupled with characteristics such as sloth, laziness, bigotry, cruelty by the imperial ruler (Herr and Pont, 1989, p. 210). Fernand Braudel contrasts the pride of the Spaniards, which makes them unwilling to borrow technology or the work habits of others and happy in sloth (1966 [1975], p. 764), with the vanity of the French. Pride means that you don't care about the opinions of others and are unwilling to imitate them; vanity calls for taking others' opinions into account and working well to earn esteem (Ortega, quoted by Ilie, 1989, p. 161). But one must be careful with such stereotypes. Maria Carmen Ingesias credits Montesquieu with spreading these notions that became widely accepted abroad and to a considerable extent within Spain, as Ortega and Brenan testify. She quotes Montesquieu's *Spirit of the Laws XIX*: "To the last detail, Spain was a reverse image of English vitality" (1989, p. 145). Faulting the country for building an empire on gold and silver of the New World and rehashing a few platitudes about the Inquisition and expelling the *moriscos* were shortsighted, she thinks, as was Montesquieu's treatment of pride and sloth (ibid., pp. 147, 149). None of these generalizations made allowance for the possible change (resilience) with the spread of the Enlightenment into Spain from France in the eighteenth century.

Slowdown

Economic historians frequently devote attention to singling out particular causes and particular turning points in the path of economic decline. In the economic decline of a state, many causes may work at various paces in the aging process leading to decline at a late stage of the nation cycle, including in no particular order: a shift from accumulation of wealth to resisting its decline; risk aversion; conspicuous consumption; loss of monopoly, including a loss of status as a leading intermediary to direct trading; exhaustion of resources; a weakening of entrepreneurial dynamism and innovative capacity; rent-seeking; loss of tolerance of particular groups for the public good, leading "distributional coalitions" to fend off their share of national burdens by unwillingness to pay taxes; unions pushing up wages; overstretch, that is, overweening ambition that tries to achieve too much with given resources. The rapid decline of Spain in the seventeenth century, especially under the catastrophic ministry of Olivares, was the result, Gerald Brenan maintained, of the usual Spanish attribute of "attempting ambitious projects without considering the economic and material means.

The Spanish national vice had always been over-confidence and optimism" (1950, p. 2). A present-day business economist, writing on his own heretical views, suggests that financial troubles arise partly from errors because of the difficulties of forecasting, but are "mainly due to the fact that human beings are genetically wired to be unduly optimistic gamblers, to be myopic and to tend to addiction . . ." (Wojnilower, 1992). Wojnilower was writing of financial markets, and his view can be illustrated over the years by the Fuggers, Medici, Barings, and today Bunker Hunt, Ivan Boeskey, Michael Milken, et al.

The Role of War

The subject of war belongs primarily to the next chapter, which outlines the shift of economic primacy from one country to another. I have, moreover, mentioned the view that defeat can stimulate, and also the Organsky and Kuglar "Phoenix theory" of the recovery of losers in war ten to fifteen years after defeat. But there is something to be said for the hypothesis that war is a hothouse for growth or decline, accelerating the speed of upswing of rapidly growing economies and the decline of those wilting or slowing down, without regard to winners and losers. The notion derives perhaps mostly from Anglo-American experience after World Wars I and II, which accelerated both growth in the United States and relative decline in Britain. Examples can be multiplied. Venice declined in the last quarter of the sixteenth century despite the 1571 victory over the Turks at Lepanto. Dutch growth was only mildly interrupted by French occupation in 1672 because the country was close to its zenith (in most views), but Holland was finished off as a leading economic and political power by French conquest in 1793. War puts heavy pressure on resources. How that pressure affects the economy depends importantly on the capacity of society to respond, especially in the adjustment of ancient rights over forests, water, mines, and roads as change occurs (Cipolla, reference misplaced). The response to disaster, epidemics, and epizoötics (animal disease) equally required social coordination; Europe had it in abundance, including public subsidies for killing and burying dead animals and quarantining vessels and houses at great expense in medieval Europe; but Islamic countries and the Far East did not, their governments remaining passive in similar dire circumstances (E. L. Jones, 1978).

The physical destruction of war was widely regarded as its most serious economic consequence until the German and Japanese miracles after World War II, when it seemed clear that casualties, war damage, and dislocation were relatively unimportant compared with responsiveness. Responsiveness falls under the heading of social innovation in the Central Planning Bureau of the Netherlands model. The Thirty Years' War in the Holy Roman Empire has been blamed for the setback in central European economic progress for a long period, including especially the succeeding necessity to rely on foreign merchants. Even here, however, a few observers believe that the currency debasement of the period was more destructive than the loss of capital and manpower (G. Parker, 1984, p. 214; Steinberg, 1966, p. 1060).

Policy

Just as widespread war can stimulate or set back economic growth, so economic policy can produce different results depending on the responsiveness of a country at the relevant levels. Most economists have favorite therapies for particular economic problems—monetary, fiscal, trade, industrial—especially taxes and subsidies, without emphasizing that the medicine works well or badly depending on the vitality and resilience of the society. Hamilton claimed that in the seventeenth century every wound in Spain healed (quoted by Braudel, 1979 [1984], p. 86). In 1956 West Germany lowered tariffs on imports to correct an export surplus, but found such a dynamic response in Hume's law (that imports create exports) that the balance of payments remained in surplus at higher levels of trade. A still more apposite example is that of Venice, which undertook various measures to support shipping one-hundred years apart, in 1502 and again in 1602. In the earlier instance the medicine worked and could be withdrawn; in the second case, as explained hereafter, it failed to help.

Conclusion

In thinking about economic decline there is a temptation to focus on different functions—debt (Veseth, 1990), technology (Rosenberg and Birdzell, 1986; Mokyr, 1990), coal (W. Parker, 1984, part iii), property rights (North and Thomas, 1973), loss of preeminence in shipping, and the like. In discussing the Mediterranean after 1580, Ferdnand Braudel points to the collapse of vital sectors: public finance, investment, industry, and shipping (1966 [1975], p. 1240). Jaime Vicens Vives laments the passing of Spanish external trade and shipping into foreign hands (1970, pp. 143–45). And yet the leading student of Venetian shipping compares the decline of shipping in Venice with that in the United States, each lost after an early start and brilliance in such an innovation as the clipper ship. But the decline of American shipping after 1860 to competitors with cheaper labor and excellent technology by no means fatally damaged U.S. economic growth (Lane, 1973, p. 337).

In the life cycle of growth and relative decline, the experiences of different countries show somewhat different features, as one factor in growth substitutes for another. But it is the vitality and flexibility giving way to rigidity that determines the pattern.

3

Successive Primacies

Postulate that there is a national life cycle—though it ends in quiescence, not death—with youth, vigorous adulthood, maturity, and eventually aging, somewhat like the process in individuals but with much variance, chaos, path dependency, and unanticipated outcomes of both unplanned events and policy choices. The question raised in this chapter is why one dominant, primary, or leading country is followed by another. I remind the reader that there are some who say this does not happen, and that the various countries of Europe, after 1400 when China stopped growing and before growth spread abroad from Europe to North America and across the Pacific, were more cohesive than disparate in their growth (Elliot, 1961 [1970], p. 172; E. L. Jones, 1981 [1987], p. 236). This is one of those questions the answer to which depends on the choice of the counterfactual: what is being pointed to as the basis of comparison. I choose, however, to follow the model of a Dutch historian who propounded "the law of interrupted progress," holding that "any country pioneering in a new, more highly developed phase of civilization reaches a threshold or barrier beyond which it is extremely difficult to proceed, with the result that the next step forward in the progress of mankind has to be made in another part of the world" (Jan Romein, quoted in Swart, 1975, pp. 47–48). This leaves, to be sure, the question why progress resumes at all instead of countries remaining static, as in the Middle East a century ago, the Far East (except Japan) before World War I, and Africa today. Casual observation attests, however, to the successive economic primacy of the Italian city-states, the Spanish-Portuguese empire, the Low Countries, Great Britain, and the United States, with failed challenges and impressive growth in France and Germany.

Fernand Braudel and Immanuel Wallerstein put the matter in terms of a center and the periphery, or sometimes as the center, pole, or core around which growth proceeds; a semiperiphery; and a periphery beyond that (Braudel, 1979 [1984], chaps. 2, 3; Braudel, 1977, pp. 81–82; Wallerstein, 1980, see index under "core," "periphery"). Wallerstein is especially interested in the exploitation of the periphery by the core; Braudel expresses much the same thought in saying that every time the center extends the periphery it builds up the center (1979 [1984], p. 322). Of more immediate interest is the view that centering is followed by decentering, and "every time a decentering occurs, recentering takes place, as though the world cannot live without a center of gravity" (Braudel, 1977, p. 85). This is denied by a British historian writing on the Netherlands, who takes occasion throughout his study of Dutch trade to oppose many of Braudel's generalizations. He claims that the Renaissance and Reformation constituted an age of great dispersal of economic power, polynuclear in its expansion (Israel, 1989, pp. 1, 3). The issue is the important one of timing. By the early seventeenth century the Dutch Republic had established a *Pax Neerlandica* over the waters of the Baltic and North Sea (ibid., p. 95), and Israel notes the "Dutch world-trade hegemony during the seventeenth century" (ibid., p. 158). It is also worth observing that a British journalist who knows Japan asserts that it is "misleading to infer from British dominance in the nineteenth century and American in the twentieth that the world must now look for a dominant power or a dominant peacekeeper" (Emmott, 1989, p. 16). Two cases do not build a political law, to be sure, but as this book attempts to show, the pressure for hierarchy, hegemony, or leadership, whatever one chooses to call it, is more general than the British and American cases alone.

Catching Up and Leapfrogging

Much of the discussion of economic growth among developed countries after World War II ran in terms of "catching up." Some country got ahead in a war, Britain during the Napoleonic wars, the United States in World Wars I and II. When peace returned, other countries gained an opportunity to catch up. New technology was readily available to them, as free riders on the innovation successes of the leaders. The leader or leaders slowed down. Followers were assumed to catch up (Abramovitz, 1986 [1989]), and income per capita in various economies tended to converge. Some considerable econometric energy was expended in testing national incomes for convergence, finding some after World War II as the United States rate of growth slowed relative to that of especially Japan, Germany, France, Italy, Spain, Sweden, and Switzerland, but finding little before World War I.

It was early evident that there was no obvious reason why a rapidly growing country should slow down as its level of living approached that of the erstwhile leader, and attention turned to "leapfrogging." *The Economist* devoted an article to the subject (October 16, 1993). A trio of international trade economists has recently produced a model in which lagging countries produce "occasional" new technologies which, with lower wages, enable the countries to pass the leader in income per capita. The model is admittedly simple, with only two countries; a little potted history; citations from Adam Smith, Alfred Marshall, and David Landes; and a mention but no admixture of social forces such as conspicuous consumption, changes in risk-bearing, or chaotic events such as war (Brezis, Krugman, and Tsiddon, 1993).

Centralization and Pluralism

There is tension in many or perhaps most forms of economic and social organization between centralization and pluralism. Centralization is readily seen within a given country. It is partly a result of specialization of function with an admixture of other processes such as location theory, economies of scale as modified by chaos theory, and the power of the strong. Peoples, institutions, cities, nations, even continents arrange themselves in a hierarchical order. "Inside a given civilization, an . . . interaction may be detected . . . between center and periphery, capital and provinces, upper and lower classes. . . . Varying skills and conflicting interests therefore divide civilized communities among themselves" (McNeill, 1983, pp. 10–11). Specialization and economies of scale mean that differences of function widen between cities and areas producing primary products, pinned to particular resource-bound locations. Cities administer. Central-place theory assembles buyers looking for supplies, and suppliers looking for buyers. The process gives rise to theater districts, market areas, insurance districts, financial districts. The same city-state or nation need not be ahead in every function. Some countries have government, finance, and trade located in a single city—the primate arrangement—as in Paris and London. In others more federal arrangements prevail, with a division between government and economic leadership: Milan and Rome, Amsterdam and the Hague, Washington and New York, Ottawa and Toronto, Canberra and Sydney, Sao Paolo and Brasilea. The process can be seen in slow motion especially in the field of finance, as banks started locally, grew, and then gravitated to financial centers, often in the face of government pressure to maintain the system on a pluralistic basis (Kindleberger, 1974 [1978]).

Centralization can be a deliberate policy, as illustrated by Louis XIV bringing his nobility to Versailles away from their scattered chateaux. Its Darwinian manifestation is the coagulation of financial centers, largely through the movement of banks, when political constraints are lifted. The unification of Italy in 1860 produced a movement of bank concentration, first from Turin to Florence when the government moved there, then to Rome as the capital went that extra step, finally back to Milan when it became clear that Rome, for all its attraction for papal revenue, was not a business center. In Germany banks in Cologne, Frankfurt, Darmstadt, Dresden, and most reluctantly Hamburg found themselves pulled to Berlin after unification in 1871. The process was repeated after 1945, when the occupation authorities in Germany first established central banks in the *Laender*—at Hamburg, Düsseldorf, and Frankfurt; then yielded to their merger into a *Bank deutscher Laender*; and finally gave up and permitted the creation of the Bundesbank, a **central** bank, despite the word *federal* (*Bund*) in its name. Similar populist resistance to a central bank had been shown in the United States in 1913 when the Federal Reserve Act created twelve ostensibly regional financial markets, each with its regional central bank, only to find financial power gravitating to New York and the Federal Reserve Bank of New York, which ultimately yielded much of its clout to a political unit, the Federal Reserve Board in Washington.

Resistance to centralization occurs in finance when centripetal force is matched by an outside pull. Hamburg was an international, not a highly nationalistic, city and held out against the Zollverein—the 1834 customs union among German states—and the attraction to Berlin of its banks as long as it could. Regarded as an English city, its merchants forbade their daughters to marry Junkers, and when the pull of the Commerzbank to Berlin proved irresistible, it chose to disguise its ignominious surrender by merging first with a bank in Frankfurt and moving to Berlin only thence. The federal structure in Switzerland for a long time proved too strong for centralization of banks and money markets—Geneva was pulled to France, and Basel to Alsace and the upper Rhine in Germany—which countered the ultimate centripetal force of Zurich. The resistance in Germany to the centralizing pressure of London at the international financial level after 1872 is mentioned below.

The classic example of centralism versus pluralism is the United Provinces of the Netherlands, where Holland dominated the seven provinces; directed much of the military, naval, and commercial activity; and paid for the privilege of leadership among the provincial "free riders" by paying a disproportionate share of the taxes. Jonathan Israel objects to Fernand Braudel's characterization of Holland, essentially Amsterdam, as a center or pole of economic development, insisting that the United Provinces were fundamentally decentralized or federal, with the other provinces preventing Amsterdam from controlling foreign policy, shipping, trade, and fisheries, or dominating the Dutch East India Company (Vereinigde Oostindiche Compagnie, VOC) (1989, pp. 187–89). In 1622 Amsterdam had 122,000 inhabitants, but Leiden had 44,000, Haarlem 39,000, Delft 23,000—closer to the log-normal than to the primate pattern. As the United Provinces declined in the eighteenth century, the reluctance, even refusal of the other provinces to allow greater centralization of decision-making, especially in taxation, in the wars against Britain and France revealed how decentralization obstructed effective decision-making, thus hastening the speed of decline (Boxer, 1965, p. xxiii; Schama, 1977 [1992]).

Pluralism within an overarching unity is capable of yielding advantages. Italian art, German music, British invention were grounded in local rivalries and initiatives. In a recent treatise on historical economic growth, John Powelson (1994) introduces the power-diffusion process, which distinguishes centralized societies where decisions come from the top down, as opposed to the process in pluralist societies where change may come from the bottom up. He claims that the power-diffusion process does not supplant theories based on Smithian exchange, Schumpeterian innovation, resources, culture, and the like, and is relevant today largely to less-developed countries where change is applied by government or from outside as in the conditionality coming from the International Monetary Fund. The issue is complex. Such a loose organization as the Hanseatic League "could not act to develop the latent economies of concentrated trade to the full extent" (Marshall, 1920, p. 692). Centralization can be defended by the metaphor that a post office is cheaper than messengers (ibid., pp. 693–94).

Hierarchical ordering is most clearly seen in international monies, whose use involved centralization well before such centralization was possible in trade in commodities. In the Mediterranean, trade was conducted within a changing series of national or local currencies—the Byzantine bezant, Venetian ducat, Florentin florin, Genoan genoin, Spanish maravedi, Dutch rixdollar, British pound sterling, and U.S. dollar. Before the sixteenth century with slow communication it was necessary to have stores of commodities in many regional markets. By 1590, Amsterdam emerged at the head of "a hierarchy of exchanges" and became the world's central store and hub of commercial finance (van der Kooy, 1931, quoted in Israel, 1989, p. 73). Selection of which money is used in international trade (as unit of account, to be sure, not necessarily medium of exchange or store of value), of the "top money" in the phrase of Susan Strange (1971), is made by the market, in Darwinian fashion. Political leaders propose, markets dispose. One cannot necessarily measure the primacy of an economy by the standing of its currency because of lags in recognition of decline; finding a suitable alternative may stretch out over a long period. When a top currency starts to depreciate, however, some recognition of decline is signaled, as the depreciation of the genoin (Braudel, 1979 [1984], p. 159) (which replaced the Byzantine bezant [Lopez, 1951]), the Flemish and Brabant groat (Davis, 1973, p. 98), the French franc from 1914, the pound sterling (after 1931) and the U.S. dollar from 1973 suggest. Money markets arrange themselves in hierarchical order, though exact rankings are not always completely clear, and rivalry persists (Coste, 1932; Kindleberger, 1984 [1993], pp. 115–17, 260–63).

Cooperation and Rivalry

The hypothesis that there is usually one economic leader rather than two or more operating as equals must be modified for cooperative relations between or among countries or their nationals, although such relations may have an element, perhaps sizeable, of imbalance and exploitation. Bankers from Lucca and Siena in Britain; Venetian and Genoese bankers in Augsburg; Florentine bankers in Bruges, then Antwerp and Lyons; the Genoese in Seville and Lyons made clear that trade and finance flowed in channels rather than spread evenly over broad surfaces. A relationship between countries might transcend the mercantile and banking realms. The Treaty of Methuen in 1703 between Portugal and Great Britain dealt with cloth and wine made famous by David Ricardo's discussion of comparative advantage, and seems to have been a response to the discovery of gold in Brazil in 1680. It has been attacked as unusually exploitive in formal colonialism (Sideri, 1970). The "special relation" between the United States and the United Kingdom dates primarily from World Wars I and II when the countries were allies, deriving its strength from the colonial past and common language.

The greater the degree of equality between cooperating parties, the more likely a struggle between them for ascendancy. An editorial in the *New York Herald Tribune* in connection with the financial crisis of 1857 read:

> Each panic has resulted in making the city of New York the centre of finance and trade for this continent. In 1837 it stood on a sort of struggling emulation with Philadelphia and Boston. . . . The rivalry between New York and other cities has ceased. The late struggle in 1857 was in great degree between New York and London, and has been terminated in the advantage of the former city. And the time must not ere long arrive when New York, not London, will become the financial center not only of the New World, but also, to a great extent, of the Old World. (Quoted in Evans, 1859 [1969], pp. 113–14)

This of course was *chutzpah*; "not ere long" proved to be more than half a century. As change appeared on the horizon, however, the United Kingdom became acutely conscious of the decline of London and the rise of New York. In speeches announcing and defending the restoration of the pound to par on April 28 and May 4, 1925, Winston Churchill, chancellor of the exchequer, said:

> . . . this island . . . which is the centre of a wide Empire and has . . . if not the primary, at any event the central position of the world (1925 [1974], vol. 4, p. 3362)

and

> If the English pound is not to be the standard . . . the business of not only the British Empire, but of Europe as well, might have to be transacted in dollars instead of pounds sterling. I think that would be a great misfortune. (ibid., p. 3599)

Prestige dominates profit in such remarks as this, and in the rivalry for primacy generally. Other ambitious statements come from Germany in the half century before 1914. Germany must be prepared to fight for "a place in the sun to become a world power" (Böhme, 1968b, pp. 106, 111). Georg von Siemens spelled out the details to his father as early as 1866 à propos free trade and the 1862 tariff treaty with France:

> If we don't want to be colonies like Portugal, Turkey, Jamaica, etc., if we don't want to remain an agricultural state, sending out products through England, and if we don't want to deal with foreign trade people, etc., then we must have Schleswig-Holstein and then must the Zollverein and Prussia be identical. (Böhme, 1966, p. 205, from Helfferich, 1921, vol. 1, p. 46)

Challengers

The German case illustrates an ambitious power ready to challenge the leader for primacy. Perhaps the classic example is that of Britain in the seventeenth century and its challenge to the Dutch. The Dutch, according to Jonathan Israel, broke through to world trade hegemony in 1590 to 1609, and were the "most hated, and yet the most admired and envied commercial nation of the seventeenth century" (Heckscher, 1935 [1983], vol. 1, p. 351, quoted in Israel, 1989, p. 13, note 1). The hate, envy, and admiration shine forth in the writings especially of English contemporaries—Mun in the 1620s, a series of commentators on trade in the middle of the century, Sir Josiah Child in the last third. In some instances, the same difference between Britain and the Netherlands brought envy, admiration, and scorn; for example, Dutch shipping, which was cheaper, efficient because ships were built lightly, and protected by convoys, was "weak." Particularly admired were the Dutch industry; frugality; the patent system; government support of trade, including standardization of output and control of its quality; the low rate of interest coming from thrift; and the aggressive fishing in specially built busses (Letwin, 1969; Mun, ca. [1622, 1664], pp. 182, 198–206; Thirsk and Cooper, eds., 1972, pp. 21, 45, 56–57, 69, 71, 432, 506). Early in the century Alderman Cockayne tried to break the Dutch monopoly on finishing woolen cloth by sizing, fulling, and dyeing it in England (Thirsk and Cooper, eds., 1972, p. 194ff). The Dutch defeated that by a boycott. War between the Dutch and English broke out in the Far East but was over quickly in 1619 without spreading to Europe. The remark of Charles Boxer about the attitudes of the companies in the Far East applies as well to the Dutch and English in Europe:

> There is a remarkable contrast between the attitude of the directors and servants of the Dutch East India Company toward their English counterparts and rivals in the seventeenth as compared to the eighteenth centuries. Down to about 1670, the Dutch considered themselves superior in energy and ability, as well as in capital and material resources to the English. Moreover, the British frequently admitted their relative inferiority. In the last quarter of the seventeenth century the relative attitudes of the two rivals began to change. We find the English growing more aggressive and self-confident, and the Dutch becoming doubtful of their ability to compete. . . . (Boxer, 1970, p. 245)

English bashing of the Dutch produced such pejorative expressions as Dutch courage (alcohol), Dutch treat (where the guest pays for his own meal), Dutch uncle (a severe disciplinarian), and the like (Partridge, 1967, pp. 250–51).[1] The tension between the two countries was of course accentuated by the three Anglo-Dutch wars of 1652–1654, 1665–1667, and 1672–1674, and the English navigation acts of 1651, 1660, 1663, and thereafter. After the Restoration of the Stuarts in 1661, the Duke of Albemarle said, "What we want is more of the trade the Dutch now have" (E. N. Williams, 1970, p. 484). And Sir Josiah Child in the same era expressed both British envy and its consequences: "The prodigious increase of the Netherlanders in their domestic and foreign trade, riches and multitude of shipping, is the envy of the present and may be the wonder of all future generations" (1668, quoted by Letwin, 1969, p. 41); and "All trade is a kind of warfare" (ibid., p. 28).

The Invasion of Monopolies

One means of pulling down a country enjoying economic primacy is to invade its monopolies, skirting its dominant entrepôt by trading directly with customers, stealing its industrial secrets, copying its successful methods, enticing its skilled workers and entrepreneurs, and the like. Success in these efforts brings a challenger up to equality. Overtaking and passing requires improvements of existing techniques and innovation in new. The challenged country will try to stay ahead by resisting the loss of machinery, skilled workers, and entrepreneurs, and if still possessed of economic vitality, pushing forward in further improvements in product and process. Details about all of these will appear in the country studies. The processes may involve war, especially when interlopers seek to invade a trade monopoly: Genoa against Venice in the Levant; the Dutch and British against the Portuguese in Asia; French, Dutch, and English in the Spanish and Portuguese monopolies in the New World. The outcome of the armed conflict may determine whether economic hegemony is maintained or changes. War is not necessary, however, for newcomers to threaten the old:

> Even countries with a glorious industrial past . . . were bound to suffer severe losses at the hands of their younger rivals and to lose the lead they had traditionally enjoyed in a wide variety of activities . . . cloth-making . . . ship-building, iron metallurgy, silk-making. . . . In all such cases long-established and comfortable supremacies were challenged and toppled as newcomers steadily caught up in field after field and, by dint of greater efficiency, lower costs, or better design, often left the older nation far behind. (Sella, 1970 [1974], pp. 418–19)

---

[1]Eric Partridge observes that many of these expressions came into common use in the eighteenth and nineteenth centuries, but that "Dutch" became a pejorative noun and adjective in England in the seventeenth and early eighteenth centuries as a consequence of trade rivalry and naval jealousy.

Recentering in the Absence of Challengers

At a given time there is likely to be some country or countries that are continuously challenging for political and/or economic primacy even though their chances of success may not be high. France in the nineteenth and twentieth centuries offers perhaps the outstanding example. But there are questions whether "recentering," as Braudel calls it, always takes place quickly, whether two centers can coexist, whether in the absence of a serious and aggressive challenger there may not be an extended vacuum of power, resulting in international anarchy. Braudel discusses the issue at some length in *Afterthoughts on Material Life and Capitalism*, lectures delivered at Johns Hopkins University in 1977 following the completion (in French) of the mammoth three-volume book *Civilization and Capitalism* (1981, 1982, 1984). The argument is not completely clear. The world economy always has a pole, or center, represented by a dominant city. Two centers can exist simultaneously and for a prolonged period (Rome–Alexandria; Venice–Genoa; London–Amsterdam). Centers shift—"In 1500 there was a sudden and gigantic shift from Venice to Antwerp and then in about 1590–1610 to Amsterdam. London moved ahead 1790–1815, and in 1929 the center moved to New York. If New York were to succumb—but I don't think it will—the world will have to find a new center" (Braudel, 1977, chap. 3, esp. pp. 80–86).

Braudel's discussion does not settle the question of how transitions from one center to another are made, as a rule. I assume that the Soviet Union was not included with New York as a case of two centers existing simultaneously, since the socialist bloc was largely outside the world economy in the capitalist mode that Braudel was interested in. If decentering produces two centers, there is a question whether they exist in tension and competition, as Genoa and Venice before the war of Chioggia (1378–1381) and London and Amsterdam, as shown above, or whether there is a gap. The year 1929 as a time when the center moved from London to New York seems abrupt. In the usual view Britain started to decline in the 1870s, 1880s, or 1890s while the United States behaved in isolationist fashion until 1936, 1941, or 1945. Certainly it did not assert any hegemony in 1933 at the World Economic Conference of 1933, which it broke up.

Currently a further slow transition from New York as center to a recentering seems in prospect, even though New York's decentering (its decline, widely discussed) is not certain. With the collapse of the Soviet Union and its satellites, however, no new center is in sight. Germany and Japan have grown faster and have been more innovative than the United States, but both, after defeat in challenges to U.S. primacy in World War II, have been loyal followers of the United States, unwilling to contest for the position of leader. Neither has been aggressive in pushing its currency as international money—for a leading position as a vehicle currency in trade and short-term capital movements or for the issue of foreign loans. On the contrary, after a period when much of the world but especially France regarded the dollar as extracting seignorage from its trade and banking partners, no other country, except possibly France (which is unlikely to have taken its challenge seriously), has vied for the position (Tavlas, 1991; Tavlas and Ozeki, 1992). The contrast is with the British in 1763, who were anxious to establish direct links in foreign exchange with Russia rather than having to deal through Amsterdam in rixdollars; and with Germany which, after 1871, established the Deutsche Bank to compete with London in world finance and felt shame when the German navy had to continue buying foreign exchange from London (Helfferich, 1923–25 [1956], p. 51–52).

War

Wars are often turning points in the rise of one country to world economic primacy and the decline of another. This is especially the case with trade wars, like the five between Venice and Genoa from 1250 to the battle of Chioggia in 1380 that ended the fourth war; the defeat of the Venetians in 1431, which was primarily an incident in the war between France and Milan; and, to mention them again, the four Anglo-Dutch wars, three in the third quarter of the seventeenth century and the fourth a century later. W. W. Rostow distinguished colonial wars, wars of regional aggression, and balance-of-power wars. He did not include trade, dynastic, or religious wars in his taxonomy, which was designed to fit into his analysis of stages of economic growth. He explicitly excluded wars that rest fundamentally on nationalism (1960, chap. 8). Richard Rosencrance, a political scientist, divides states, especially nation-states, into those focusing on military-political power, interested especially in acquiring more territory and willing to fight to gain more or defend what they hold, and "trading states," which expect to gain their economic ends by trade. Germany and Japan exemplify the former before World War II and the latter after defeat in 1945 (1986).

Any classification runs risks, however. Before the first Venetian-Genoese war in 1250, rivalry between the two city-states had been dampened by their fear of Pisa. When Pisa was overcome by Genoese victory, the Genoese became "more and more energetic as commercial competitors. In the wars that followed, profits were at stake but the wars were kept going more by hate and vainglory than by economic calculation" (Lane, 1973, p. 73). On the other hand, the War of the Spanish Succession from 1700–1713, although ostensibly a dynastic one, as Louis XIV sought to place a Bourbon on the Spanish throne after the Hapsburg line had dwindled, was actually a war to capture European trade with Spanish America for France, victory over Spain being only a stepping stone (Kamen, 1969, p. 135). The English and Dutch involvement in that war was also motivated by their interest in future trade with the Indies (ibid., p. 9). Rostow's colonial wars related mainly to trade and finance, first wars of a metropolitan power against a less developed part of the globe, then those between European powers as they contested for a monopoly or shares in access to the wealth of particular portions. The Spanish and the Portuguese fought against one another in 1580 in a war mostly of regional aggression, but in part over rights in the East Indies and the Americas. England, the United Provinces of Holland, and France tried to carve out portions of both extra-European areas for their own exploitation and to defeat the Portuguese in the east, so that the conflict, coming a decade after the Battle of Lepanto in the Mediterranean between Venice, Genoa, and Spain on one side and the Ottoman Empire on the other, has been called "the first world war" (Lane, 1973, p. 293). Similarly, if a century later, the War of the Spanish Succession with France and Spain against the English, Dutch, and Austrians, the last actually interested in the succession rather than trade with the Americas, has been called "a vast world war" (Israel, 1989, p. 363). While they fought together, relations between England and the United Provinces were strained when it came to making peace at Utrecht in 1713. The Dutch were bitterly opposed to a Frenchman on the throne of Spain, on the grounds, thought to represent the views of merchant members of the Dutch Jewish Sephardhim, that trade in Peruvian silver would be moved from Amsterdam to France. The British failed to support the Dutch position, and the loss of the latter contributed to, or marked a step in, Dutch economic decline (ibid., p. 375).

Economists are interested for the most part in the effects of war on economies and especially on technological change for the better, rather than in the economic factors that contribute to war. In *War and Economic Progress*, for example, John Nef maintained that war is a disease of human nature that has afflicted all societies, and not just a product of capitalism (1952, p. 113). War in his view is a mark of humanity's sin. "Warlike impulses—fear, hatred, cruelty, revenge, pleasure in destruction and human suffering" have a positive side—"competition, religious conviction, and the courage and sense of honor aroused by the obligation to fight" (ibid., p. 115). The negatives are stronger. Nef quotes Voltaire to the effect that men have corrupted nature, since they were not born as wolves but became wolves (ibid., p. 165). There is a hint of the reverse causation, however: "Peace breeds production, but production breeds war" (ibid., p. 113). It may well be true that economic progress brings with it more deadly weapons (McNeill, 1982). That economic progress leads to war is a critical tenet in theories connecting the Kondratieff cycle and the hegemonic cycle to war cycles. The theory does not seem plausible in the light of its tight causal links with no room for chaos.

Kondratieff Cycles, War Cycles, and Hegemonic Cycles

Many economists, economic historians, and political scientists have followed Kondratieff in his discovery of the fifty-year cycle in prices, starting with the Napoleonic wars. Schumpeter, Rostow, Forrester, Goldstein, and Berry extended the long wave, sometimes called "the trend period," from prices to production. Goldstein and Berry went further and linked prices and production to war. George Modelski (1983) went further still and added hegemonic cycles.

There is not much of a problem in connecting prices with production, although the explanations of individual analysts tend to differ, in some cases widely. Schumpeter and Forrester, for example, view the Kondratieff cycle as the outcome of widely spaced major innovations such as steam and electricity plus chemicals, whereas Rostow ties it to shifting relationships between population and primary resources. Prices in turn can be linked to wars, especially the inflations of the Napoleonic wars and World War I— one-hundred years apart, with a lesser peak more or less halfway in the Crimean War in Europe and the Civil War in the United States. The notion that the causes of these wars lay in economic rhythms rather than in political issues of balance of power, exorbitant ambition, or in the case of World War I overstretch plus accident, strikes me as implausible.

Joshua Goldstein, who ties prices, production, and war together in a repeated cycle of fifty to fifty-five years, is properly modest about his conclusions, which do not cohere around a single theory, "as it is necessarily the case in an immature field" (1988, p. 152). He extends Kondratieff's price series back three-hundred years to 1495, and hypothesizes that production cycles with a five-year lead to war cycles produce the price rhythms detected by Kondratieff. Twenty-five years of price decline induce a wave of innovation, following more or less Schumpeter's view of creative destruction, which leads to recovery, a rise in real wages, higher output, war, and a peak of prices. War, Goldstein maintains, lags production by about ten years, and leads prices by about one to five years (ibid., pp. 214, 255). The cycle is shown as a graph in Figure 3–1.

Goldstein admits that Paul Samuelson regards all Kondratieff analysis as "science fiction" (ibid., p. 21); that some Kondratieff analysis belongs to "crackpot" theories; that the most he can say is that the existence of long-wave theories cannot be rejected (ibid., p. 164). In commenting on the terse version of the Goldstein analysis, Richard Goodwin (1991) says he is convinced of an intimate connection between long waves and wars, emphasizing that a buoyant economy makes war more possible. He is unhappy, however, in trying to explain long waves by wars, which requires a theory of why wars occur periodically, any theory of which seems less plausible than one based on economics (ibid., p. 326). This approaches the extreme view that economic results have to have economic causes, if indeed the Kondratieff cycle ever really existed.

Brian Berry has surveyed the Kondratieff/war/hegemon cycle with thoroughness, but concludes that the fifty- to fifty-five-year Kondratieff cycle is much less plausible than the Kuznets cycle of twenty to twenty-five years, two of which are contained in each fifty- to fifty-five-year cycle, one expansionary, one contractive. But he is deeply skeptical of relating any economic cycle to cycles in war (1991, pp. 164–66).

Hegemonic cycles are the hypothesis of George Modelski, which I have not pursued. As I understand it from Goldstein and Berry, Modelski believes

Figure 3-1 Goldstein's idealized long wave of sequences of investment, growth, inflation, and wars in "cycle time." *Source*: Berry, 1991, p. 161. Reprinted with permission of Johns Hopkins University Press.

that global wars occurred every one-hundred years or so, with one world power emerging as hegemon, followed a century later by another. Each hegemon in turn is tempted into overambitious plans and ultimately faces delegitimization and defeat, leading to "deconcentration." Modelski's historical depiction of global war, followed by world power, delegitimization, and deconcentration, is shown in Figure 3–2. Five cycles last from 1491 to 2000, the first Portuguese, the next Dutch, then two British, and one United States. Measured on the vertical axis is naval power, which involves a military bias against ground forces of such powers as France and Germany. The global war that brought U.S. hegemony consists of a telescoping of World Wars I and II. Delegitimization of the U.S. hegemony comes in 1973, followed by, in prospect, a sharing of power with Japan and the Soviet Union contesting (Goldstein, 1988, pp. 347, 365).

Berry emphasized that the Kondratieff discussion is rhetorical rather than statistical on the whole, Goldstein that the future is indeterminate. Kondratieff theorists provide ample evidence to support both views. Rostow and Forrester, relying on Kondratieff, asserted in the 1980s that the world economy was turning up (Rostow) and that it was turning down (Forrester). The forecast of the Soviet Union as the challenger for world hegemony seems to have been falsified immediately by the collapse of socialist Europe in 1989. I judge it more fruitful to look at the separate instances of world economic primacy since 1350, without trying to force them into a tightly knit analysis of succession, all the time recognizing that there seems to be a national life cycle; that at any given time the world seems to be moving

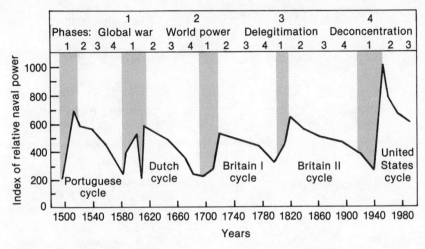

Figure 3–2 Modelski's long cycles of global power. *Source:* Berry, 1991, p. 160. Reprinted with permission of Johns Hopkins University Press.

toward a hierarchical order, which may deteriorate as the leader encounters difficulties and moves down in relative decline; and that sooner, with major wartime challenges, or later, in peaceful interludes, a new country is likely to move into the leading position.

Timing

I am not particularly interested in exact timing, or in spotting "turning points" with precision. Many historians are, and some go in for rounding as an aid to memory. At the simplest level one could hold that the Italian city-states had primacy in the fifteenth century, Portugal and Spain in the sixteenth, the United Provinces of the Netherlands in the seventeenth, France in the eighteenth, Britain in the nineteenth, and the United States in the twentieth, at least for a considerable distance. This mistakenly leaves out Bruges and Antwerp, which flourished as world trade centers in the fifteenth and sixteenth centuries, simultaneously with the Italian city-states and Portugal–Spain respectively. There is a question, too, whether France ever had economic primacy. Braudel notes that France was always contesting for the laurel but never achieved it (1986 [1988], vol. 2, p. 328). France grew rapidly in spurts in the eighteenth century (after 1720 and before 1789, as discussed in chapter 7) and has been said to have been as rich as Britain in 1780, although following a different path to economic growth (O'Brien and Keyder, 1978). Many have doubts about the standard-of-living comparison, if not about the paths. The Modelski designation of Britain as having had two cycles of global power, the first starting in 1688 with the arrival of William and Mary from Holland with the Glorious Revolution, the second after the Napoleonic wars, squeezes out the economic domination of the

French. Another cyclical pattern comes from Hopkins, Wallerstein, and colleagues, and runs in terms of ascending hegemony, hegemonic victory, mature hegemony, and declining hegemony. It is reproduced in Table 3–1, borrowed from Berry (1991, p. 162). It is notable for leaving an extended gap from 1672 (when France briefly occupied Holland) to the start of the Napoleonic wars in 1798, reinforcing skepticism about France as a leading power in the eighteenth century, or in the seventeenth century under Louis XIV for that matter.

One can collect a long string of pronouncements over the rise, peak, and decline of this country or that, and some of them will appear in the country studies in this book. One can argue about whether the United Provinces started to decline in 1672 or whether they were still safely ahead of Britain half a century later, about 1730; about when Britain should be taken seriously as a contender for economic primacy, with its initial rivalry in the seventeenth century, or the industrial revolution of the eighteenth, if indeed there was an industrial revolution. Much depends on the series examined. It is now fairly clear that income per capita grew more slowly than first thought, for example, by Deane and Cole (1962); that capital formation and savings did not make discontinuous jumps that were revolutionary rather than evolutionary, but that exports soared after the American War of Independence; and that technical innovation, measured by patents from 1766, moved up sharply with revolutionary force. The debate continues.

Similar controversy can be found in the timing of British decline. Concern that the British economic leadership was slipping was voiced as early as the Great Exhibition of 1851 but mainly at the end of the nineteenth century. Study of the issue came in the late 1960s and 1970s, when a wave of econometric studies undertook to decide whether British entrepreneurs could be blamed for any decline that had occurred relative to other coun-

Table 3–1 Wallerstein's Cycles (I–IV) of Global Hegemony

Hegemonic power	I. Hapsburgs	II. Netherlands (United Provinces)	III: Great Britain	IV: United States
Ascending hegemony	1450–	1575–1590	1798–1815	1897–1913/1920
Hegemonic victory	. . .	1590–1620	1815–1850	1913/1920–1945
Hegemonic maturity	–1559	1620–1650	1850–1873	1945–1967
Declining hegemony	1559–1575	1650–1672	1873–1897	1967–(?)

Source: Hopkins, Wallerstein, et al. "Cyclical Rhythms and Trends of the Capitalist World Economy." *World-System Analysis: Theory and Methodology,* 1982. Reprinted by permission of Sage Publications, Inc.

tries. Defense of the entrepreneur was undertaken with studies that indicated that the entrepreneur was maximizing income but was subject to constraint in the form of resources unsuited for contemporary technology, that is, that he was following the "equilibrium model" of the Central Planning Bureau (see chapter 2). The argument against the entrepreneur was that he was following this model, a static one instead of a dynamic one, known in Central Planning Bureau terms as the "free-market model with vigorous innovation." The trouble with the British businessman in this view was intrinsic rather than extrinsic. The question was not whether there were bottlenecks as the economy encountered conditions that differed from those in the past, but whether entrepreneurs were sufficiently energetic to break through those bottlenecks, as they had done with those of the eighteenth century. On one showing, the new industries of the period were started for the most part in other countries, and in many cases their founding in Britain was undertaken by foreigners, testifying to the absence of new men in Great Britain. The topic is renewed here. The reality of British decline became clear, despite the econometric defenses, when in the 1980s and 1990s British income per capita was progressively passed by incomes in Germany, France, and Italy.

The same questions—whether the U.S. economy is declining relative to Germany and Japan, and whether American economic hegemony is mature or at an end—is currently debated strongly, especially since publication of books by Mancur Olson (1982) and Paul Kennedy (1987, 1993). At issue are whether the narrowing gap is only "catching up," or whether the structural character of U.S. growth is changing with declining invention, innovation, productivity, and savings. Pinpointing exact timing is probably futile. More later.

This scheme of timing in which economic primacy is ascribed to a single state or nation, with differences rather than similarities being emphasized, is sometimes countered by a north-south instead of a clockwise pattern: the Italian city-states declined in the seventeenth century and the United Provinces and Britain were taking over simultaneously and contesting for leadership. Or the issue may be put in terms of the seas, the primacy of the Mediterranean giving way to that of the Atlantic, the English Channel, the North Sea, and the Baltic, with some doubt about the last increasingly after 1580. McNeill states that by 1600 all the techniques of the Italians had been imitated in northern Europe; as the importance of wood, peat, and coal grew, Italy found itself, because of deforestation, in a fuel shortage (1974, p. 139).

Mention of the clockwise pattern of successive economic primacy brings up a theory that has dropped out of the literature, and that, in any event, I am unable to evaluate. Just before World War I, a Yale geographer and climatologist, Ellsworth Huntington, advanced a thesis that civilization was strongly affected by high-pressure zones, which moved slowly, century by century, from the Middle East to northern Europe, starting in Mesopotamia and moving clockwise to Persia, Greece, Italy, Spain, northward into the

Atlantic, and then into the North Sea and the Baltic, bringing with them economic vitality (1915). Development is well known to have been largely restricted to the temperate zone, as contrasted with arctic and tropical areas. The notion of causal linkages between climate and economic development is thus plausible, but I have no way to judge the Huntington thesis, which seems not to have survived in the historiography.

The attempt to fit successive economic primacies, with or without tight temporal links between them, into the Procrustean bed of theories that encompass national life cycles and most of economics and politics, is one to be put aside as excessively ambitious, in my judgment, at least until one takes a look at the history of the separate entities, as done in the chapters that follow.

4

The Italian City-States

The Dark Ages in Europe from about 800 A.D. came to an end with the commercial revolution of the eleventh and twelfth centuries. The stimulus came largely from the Crusades to the Middle East, which brought western Europe into contact with new and different, many of them luxury, goods, brought to the Middle East partly from India and China by sea to the Persian Gulf and Red Sea and the rest of the way by caravan. Venice and Genoa provided the Crusaders with shipping, and grew rich in the process. The two cities fought with Byzantium, with each other over ports of call and the colonies of Cyprus and Crete, and with the Turks after they had captured Constantinople. Genoa early eliminated Pisa, a port used by Florence, and Amalfi as rivals for the trade. Genoa was also the first to break out of the Mediterranean into the Atlantic and thus to northern Europe in 1278, with Venice following a century later. Slowly, with fighting, Venice and Genoa concentrated their trade, Venice more to the east, Genoa to the west; and in the East Genoa to the north, especially the Black Sea, Venice to the south in Syria and Egypt (Heers, 1964, p. 101). From the east Venice brought mainly spices, silk, and cotton; Genoa brought alum for preparing woolen cloth for dyeing, silk, sugar, raisins, sweet wine, and dyes. From the western Mediterranean, after the fall of Constantinople had cut off the Black Sea, Genoa carried wines, wheat, fruit, and alum from the mines at Tolfa in the papal states to compete with alum from the east. Venetian galleys headed east carried woolens, some timber for shipbuilding until supplies in the upper Adriatic ran low, and especially silver mined in south Germany, the Tyrol, Bohemia, and Hungary.

For a time Venice had few products of its own save for fish and salt, until it began manufacturing woolen cloth, glass, leather goods, and printing. Secure at the head of the Adriatic from which it had cleared potential adversaries and Barbary pirates, its principal advantage lay in intermediary trade between the Levant and south Germany, most notably Augsburg and Nuremberg by means of Alpine passes, largely the Brenner. At first an isolated island in a lagoon, it gradually acquired a hinterland in the Po valley flowing throughout the year with glacial water. Across the Apennines, ringed by mountains, Genoa had no hinterland but was connected to eastern France, the Franche Comté, and Burgundy through the Mt. Cenis and St. Bernard passes leading to the fairs of Champagne. Pack trains through the mountains were expensive and could carry only luxury products. Bulk products came by ship from Genoese colonies in Sardinia, Sicily, and Naples and from Spain.

The commercial revolution led in one direction to shipbuilding and in another to finance. Both city-states without arable land escaped feudalism as Florence did not, and were served by governments in the form of republics, with elected officials, in Venice a doge. Venetian shipbuilding was carried on in the governmental *Arsenale*, built in 1104, that assembled galleys for the navy and "great galleys" for trade. Private yards constructed round (sailing) ships. With three-thousand workers, the *Arsenale* was the largest industrial establishment for its time in Europe (Lane, 1973, pp. 163, 252). Ship timbers were first brought to the lagoon from the lower Alpine slopes in the vicinity, and increasingly from farther away, from mountains to the north and south in the Adriatic and Ragusa (modern Dubrovnik) (ibid., p. 28). Government officials used care in selecting logs of the proper grain and strength. Naval galleys were built to standard design and size, with interchangeable planks and specialized workmen; and spares were located at ports along the coast to permit rapid repair (ibid., p. 363; McNeill, 1974a, pp. 5–6). One such galley was assembled in 1574 under the eyes of Henry III of France in less than an hour (McNeill, ibid., p. 244 [note 9 to p. 6]; Romano, 1968, p. 62, says "a few hours").

The maneuverable galley, manned by rowers, was used to carry valuable cargos, frequently on scheduled voyages. Round sailing ships carried cargos of bulk. The round ship was copied from the Hanseatic cog, about 1300, and was continuously improved. A square sail was substituted for the lateen for greater ease in coming about. Over decades the single mast was replaced by two, later by three (Lane, 1968, p. 36). The stern post rudder in place of the steering oar allowed ships to be built larger, with stronger rigging, armament, and better means of navigation—enough so that over one-hundred years to about 1300, the commercial revolution had led to a nautical revolution (Lane, 1973, chap. 10). The peak of gradual improvement was reached about the middle of the fifteenth century, and Lane comments that the three-masted full-rigged round ships of Venice in 1485 looked more like the ships of 1785 than they did those of 1425 (1968, p. 36).

The Genoan "nave" (in French *nef*), similarly rigged, grew in size to as much as 1,000 tons, making it difficult or impossible to penetrate silted estuaries to ports such as Aigues Mortes, Bruges, Cologne, Pisa, Rome, and Seville.

The commercial revolution involved more than the improvement in ships. Specialization went forward. The merchant-traveler, sailing with his cargoes, gave way to a sedentary merchant who stayed in his counting house and warehouse while his goods were entrusted to the ship captain, who delivered them to an agent at the port of call. In contrast to the modern cynical view that the principal had to closely monitor and bond the agent, who was more interested in his own short-term gains than in the welfare of his principal (Jensen and Meckling, 1976), the vast majority of agents seem to have served honestly, "investing in reputation" as a way of earning the respect of their profession and repeat business (Greif, 1989). The merchant equally became separate from the merchant-craftsmen who produced the goods, although as buyer he checked the goods for quality. Early in the commercial revolution sailors were at the same time rowers, warriors, and small-time merchants with their own goods for sale in foreign ports. Venetian rowers were frequently members of a guild ashore, recruited for sea duty when called by the Venetian Council because of war or the need to repress piracy. Eventually specialized arms and armor required specialized militia; the need for greater discipline also reduced opportunities for sailors as traders. Over time, sailors were reduced to a proletariat, often emigrating, revolting, accepting advances, and then failing to appear. The shortage of seamen was accentuated by the Black Death, brought to the city from Romania in 1347 and wiping out half of the Venetian population, with similar devastation elsewhere in the Mediterranean. To fill the rowing benches Venice had to recruit local convicts, men from the colonies, and from Dalmatia, and even to hire galleys from Aragon, complete with crews, for 1,000 ducats a month. The third and fourth wars with Genoa in 1340–1355 and 1378–1381 dealt heavy blows to the class structure, which began to rigidify, and even within the elite there were splits along class lines and by financial interest (Lane, 1973, pp. 174–76). Desertion of Venetian sailors to Pisa, to English shipping, and even to pirate vessels sped the movement away from galleys to round ships, and the hiring of Greeks and of landsmen from the Po valley, who proved to be poor sailors.

Venice

Venice won out over Genoa in the battle of Chioggia in 1380, in the Fourth Venetian-Genoan War. With Genoa exhausted, the fifteenth century brought military and economic dominance to Venice. Old nobles were beginning to abandon the sea and come ashore, acquiring estates in the Terra Ferma, especially in Padua and Verona. New merchants became active in trading with the Levant, with Cyprus and Crete, with south Germany, and with Bruges and Britain. An exemplar of this trade was Andrea

Barbarigo, trading from 1418 to 1445, whose operations were mobile and fluid, allowing him to dodge in and out among the operations of the great families (Lane, 1944, pp. 135–36). Barbarigo dealt with agents in various markets—Germans at the Fondaco dei Tedeschi (warehouse of the Germans) in Venice, cotton buyers in Ulm or Augsburg, cotton sellers in Syria, wool merchants in England, and merchant employers in Venice. According to Frederic Lane, and despite the slow pace of shipping, none could adapt to changing market conditions as rapidly as Venetian merchants with international connections (ibid.). Barbarigo's son, however, was not an active merchant, despite having studied the abacus. He lived off the income from his estates in Crete and the Veronese. In 1483, his profit of 15,400 ducats came mainly from his estates and included only 700 ducats from mercantile operations (Lane, 1944, pp. 170, 179).

There is considerable controversy over whether the move from trade to estates in the Terra Ferma was a symptom of decline. There seems to be little doubt that the change from sea to landed estates took place and that it reduced risk, producing a smaller but less variable income than trade. The central question is whether Venetian nobles were "improvers," as British merchants were said to be by Adam Smith, or were indulging themselves. In some views they earned low yields, splurged in a manic wave of speculation in land, and eager for income permitted deforestation and soil mining (Woolf, 1968; Berengo, 1963, pp. 15–18). In others the move to the land from the sea was a response to higher prices of grain, as population increased and new crops like maize made agriculture production more rewarding. Fernand Braudel expresses doubt that the move from intermediary trade in the city to land in Terra Ferma was a sign of commercial and financial decadence (1979 [1982], p. 286). and Brian Pullan asserts that historians no longer accept the facile suggestion that investment in villas was pointless and cowardly (1968, p. 19). But Peter Burke states the general belief that Venetian landowners took less interest in land as enterprise and more as rentiers. He found it surprising not that Venice (and Amsterdam) shifted from bourgeois to noble pursuits, as did successful merchants in England, France, and Spain, but that the transition was delayed so long (1974, pp. 107–11).

Venetian nobles turned from the sea also to public office. Land and public office contributed to noble status in most European countries, and in Lombardy patrician status was even lost if no family member had held a civic post for three generations (Roberts, 1953, p. 65). The Council of Venice was concerned not only with trade and its protection by the navy, but also with ensuring the feeding of the city. A Grain Office was established with stocks. In the crop failures of the 1590s, attempts were made to bring grain overland from Prussia and Poland, with great difficulty and at great expense. The pressures were reduced as Dutch and English ships reentered the Mediterranean after 1590 and slowly built up a regular traffic (Aymard, 1956, pp. 155–62). The trade required planning as grain harvested in the fall went downriver mainly to Danzig on the Vistula and then had to wait for shipment for the following spring, after the Baltic ice broke up.

In the heyday of Venetian commerce with the Levant and Germany in the fifteenth century, not only did Germans reside in the Fondaco dei Tedeschi in Venice, but north of the Alps Augsburg was said to be half Italian, divided into Venetian and Genoan quarters (Braudel, 1966 [1972], vol. 1, p. 316). Venice was also a center of attraction for Marranos—Spanish and Portuguese Jews—who chose not to convert to Christianity, and who contributed to the intellectual life of the city.

Wars were practically continuous, with fairly rapid recovery between them until the fourth war with Genoa ended with the Battle of Chioggia in 1380 and class lines began to rigidify (Lane, 1973, p. 174). Lane comments that the Genoans were perhaps better sailors, but the Venetians better organizers (ibid., pp. 84–85). The War of the League of Cambrai, when Pope Julius II enlisted the French in an effort to humble the arrogant Venetians and succeeded in defeating their army outside Milan in 1409, constituted a turning point on land (ibid., p. 245). A turning point at sea was the defeat by the Turks in 1503 (ibid., p. 241). Lane dates the beginning of Venetian decline to 1430, and notes that such decline was evident from the third quarter of the fifteenth century as south German merchants shifted their activity to Antwerp. The great Battle of Lepanto one-hundred years later, with the pope, Genoa, and Spain lined up with Venice against Turkey, occurred well after Venetian power had peaked. Testimony to decline is furnished by the fact that Genoa was called on to provide crews for Venetian ships. Rapp's dating of the peak of Venice's undisputed world commercial leadership at 1550, and decline to insignificance by 1700 (1976, p. 164) appears to be a little late.

The decline was drawn out, and not without comebacks. A contrast in resilience is furnished by two "navigation acts" a century apart, requiring goods to be carried in Venetian ships to and from Venice, and sold to or bought from Venetian intermediary merchants. One such set of controls was applied in 1502 and proved so successful in inducing recovery in Venetian shipping that it was given up after a decade (Lane, 1968, p. 31). The navigation act of 1602, on the other hand, proved to be "ill-fated" and "disastrous," as trade moved to other ports where Genoese, British, and Dutch ships were free to conduct it unhindered (Sella, 1968a, p. 91; Lane, 1973, p. 389). Early in the sixteenth century Venice was sleeping the sleep of the rich. By 1600 its coffers were overflowing with money. But while it was richer in the sixteenth than in the fifteenth century, and caught up in finance, it was no longer the center of Mediterranean trade (Braudel, 1966 [1972], vol. 1, pp. 389–91). The transition was not only from trade to finance, but to conspicuous consumption, to art, and to architecture. There was innovation in art, such as the shift of painting from frescos to canvas. The peak of visual art came perhaps a century after that of trade, with the death in the last quarter of the sixteenth century of Titian, Tintoretto, and Palladio.

Venetian decline, to which we recur shortly, has been ascribed to many causes. More than decline, perhaps, what needs to be explained is its success in primacy in the west that lasted from some such time as 1200 to the end of the fifteenth century, or perhaps as late as 1550, "in the face of revolutions in nautical and commercial technologies and in trade routes" (Lane, 1973, p. 2). The greater part of these revolutions was the product of Venetian vitality—in trade, insurance, shipbuilding. Much was owed to effective government of the Republic, led by the Council and the elected doge, who did not hesitate to regulate trade and industry, initially successfully, later less so. After the exhausting fourth war against Genoa, thirty new families were added to the Great Council, the *curti* (short) to distinguish them from the old families (the *longhi*). The new men took over. In the next two and a half centuries no *longhi* achieved the dogeship (Lane, 1973, p. 196). The Republic had always been run by an oligarchy, twenty or thirty great families at the top, plus another hundred or so among the nobility below them (ibid., p. 151). Quarrels were endemic among them, especially because of the haughty manners of the old nobles. Many of these quarrels were over the financing of wars, and the turbulence of the prices of bonds used to finance the wars and of real estate, some of which assets had to be dumped from time to time at ruinous prices to pay for the forced loans levied on holders of wealth. In crises, however, the Venetians managed to pull together.

Venice was essentially a commercial city, There was some transition to industry and finance, but in the latter case not nearly to the extent of Florence. Venice did not innovate in the bill of exchange and double-entry bookkeeping as did Florence, and much of its trade was financed in that city.

Florence

Florence was largely a financial city. It started dyeing woolens bought from the Champagne fairs in the thirteenth century, and gradually developed its own spinning, weaving, and dyeing of wool in the customary practice of import substitution. Its merchants moved mainly into national and international banking; for example, collecting monies for the papacy in Rome and for the other pope in Avignon during the schism of the fourteenth century. There were other Italian banks in Tuscany. The Ricciardi bank of Lucca loaned £400,000 to the British crown, starting in 1272, and failed when it could not collect its debt. The Bardi, Peruzzi, and Aiccuoli banks of Florence helped Edward III finance the Hundred Years' War against France and were similarly bankrupted when that monarch defaulted in 1348. The lending was not for interest, forbidden by usury laws, but for privileges such as nominal rent on some manors, exemption from particular taxes, the right to nominate candidates for ecclesiastical offices, and permission to export wool at favorable exchange rates in competition with the English Merchant Adventurers (Prestwich, 1979, pp. 87–93). The wool was sold to spinners and weavers in Flanders producing for the Champagne fairs.

These fairs—at Troyes, Bar-sur-Aube, Provins, and Lagny—were the center of what Braudel calls "the first world economy" (1986 [1990], p. 148). For two centuries the fairs exchanged English (later Spanish) wool, German linens, and Italian cloth, and alum, spices, and silk brought from the East by Italian merchants.

Florentine bankers were everywhere—Rome, Venice, Genoa, Naples, Milan, Pisa in Italy, and Geneva, Lyons, Avignon, London, and Bruges outside Italy (de Roover, 1966, chaps. 12, 13). Those who went abroad returned home to marry and later to die (Brachtel, 1980; Origo, 1957, p. 124). The zenith of the power of the Medici bank, smaller as it happened than that of the earlier Bardi, was reached about the middle of the fifteenth century, following which the bank got into trouble lending to monarchs, as Franceso de Marco Datini, a humbler merchant-banker of the fourteenth century, was careful not to do (Origo, 1957, p. 95). The Medici bank went bankrupt at the end of the fifteenth century.

Florence had no port beyond Pisa at the mouth of the Arno river, with which it fought from time to time in the struggles between the Guelphs and the Ghibellines (it also fought with Genoa). Florentine galleys carried alum and cloth to Bruges and Southhampton, though Florence had no navy nor any substantial merchant fleet. Part of the reason was that it had an agricultural hinterland, the Maremma, growing wheat, just as the inland city Milano, also without much of a fleet, had the first irrigated lands of the upper Po valley producing rice. Venice and Genoa, without hinterlands, had to rely mainly on imported wheat from Sicily, until Venetian nobles displaced themselves to the Terra Ferma. The Medici established another Tuscan port in Livorno (Leghorn), a fishing port with a castle that the Duke of Tuscany made a free port in 1590. It flourished for a time when the Venetian navigation acts led especially the British to make use of it. Thomas Mun was a commission agent there for the greater part of his stay in Italy from 1597 to 1607, dealing in tin, lead, and cloth from England (de Roover, 1949). A British sailor, Edward Barlow, complained in his diary of the brothels there, sometime before 1670 (Barlow, 1934, p. 163).

Genoa

With the Ligurian mountains close at its back, Genoa was really an island in an economic sense, entirely a medieval creation, without a Roman history, and no state worthy of the name (Heers, 1964, p. 87). Most of its economic history took place outside its borders, partly in Naples, Sicily, and Corsica, partly in the eastern Mediterranean, and in the late sixteenth and early seventeenth centuries in Seville, the Franche Comté, Geneva, and the Spanish Netherlands. It was derided as having a "sea without fish, mountains without wood, men without probity, and women without shame" (Berner, 1974, p. 20). It had some silk production, but its real businesses were trade, war, and finance. Specialization in trade has been discussed, along with the pioneering breakthrough into the Atlantic and joining the

Mediterranean to the North Sea. Its bankers were not strong on double-entry bookkeeping, developed in Florence, but in 1272 they pioneered the first gold coinage since Roman times, the genoin, followed quickly in Florence by the florin, and other modern financial techniques for handling deposits and traffic in bills of exchange (Heers, 1964, pp. 95–96).

Italian bankers worked the fairs that developed after the decline of the fairs of Champagne, Florentine bankers especially in Lyons, the Genoese outside of French jurisdiction in the Franche Comté and Geneva, both on the western north-south axis between Italy and the North Sea, with Geneva on an east-west axis from Lyons (and Marseilles) to Lake Constance and beyond it to Ulm, Augsburg, and Vienna (Bergier, 1963, pp. 40–41). In 1464, Louis XI ordered French bankers to move from Geneva to Lyons, and the Florentine bankers, later and reluctantly the Genoese, followed them. Excluded from the Lyons fair in 1535, the Genoese moved to Besançon under the jurisdiction of the Duke of Savoy. Gradually fairs became more concerned with trade in bills of exchange rather than goods. But Besançon was out of the way, and the fair moved from place to place in the next few years, ending up in 1579 at Piacenza, near to, but outside, Genoa. It could not move to Genoa itself because that would have involved complications over usury (da Silva, 1969, vol. 1, chap. 1). It continued to use the name Besançon, Italianized as Bisenzone. Venice started downhill in economic dominance about 1450, Florence half a century later. The economic success of Genoa lay still ahead when it first competed with, and then replaced, the Fuggers as the bankers of the Hapsburgs in Spain.

Genoese involvement with Spain began with ships sailing to England and Flanders, stopping off en route at Barcelona, Seville, and Lisbon in Portugal. Genoese mariners and merchants woke up Spain commercially, as well as England and Flanders. Some settled in Portuguese colonies and in Lisbon, and especially in Andalusia in Spain, the province in which Seville was located, where they married daughters of Castillian nobles and stimulated trade in sherry, tuna fish, olive oil, and mercury. Gold from West Africa was shifted to Genoa from Lisbon and Seville. When Genoese sailors ran short, Genoa's vessels signed on those from Portugal, from Galicia and from Vizcaya on the Spanish north coast. This early trading relationship paved the way for finance in the latter part of the sixteenth century (Heers, 1964, pp. 99–100), and especially for Genoese dealings in Spanish silver. "The Genoese businessman was remarkable, it has been said, for his adaptability, versatility, 'weightlessness,' and that 'total absence of inertia' admired by Roberto Lopez. Time after time Genoa changed course . . ." (Braudel, 1979 [1984], p. 162).

Columbus's discovery of America in 1492 was followed immediately by some looting of Indian gold, but the main precious metal was silver, which began to arrive from the Americas in volume in 1580 or so. The silver mountain, Potosí in Peru (today's Bolivia), was discovered in 1545 but could not be fully exploited until mercury for the amalgamation refining process was found at Huancavalica, saving the laborious task of importing it from Almadén in Spain (Vilar, 1969 [1976], chaps. 12–15). Europe had undergone a bullion famine in the fifteenth century (Day, 1978 [1987]). Bullion was needed to replace the dwindling production of central Europe, to pay Spanish mercenary troops in the Spanish Netherlands fighting the Counter-Reformation, and especially to pay for unrequited imports— imports that were not offset by European exports—from the Far East and the Baltic. The transfer of this silver was dominated by Genoese bankers, since the Fuggers were bankrupted by the successive bankruptcies of the Spanish monarchy (Ehrenberg, 1896 [1928], p. 334) until they finally collapsed in 1627, closely followed by the Genoese. With the decline in Spain from 1620 or 1640, Genoese wealth was invested more widely; in the early eighteenth century, Genoese foreign investments were the largest in Europe after those of the Dutch (Zamagni, 1980, p. 125).

In social terms Genoa was a city of rich and poor with only a small bourgeois middle class to intermediate between them. The gap in income between the wealthy merchant-nobles and the impoverished masses meant there was little demand for investment at home, which pushed the rich to invest abroad (ibid.). Like Venice, Genoa experienced a rift between old nobles and new, the former partial to French financial markets such as Lyons, the latter to Spanish. Other social tensions ran between the rich oligarchy and its collaterals—younger sons and members of families that lost their fortunes, with no function to play as they were excluded from public office (Bulferetti and Costanti, 1966, p. 15). The nobility had gradually withdrawn from trade into finance. How much this withdrawal was the consequence of spontaneous risk aversion and how much the response to foreign competition is hard to determine. Luigi Bulferetti and Claudio Costanti observe that the trade crisis in Genoa came from loss of its ancient function as intermediary between the Mediterranean and the west. In the seventeenth century, ships of Britain, Holland, and France sailed directly to Sicily, Naples, Sardinia, and Catalonia with goods that used to be distributed from Genoa; and Flemish, Portuguese, and Lombard merchants, along with the British, Dutch, and French, began to make increasing use of Marseilles and Leghorn, rather than Genoa. By the end of the seventeenth century there were more Dutch merchants in Leghorn than in Genoa. The governing oligarchy of Genoa debated whether to make Genoa a free port like Leghorn and later Spezia. This was finally done for packages (but not for bulk goods?). The action had the result that income from taxes in the port fell by 45 percent, and the experiment was abandoned (ibid.).

Milan

The fourth city in northern Italy was Milan, thought by Arthur Young, the English agronomist, when he traveled to the Continent in the late 1780s to be the richest spot in Europe (1790 [1969]). Young was impressed by Lombardy's flourishing agriculture, irrigated by the Po river which flowed continuously from its glacial origin and fell only 260 meters in 200 miles from the source to the sea (Greenfield, 1965, p. 18). The wealth of Lombardy was largely agricultural. One percent of the population owned 50 percent of the land and the elite retained it with the institutions of mortmain and *fideikommis* (forbidding the alienation of land holdings outside the family, restricting sale to outsiders) (Roberts, 1953). The nobility lived sumptuously in the city, renting out their farms to tenants. They were, however, interested in improved productivity, and produced rice and flax in water meadows along with grain specifically stipulated in leases so as to provide food for the city.

Located like Paris, Lyons, and Geneva at the junction of east-west roads (through Italy) and north-south routes through the Gotthard and Simplon Alpine passes, Milan was prominent in trade, industry, banking, and communications, but not outstanding in any one, as were Venice and Genoa in trade, Florence and Genoa in banking. The rich bottomland grew wheat and rice, the hills mulberry trees for silk cocoons. Along with Como, the city was a leading market for silk and sought from time to time to forbid the export of cocoons to keep their prices low at home and high abroad and to expand foreign markets for silk yarns and cloth.

Part of Milan's problems came from continuous warfare and intermittent foreign rule. Early there was fighting between the Guelphs and the Ghibellines, and between rich and poor. The French attacked in 1495. The Spanish took over in 1535 as a winner after the Italian wars among Venice, the papal states, Florence, and the French. Later Austria displaced the Spanish. Spanish misrule produced famines, epidemics, continuous warfare, and loss of foreign markets (Sella, 1974a, p. 11). From a stimulus through export-led growth, foreign trade turned into a debilitating factor as Milan lost to foreign competition in markets abroad and within Italy itself (Cipolla, 1974, p. 10). Milan, Cremona, and Como showed little resilience in intervals of peace. Inability to compete, partly as a result of high wages owing to guilds plus conspicuous consumption in the cities, made it a good strategy for the wealthy to divert their capital from the city to the more vital rural areas (Sella, 1974a, p. 13). While Sella stresses the damage of Spanish rule, he does note that the Spanish diverted some capital from another colony in Naples to Lombardy, thus widening the north-south disparity in productivity in Italy (1974b, p. 31).

Causes of Decline

The successive declines of the Italian city-states have been ascribed to a variety of causes by no means independent of one another: deterioration of shipping, of trade, of manufacturing; the loss of monopolies to competition abroad; depletion of timber; the movement from trade and shipping to finance, to rentier status, landed estates, conspicuous consumption, and prestige through public office. Within each broad category a number of contributing factors can be isolated.

In shipping, for example, the intermediary functions of Venice in the Adriatic and Genoa in the Tyrrhenian Sea were lost to direct trading. In the fifteenth century there was little problem of recruiting oarsmen for the galleys: guilds were required to provide rowers, and freemen served compulsorily when called for. In the sixteenth century the shortage of oarsmen was not serious, because the demand for galleys was limited by the move to round ships. But the shortage of crews proved to be a greater and greater problem, despite continuous appeal to the tradition of the past. Convicts were pressed into service, including those from colonies such as Malta. Slaves were bought in Turkey. Real sailors migrated to Pisa and even to the English fleet. The officer staff wore elaborate uniforms—cloth of gold with ermine linings in some instances—and became increasingly corrupt (Romano, 1968). Seamen's wages doubled from 1550 to 1590 but this did not elicit an increased supply.

The problem in shipping extended to the *Arsenale*. Timber ran short, and it was necessary to procure it from farther and farther away. In Roman times the peninsula had great forests of fir preferred for warships (Starr, 1989, pp. 55, 80), but scarcity was apparent as early as the late fourteenth century (McNeill, 1974a, p. 146). *Arsenale* officers first brought it from the Alpine foothills, then north toward Trieste, and finally across the Adriatic from the vicinity of Ragusa. Private builders were required to buy their oak abroad (Lane, 1973, p. 40). As costs of shipbuilding rose, Venice clung to its sixteenth-century standards while the Dutch were innovating in lighter and more easily handled ships (discussed in chapter 6).

The step from buying foreign timber to buying foreign ships was regarded as a short one, especially when complaints were heard in the latter sixteenth century that the standards and traditions of the *Arsenale* were running down. Work was stretched out, and done poorly. Older workmen had been allowed to stop work a half hour before the regular time. In 1601 the younger workers left with them, invoking echoes of today's expression of 1980s young people who "want it all, and want it now" (Romano, 1968, p. 63, text and note). Merchants complained that the privileges reserved for Venetian-built and owned ships were first extended to those Venetians who bought ships from abroad and then to foreign-built and owned vessels. Lane observes that after the loss of ships in the victory of Lepanto and that of Cyprus, shipbuilding displayed a lack of resilience that had characterized the industry at the start of the sixteenth century (1968, p. 38).

Conventional explanation for the loss of Venetian dominance in trade is the Portuguese direct sea route to the East that replaced the overland silk road of Marco Polo from the Black Sea and the highly profitable Indian Ocean-caravan-eastern Mediterranean route to Venice. Vasco di Gama's voyage around the Cape of Good Hope to India took place at the end of the fifteenth century, and by 1502 the trans-Arabian caravan route had been cut off.

The Venetian Council finally allowed round ships to enter the trade, previously reserved for merchant galleys, reducing transport costs by one-third. Prices of spices delivered by ship from the Levant came to equal those of Portuguese vessels, but the increase in quantity with both routes in operation drove the landed price far down (McNeill, 1974, p. 128). Gradually, however, the entrepôt function of Venice for spices and silk, dyes, cotton, and African gold brought from Egypt decayed. The French in the seventeenth century refused to trade exclusively with Venetian merchants. Monopolized markets were limited to northern Italy and southern Germany, and the latter collapsed with the outbreak of the Thirty Years' War in 1618 (Sella, 1968b, p. 97).

British woolens started as cheap imitations of Venetian wool cloth, occasionally baled with a high-quality Italian cloth on the outside, just as British soap was stamped with the likeness of the doge. In the seventeenth century the quality of British woolens was improved but without slavish imitation of the Venetian standard, becoming of somewhat lower quality but cheaper and suitable to a wider range of consumers. Venetian guilds and the Venetian Council insisted on adherence to Venetian standards, in the confident belief that they would prevail, despite growing Turkish preference for the British product (Sella, 1968b, pp. 117–18). Venice held its preeminence in such luxury goods as silk cloth, glassware, some chemicals, mosaics, metallurgy, and leatherwork and innovated in printing and sugar refining. Even here there were encroachments. Sir Thomas Lombe stole the plans for a silk-throwing mill on the Bologna (not the Venetian) model, and built one in England in 1717 (Poni, 1970), this despite intense efforts to keep Bolognese methods secret, vigorous surveillance, and the death penalty for transgression. Some Venetian masters emigrated with industrial secrets to set up production in areas with lower wages and lower consciences in competition with the Serenissima (Rapp, 1976, pp. 109, 155–56). Most important in Venice's relative decline was the competition in spices from Portugal, in woolens from the British, and in shipping from the Dutch and British, leading to Venice's loss of "status, empire" and hegemony (ibid., p. 1). It was a mistake to cling to obsolete standards, a mistake on the part of both the guilds and the government, reflecting ridigity of attitudes. Little could be done by government about high wages, given the attitude of guilds, workers, and a leveling off of productivity.

Venetian and Genoese shipping started to decline from about 1530— before the entry into the Mediterranean of large volumes of Dutch and British shipping—and was clearly outclassed by the end of the century. A contemporary of Shakespeare observed that the productivity of Italian shipping had declined, compared with that of the British, because of conservatism and loss of expertise:

> I observed English shipping going forth from Venice with Italian Shipps to have sayled into Syria and returned to Venice twice, before the Italian Shipps made one more returne, whereof two reasons may be given, one that the Italians pay their Marriners by the day, however long soever the voyage lasteth, which makes them upon the least storms, putt into harbors, whence only a few wyndes can bring them out, whereas the English are payde by the voyage, and so beate out storms at Sea, and are ready to take the first wynde any thing favourable unto them. The other is that Italian Shipps are heavy in

sayling, and great of burthen, and the Governors and Marriners not very expert, nor bold. . . . (*Fyndes Moryson's Itinerary*, quoted by Cipolla, 1968, p. 144)

The matter goes deeper, as the last sentence suggests. Italian sailors were deserting and emigrating, their ranks filled with conscripts. Captains, no longer recruited from the ranks of nobles, were weak on navigation. Emphasis shifted from military tactics and fighting spirit to orderly administration. Venetian seamen stopped fighting and even resisting pirates helping themselves to cargo in the northern Adriatic. The navigation acts of 1602 forbade the use of western-built ships, but by 1627 the government was offering subsidies for the purchase of ships built abroad (Lane, 1973, chap. 26).

Finance

Venice and Florence were hindered in economic development by debt, which rose in wars and sometimes fell because of taxes, sales of offices and titles, and forced reductions of interest. Simple tables of debt and revenue are virtually impossible to compile because of confusion between payments on principal and those on interest, and would be relatively meaningless because of the element of compulsion on loans and reductions of interest in crisis. Venice had old loans, new loans, newest loans, and subsidized loans, Florence in its turn communal loans, dowry loans, and special war loans. The shortest term loans in Venice paid interest rates as high as 20 percent a year, but were available only to the wealthy members of the oligarchy. Despite these complications, Frederic Lane has produced a table comparing Venetian debt payments on interest and principal with government revenue from 1313 to 1788, showing wide fluctuations. The first entry, for 1343, shows that debt payment took 31 percent of government revenue, a ratio that fell to 7 percent the following year, rising back to 20 percent about 1500 and to 40 percent after the Battle of Lepanto (Lane, 1973, p. 426). In the next decade, the formal but not the short-term debt was entirely wiped out through heavy taxes, depriving charitable foundations of the securities they needed for income, a result leading to the establishment of deposit accounts paying 4 percent (ibid., p. 326). The taxes used to pay off the formal debt were levied mainly on consumption, foreign trade, and cities on the mainland. Risk-averse merchants took their money out of shipping and put it into houses, shops, and government bonds (Lane, 1965, p. 60). The rich in Venice earned more on their short-term holdings than they paid in taxes (ibid.). Similar governmental policies on taxing and borrowing in Florence hurt the poor and favored the well-to-do (Veseth, 1990). Braudel asserts that the divisions in Genoa between the rich and the poor, and within the rich merchant class turned aristocratic between the new and old nobles, were largely social but had strong political overtones (1966 [1975], p. 1134). As noted earlier, the new nobles loaned mainly to Spain, the old to France.

Bankers and rentiers lent little to domestic industry, somewhat more to foreign trade, but increasingly to foreign borrowers whose defaults, in the case of Florence and Genoa, proved their undoing. The Medici bank failed in 1494 because its representatives abroad, insufficiently controlled from Florence, loaned too much to princes and sovereigns in Bruges, Lyons, and London. Tax-farming, says de Roover, failed to protect advances to such a prince as Charles the Bold of Burgundy, since advances on anticipations of revenue tended to be excessive and led to debtor default (1966, chap. 14). The financial type of sedentary merchant analyzed by N. S. B. Gras (1939) tends inevitably to drift from private banking into government finance.

Conspicuous consumption plays a role in all this—consumption in dress, country estates, urban palaces, public offices, and art (Lane, 1973, chap. 18; Veseth, 1990, pp. 55–63, 65). Lorenzo the Magnificent delegated power of the Medici bank branches to Francesco Sassetti as he turned to high life, but Sassetti himself did not keep close control over the foreign branches, as he had advised Lorenzo to do, perhaps because he was interested in a family chapel for which he commissioned Ghirlandaio to paint an altar piece (de Roover, 1966, pp. 362–63).

5

Portugal and Spain

Throughout this book we encounter the question whether the decline of a given country was relative or absolute, that is, whether the income and wealth of the country did in fact slip back. With Spain there is little doubt. Three distinguished historians have each written papers entitled "The Decline of Spain" (Elliot, 1961 [1970]; Hamilton, 1938 [1954]; Vicens Vives, 1970). The decline was perhaps more political than economic, for although it was rich because of conquest and of wresting of treasure from the New World, Spain was never really economically developed in the early modern period. Castilians, said Gerald Brenan (1950, p. x), had an industrial and commercial apathy. Except for shipbuilding in the north along the Bay of Biscay and fine woolens, trade, industry and finance were largely in the hands of foreigners until Spaniards made some progress in winning it half-way back in the eighteenth century (Herr, 1958, pp. 147–48). But first we turn to Portugal.

Portugal

Portugal started the process of becoming rich by going beyond the confines of its coastline in the first half of the fifteenth century. With the help of an arsenal for shipbuilding and a school for navigation, Henry the Navigator sailed around Cape Bojador in West Africa to trade for gold and slaves, and launched the Age of Discovery. Bartholomew Diaz reached the Cape of Good Hope in 1488, and Vasco di Gama sailed to Calicut on the west coast of India in 1497–1498. After the voyage of Columbus, Brazil was claimed for the Portuguese crown in 1500, and trading "factories" were established in Asia; in Goa, India (1510); in Malacca (1511); in Hormuz, Persia (1515); and in Macao (1557). Magellan went westward through the straits later named for him in 1520, and reached the Philippines (where he met his death) in 1521. Pope Alexander VI from Spain divided the world overseas on a north-south line that gave Brazil and Asia to Portugal and the rest of the New World to Spain (Miskimin, 1977, p. 34). The division failed to last.

The conquest of Hormuz at the entrance to the Persian Gulf was intended to cut off the Venetian route for spices and silk from India by ship to Persia, by caravan to Aleppo in Syria or Alexandria, and then by merchant galley to Venice, creating a Portuguese monopoly for the trade to Europe around the Cape of Good Hope. When pepper first reached Venice from Lisbon rather than from the Levant in 1589, it was thought that the Adriatic city was ruined (Steensgaard, 1973, p. 55). Such proved not to be the case. The caravan route competed with that of the Portuguese carracks well into the seventeenth century, as the "glorious peddling trade" of the caravans bought protection from the Persians and galleys gave way to sailing vessels (ibid., p. 171). In due course both routes produced a surfeit of pepper, bringing about a shift to other spices, silk, and cotton.

Portuguese interests in Asia were divided among private settlers who conducted local trade among China, Japan, the islands that later became Indonesia, and India; the king and nobles who were interested in customs duties and mercantile profits respectively; and the Catholic Church, concerned to win the infidels to the true faith. In one view, it was an open question how much religious conversion, and how much trade opportunities, motivated the conquests (Meilink-Roeloesz, 1962, p. 117). Marketing of pepper in Europe was first conducted in Antwerp, and merchants and bankers from Italy, France, Germany, and England gathered there. When Antwerp went into decline after the middle of the sixteenth century, some moved on to Amsterdam, some back to Lisbon (Steensgaard, 1973, p. 96).

The success of Portuguese trade, lasting almost a century and a half, in retrospect strikes many observers as surprising. It was one thing to push Chinese junks with their small size and limited armament out of the way (Landes, 1989, pp. 155–56), quite another to sustain a significant portion of the trade in the seventeenth century after the British East India Company (EIC), founded in 1600, and the Dutch Vereinigde Oostindiche Compagnie (VOC), of 1602, moved into the area to contest for it. The population of Portugal was little more than two million. Apart from Lisbon on the Tagus river, there were only two ports, Setubal shipping salt to the Baltic and Oporto exporting wine. Deep-water sailors were scarce. Boxer states that as early as 1505 the crews of the Casa de India sailing east consisted primarily of raw landsmen and foreigners. There was a persistent problem of command as well, since *fidalgo* officers, of quasi-noble status, refused to serve under professional seamen who lacked social standing

(Boxer, 1969, pp. 211ff). Losses of seamen to disease and accident were heavy. It was easier to man ships for the much shorter run to Pernambuco in Brazil and return than those to the Far East, but by the eighteenth century even crews of the former ships were made up largely of Negro slaves (ibid.).

Portuguese trade began to prosper at the beginning of the sixteenth century. Young men were attracted to Lisbon, especially in the 1510s and 1520s. Most were younger than 22 when they arrived, according to a noted Portuguese historian, and might hope to get rich through marrying wealth or through a series of deals pushed by audacity and blessed with luck (Mauro, 1990, p. 262). A speculative boom with considerable dishonesty peaked in 1550 and then collapsed, leaving a series of bankruptcies. But Frédéric Mauro regards Portugal as the center of the world economy "in the European context" to the end of the sixteenth century (ibid., p. 283), and the Spanish historian Jaime Vicens Vives holds that the United Empire of Portugal and Spain (formed in 1580 by the Spanish conquest of Portugal) was the center of world trade up to 1640, with Seville and Lisbon the "chief points of contact between the colonial world and continental Europe" (1970, p. 144). The question can be raised, however, whether a country whose trade is conducted to a great extent by foreigners (Spain) can properly claim to be the center of world trade.

While the king controlled and taxed trade, much trade was actually conducted by foreign merchants and financed by Jews. The Jews were forcibly converted to Christianity by baptism as "New Christians" after the expulsion of Jews from Spain in 1492. With the arrival of the Inquisition in Portugal in 1536 there was a "mania" of accusations against New Christians for petty violations of Catholic religious practices (Shaw, 1989). Many were imprisoned; others emigrated, some to Seville where their experiences in foreign trade made them especially valuable.

Despite the disadvantages of fewer ships and poorer sailors, the Portuguese hung on against formidable British and Dutch opposition until about 1640, retaining all Asian outposts except Hormuz which fell to combined British and Persian assault in 1622 (Steensgaard, 1973, p. 117). In one view its staying power rested on its success in colonizing, its citizens settling abroad for life, mingling and marrying with the native population, whereas the Dutch returned to Holland from the Far East after six years (if they survived) (Boxer, 1969, p. 120). A somewhat different opinion credits Portugal's survival as a colonial power against sizeable odds to courage, resolution, and stubbornness (Meilink-Roeloesz, 1962, p. 125). Even with better ships, better naval strategy, better commercial organization, and less corruption, it took the Dutch sixty years to displace the Portuguese in Asian trade to Europe, and they never succeeded in driving them out of Brazil. It should have been easy. The Portuguese were not good merchants. As in Spain, nobles detested both physical work and commerce. Albuquerque said that a clerk trained in a Florentine counting house was of more use than all the factors the king of Portugal sent to India (ibid., p. 178). In the circumstances it is a wonder that the Portuguese seized the opportunities of long-distance trade to move from commerce dominated by fish, wine, and salt sold to the north, to gold and slaves from Africa and spices from the East (Parry, 1966, p. 40). Cultivation of sugar moved from the Middle East to the Portuguese Atlantic islands to Brazil, and coffee from Mokka at the entrance to the Red Sea was successfully cultivated in Java and Brazil.

Profits in importing from Asia and Brazil were initially high but were competed down. What Portugal sent to pay the little needed to acquire the imports was precious metals, partly for coining and partly for hoarding. Another export product, especially for Africa, was copper brought to Antwerp from Hungary, and especially valued in the form of brass. Miskimin notes that early in the sixteenth century the price of a slave in West Africa rose from two to four or five barbers' basins made from brass (1977, p. 127). In *Don Quixote,* it may be remembered, the hero mistakes a barber's brass basin for the golden helmet of the Saracen Membrino (Cervantes, 1606 [1950], pp. 140ff).

After peaking first in the middle of the sixteenth century and a second time after the discovery of gold in Brazil in 1680, Portugal lost out in economic competition. Decline was blamed on many factors—the difficulty of driving the Dutch out of Brazil in 1625; the fall in the prices of sugar and tobacco with the boom in their cultivation in the Caribbean by the Dutch, French, and British; and especially the 1703 Treaty of Methuen between Portugal and England, which relayed Brazilian gold from Lisbon to London in payment for the English goods needed in Portuguese colonies that the Portuguese could not produce for themselves. This treaty has been regarded in some quarters as the application of force in making Portugal into an English colony (Sideri, 1970). Still another factor has been singled out: the persecution of the New Christians and the confiscation of their wealth on imprisonment by the Inquisition or if they emigrated. This put the British merchants with whom they dealt in a cleft stick: they feared to keep selling to New Christians in Portugal for fear that new debts would not be paid, but feared also to stop trading because of the risk that such action would induce their debtors to default (Shaw, 1989, pp. 426–28).

Still another force weakening Portugal was that after its defeat by Philip II in 1580 the country was taken over, and the Portuguese, with few numbers to begin with, were forced to contribute manpower for Spanish military adventures (Boxer, 1969, p. 140). The Iberian peninsula was not a cooperative place. Soldiers detested sailors, nobles scorned commoners, all Portuguese united in hating the Spanish. Both Spanish and Portuguese reviled Jews and Moors. The recipe was not one for success despite victories in the East in the short run and in Brazil until the nineteenth century. What is perhaps remarkable is that the empire hung together for one century in Asia, and more than two in Brazil.

Spain

The peak of power in Spain is generally given as the sixteenth century in the reign of the Hapsburgs, Charles V, and Philip II, with decline at some time in the seventeenth. There is another view, expressed long after the event at the end of the eighteenth century in a revival of interest in Spanish history—already a sign of aging. Richard Herr calls it a peculiar interpretation, based on a surge of attraction to democratic rule. Spain in this insight was at its greatest in the Middle Ages and started to decline in 1520 when, after the deaths of the Catholic monarchs, Ferdinand and Isabella, Charles II of Burgundy and the Hapsburgs took over the throne of Spain and embarked on absolute monarchy. Charles's son, Philip II, then suppressed the Moors, crushed the pride of Aragon, promoted the Inquisition, and was "the origin of decadence" (Herr, 1958, chap. 12). It was held that the Hapsburgs of the sixteenth century destroyed the capitalists and the factories of Castile. Thereafter the corruption of American gold and Spain's foreign wars completed the process (ibid., p. 347, quoting an economist, Joaquin Maria Acevedo y Pola, writing in 1799).

This judgment runs contrary to the understanding of modern historians who regard the sixteenth century in Spain as a time when every wound healed (Braudel, 1979 [1984], p. 86, quoting a conversation with Earl J. Hamilton) and takes me well beyond my historical understanding. I do not pursue it. In the conventional view, the period from the marriage of Isabella of Castile and Ferdinand of Aragon (and connections with Catalonia) in 1479 to the death of Philip II in 1596 was a golden age. Spain, which had been a loose assortment of provinces, coalesced as a nation. The Moors were driven from Granada, the Jews driven abroad from especially Seville, Columbus discovered America and claimed an empire for the Catholic monarchs. After a small amount of gold had been collected in the Caribbean, the silver mountain of Potosí was discovered in Peru in 1545 and its bullion began to flow to Spain in the 1560s. Portugal was annexed to the crown in 1580. The Spanish fleet recovered with some speed after the disastrous defeat of the Armada in 1588. The decline of Spain has been variously dated as starting in 1580 (Ortega, 1937, p. 34), 1598, 1620, 1640, and 1680 (Braudel, 1966 [1972], vol. 2, p. 1240). In one view the peak of Spanish power came in 1625, a miraculous year when the Spanish defeated one of a series of English, Dutch, and Anglo-Dutch attacks on Cadiz and also pushed the Dutch out of Brazil (Carla Phillips, 1986, p. 18).

The location of Spain on the Mediterranean, the Atlantic, and the Bay of Biscay was both a plus and a minus, a plus as it was connected by water with the Levant, the Americas, and north Europe, a minus because, while it could trade and attack on three fronts, it was also obliged to defend on them. Spain was able to participate in the battle of Lepanto because the west was quiet. With the victory there it was able to concentrate on the Atlantic front. Fernand Braudel thought Philip II made a fatal mistake in moving the capital back to Madrid from Lisbon three years after his victory of 1580, a mistake because the future lay in the Atlantic (1979 [1984], p. 32). It was true that Madrid was better connected to European capitals, but the north was rising, the Mediterranean slipping. Lisbon, however, like other cities on the Atlantic—Nantes, La Rochelle, and Barcelona in Catalonia—lacked a hinterland and was therefore limited in its potential for economic growth (Carla Phillips, 1990, p. 36). Victory at Lepanto following the arrival of the first major shipment of silver from Potosí in 1566 encouraged Philip II to try to wrest the Spanish Netherlands back from Luther in the Counter-Reformation, or in another view, mainly to put down the revolt of the Netherlands against the Hapsburgs, to which the lands belonged by right of succession of Charles II of Flanders (Charles V of Spain), rather than it being a holy war (Elliot, 1968 [1982], p. 165).

Resources

Spain was arid. Castile was so dry that it rained upward (Ortega, 1937, p. 161). Aragon, Granada, and Andalusia were cultivated from the time of the Moorish conquests by irrigation and were managed by communal groups, in opposition to the view that private property is needed to provide the incentive for efficient production (Glick, 1970). Expulsion of the *Moriscos* in 1609–1614 led fairly directly to the decline of agriculture on the Mediterranean rim as *hidalgos* (gentry below the grandees) gobbled up the vacated land, served as absentee landlords, and let the irrigation works decay. The dry plains of Castile were a sheep run, with large flocks that went north to the mountains in the summer and south in winter. By ranging widely into arable land, the sheep inhibited crop raising, grazed young seedlings, and contributed to deforestation. The sheep breeders were organized into an association called the *Mesta*, which was granted wide rights by Ferdinand and Isabella in a mercantilist effort to promote the export of fine wool. Export of the merino sheep themselves was forbidden to preserve the monopoly for Castile and Aragon. The *Mesta* began to lose power in the sixteenth century but survived until the eighteenth (Klein, 1920, p. 39). Much of the land was owned by nobles who had acquired it when the Black Death killed off peasant owners, and also with the expropriation from the Moors.

The *Mesta* owned consulates in Bilbao and Burgos. It also maintained marketing "factories" abroad in La Rochelle, Bruges, London, and Florence. Close outside Burgos was the fair of Medina del Campo, which for long was the financial center of Spain, dealing with bills of exchange from wool exports (ibid., esp. chap. 3), and *asientos*, special bills to transmit funds to the Spanish armies fighting in the Spanish Netherlands to pay their mercenaries. Genoese merchants took over the *Mesta* in the 1540s, and by 1577 it was starting to decline as Philip II raised the export taxes that he had farmed to Genoese bankers in 1552 and 1564.

The interior of Spain presented an obstacle to economic development. Roads were poor; mule pack trains and oxcarts failed to integrate the separate provinces. Domestic production was limited in amount and by the distances it could travel except by ship. In the famine of the 1590s it was necessary to rely on grain brought from the Baltic, largely in Hanseatic ships, often Dutch vessels sailing under Hamburg or Lübeck colors because of the Eighty Years' War. It was easier and cheaper to bring goods for the 100,000 or so settlers in Spanish America by ship from France, especially Brittany, England, and the Low Countries, than to haul them down from the mountains and through the hot dry plains.

Madrid, the capital city of Spain located in the center of Castile, was a political rather than commercial city, drawing on the rest of the country for grain, taxes, and rents but providing little stimulus to the Spanish interior. Like Rome in Italy, it was parasitical, housing the court, grandees, *hidalgos*, and bureaucrats but consuming, in addition to grain for its poor, luxury goods from abroad and semiluxuries from local crafts. It failed to galvanize Castile (Ringrose, 1983). The various coasts were more closely tied to one another and to foreign countries—Barcelona to the east, Seville to the colonies, Bilbao to France and northern Europe—than to the center of the country. Ringrose observed that of several hundred bills of exchange in the largest house in Seville in 1803, only twenty-five or thirty involved trade with Spain while the vast majority came from England, France, the Low Countries, and Germany (ibid., p. 231). The collapse of colonial trade later changed these proportions. The country as a whole was described by Ortega as "invertebrate" (1937).

An added drawback to internal trade was a set of internal customs duties. Barcelona was the port for trade with the Mediterranean, but the Catalans were forbidden to export wool or woolen cloth at the instance of the *Mesta* or even to trade at Medina del Campo on an equal footing with Castilians. Taxes made it impossible to ship woolens from Burgos to the colonies through Seville (Parry, 1966, p. 239). The execution of interior bills of exchange was prohibited by the religious injunction against usury, making it difficult for Seville merchants to get credit to provision the fleet for the Americas. Even exchanges between Seville and Cadiz, on the one hand, and the north, including France, on the other required gold shipments (da Silva, 1969, pp. 603–5). The difficulties in dealing in goods and finance within the country turned the attention of Spanish and foreign financiers to the market for silver, and to external transactions, especially the transfer of funds for the war in the Spanish Netherlands (ibid., p. 620).

Shipping

Barcelona was the port for Mediterranean trade in galleys and did some galley construction, but fairly rapidly exhausted its supplies of timber and oarsmen and had to turn either to Genoa in the Mediterranean or to Viscaya on the Bay of Biscay. Seville, in Andalusia and on the Atlantic, close to the favorable trade winds and readily accessible to Gibraltar and the Mediterranean, was the principal Spanish port for the Americas. It had little timber and little shipbuilding. Unlike Viscaya on the north coast, however, it had access to a hinterland, irrigated by the Guadalquivir river, and rich with grapes for sherry, citrus fruit, grain, and olive groves for oil, used notably in cleaning wool. As ships grew in size and draft, however, the shifting of the bar in the river at San Lucar about 1630 presented an obstacle, requiring the transfer of activities to the harbor of Cadiz on the ocean, readier of access but vulnerable to attack by foreign men-of-war. Francis Drake and John Hawkins slowed down the assault of the Spanish Armada on British ships barring access to Flanders by an attack in 1587 that burned a number of ships in the fleet at Cadiz, and especially the store of cask staves accumulated for provisioning the fleet. Columbus would have sailed for "the Indies" from Cadiz instead of from a small fishing port to the northwest had not the harbor been filled with ships carrying Jewish expellees away from Spain (Parry, 1966, p. 53). Seville (and Cadiz) was the intermediary between northern Europe and the Americas, designated such by the government, which established the Casa del Contratacion to record all goods in and out of the Americas, especially silver (Vicens Vives, 1970, p. 147). The profits of the trade were attacked on all sides, by British, Dutch, and French "interlopers" who sought to evade the Seville monopoly by sailing direct to the New World; by smugglers who escaped the taxation of one-fifth the value of silver imports by bringing it to Lisbon instead of Seville or by selling it at Cadiz to ships of the Dutch or British East India companies, which needed it to buy goods in Asia; and on one occasion in 1628 by the attack of the Dutch admiral Piet Hein on the silver fleet at anchor in Matanzas Bay in Cuba—"the first and only time an entire fleet had been lost to an enemy" (Carla Phillips, 1986, p. 3).[1]

Spanish shipping strength derived largely from its north coast, from Asturias to Viscaya, with excellent harbors at La Coruña, Santander, and above all Bilbao in the Basque country. The last was the center of shipbuilding, originally with abundant timber (except for masts), plus iron for anchors, chains, and armament and superb sailors (ibid., p. 19). Naval stores were handy in the pine forests of the Gironde in France, along with hemp and cables for rigging, and linen for sails from across the Bay of Biscay in Brittany. In 1551, foreigners were forbidden to build ships in Viscaya, because Italian and Ragusan builders were beginning to deplete the forests. In 1625 as mariners ran short, the government instituted a system of conscription, requiring the registration of sailors, town by town, even those on small fishing boats (ibid., pp. 21, 141).

Shipbuilding was undertaken under the close supervision of a surprisingly effective bureaucracy to hold prices down, keep quality up, and guard against malfeasance (ibid., pp. 91, 95). The problem lay in numbers, with

---

[1]This judgment runs counter to that of Keynes in *The Treatise on Money*, that the booty brought back by Sir Francis Drake from his three privateering expeditions ending in 1573, 1580, and 1586 produced a large part of the imports of bullion into Britain, estimated at perhaps not more than £2 million or £3 million, and "may fairly be considered the fountain and origin of British Foreign Investment" (Keynes, 1930, vol. 2, pp. 156–57).

large losses owing to privateers and raiders, battles such as that of the Armada, and normal wear and tear. The loss of ships in 1588 was less serious, given the resilience of shipbuilding, than that of sailors. But ships were nonetheless a continuous problem. There was the Atlantic squadron that took soldiers and money to the captains general in Flanders; and the Carrera de la Indias, with the Armada de la Guardia to protect it in returning to Seville with its treasure. Time at sea was limited because of the necessity to careen ships to keep their bottoms free of seaweed and barnacles before the days of copper plating. In addition to naval battles and storms, there were further losses from wear. The Indies were a graveyard for ships that, as a rule, could make only four round-trips across the Atlantic in a lifetime. Some usable ships, moreover, were retained in the Indies for storage or were broken up for their timbers to use in building housing, along with hulks ferried to the West Indies for these purposes.

When shipbuilding was undertaken on the west coast of South America to provide still another fleet there, and to avoid the necessity to sail through the straits to the Pacific, valuable brass and iron fittings were stripped off Atlantic vessels for Pacific ships (Parry, 1966, p. 121). I come later to the causes of Spanish decline, but call attention to the numbers of authors who cite the collapse of shipping between 1566 and 1603 (McNeill, 1982, p. 103), the loss of confidence of merchants following the Drake-Hawkins attack on Cadiz and the defeat of the Armada, and "the fundamental cause of seventeenth-century decline, the fall of maritime trade into the hands of foreigners" (Kamen, 1969, p. 31; Vicens Vives, 1970, pp. 144–45). This of course is the thesis of Admiral Mahan, the American naval strategist, that national power, and to some extent economic strength, depends on naval forces.

Spanish Silver

With the discovery of the silver mountain Potosí in 1545 and that of mercury deposits at Huancavelica, the annual average of world silver production rose from 2.9 million ounces between 1521 and 1544 to 10 million in the following fifteen years and to 13.6 million in the first two decades of the seventeenth century (Vilar, 1969 [1976], p. 351). As already noted, the arrival of a huge amount of silver in 1566 and the victory at Lepanto encouraged Philip II to seek to win back Flanders for the Hapsburgs and Spain in the Eighty Years' War (1568–1648) (Elliott, 1968, p. 165). The war was fought hundreds of miles from Spain by mercenaries who needed to be paid with coin. Getting silver to Flanders was awkward when the British controlled the channel and were warring with Spain. The alternative to this "Dover Road" was the "Spanish Road" to Barcelona, then to Genoa, by pack train through the Alps to the Franche Comté (G. Parker, 1972). Financial rather than physical means were available through *asientos*, bills drawn from Flemish bankers on the court at Madrid, or from bankers in Antwerp, Lyons, or Frankfurt and Besançon (Bizenzone) or the Genoan fairs. A third way was sending silver to Nantes, to Paris, to Flanders with French safe-conducts, which required one-third of the specie to be left in France. Bankers paying monies in Flanders on asientos were granted rights to export silver from Spain. But Philip II and his successors Philip III and Phillip IV often overissued asientos on which they were unable to pay in silver, and forcibly converted their obligations into *juros*, or bonds payable only in paper money (Vilar, 1969 [1976]; Lapeyre, 1953, 1955). These bankruptcies occurred at frequent intervals—in 1576, 1596, 1607, 1627, 1647, and 1653—and brought down the Fuggers and the Genoese bankers (Lapeyre, 1953, chap. 4). In these traumatic events, the king would cancel licenses to export silver and seize any silver belonging to merchants and bankers he could get his hands on, even beyond his regular tax of one-fifth. The arrival of the fleet from America was waited anxiously by bankers in Spain and throughout Europe. When silver safely arrived in Spain, it did not stay long; it poured out through various means to the Far East, the Baltic, the Levant, and the money markets of Bruges, Antwerp, and later Amsterdam. That part of it that stayed in Spain was thoroughly disturbing to the economy in many ways.

Inflation, Conspicuous Consumption, and the "Dutch Disease"

Earl J. Hamilton, the University of Chicago economic historian who produced the first wide-ranging data on the "price revolution," blames the silver for inflation in Spain, and the inflation for economic setback because wages rose as fast or faster than prices. Since his classic study was produced (1934), considerable doubt has arisen whether the price revolution rose from the money side or from supply, because population, increasing faster than agricultural prices, drove food prices up early in the century well before much silver had in fact arrived (North, 1990, pp. 224–30; Outhwaite, 1969). In addition, Hamilton's data on Spanish prices have been questioned on the grounds that they were exclusively urban, biased by the omissions of some regions, and unrepresentative in being taken largely from hospital records derived from bureaucratic forms filled in routinely without a real attempt to record prices accurately (Lynch, 1964, p. 123, note 43; see also a similar complaint about the use of hospital records in the determination of French diets in Kindleberger, 1992b, p. 45 commenting on Hamilton, 1969).

As a slight digression, it is worth noting that Hamilton made a valiant effort in securing price material to compare quantities of goods in different places in a full chapter devoted to metrology, especially of weights and measures (1934 [1965], chap. 7). Common standards of measurement needed to reduce transaction costs in economic exchanges are, of course, a public good that must be produced, as a rule, by government. Two millennia earlier, for example in 449 B.C., Athens promulgated a Currency Decree ordering the use of Athenian coinage, weights, and measures throughout the Greek Empire (Starr, 1989, p. 40). Hamilton recounts the efforts not only of the Hapsburgs but also of the Bourbons to systematize weights and measures in Spain, and notes that even in the nineteenth century when Castilian standards were finally adopted for the country, Valencia was exempted. Complaints to the Cortes over the failure of provinces and especially of the smaller towns and villages to adhere to standards included charges that even where the promulgated standards had been adopted, inspection of scales and yardsticks was woefully lacking.

That there was inflation in Spain because of the inflow of silver, although not unconnected with the earlier rise of prices throughout Europe, cannot be doubted. That the inflation led to economic decline because of the faster rise in wages than in prices is questionable. But the silver had another pernicious effect. In the first place, the opportunities opened up in Spanish America led to the emigration of 100,000 (in very round numbers) Spaniards to the New World in the sixteenth century, a high proportion of them young people of vigor and initiative (Parry, 1966, p. 235), "some of its most vital elements" (J. H. Elliot, 1961 [1970], p. 177). Almost half were gentry (*caballeros*), less than a quarter farmers, 15 percent craftsmen, and a scattering of officials (*letrados*), merchants, and clergy (Menéndez Pidal, 1941, map 22). A number remained in Spanish America, became rich, and demanded European goods. Others, "Indianos," returned to Spain, many to Seville, and with wealth bought offices, estates, elegant houses. Along with New Christians from Portugal, *conversos* of Spain, and Genoese merchants and bankers, they lived well, invested in real estate, in financing of trade to the Americas, sugar and pearling in the Americas, and ultimately, for the Genoese and conversos, in lending to the crown (Pike, 1972).

The sons of merchants went into commerce only in small numbers, which favored the nobility. Merchants spent money on the education of their children, who proved to be a "worthless generation," according to Pike, addicted to wine, women, and gambling. The first generation could have spent for three good villas, dowries of as much as 240,000 ducats, but few of the next generation left estates of 200,000 to 400,000 ducats (ibid., pp. 114–18).

One industry in Seville flourished: silversmithing. Silversmiths, along with pharmacists, were the highest class of artisans, and some silversmiths were rich (Pike, 1972, pp. 132–47). While most silver went through Spain north and especially east, considerable amounts remained in the form of plate. Fernand Braudel notes that the Duke of Alva of Toledo, a captain general of the Spanish forces in the Netherlands and later a grandee at the court of Philip II in Madrid—a man without a reputation for wealth—died in 1582 leaving six-hundred dozen silver plates and eight-hundred silver platters (1979, [1981], p. 463).

In addition to inflation, plague, expulsion of the Moors, guild restrictions, taxes, state mercantilism, and aversion to manual labor, still another effect is charged to silver as an explanation, or a partial explanation, of Spanish decline. This reason has the possible merit of fitting an economic model. Peter Forsyth and Stephen Nicholas maintain that under ordinary circumstances, discovery of resources enriches an economy, but that with a large rise in income from an outside resource, spending increases for tradeables (exports and imports) and nontradeables (domestic goods and services) alike. With full employment, an increase in output of nontradeables can come only from a reduction in output of tradeables, that is, exports and goods that compete with imports. In this fashion, output of exports and import-competing goods is bound to fall to release labor and capital to increase the output of nontradeables. The modern analogue is the so-called "Dutch disease" arising from the discovery of North Sea gas in the twentieth century. The rise in income from gas output leads to a decline in other domestic production through the balance-of-payments adjustment mechanism. The increase in demand for domestic goods and services diverts spending from exports and import-competing lines (Forsyth and Nicholas, 1983). This is not very different from the Hamilton thesis of inflation raising wages faster than profits, thus reducing profits and squeezing manufacturing, leaving out the balance of payments.

Forsyth and Nicholas state that the real question is why manufacturing output did not revive after the silver flow slowed down (they say "stopped"). Such a revival did occur in the eighteenth century under Carlos III, however. Before its interruption by the French Revolution and the Napoleonic wars, Spanish goods shipped to the New World rose from one-eighth of the total (about 1700) to 45 percent in 1784 and 53 percent in 1788. It leveled off at 50 percent in 1789 (Herr, 1958, p. 147). In the early seventeenth century, however, Spanish exports were being displaced widely, both the raw materials sold in Europe and the manufactured goods exported to the New World. Irish wool was displacing Spanish wool in northern markets; in 1622 Santander shipped 505 sacks of wool in eleven ships, contrasted with 17,000 sacks and sixty-six ships half a century earlier. Swedish iron was competing with Bilbao's product in France and Britain; Piedmont silk was edging into the Spanish market (Vicens Vives, 1970, pp. 146–47). Foreign workers entered in many fields: German miners and engineers for building and operating a water-propelled mint at Segovia (Hamilton, 1934 [1965], p. 166, text and footnote); Genoese shipwrights to revive the Catalan industry (Lynch, 1964, p. 77); and Flemish workers in cloth, French in glassmaking and silk, both helped by the Bourbon occupation of the Spanish throne and despite Louis XIV's concern that French workers would start manufacturing in Spain in competition with France (Kamen, 1969, pp. 124, 134). Writing about eighteenth-century Spain, Richard Herr asserted that ever since the end of the seventeenth century, the depressed and depopulated country had served to attract enterprising businessmen and laborers from abroad (1958, p. 78). And as already noted, foreign merchants dominated trade with America. In the sixteenth century, five-sixths of the outbound cargos were supplied by foreigners (Haring, 1918, p. 113). In 1702, before the Bourbon takeover, Cadiz had eighty-four commercial houses, twelve of which were Spanish, twenty-six Genoese, eighteen Dutch and Flemish, eleven French, ten English, seven from Hamburg. At the end of the eighteenth century, 8,734 foreigners were resident in Cadiz, 5,018 Italian, 2,701 French, 272 English, 277 German and Flemish (Dornic, 1955, p. 85).

War

Spanish soldiers were superb fighters and found ample opportunity to exercise their profession. The war to expel the Moors lasted eight centuries and was finally won in 1492 when Granada was retaken by the Castilian armies of Ferdinand and Isabella. The revolt of the Netherlands, which Charles V continued to claim after his election as emperor of the Holy Roman Empire and accession to the throne of Spain, lasted eighty years, from 1568 to the Treaty of Westphalia in 1648, when Spain was exhausted and dispirited. Lynch insists that it was less a war of Counter-Reformation—much of the time Charles V and Philip II were at odds with Rome—than an attempt to retain territories that belonged to them (1964, chap. 7). During the eighty years there were side wars with the Ottoman Empire, won at the battle of Lepanto in 1571; with Britain, which subsidized the Dutch from time to time; and with France. A truce with the Dutch that lasted twelve years (1609–1621) was regarded as a humiliation on the one hand and broken off when it became clear that the Dutch were advancing rapidly in economic terms. Pride required that the Spanish negotiate only from strength, after winning a battle, and that they keep on fighting to avoid humiliation when falling behind (G. Parker, 1972, pp. 131–32). Inability to compromise precluded negotiations on the religious question between South Netherlands (Catholic) and the United Provinces (largely Protestant), even when continued fighting required enormous financial sacrifice and strain (ibid., p. 268). This was overstretch, undertaking objectives beyond the country's capacity to achieve them.

The War of the Spanish Succession from 1702 to 1713 was ostensibly dynastic but in reality was motivated by French desire to invade the Spanish monopoly of trade with America (Kamen, 1969, p. 135). The peace left France with an *asiento* to trade with the Americas, but yielded one to the British as well, which led to the South Sea bubble. Kamen notes that while the war increased the economic problems of the Spanish, the economy of which had been in decline since the late seventeenth century, and led to the humiliation of the loss of Gibraltar, it vitalized the bankers who had to provide funds for French and English troops (1969, chap. 2, p. 74).

Overall Decline

A host of factors contributing to Spanish economic decline in the period 1580 to 1620 has already been mentioned: inability to compete at sea; warrior temperament; disdain for work and preoccupation with *hidalgo* status; strong hatreds not only of the Jews and Moors but also of the Genoese, referred to as "White Moors" (Elliot, 1961 [1970], p. 190); wars; their finance; inflation; the Inquisition; guild restrictions which earlier had

been helpful (Vicens Vives, 1970, p. 142); the loss of demographic "buoy-
ancy and resilience" (Elliot, 1961 [1970], p. 179); support of the *Mesta* at
the expense of arable land; and a wide gap between grandees, basking in
land acquired from the Moors and church sales and held through mortmain,
and the peasantry, driven into cities to beggary by plague and inability to
earn a living on the farm. Many of these factors have been held by various
historians to have been overemphasized by others. Whatever the emphasis,
the totality makes for a dismal picture.

The sixteenth century was the golden age of Spain, the seventeenth one
of decline. In many accounts, the change was the result of the weak kings
following Philip II, but he used his strength unwisely. Already by 1600,
Spanish economists were discussing decline and the cyclical shape of history (ibid., p. 170). *Arbitristas,* as the economists of the seventeenth century were called, "denounced primogeniture, mortmain, vagabondage,
deforestation, redundance of ecclesiastics, contempt for manual labor and
arts, indiscriminate alms, monetary chaos and oppressive taxation" and
proposed technical education, immigration of artisans, monetary stability,
extension of irrigation and improvement of internal waterways (Hamilton,
1938 [1954], p. 224). Earl Hamilton goes on to say that history has few
examples of such able diagnoses or such utter disregard of sound advice
(ibid.).

Some headway was made in these and other positive directions in the
eighteenth century, especially in the second half under Carlos III as the
French Enlightenment spread into Spain despite the efforts of the Church
and the conservative elements in the universities to oppose it, especially by
banning the importation of French books and periodicals. Immigration
increased, and students went abroad to study architecture, medicine, science, and engineering (Herr, 1958, chaps. 6–13). Catalonia, which had been
flourishing through trade early in the millennium, diverted its capital into
banking and land and went into a decline of almost two centuries (Braudel,
1966 [1972], pp. 145, 147). In the fifteenth century it was regarded as
"devitalized" (Vicens Vives, 1952 [1967], p. 95). In the eighteenth century the east and north of Spain experienced a renaissance (ibid., chap. 5).
As elsewhere in Europe, mercantilist policies were adopted, applying tariffs on cotton textiles to help Catalonia as early as 1718 and again in the
1760s, tariffs on silk for the benefit of Valencia, and restrictions on metal
goods such as hardware for the benefit of the Basque country. In Richard
Herr's words the country flourished in commerce and manufacturing "in a
way unknown for centuries" (ibid., p. 147). It was not to last.

With the beginnings of a bourgeois middle class in trade and industry
supported by Carlos III and enlightened views arriving from France, the
Church and the aristocracy organized in opposition. The French Revolution accentuated the division in Spain between those who favored change
and those who dug in to resist it. Invasion by Napoleonic forces, and by
the English warring against France, cut Spain off from her colonies, which
revolted from 1808 to the early 1820s. The collapse of factories released

workers who joined peasants in fleeing into the big cities. One is forced to conclude that Spanish resilience, exhibited on a number of occasions, was insufficient to bring the country back to stability. The "failed transition" from feudalism to modern capitalism of Frederick Kranz and P. M. Hohenberg describes Spain of the eighteenth century better than Italy and Holland, to which their book is devoted (1975). Foreign intervention perhaps cut revival short, as did the death of Carlos III, but the deep-seated elements of decline—lack of social cohesion, inflation, guilds, overstretch in warring against especially the Dutch but also Britain, France, the Italian provinces, plus the Ottoman Empire, and the "Dutch disease" occasioned by the flood of silver—made the decline evidenced from 1590 to 1720 impossible to overcome even with the best of policies. Spain and Portugal under Philip II may have held world economic primacy. They were incapable of holding it for long for a host of causes, none sufficient, and most perhaps not necessary.

6

The Low Countries

North Europe

Before the thirteenth century and for some time thereafter, the North Sea and the Baltic were one trading system separate and for the most part distinct from the Mediterranean. The major network holding it together was the Hanseatic League, a loose collection of largely German cities, such as Lübeck, Hamburg, Cologne, Rostock, which traded from Bruges to Novogorod, and occasionally through Russia to the Black Sea, continuously northward to Bergen in Norway, and sporadically by way of the Atlantic and the Bay of Biscay to Iberia and the Mediterranean. Herring from Scania, cod from Bergen, honey and furs from Russia, ales from Hamburg, salt from Lunenberg, plus grain and timber from Danzig and Königsberg, were shipped west to *Kontors* (counting houses) in Bruges and the Steelyard in London. Going eastward, the Hansa's cogs brought especially salt from Portugal and France to cure the herring and cod, woolen cloth from Bruges and metals from London.

Hanseatic trading practices were primitive. The bill of exchange available from the North Italian city-states was resisted. Ships making a given port would sell for local money and buy what they could with it. Differences would be paid in specie. The League was also distinctive in its loose political organization, with responsibility widely diffused. Alfred Marshall said that "the scattered forces of the Hanseatic Federation could not act to develop the latest economics of concentrated trade to the full extent" (1920, p. 692). Only Lübeck, Hamburg, and two or three other towns paid their dues in full; the rest were free riders. Decentralization went well beyond that of the Dutch who were trade rivals (Dollinger, 1964 [1970]). Sweden on the periphery marketed its copper originally through Lübeck; later, in an effort to liberate itself from dependence on the League, shifted to Amsterdam, which had the advantage of lending it the money to pay off an indemnity to Denmark called for by the 1613 Treaty of Knared (Heckscher, 1954, pp. 63–64).

Bruges

The principal western port to which the League traded, Bruges had emerged as the leading commercial and financial center of Flanders at the end of the Middle Ages, serving as an intermediary between England and the Champagne fairs on the one hand and the Mediterranean and northern Europe on the other. The kings of England transferred the staple (for wool) among Dordrecht, Antwerp, Bruges, and finally to Calais where it remained from 1363 to 1558. The wool was reexported to Bruges, however, for sale to the Flemish spinners and weavers, until the British finally stopped exporting wool in favor of cloth, producing a loss for Flemish home industry. In similar fashion, the Hansa moved its *Kontor* from Bruges to Dordrecht (on the German river system), to Bruges again, back to Dordrecht, to Antwerp in the Brabant, to Utrecht, and back to Bruges, as quarrels broke out, were resolved, and broke out again over taxes, loans, and monopolies.

To Bruges from Italy came Venetian and Genoese galleys carrying mostly luxury goods, Italian silks, and velvet plus, from the Levant, Greek wines, Oriental silks, and spices. Spanish trade was mostly wool and hides, the former needed to replace the dwindling English supply, plus Basque iron, and from south Spain and Portugal fruit, olives, rice, and wine. In the first half of the sixteenth century Lisbon delivered spices, especially pepper, which it obtained from the Asian islands. From Bruges to the North Sea and Baltic went Flemish cloth, linens, and woolens, plus luxury goods like French wines sought by the rich in the Baltic.

Most is known about the Genoese "nation" in Bruges, the latest to be granted privileges—in 1395—but there were more Germans (Hanseatics) in Bruges than Italians or Iberians, and no French nation because Flanders was regarded by the French as French. When Philip the Good entered Bruges in 1440, the parade included 136 Germans, 48 Spanish, 30 Venetians, 30 Milanese, 35 Genoese, 22 Florentines, 12 merchant-bankers from Lucca, and an unknown number of Portuguese and Catalans (van Houtte, 1967, p. 67). A description of a similar procession to celebrate the wedding of Charles the Bold of Burgundy in 1468 mentions that the merchants came behind the ambassadors and clergy with 10 Venetians on horseback, then 60 Florentines on foot, 24 Spanish again on horseback, 108 Genoese, and 108 Easterlins (Hanseatic merchants), all resplendent in bright colors, each nation with a retinue of servants, and again no English or French (Mollat du Jourdain, 1993, p. 78). Van Houtte expresses astonishment that there were no English in the 1440 parade, and speculates that the festivities may have taken place at the time of an embargo. He went on: Bruges at the time constituted a turning place for world commerce in the Middle Ages. If it was not the world market, it was nevertheless a great market, perhaps the greatest market in Christendom of the fourteenth century (ibid., p. 68). Most foreigners (those not born in Bruges) had permission to trade with other foreigners, but the fact that most disputes took place between foreigners and Brugeois suggests that for the most part, natives of Bruges intermediated between foreign buyers and sellers.

Trade gradually evolved into finance. There were three groups of financiers: pawnbrokers who loaned on collateral, exchangers who after a time dealt in transferable deposits as protobankers, and merchant-bankers who transferred funds from place to place through bills of exchange. The money market was located at the Bourse, named after a hotel belonging to a man named van der Burse. Exchange rates were quoted on Venice, Genoa, Florence, Barcelona, London, and Paris. When Burgundy was at war with France, bills for the Parisian capital were drawn first on Geneva and then on Lyons (ibid., pp. 70–74). There were no quotations for Lübeck, Hamburg, or other Hansa towns, which did not use bills. When remittances to Rome from north Germany, Poland, and Scandinavia were required, the Hansards would buy goods in those places, ship them to Bruges, sell them for local currency, and buy bills on Rome from an Italian banker.

One great Florentine banker, Cosimo de Medici, got into trouble lending to Bruges and London, the latter a satellite of Bruges in the fifteenth century, as the bank's agents violated their instructions by lending too much to Edward IV in London and to the Duke of Burgundy, both from Bruges. The bank had representatives in Bruges, though not a branch in the early part of the century. It formed a branch in 1439, with the London office as a subsidiary until 1451 when it, too, was constituted as a branch. The Bruges branch did badly to 1450 with unpaid debt, especially in claims on Barcelona. Other debts in London and Bruges included £8,500 from Edward IV on wool assignments plus £2,000 on other pledges, £9,500 outstanding from Charles the Bold (Duke of Burgundy) at the time of his death in 1477, and further a loan to John II of Portugal to explore the coast of Guinea. In all, the losses of the Bruges and London branches came to £19,000, a "fantastic sum" for those days (de Roover, 1966, chap. 13).

The Decline of Bruges

The decay of Florence in banking, with the collapse of the Medici bank in 1494, was only one of many causes of the decline in Bruges, and not the foremost. The city's possible claim for world economic primacy dates back to the first half of the fourteenth century. The beginning of decline has been traced to 1350; the pace picked up in the fifteenth century. J. A. van Houtte states that there was no clear turning point, and that the down gradient was attributable to many causes. Some, such as the increasing conservatism of Brugeois traders and bankers, were internal; others, such as the frequent quarrels with foreign merchants, especially those of the Hanseatic *Kontor*, external. The two sorts are not unconnected, in all likelihood, with greater and greater unwillingness on the part of merchants to take risks. States and provinces in Holland stopped borrowing in Bruges in the sixteenth century because of fear that Dutch goods would be seized at Sluys if the interest had not been paid, as occurred in 1530 (Tracy, 1985, pp. 112, 129).

An important factor contributing to the decline was the silting up of the Zwin river, which forced larger ships to unload at Sluys, the foreport on the North Sea, which in turn silted up. Canalization and dredging proved expensive and of limited effect. Larger ships were forced to anchor in the bays of Walcheren Island and to lighter their goods to the market in Bruges. It became easier to handle vessels in Bergen-op-Zoom, the foreport of Antwerp, until a tidal wave in 1530 ruined that port but enhanced access to Antwerp itself.

Another problem was probably the decline in Flemish cloth in competition with that of the Brabant, in part, but especially with the British "new drapery," an innovation at the beginning of the seventeenth century producing lighter and cheaper woolens. Van Houtte notes that the British exported only 5,000 pieces of woolen cloth in 1350, but that two centuries later the volume was up to 150,000 pieces, much of it dyed in Antwerp and Malines (1967, p. 80).

The real force behind the decline of Bruges, however, was its inability to meet the competition, and the failure of the city's monopoly. The cost of Flemish cloth rose. The Duke of Brabant sought to take the wool staple away from Bruges, which led some merchants to move to Antwerp. When in 1496 the two fairs of Antwerp were combined with the two financial fairs at Bergen-op-Zoom, making four a year, Italian merchants began to move seasonally from Bruges to Antwerp to participate. The Portuguese factory in Bruges shifted to Antwerp a few years later (Subrahmanyam and Thomas, 1991, p. 302, note 7). German wine merchants from Cologne and copper merchants from central Europe carrying the metal down rivers to the North Sea stopped at Antwerp to meet the Portuguese there. The Hanseatic League, which was losing out at best as ships grew too large for the port of Lübeck, finally moved. By the opening of the sixteenth century there was little left in Bruges.

Hansa assemblies in 1442 and 1447 at Lübeck had tried to restrict purchases of Low Country cloth to those from Bruges, but failed. Bruges itself tried fiercely to retain its monopoly, building a fort to block trade (unsuccessfully) with Antwerp, promulgating ordinances to compel foreigners to remain in Bruges except during the four Antwerp fairs. When these fairs became permanent and year-round, that effort was abandoned. A new "nation" for Andalusia was formed by Ferdinand and Isabella to mark the Spanish reconquest of Granada, but moved to Middleburg in 1500. The Florentine bankers Frescobaldi and Gualterotti shifted to Antwerp after 1488, and the Venetians withdrew altogether (Bergier, 1979, p. 113). The

Portuguese moved to Antwerp early in the sixteenth century—their first shipment of pepper was unloaded there in 1501. About 1516 the financial nations of Genoa and Lucca joined the exodus. Bruges, tied up in bad loans to the Duke of Burgundy and to Maxmilian, the Holy Roman Emperor, lacked capacity to lend. The Italian bankers returned to Bruges for a while, possibly because, Herman van der Wee suggests, Bruges was in liquidation as a financial center (1963). Only the market for Spanish wool remained there. Numbers of Hansard merchants dwindled from twelve in 1511 to three in 1540, then two, lastly one who died in 1554 (van Houtte, 1967, p. 90).

Antwerp

Like Bruges, Antwerp was a world market without much in the way of shipping, the two relying primarily on the ships of the Hanseatic League, the Italian city-states, and the Iberian peninsula. Antwerp was not a new town when the foreign merchants and bankers resident in Bruges joined the Germans from Augsburg and Nuremberg there at the end of the fifteenth century. Its commerce had gained on that of Bruges as northern commodities gave way to southern—sugar displacing honey; silk, fur; ale, mead—and as flax expanded in Flanders and Zeeland (van der Wee, 1963, vol. 2, p. 120). German silver production and copper from Hungary and the Tyrol moved north to Antwerp rather than south to Venice, paving the way for Spanish American silver, which picked up volume after 1560. Early English woolens were also dyed at Antwerp. While Bruges traded local products against imports, as well as serving as an entrepôt, Antwerp was mainly a market, not deeply engaged in production. Major commodities were English cloth, German metals, and Portuguese spices (van Houtte, 1964, p. 304). In addition, Antwerp had a position in the grain trade that made the Dutch nervous (Tracy, 1985, p. 118). "For the first time in history, a world market [came into being] in the sense that the bulk of certain commodities was traded in one spot" (van Houtte, 1964, p. 384). Richard Ehrenberg goes further in an extravagant statement: "In four decades from 1446, Antwerp developed into a trading center such as the world has never seen before *or since*" (1896 [1928], p. 223, emphasis added). As merchants and bankers emigrated from Bruges to Antwerp, Antwerp's population grew from 20,000 in 1444 to 50,000 about 1500 and to 100,000 by 1560, equal to the numbers in Seville and exceeded in Europe only by Naples, Milan, Venice, and Paris (van Houtte, 1964, p. 305).

Four decades of trade is one thing. By the sixteenth century, however, transit trade had diminished in size and importance; finance had risen. Some of the change may have been owing to the influx of Italian bankers. The reasons went deeper, however. Fernand Braudel observes that in contrast with Venice and Amsterdam with successful runs of a century and more, Antwerp between 1500 and 1565 had a series of ups and downs and never "found its cruising rhythm or its long term equilibrium" (1979 [1984],

p. 48). Jean Bergier observes that a new economic world was opening up. The Italians of 1450 were satisfied with their merchant-banker techniques. Competition was minimal and they had settled into a comfortable routine. "The forms of their undertakings show all the signs of a smoothly operating capitalism, but the spirit is lacking" (Bergier, 1979, pp. 107–11. The quotation is from p. 111). Bergier asks why the place left by the Italians was not filled by the French, say at Lyons, which like Antwerp was heavily populated by Italian bankers. He concludes that the vacuum was filled by south German bankers operating not only in Nuremberg but in Lyons, Madrid, and especially Antwerp because they had a "fierce will to win the big markets and to dominate international commerce and finance—in a word, to succeed" (ibid., p. 111). The German bankers—Fuggers, Welsers, Hochstetters, Seilers, Kleberg, Tucher—were beginning to spread into the rest of Europe with their fortunes based on trade with Venice, production of metals, and loans to electors of the Holy Roman Empire, just at the time when the spices from the Far East were arriving in Europe in Portuguese ships. Bergier asserts that the Italians made a mistake in starting up operations in Lisbon, where the spices first arrived, rather than in Antwerp where they were distributed (ibid., p. 115).

The development of yearly trade fairs from two to four to a permanent year-round fair has been mentioned. Antwerp went further in tying credit tightly to goods at first, then developing purely financial bills of exchange that ran from fair to fair at 2 or 3 percent for three months equal to 8 to 12 percent a year. By 1630, Ehrenberg claims, the richest firms no longer dealt in commodities; it was too much trouble, too risky. It was easier to deal in bills of exchange (1896 [1928], pp. 242–43). Germans, and to a declining extent Italians, borrowed and lent money, while some merchants, but increasingly agents of the crowns of England, Spain, and France, borrowed it. London had finally driven out the hated Italians from whom it borrowed early and to whom it defaulted. An agent of the Tudors, Stephen Vaughn, settled in Antwerp but began borrowing for the throne only in 1545. His successor was discharged for incompetence and was followed in 1552 by Thomas Gresham, a London merchant rather than a banker. Ehrenberg comments that the Tudors were forced to borrow abroad after the expulsion of the Italians because the usury laws of the time prevented dealings among their subjects (ibid., p. 253).

War, especially fought by mercenary soldiers, increased the demand for loans but failed to help with their repayment. Most of Antwerp's troubles were caused by the mutinies of unpaid mercenaries, who sacked Antwerp in 1576, killing six thousand people, following the devastating attack by the Zeeland Protestant "Sea Beggars" on Brill in 1572, and starting an exodus. The siege of 1584–1585 finished the job of depopulation, as numbers fell from 90,000 in 1566 to 60,000 in 1585. In all, 100,000 people left Brabant and Flanders after the blockade of the Scheldt in 1585, mostly merchants and skilled artisans, taking with them mobile capital and industrial technique. They left not only for the northern Netherlands but for

Germany, England, Sweden, Italy, central Europe, and the New World as well. The largest numbers went to the United Provinces and the neighboring cities of the Rhineland, but as many as 10,000 emigrated to London (van der Wee, 1988, p. 348). Despite these numbers it has been remarked that some merchants quit commerce altogether, investing their wealth and land to join the local nobility, and, as in Portugal near Lisbon and later in England, became agricultural improvers (Arruba, 1991, pp. 361–62). It is not made clear in this Portuguese account whether the impetus came from economic motives or social ambition.

Holland

The seven United Provinces of the northern Netherlands, dominated by Holland, received an enormous stimulus from the troubles of Antwerp, the finishing blow of which was the blockade of the Scheldt in 1585. The spurt of growth that ran from 1590 to 1620 has been called an economic miracle (Slicher van Bath, 1982, p. 23). Its roots went back a long way. Some of the favoring factors were locational: ready access like Bruges and Antwerp had to the Atlantic, the North Sea, and the Baltic; a rich hinterland from which a series of broad rivers flowed (Alfred Marshall pointed out that in England all rivers flow away from one another [1920, p. 39]); the availability of peat, which could serve as fuel in the absence of forests. Other factors were structural: lack of a strong nobility, a condition produced along the north coast of Europe where heath and moor were separated from the sea by dikes that needed tending, with little time left for cities, noble knights, artists, or thinkers (Kellenbenz, 1963, pp. xxii, xxiii); and lack of a powerful church, a product of the incomplete Reformation. Another feature of the United Provinces, missing in many countries of Europe, was widespread education that produced a school in every village in western and northern Netherlands at the end of the Middle Ages, with the arithmetic necessary for a money economy widely taught (Slicher van Bath, 1982, p. 32). In addition to such structural factors, there was a series of accidents. The weakness of other leading European powers left room for the United Provinces to forge ahead (ibid., p. 32). Defeat of the Spanish Armada by the British in 1588 weakened two navies and created an opening for Dutch shipping. One could mention the move of herring from the Baltic to the North Sea in the fourteenth century, favoring Dutch fishermen over the Hansards, providing a "primitive accumulation" of capital for subsequent investment, and enabling the building of Amsterdam on a bed of herring bones (Marshall, 1920, p. 693). Thomas Mun, writing in the 1620s, said that it was not the *Place*, but the *employment*, not the barren Netherlands but the *rich fishing*, which gives foundation, trade, and subsistence to those multitudes of Ships, Arts and People . . ." (1620s [1664], p. 190). Mun objected especially to the fact that Dutch fishing for herring, ling, and cod took place in "His Majesties' Seas" (ibid., p. 188). There was also the accident of the influx of talent, capital, and drive to make a new economic life.

This recital of locational, structural, and accidental causes of Dutch commercial greatness fails to do justice to the mentalities that drove its citizens. Alfred Marshall wrote "[t]he Dutch, like their pupils the English, were slow of invention" (1920, p. 692). This seems less than generous to both countries, taking into account, with regard only to the Dutch, their methods of drainage and land reclamation, of ship design and building, of using windmills for milling grain and sawing ship timbers; the invention of the *trekvaart* for moving businessmen and officials between towns by horse-drawn personal barges, a feat comparable to making the trains run on time three centuries later (De Vries, 1978); the organization of the Dutch East India Company (VOC); the creation of an effective convoy system for small merchant vessels; the development of a panoply of financial instruments, and many other innovations. Marshall does say, however, that "their tough-ness of fiber was unsurpassed, they possessed a singular self-control and remained frugal and persistent for more generations than any other rich people had done before them" (ibid.). Again one could question whether Dutch abstinence had outrun that of, say, the Venetians. Simon Schama emphasizes that Dutch austerity gradually broke down and acquired a dark side: "By the 1660s, it was commonly said, the frugal and modest habits which had originally created the foundations of Dutch prosperity, were being squandered in a show of world vanity and luxury." He went on to add: "This was no more than the latest version of the Roman stoic lament for the syba-ritic corruption of republican virtue" (1988, p. 293).

A central problem in Dutch history is the extent to which its early dynamism grew out of its decentralized character. Holland, with Amsterdam as its economic center, was the leading province of the Dutch republic, but it did not rule. Each province was governed by an oligarchy of regents, originally drawn from merchants, later from their progeny. The total tax burden was determined by the States General, which represented the seven provinces, and was apportioned to the provinces, which in turn apportioned their shares to lesser units down to cities and villages. The system seemed to function much as a Quaker meeting that reached conclusions by "the sense of meeting" without direction from the top or initiative entirely from below. Immanuel Wallerstein's application to the United Provinces of his theory of economic hegemony, with a world "core" that lays down the conditions of trade with the "periphery" and the "semi-periphery" and captures the surplus for itself, which he applies to the United Provinces (1982), was challenged by Peter Klein, who insisted that hegemonic theory called for a strong nation-state, and this the United Provinces was not (1982, p. 85). Holland was the leader among the seven provinces, however, and as in political science theories of leadership, had to pay for the privilege of leading and being repaid in prestige, by taking on a disproportionate share of the costs of the totality (Froelich and Oppenheimer, 1970). During the Dutch golden age of the seventeenth century, the issue was not trouble-some. It became salient in the decline of the eighteenth century, however, as Holland needed to raise more funds for military operations on land and sea, especially after 1789 when first the French Revolution and then the Napoleonic occupation levied heavy indemnities on the country (Schama, 1977 [1992]). I return to the issue below.

Commerce

In the traditional account, the Dutch profited primarily from the "mother trade," having outcompeted the Hanseatic League in fierce competition at the end of the sixteenth century. It brought grain, timber for shipbuilding, and naval stores from the Baltic through the Kattegut and the Skaggerak and paid for them with English and Flemish wools dyed in Leiden, linens made from Silesian flax woven in Haarlem, salt and wine from the Bay of Biscay and the Iberian peninsula, plus silver to balance the accounts. The traditional account is set out, for example, in Braudel's three volumes, *Civilization and Capitalism*, but is strongly attacked by Jonathan Israel, who tends to disagree with much of Braudel's interpretation and insists that the real Dutch advantage was in the "luxury trades" with the Far East and Spanish America (1989). Sir George Downing, who was British minister at the Hague in the middle of the seventeenth century, equally made a distinction between the "rich trades" in the Mediterranean and to the Far East, with little bulk but considerable risk, and the "lost trades," in which the Dutch outcompeted the British in the Baltic and in fishing (Barbour, 1930 [1954], p. 231). The Baltic was frozen seven months out of the year, and Atlantic storms increased the dangers of sailing north-south in late fall and winter. During this time the Dutch accumulated stores of rich products headed north and of bulk products en route south to Spain, becoming a great storehouse. Goods were brought to Amsterdam and taken away by the "First Hand," sorted, graded, repacked (for example to avoid spontaneous combustion of grains under hot Mediterranean skies) and stored by the "Second Hand," with a relatively small amount distributed locally by the "Third Hand." P. W. Klein holds that as "a very daring guess," at least 25 or 30 percent of gross domestic capital formation consisted of investment in stocks, which was more important than investment in the processing industry (1970a, p. 14).

Not all timber products came to deforested Holland from Norway and the Baltic. A great deal came from the forests bordering the Rhine and its tributaries, on both the French and German banks. Pilings, firs for masts, oak for planking came down the Rhine in enormous rafts, compromising as many as 24,000 logs, operated by collectives joined by residents of the towns along the river. As many as six hundred to a thousand workmen assembled the awkward craft, and crews of five to six hundred men took them down the stream in thirty days or so, bringing their own provisions (Dufraise, 1992).

In addition to stapling foreign commodities, the Dutch enjoyed an advantage in trade from the fact that government set standards for goods produced at home and saw to it that they were adhered to. (This argues, to be sure, in favor of centralization and against pluralism.) Government standards were noticed in Britain by Sir Josiah Child in his *Brief Observations Concerning Trade and Interest of Money* of 1668. The third of fifteen observations explaining the "prodigious increase of the Netherlanders in their domestick and forreign Trade, Riches and multitude of Shipping" is given as "the exact making of all their Native Commodities. . . . That the repute of their said commodities abroad continues always good, and the Buyers will accept them by the Marks without opening" (Letwin, 1969, pp. 41–42).

In a study of Dutch primacy in world trade, 1585 to 1740, Jonathan Israel divides the century and a half into seven segments. In the first, from 1590 to 1609, the country made its breakthrough into a leading position in world trade, first entering the Mediterranean with the British in 1590; establishing the Dutch East India Company (VOC); gaining indirect access to Spanish silver, which was arriving in Seville in increasing amounts in the 1590s; and establishing the Bank of Amsterdam to expedite trade finance (Israel, 1989). Truce in the war with Spain in 1609 led to a suspension of the Spanish embargo and a further surge in Dutch trade, as Dutch ships could run to Seville and Cadiz carrying northern European goods for reshipment to Spanish America. The numbers reached four to five hundred ships a year (ibid., p. 125). In addition, command of the Baltic was gained from Denmark and Sweden. The third phase, from 1621 to 1647, was less successful. War with Spain was renewed and trade with Spain had to be shifted to Hamburg ships to the extent that it could be maintained. Another setback was being driven out of Brazil to the West Indies in 1625 at a time when trade with the East and West Indies was otherwise flourishing. The period came to an end in 1647 with the renewed lifting of the Spanish embargo.

In the second half of the seventeenth century there followed a series of commercial challenges and wars—the British Navigation Act of 1651; three Anglo-Dutch wars, in the second of which Holland lost New Amsterdam to the British; and a tariff war with mercantilist France under Colbert, culminating in the French invasion of Holland in 1672. The French tariff war provided an example of import substitution of the sort that dynamic economies undertake: in an effort to inhibit Dutch shipbuilding, the French cut off exports of Breton canvas for sailcloth. In a short time, Haarlem and Enkhuizen produced enough linen canvas not only to satisfy Dutch needs but to replace the French in English and Spanish markets (ibid., p. 264). The period also witnessed a growth in Dutch imports of colonial goods— sugar, tobacco, tea, coffee, dyestuffs, and materials that were processed to a limited extent in Holland for domestic use and export.

The turn of the century saw intense competition in trade, the British, French, and Dutch trying to break the Spanish monopoly of trade between Europe and the Americas by interloping, that is, by dealing directly rather than through Cadiz. They succeeded in the War of the Spanish Succession as the Bourbons replaced the Hapsburgs on the Spanish throne and Madrid granted an *asiento* to the English for trade in the South Sea (dealing with

Peru through Buenos Aires). Competition between the Dutch and the English was particularly intense. A popular jingle in England ran: "Make wars with Dutchmen, Peace with Spain, Then we shall have money and trade again" (Letwin, 1969, p. 1). Josiah Child, writing in 1668, put it "The prodigious increase of the Netherlanders in their domestick and forreign Trade, Riches and multitude of Shipping is the envy of the present and may be the wonder of all future generations" (ibid., p. 41). Child's fifteen reasons for the superiority of the Dutch over the British in the last third of the seventeenth century emphasized especially their high rate of savings and low rate of interest (ibid., p. 42). He failed to see, however, that Dutch trade was based on intermediation, in which their monopoly was destined to diminish as knowledge of the profits to be made and of the costs of packing and repacking in the central emporium became diffused. Adam Smith made one of his rare errors in suggesting that the Dutch merchants brought their products to Amsterdam because they were uneasy at being separated from their capital and wanted to see it with their own eyes (1776 [1973], p. 422). This overlooked the stapling function of grading, packing, and storing and the economies of scale of broader markets. In one view, Dutch intermediary trade was necessarily transient. As knowledge of quantities, qualities, and prices becomes widespread, and volume rises, direct trade becomes economical and the intermediary is passed by (Butter, 1969, p. 6).

Here, more than knowledge was involved. Seas became safer from pirates, ships larger, and nations sought to acquire their own merchant marines (Charles Wilson, 1941, p. 17). Writing on the eighteenth century, Wilson cites case after case of direct trade substituting for intermediation in Amsterdam in trade between Britain and Germany on the one hand, and between Britain and Spain on the other (ibid., pp. 38, 44, 51, 61ff). Gradually exports of French wine to the United Provinces declined from their peak in the seventeenth and early eighteenth centuries, for example, from 67 percent of the total in 1717, to 10 percent in 1789, while that to the "Nord," largely Hamburg, rose from 13 percent to 46 percent (Crouzet, 1968, pp. 250–57). A British merchant explained to his Dutch colleague in 1714: "It is needful to buy Goods at the Fountain and save all superfluous Charges, for that divers merchants draw directly from Hambro and Bremen, German linens: it saves much" (quoted by Wilson, 1941, pp. 52–53). Wilson ascribes much of the motive for moving from trade into finance to the loss of Amsterdam's role as an intermediary in trade.

Industry

Dutch commerce dealt not only in the products of other countries and colonies. Exports consisted of butter and cheese produced in rural areas reclaimed from the sea on farms that relied on imported grain for human food, and of herring caught from the North Sea in 500 busses that shipped their catches back to Dutch ports for salting and other processing in buy-boats that transferred the catch at sea. Holland's major industry, however, was shipbuilding. Large ships were needed for long ocean voyages to the East and West Indies, ships large enough to carry provisions for long voyages, personnel to populate the "factories" overseas, and guns and gunners to defend against pirates and privateers when sailing alone without armed escort. In this, the British competed closely with the Dutch. In the Baltic trades, however, they were far from competitive. Prices for timber, deals, hemp, flax, and pitch were higher in England than the prices of supplies from the Baltic brought to Zaandam, partly because of British customs duties and partly owing to the navigation acts that restricted imports of naval stores to British ships (Barbour, 1930 [1954], esp. pp. 232, 234). A Dutch *fluyt* (flyboat) that would cost £1,300 to build in England would come to only £800 in Holland. In larger ships the differences ran from £1,400 to £2,400. Both French and British held the *fluyt* in some disdain as flimsy and weakly built, but with a crew of nine or ten mariners for the thirty required in a British vessel of the same size—Wilson says eighteen for the Dutch as against twenty-six to thirty for the other nations (1941, p. 6)— Dutch freight rates were one-third cheaper. One contribution to the cheapness was that the Dutch bought much provision for crews in Ireland, where beef and butter, kept out of Britain, were particularly inexpensive. Still a further private economy at public expense was the naval convoys sought by merchants from the Admiralty in Holland to protect their ships against privateers and pirates. Dutch ships to the East and West Indies were large enough to carry their own armament and sailed for the most part singly, but British ships of all sizes had to carry both goods and guns.

Finally, in commenting on shipbuilding, as noted earlier, a Dutch writer of a treatise on shipping in 1671 asserted that foreigners who studied Dutch practice could not succeed in imitating it, working as they did in an alien environment with alien artisans. "The workmen lacked the thrifty and neat disposition of the Hollander" (Barbour, 1930 [1954], p. 234). These workmen were further characterized, along with sailors, dockhands, and farmers, as "the most educated, spirited and outspoken workingmen in Europe" (E. N. Williams, 1970, p. 31). British navy commissioners consulted Dutch shipwrights, and Colbert in France sought to recruit forty of them to instruct French shipbuilders in their techniques (Barbour, 1930 [1954], pp. 235, 239). Barbour further hypothesized, however, that the lack of the advanced techniques of Dutch sawmills and shipyard cranes may have induced certain Dutch carpenters to decline the French invitation (ibid.). About a century later the States General forbade the emigration of skilled workers sought by foreign countries, especially sawmill operators, ropemakers, and textile-finishers, though these restrictions were easily evaded (Williams, 1970, p. 257).

In addition to shipbuilding, finishing textiles, and processing colonial products, Dutch industry went in for brewing beer, distilling gin and brandy, refining sugar and salt, boiling soap, milling vegetable seed for oils, and diamond cutting. The last of these, along with other industries, had been largely transferred from Antwerp. While later Dutch failure to make the transition to modern industry before about 1880 was widely blamed on lack of coal—though in the twentieth century coal for steel was readily imported by barge from the Ruhr—the Dutch were able to provide the requisite energy for their early industries, especially brewing, distilling, and faience and brick-making, with peat, which was abundant in the country at or even below water level and accessible to canal transport. Peat provided the Dutch republic with "cheap fuel" despite its early deforestation (de Zeeuw, 1978). Some peat was even exported to Antwerp and other Flemish cities in one direction, to Emden, Bremen, and Hamburg in the other. At the same time a small amount of coal was imported from England and Scotland (ibid., pp. 14–15). After the seventeenth century, peat became less accessible at appropriate altitudes, and more expensive in consequence. J. W. De Zeeuw calculates that through windmills and peat the Dutch were able to produce the energy equivalent of 0.8 million hectares of forest, and 1 million hectares of arable land would have been needed to produce fodder for horses to replace peat (ibid., pp. 22–23).

Apart from commerce, shipping, and fishing, however, there was not much entrepreneurial verve in Holland after the initial half century from 1590. There was quite a burst of innovation—at a fairly low level of technology—in the first four decades of the seventeenth century, with half of all the patents issued from 1590 to 1790 being granted in that period. After 1640, however, invention slowed down (Klein, 1970a, p. 11).

Dutch shipping continued to be profitable despite the rising wages of sailors until the Fourth Anglo-Dutch War in 1780, but commerce began to give way to finance much earlier. Writing on Anglo-Dutch trade in the eighteenth century, Wilson asserts that commerce held up until about 1730 (1939 [1954], pp. 254–55; 1941, p. 17). He noted the view that trade had started to decline in the last quarter or third of the seventeenth century, but asserted that "new research" has modified that view (1939 [1954], p. 254). Still newer and more detailed research by Jonathan Israel puts the decline earlier, as Dutch/French rivalry from the 1680s and successive wars between the Dutch and the English on one side and the French and Spanish on the other took a heavy toll of Dutch trade, especially with Cadiz and via Cadiz with the New World, a toll not fully made up by interloping (1989, pp. 340ff, chaps. 8, 9). Israel notes that other commentators went wrong in focusing on the bulk trade with the Baltic, which held up, and overlooking the luxury trades with the Far East and West Indies, which did not (p. 379). The contemporary debate has been over whether the decline was relative or absolute at the turn of the century.

Finance

By the time of the Nine Years' War and the War of the Spanish Succession on each side of 1700, Dutch finance was well advanced. James Tracy in fact postulates a "financial revolution" in the middle of the sixteenth century when Dutch provinces shifted from borrowing from merchant-bankers to marketing *rentes* directly to wealthy individuals (1980). This "novel expedient" preceded another financial revolution in London after the Glorious Revolution of William and Mary of Holland replaced the Stuarts (Dickson, 1967), and preceded by three centuries the technique by which Jay Cooke, the Philadelphia banker, made his reputation in the U.S. Civil War by marketing Union bonds directly to northern savers, rather than through the banking establishment (Kindleberger, 1990, pp. 78–79).

Merchant-bankers fleeing Antwerp for Amsterdam and elsewhere in 1585 brought with them Italian, Flemish, and Brabant techniques that closely joined commerce and finance. With the boom in commerce from the breakthroughs into the Mediterranean, the Far East, and the Baltic from 1590 to 1609, and especially the monopoly profits in trade achieved in the twelve-year truce to 1621, frugal Dutch habits created an enormous pool of savings that went beyond the needs of ship-owning, holding stocks of commodities in the storehouse of Amsterdam, reclaiming polders for agriculture, and the like. The profits of farmers producing industrial crops on diked fields even spilled over into the finance of herring busses and *fluyt* ships, shares that were divided in binary fashion in fractions down to 1/256 (Lambert, 1971, p. 186). The Dutch capital market grew apace. Foreign lending started with help for the Swedish and Danish crowns for their participation in the Thirty Years' War (1618–1648). Klein attributes the movement from trade to finance to a change in mentalities, owing as much to indolence as to the spirit of speculation (1970b, p. 33).

Along with their borrowing of financial techniques from the Spanish Netherlands, the Dutch inherited the Antwerp love of gambling (Schama, 1988, pp. 347–50; van der Wee, 1963, p. 202; van Houtte, 1964, p. 311). Frugality and gambling formed one of the many anomalies, contradictions, and paradoxes that Schama found in Dutch character of the period (1988, pp. 503, 505). An early climax was the Tulip Mania of 1636, described at length by various historians (ibid., pp. 350–66; Posthumus, 1928 [1969]; and more recently viewed, rather oddly, as rational investment in response to "fundamentals" [Garber, 1990]). Antwerp and Amsterdam both went in for lotteries, Amsterdam especially toward the end of the eighteenth century when Jacques Necker, the French director-general of finances, sold annuities based on multiple lives (Harris, 1979, pp. 125–33).

Somewhat less in the spirit of gambling but financially impressive as technique were markets in futures, options, and speculation in commodities, shares, and government bonds, even to the extent of buying and selling herring before they were caught (Barbour, 1950 [1966], chap. 4, esp. p. 74). Jewish exiles from Spain and Portugal were particularly innovative and adept in trade in futures and options, called "*Windhandel*" because buyer and seller in reality never saw real goods but dealt in air. Barbour comments that purely financial speculation began early in the first half of the seventeenth century and that by the second half it was preferred to foreign trade (ibid., pp. 74, 76). Merchants also tried to corner markets in Italian silks and marble, sugar, perfume ingredients, saltpeter, and copper.

Dutch speculators seem to have been adroit enough not to have been badly caught in the collapses of the Mississippi and South Sea bubbles (Charles Wilson, 1941, pp. 72, 103, 124). After the latter, many speculators moved to Amsterdam to speculate in the shares of newly created insurance companies, of which the Maatschappij van Assurance alone survived (Spooner, 1983).

One aspect of the growth of finance in the seventeenth century was the establishment in 1609 of the Bank of Amsterdam, patterned after the Bank of Venice. The Bank of Amsterdam received deposits of coin against which, after weighing and assaying, it issued "bank money," which generally went to a premium over coin because of its assured value. The Bank's success led to the establishment of similar banks in other Dutch provinces and in Germany. The City of Amsterdam required payment of bills of exchange over 600 florins to be made at the Bank of Amsterdam, which was known as a *Wisselbank* (exchange bank). The bank would from time to time make loans in rixdollars against deposits of specie, to enable borrowers to gain liquidity. By these means Amsterdam developed into the European center for dealing in foreign exchange and gold and silver.

In a report to the British Parliament in 1650, Thomas Violet wrote:

> It is well known to all merchants that trade from Spain that one-third part of their gold and silver at least is never registered; which gold and silver is consigned to particular merchants for the avoiding of the king's duty before it comes within the bar at St. Lucas (and generally now is sent for Holland). (Thirsk and Cooper, 1972, p. 63)

The fact that in an age of mercantilism the States General allowed the free import and export of precious metals was unique, says Artur Attman, and "helped create wealth" (1983, p. 28). Uniqueness of the policy is also attested by Jan De Vries: "Only the Dutch Republic, conspicuous for so many other reasons, seemed to have liberated itself from the Midas complex" (1976, p. 239). The market served as a public good. The East India Company was able to overcome the British Parliament's restrictions on its export of British coin by buying in Amsterdam the coin it needed for its purchases in India.

With the Glorious Revolution of 1688 and the assumption of the British throne by William of Orange, a new era of close financial ties opened between Holland and England. Early lending to Scandinavia in the century had been followed by that to German cities. The absence of loans to Britain had not been owing to the navigation acts and the three Anglo-Dutch wars, stated Charles Wilson, who called the wars "naval scuffles." There were some investments in drainage schemes, and perhaps mortgages, but the major breakthrough came with William of Orange and the British financial revolution (1941, chap. 4, quotation from p. 88). Some Dutch financiers displaced themselves to London to handle their own orders and those for compatriots at home. Dutch bankers assisted the Bank of England in meeting payments on protested bills used by the bank to finance British expenditures on the Continent in the Nine Years' War, fought by the British and Dutch against France and Spain (1689–1697). Dutch names were prominent among the subscribers to the stock of the Bank of England, of the East India Company, and of the South Sea Company. Dutch finance flourished in a more and more excited way, leading to financial crises, in 1763 at the end of the Seven Years' War, when commodity speculation and lending to Germany produced the failures of Arend Joseph (a Jewish house) and then the DeNeufvilles, requiring help from the Bank of England; and in 1772, when Clifford & Co., which had been speculating in the stock of the Dutch East India Company, failed along with the Ayr Bank in Scotland. The more lasting and traumatic event occurred in the Fourth Anglo-Dutch War, when the Dutch stopped lending to London and switched their capital to France, only to lose it and more when the Revolution, its wars, and Napoleon defeated the Republic and levied heavy indemnities on it. The crisis of 1763 marked a step in Dutch decline as the British started trading foreign exchange directly with St. Petersburg rather than through Amsterdam.

Education

Some attention should be given to the Abramovitz belief that economic growth requires labor, capital, and technology, which can be imported, plus social capability, for which a handy if rough proxy is years of education. The Dutch were committed to education long before Protestantism arrived, as far back indeed as the Middle Ages. As noted earlier, every western and northern village in the seventeenth century had a school and a schoolmaster and taught especially arithmetic, which was crucial for the money economy (Slicher van Bath, 1982, p. 32).

At the start of their economic upsurge, the Dutch founded five universities, Leiden (in 1575) being the most distinguished of them (Lambert, 1971, p. 188). Amsterdam abounded with printing houses, philosophers, historians, and scientists (ibid.). Amsterdam also attracted young merchants from abroad to learn their profession (R. G. Wilson, 1971, pp. 44, 45, 209). Between 1575 and 1700 there were 16,557 foreign students at the University of Leiden, according to Huizenga, alongside 21,528 Dutch students (Butter, 1969, p. 37). Schama devotes a dozen pages to describing attempted reform of elementary education at the end of the eighteenth century, which Goguel tackled after producing new tax laws and abolishing guilds as part of a plan for economic recovery (1977 [1992], pp. 530–41). Emphasis was on general education, as opposed to the French interest in producing engineers, military officers, and bureaucrats (ibid., p. 536). The reform seems not to have extended widely into the practical aspects of higher education. Inaugural speeches and dissertations were still produced in Latin as late as 1846 (Butter, 1969, pp. 36–37). The change occurred in the late 1840s, as one inaugural lecture by a (single) true "Smithian economist" was given in Latin in 1842 but published in Dutch in 1846 (ibid.,

p. 117). Not all of this is congruent with a recent study in Dutch, of which I can read only the English summary, that states that 25 percent of the men and 40 percent of the women born before 1800 had not learned how to read and write, whereas 100 years later literacy was universal (Boonstra, 1993, p. 449).

Migration

The Dutch Republic was well known for its tolerance in providing asylum for all sorts of peoples, in contrast to Spain, which expelled the Marranos and Moors. First, as noted, there was the mass movement of merchants, bankers, and industrial workers escaping the devastation of war in Flanders and the Brabant. Second, Jews and intellectuals were welcome. Third, at the height of the Dutch prosperity in the seventeenth century there was a seasonal migration from the Frisian Islands and Germany, as far east as Hanover, some to work as manual labor and some as soldiers and sailors for the Dutch East India Company. Before 1650, the migration from July to December was on herring busses and the merchant marine, and from March to May in south Holland it was in hay-making and grass-mowing. Some of the herring fishermen worked on the polders, in peat, and in brick-making in the off season. Work for the Dutch East India Company was regarded as the least attractive in Holland because of the long time away from home and the high chance of dying en route or abroad (Lucassen, 1984 [1987], chap. 8). The VOC hired Dutch when it could, and did better when business in Holland was depressed. The Dutch it managed to hire were mostly from the maritime provinces of Holland and Friesland, whereas the Germans were farm boys, "uneducated louts from the heart of Germany" less able than those of the East India Company (Boxer, 1970, p. 246). Fourth, in the events leading up to and following the Revocation of the Edict of Nantes, Huguenots came with their capital and skills to Amsterdam as well as to London, Geneva, and Hamburg.

With economic decline, skilled workers reversed direction and went abroad, while migrants increasingly filled unskilled tasks as the Dutch, leaving Leiden, Haarlem, and similar industrial towns, emigrated or stayed to receive charity. The attempt to restrict the emigration of skilled artisans has been mentioned, along with its lack of success. A German historian notes that in 1767 there were 27,000 Germans in Holland as mowers, peat-cutters, fishermen, and whalers, a number that declined to 4,000 or 5,000 by 1860 (when German industry was booming). By 1900 Dutch went to work in the Ruhr, and Oberhausen had not only a Dutch quarter, but a Dutch "worker borse" (Brepohl, 1948, p.91)

High Wages, Taxation, and Debt

A great many historians blame Dutch decline on high wages caused by high taxation on cost-of-living items, such as housing, clothing, and food. Taxes had to be levied on someone, and the Dutch burghers were resistant to income taxes in their separate provinces and to duties on imports and exports that might interfere with their carrying trade. Tax farming continued in Holland after it had been abandoned in favor of government collection in England. Ehrenberg claims that it died out only in the middle of the eighteenth century, but had not been scandalous before that (1896 [1928], p. 351); Klein put forth a different view, calling it chaotic, leading the public to revolt against it openly, and paying the government only 60 percent of the amounts collected, the rest accruing to the tax farmers (1970a, p. 16).

High wages are blamed for Dutch inability to make the transition from trade to substantial industry until the late nineteenth century by a long list of historians—Adam Smith (1776 [1937]), Charles Wilson (1941), Joel Mokyr (1977), H. R. C. Wright (1955), and many others. In a later paper, however, Mokyr points out that wages have one effect in a static model, where entrepreneurs maximize profits within the existing price structure, and another when entrepreneurs respond dynamically to seek to overcome handicaps (1991b). In a well-known book, H. J. Habakkuk suggested with mild diffidence that invention in the United States was labor saving because of high wages, while that in Britain saved resources, which were scarce and high priced (1962). That the W. Arthur Lewis model of growth with unlimited supplies of labor (and low wages) conflicts with the neoclassical model in which scarce labor stimulates labor-saving innovation emphasizes the need for caution in drawing conclusions from a single model without forethought.

The fact that the Netherlands taxed the laboring class rather than merchants, bankers, and the limited number of industrialists meant that funds could not be readily raised in wartime, and resort had to be taken to borrowing. Low interest rates favored this borrowing in the short run, but mounting debt required higher taxes in the longer, and gave rise to a fiscal crisis over whether and how to centralize taxation and meet the burdens of war and debt service.

Timing of Decline

There is in economics much debate over the timing of both rise and decline. With the Dutch the rise is dated with clarity from 1585 and the infusion of merchant-bankers from abroad, leading, with the Dutch tradition of asylum, to more expellees seeking refuge—Marronos from Spain, Jews and New Christians from Portugal, in due course Huguenots from France—each adding skill and drive to Dutch economic growth. The timing of decline is less settled, as different observers focus on different sectors and segments of the economy. "In 1650 the center of the world was tiny Holland, or rather Amsterdam" (Braudel, 1977, p. 91). In Jonathan Israel's taxonomy the period from 1647 to 1672 was the zenith in Dutch economic primacy in world trade, but the author explains that while Baltic trade was declining from 1650, trade with the Mediterranean and with the East and West Indies continued to flourish and that emphasis on 1650 was based on the exaggerated importance attached to the mother trade (1989, chap. 4, esp. pp. 214–15). There is much to support this timing, especially the views that the golden age ran from 1580 to 1670 (Schama, 1988, p. 283), the fixing of the beginning of the decline somewhere in the last third of the seventeenth century (De Vries, 1984b, p. 149), or in 1675, making it the last quarter of the century (ibid., p. 167). A more precise date in this period, 1672, is often given, the year in which the French occupied Holland, as they were to do a century later. But there is evidence in support of earlier and later dates: In a much quoted remark, the Dutch historian Aitzema records a complaint made in Amsterdam in 1652 that "the regents were not merchants, they did not take risks on the seas, but derived their incomes from houses, lands and securities (*renten*), and so allowed the sea to be lost" (Burke, 1974, p. 104). Burke comments that this was a political statement, rather than a judicious attempt to ascertain the facts. He further reproduced a table (Table 6–1) from two sociologists showing regents without occupation, suggesting rentiers rather than active entrepreneurs or financiers, and those with a country house:

Table 6-1 Dutch Regents

Period	Without Occupation	With Country House
1618 to 1650	33%	10%
1650 to 1672	66%	41%
1672 to 1702	53%	30%
1702 to 1748	73%	81%

Source: Burke, 1974, p. 106.

Burke suggests that the figures show the movement to have been gradual and concentrated more about 1700 than 1650, although the doubling between the first two periods for those without occupation and a quadrupling for those with country houses argue for the earlier date. The table helps explain a contradiction in various histories. In one view neither public office nor land attracted the Dutch (nor nobility the bourgeois merchants in a city such as Hamburg, for that matter [Schramm, 1969]). "The fatal urge to possess land for social status was little felt" (Davis, 1973, p. 189). This presumably reflects an early reading. In other reckonings:

> . . . Merchants who waxed rich made large purchases of land, an investment which also attracted them because of the social status and lordly rights and titles attaching to it (Geyl, 1961, p. 164).

John Hope was entering upon a process of aristocratization which was gradually alienating him from everyday affairs of the firm. In 1767 he bought Groenendaal estate, Bosbeek added in 1784, in 1774 acquired Nederhorst den Berg castle. In 1772 assumed occupation of family house but in 1782 moved again, this time to a house on the Herrengacht . . . also one on the north side of Korte Voorhout in the Hague. Widely scattered property and life of travel among them. (Buist, 1974, p. 18)

Charles Boxer observes that in the last quarter of the seventeenth century the old, severe, and frugal way of merchants gave way to lavish style, country houses, and the life of the grand seigneur, and cites a pamphlet in this vein from 1662 (1965, p. 38). John Hope may be explained away as a Scot, rather than a Dutchman. Alice Clare Carter quotes Montesquieu as noting in 1729 that in Amsterdam people withdraw their money from commerce to put it into structures (*pierres*), and "I see that it will be as in Venice, beautiful palaces instead of fleets and kingdoms" (1975, p. 40n).

Decline proceeded at different paces, slowly in finance despite the financial crises of 1763 and 1772, more rapidly in industry because of imports of finished cloth that undermined the work of Leiden and Haarlem, and in-between in fishing and shipping, hurt by competition, higher wages, emigrating fishermen, and import restrictions abroad, and perhaps by a change in diet favoring meat as against fish (Boxer, 1965, p. 273). French privateers in the war of 1702 to 1712 also hurt the herring fishery, but in whaling the Dutch were outstripped by the British and Germans using new techniques while they clung to their old ways (ibid., 1970, pp. 244–45).

The decline of the Dutch Republic in the second half of the eighteenth century is covered brilliantly, in detail and at great length, by Simon Schama in a book written at an early stage in his career but reprinted recently, *Patriots and Liberators: Revolution in the Netherlands, 1760–1813* (1977 [1992]). The second chapter marks the Dutch "dotage" from 1747 to 1760, and lists the usual suspects responsible for (relative) economic decline: estrangement from the sea; direct trade that bypassed Amsterdam; guilds; old-fashioned methods of ship-building; emigration of skilled workers; the move from commerce and industry to finance, with its divisive effect insofar as merchants and industrialists fail to make fortunes on the scale of those of bankers; the disparity between private wealth and public penury, bringing together conspicuous consumption and increasing impoverishment; the decline of industrial towns and the spread of beggary and vagabondage; the award of public offices to the widows and even babies of erstwhile regents to keep them in the family; bankruptcy of the VOC in the Fourth Anglo-Dutch War, bringing down the Bank of Amsterdam and almost bankrupting the City of Amsterdam, and so on and so on. The coup de grâce was delivered by defeat, occupation, and annexation by France. On the meager plus side were an efficient prosperous agriculture, an effective system of charity (DeVries, 1974), and the smuggling of tea, tobacco, and rum into England in the face of the continental system (Boxer, 1965, p. 281). As in superannuated societies in general, there was great nostalgia for the golden age (Schama, 1977 [1992], pp. 21, 68, 431). The central theme of the book is the loss of Dutch political cohesion, as only a few politicians at the end of the eighteenth century, mostly outsiders, sought to pull the country together to meet its problems, especially the indemnities levied on those few states that Napoleonic France permitted to exist.

One of the most interesting of the reformers was Isaac Jan Alexander Goguel, a man not of the top drawer, not of the regent class, but a merchant of the Second Hand (Schama, 1977 [1992], p. 499). He, following Rutger Jan Schimmelpennick, fought to change the federal system with its power, or at least veto power, in the provinces to a more centralized one, the better to cope with mounting political and economic problems. Federalism had worked wonderfully well during the golden century, but it was inadequate to the changed circumstances. Schama observes that the Dutch lacked a great dramatic event like the storming of the Bastille to electrify the populace and galvanize action (ibid., p. 216). As Schimmelpennick observed, some kind of new system was needed "to trim the fat from the Obese Old Republic" (ibid., p. 214), necessary perhaps but difficult to obtain. The Dutch transition to modernism came late in the nineteenth century, after almost one hundred years in which the country failed to emulate the industrialization processes at work in Britain, Belgium, France, and Germany.

In some views, the prosperous times of the seventeenth century were a miracle, and decline signified merely a return to its rightful place in Europe of the tiny Dutch Republic of two-million souls (Kossmann, 1974, p. 49). In other opinions, the rise of the Dutch Republic after 1570 or 1585 was the consequence of a society with originality and vitality that was able to seize the opportunity the world presented it. On this showing decline followed the deaths of a long list of creative geniuses who died more or less about the same time in the 1670s, and were not replaced. Originality was lost (ibid., pp. 51, 54). The Dutch shifted into conservatism, losing the self-confidence that bordered on arrogance (Boxer, 1970, p. 245).

Was the Cause of Decline External or Internal?

Of the various "causes" of Dutch decline—wars; foreign mercantilism (Omrod, 1974); foreign copying of Dutch techniques; the shift of Europe away from using Amsterdam as an entrepôt, first in trade, then in finance; the loss of capital in loans to France in the Revolution; and the levying of indemnities by France—these may be regarded as external, and are blamed for decline by Dutch historians (Swart, 1975, p. 44). Withdrawal from trade and industry for finance, however; the switch of lending from London to Paris; high taxes on consumption, which entailed high wages; provincial resistance to central direction, especially in matters of taxation; the persistence of guilds; loss of skilled workers; conspicuous consumption; skewed income distribution; and many more are internal. Between external and internal are such factors as the strong competition from Britain and Germany in fishing and whaling, which the Dutch were unable to meet, and the loss of skilled workers, especially sailors, to foreign parts. This last, it seems to me, holds the clue; young countries with vitality and energy challenge the old monopolized lines; the older lack the capacity to meet the challenge with innovative response.

7

France, the
Perpetual Challenger

Counterexample

France lies on but within the clockwise circle of primary economic and/or military states from Venice, Florence, Genoa, Spain, the Low Countries, and, outside the circle, Britain. Its exclusion was not a matter of design, for it was continuously striving to gain military dominance. Fernand Braudel says, perhaps sarcastically, that France never had economic hegemony except during the period of the Champagne fairs from 1130 to 1160 when French territory was the center of the European economy, with intermediate zones between it and a periphery (1986 [1990], vol. 2, p. 148). He records early attempts to escape the role of onlooker at the success of others: the attack on Italy of Charles VIII in 1494 and of Louis XIV on Holland in 1672; both fell short (ibid., pp. 163–64). The continuous wars from 1688 to 1780 were largely aggressive as well. "France failed to become, for any length of time, the leading economic power, that is, the center of Europe. . . . It lacked the essential elements: abundant economic production, plentiful credit, thriving business, a large volume of seaborne trade" (Braudel, 1986 [1988], p. 328).

But France is an exception in another respect to our complex model of growth leading to decline in a national life cycle. Not only did it not achieve dominance (despite the title of Schuker's study of the Dawes Plan in 1924 [1976]); it experienced no protracted long-term decline vis-à-vis the rest of Europe. Instead it had a series of governmental breakdowns and shake-ups, as described in a model developed by Jack A. Goldstone (1991), providing it, in the terms of Mancur Olson (1982), a series of opportunities for new starts.

Goldstone is a socioeconomic historian interested in the national pathology of rebellion and revolution in different countries, especially in how various elements combine in a way too similar to be simple analogues but sufficiently different so as not to constitute a "socio-political law." The start comes with population increase, somewhat exogenous unless produced by McNeill-type buildup in the population of antibodies that resist imported infections that had previously kept the death rate high. Population grows faster than agricultural production, leading to price increases, inflation, and hunger, both in cities and in peasant areas where rents are paid in kind. Poor harvests compound the difficulties. Population increase also leads to competition for places among the elite, frustrating the younger sons of nobles, rich merchants, professional lawyers, notaries, doctors, and the like, large numbers of whom fail to meet their expectations of finding a place among the *noblesse de robe*. War increases the demand for advancement, and may somewhat reduce the supply of candidates for it but foretells trouble if the monarch and his advisers try to pay for it with taxes, or, lacking substantial taxes, borrow and try to pay the interest on the debt with taxes. It is not completely clear whether all four elements—population increase, inflation, hunger, and crowding for eminence—are necessary, or whether clashes among sectors over debt and taxation are close to being sufficient. Successive breakdowns combine the elements in different proportions. Government control after revolt produced by combinations of these circumstances can be regained as in the *Fronde* in the middle of the seventeenth century, or lost as in the French Revolution. In either circumstance, turmoil tends to break up or loosen old interest groups and open the way for new men.

The Fronde

Population increase, inflation in the Thirty Years' War, and fixed taxation in the regency after the death of Louis XIII led first Cardinal Richelieu and then Cardinal Mazarin to try and raise funds by exacting more monies from *officiers* and *financiers* who had already bought their offices, to permit them to keep them as hereditary, and by creating as many as 50,000 new offices. Tax farming was an efficient means of raising revenue for the crown in a period when government servants were limited in number. It worked best when the farms were leased on short-term contracts sold and resold through auction, as in Britain, rather than awarded without limit so as to evolve gradually into private property. The threat to the wealth and status of the French *officiers* led to revolt among the *parlementaires*, first of Paris, and then more widely, along with variously adversely affected nobles, peasants, and Parisians in the late 1640s. The *Fronde* took its name from the French word for "slingshot," signifying attack on the Regent Anne and her adviser Mazarin, and was encouraged by the example of the Cromwell rebellion in England in 1640. The end of the Thirty Years' War in 1648 freed the royal army to enable the Regent, and then Louis XIV who ascended the throne in 1660, to put down the *Fronde*. Some contribution to the subsidence of the revolt was the shock over the beheading in England of Charles I in 1649.

Mercantilism and the Revocation of the Edict of Nantes

Religious wars in France from 1562 to the Edict of Nantes in 1598 occurred earlier than our years of interest in French economic growth. In the seventeenth century, however, there was vigorous economic growth from the end of the *Fronde*, especially under the mercantilist policies of Jean-Baptiste Colbert. Colbert started as a financial adviser to Mazarin, became comptroller-general of finance in 1665, and secretary of naval affairs in 1669. In a *Lit de Justice* (a form of court hearing) to penalize war profiteers, he repudiated some debt and tried without success to reform taxation. His greatest achievements were in what is today called industrial policy, encouraging the growth of industry through subsidies and tariffs, and bringing to France Dutch shipwrights, Swedish miners, Italian glassblowers, Flemish lacemakers, and seeking especially to rival the British and Dutch in woolens (Lodge, 1931 [1970], pp. 151–53). In naval affairs, he pushed ship-building and port-building, the latter particularly along the Atlantic coast, with planned cities at Brest, Lorient, and Rochefort, along with Nantes, and Sête in the Mediterranean for trade with the Levant (Konvitz, 1978, part 2). Braudel quotes one Malouet to the effect that Colbert was too much in a hurry in his program of trade and naval building. He had barely started on building ships for trade when he took them over for the navy (1986 [1988], p. 327). France was partly a victim of geography, needing two fleets, one for the Mediterranean, the other for the Atlantic and North Sea. Louis XIV had no understanding of the sea, and in the contest for manpower and leadership between land and sea, his bellicose nobility always came down on the wrong (land) side (ibid., p. 326). Colbert is quoted as blaming French individualism for the country's small merchant ships: "These men wish to have each his own barque, rather than to associate themselves with other *armateurs* (ship owners and/or outfitters) to possess, like the Dutch, large ships (Ministère du Commerce, 1919, vol. 1, p. xvii).

One element of the French population that might have strengthened France at sea was the Huguenots, who in addition to their success in banking, trade, and industry, notably glass, silk, and papermaking, included effective privateers who preyed on Spanish shipping in the Bay of Biscay from the Atlantic ports, especially La Rochelle and Nantes. During the first three quarters of the century the Catholic circle around the Regent and the crown kept urging restrictions on Protestants, harassing the Huguenots in various ways, including especially billeting soldiers in their homes. In 1679 government officials recommended discriminatory taxation against those who did not convert to Catholicism. Guilds and professions wanted government to oust them from their ranks, but Louis XIV and Colbert were reluctant to do so, in particular from trade and shipping (Scoville, 1960, chap. 2).

With the death of Colbert in 1683, the plight of those unwilling to abjure worsened. A sizeable portion of them emigrated, taking with them specie and skills. Warren Scoville estimated that the total number of Huguenots in France was between 1.5 and 2 million, of whom one-tenth left, beginning shortly before the Revocation of the Edict of Nantes in 1685 and continuing in the years to follow (ibid., pp. 5, 7). While France at the time of Colbert's death was "perhaps the richest, most populous, and strongest nation of western Europe," its economy stagnated from 1684 to 1717 (before the stimulus of inflation under John Law [ibid., p. 155]). Scoville is unwilling to ascribe the stagnation mainly to Huguenot emigration, but stresses rather the two wars that followed, that of the League of Augsburg from 1688 to 1697 (in England, the Nine Years' War) and the War of the Spanish Succession (Queen Anne's War) from 1702 to 1713. One could conceive that the emigration of the Huguenots actually assisted in the expansion of French trade that characterized the eighteenth century; the vast majority of Huguenots remaining at home after (largely insincere) conversion to Catholicism acquired a rapidly built network of former co-religionists, established abroad in a diaspora with whom those at home could do business (ibid., p. 446).

The Mississippi Bubble

Following the end of the War of the Spanish Succession in 1713 and the death of Louis XIV in 1715, the regent for Louis XV held a *Lit de Justice* to confiscate undue profits from the recent wars or accumulated under the reign. This became known as Visa I. A repetition of the exercise, Visa II, was undertaken at the behest of the *financier* rivals of John Law, to deal with inappropriate enrichment (by others) in the Mississippi bubble of speculators in notes of the Banque Royale, shares of the Compagnie d'Occident, and *billets d'état*. I have discussed the Mississippi bubble elsewhere (Kindleberger, 1978 [1989], pp. 93, 134–35), and choose not to deal with it again except to say that the capital levy, large profits retained by insiders, and speculative losses by those who came in too late or stayed too long produced a substantial redistribution of wealth. This may have been a contributing factor to the spurt in trade and industry in France from 1720 or so to 1789. An historian of the South Sea bubble in London thought that that episode, the confiscation of the wealth of its instigators, and the Bubble Act of 1724 requiring new corporations to obtain a Parliamentary charter, set back the arrival of the industrial revolution in England some forty or fifty years (Carswell, 1960, p. 272). I am unaware that this speculation holds wide acceptance. The successive Visas in France represent not breakdown of government, as in the Goldstone model, but effective action leading to economic growth, if not what John Law had in mind when he started his banks, took over the tobacco monopoly, and became minister of finance. He intended to reform French *financiers*, as other foreigners plus one or two French were to try to do, but the corps of *financiers*, led by the Paris brothers, defeated him. Nonetheless, the redistribution of wealth and especially large capital losses stimulated efforts by many to repair their fortunes. After the slowdown from 1680 to 1717 or 1720, the French economy picked up speed.

The Eighteenth Century

Gregory King in 1688 estimated that income per capita amounted to £8 1s 4d in Holland, £7 18s in England, and £6 3s in France (Cole and Deane, 1965, pp. 3, 4). W. A. Cole and Phyllis Deane go on to argue that the gap between England and France widened during the eighteenth century. Patrick O'Brien and Caglar Keyder assert, on the basis of later but not entirely persuasive research, that by 1789 income per capita was more or less identical in the two countries (1978). Their estimates are hedged by the frequent use of qualifiers such as "perhaps," "possibly," "plausible," "reasonable," and the like, and they insist that France followed a path different from that of Britain. "A gap of 15 percent is not very wide, and the relative backwardness of France is not obvious" (ibid., p. 197). The evidence of contemporary travelers is dismissed as superficial (ibid., p. 186).

It is hard to accept that France was the economic equal per capita of Britain at the time of the Revolution. Overall it was superior, because of its far greater population. In 1801 the British population amounted to 11 million, the French to more than 27 million (Cole and Deane, 1965, p. 6). But on qualitative grounds in industry and finance, the British had achieved a more advanced development. Where the French made their greatest gains in the eighteenth century was in trade.

Before 1600 England was an importer of technology from the Continent, hiring German miners, Dutch engineers specialized in drainage, French civil engineers and architects. Ambrose Crowley brought nailmakers from Liège in the Spanish Netherlands to his plant at Sutherland (Flynn, 1953 [1965], p. 244). With the Revocation of the Edict of Nantes, the flow of entrepreneurs and artisans from France to England grew into a flood, for religious rather than economic reasons, to be sure, largely in luxury goods of high quality as in glass, silk, and clocks, and in finance. Sir Thomas Lombe started a silk-throwing mill in Derby with plans stolen from Bologna by his brother, as earlier mentioned. At about the turn of the century, however, the movement of technology began to swing the other way. Inventions and innovations included the Nottingham knitted stocking mill, the Newcomen steam engine, the Cort puddling process in iron and steel. The British government began in earnest to enact measures to forbid the export of machines and the emigration of skilled workers, to keep industrial knowledge monopolized. In 1719, after innovations in producing and dyeing cotton cloths to compete with Indian muslin and calicos, the government again forbade worker emigration to the Continent. After the middle of the century, the balance became more uneven, and the movement of technology to France picked up despite attempts to restrain it. John Kay, the inventor of the flying shuttle, was induced by the French government to go to France to teach carding and weaving of cotton to French plants. John Holker, a Jacobite, was persuaded to set up the first of a series of cotton textile plants with the help of the French government. William Wilkinson, an ironmaster and machine maker, was drawn to France and helped start up the foundry at Creusot (Henderson, 1954, chap. 2).

In the 1760s and 1770s with the coming of the industrial revolution (to be discussed in the next chapter), the French government financed trips to England to study industrial practice. Gabriel Jars was sent in 1765–1766 to study especially iron works and collieries, followed in 1775 by de la Houllière and in 1777 by Constantin Périer, who operated a machinery plant in Paris (Blanchard, 1974). The French Revolution and the wars that followed it interrupted French technological borrowing from England but did not eliminate it altogether. Despite the war, for example, textile machinery, a steam engine, and workers to run it were smuggled from England to Ghent by way of Hamburg (Ballot, 1923, pp. 99–103; Dhondt, 1955 [1969]).

The major source of growth in France in the eighteenth century was not technology, or agriculture, in which growth barely kept up with population, but trade. In spite of three wars—the War of the Austrian Succession, the Seven Years' War, and the War of American Independence—and high ship losses, trade boomed. The gains were largely with the West Indies in sugar, tobacco, and indigo and with the American colonies in cotton, rice, tobacco, lumber, and wheat and flour. Bordeaux, Nantes, and La Rochelle served as intermediaries in colonial products between the western rim of the Atlantic and much of the European continent. Saint-Malo, engaged primarily in fishing off Nova Scotia and Newfoundland, did not do as well.

In addition, French shipping began to displace the Dutch to a considerable extent, and French shippers began to transport direct, instead of relying on Amsterdam as an intermediary. In 1717, 67 percent of wine exports from Bordeaux went to Holland, as against 13 percent to the "*Nord*," largely the Hanseatic cities of Bremen, Hamburg, and Danzig. In 1787 the set of figures had altered to 10 and 46 percent respectively (Crouzet, 1968, p. 250). Marseilles, the other great French port in the eighteenth century, was less committed to the West Indies than was Bordeaux. In 1789, 54 million livres of combined exports and imports of a total of 230 million (excluding coastal trade) was conducted with the Caribbean, in contrast to Bordeaux's 112 million of a 250-million total, almost 25 percent as against 44 percent. Marseilles trade also grew at a lower rate in the century, 1.6 percent per year in real terms, as against 4.1 percent for Bordeaux (Forster, 1975). The growth of the Atlantic trade is remarkable in light of the fact that France was at war with Great Britain in sixty of the years between 1700 and 1815.

There is some question whether financial institutions are a critical factor in determining rates of economic growth, but it is probably significant, in comparing rates and levels of growth between France and Britain, that the former lagged behind the latter in developing paper currency, banks, a central bank, a clearing house, insurance companies, and securities markets (except for *rentes*) by about a century. A list of nine institutions with comparable dates stretching into the nineteenth century is furnished elsewhere and need not be reprised (Kindleberger, 1984 [1993], p. 116), but as illustrations note the founding of the Bank of England in 1694 and the Bank of France in 1800; the widespread use of banknotes in Britain in the eighteenth century; and the debate over their utility still going on in the *Enquête sur les principes et les faits généraux qui régissent la circulation monétaire et fiduciaire* as late as 1867 (Ministère des Finances et al., 1867). I should have perhaps added to the original list that Britain levied an income tax in 1797 while France did not get around to doing so until 1917, when it enacted one to take effect after the war. It may be noted that François Crouzet maintains that 1797 goes down as one of the most lugubrious years in history with the enactment of the income tax in Britain and military conscription in France (personal communication).

One further rough-and-ready measure of development is furnished by the proportion of the labor force engaged in agriculture, fishing, and forestry. The measure is rough because it has to be adjusted for exports and imports, for the counting or not counting of women and children, and other differences. But the lag of France behind Britain receives support from the fact that probably less than 40 percent of the labor force in England was so engaged at the end of the eighteenth century (Cole and Deane, 1965, p. 43), whereas in France more than half of the working population was in these occupations as late as 1856 (INSEE, *Annuaire Statistique*, 1957, p. 3).

France may have grown faster than England during the major part of the eighteenth century, but it is difficult to accept the O'Brien and Keyder conclusion that her income per capita in 1789 was equal to that across the channel. In addition to the foregoing qualitative indications for technology, financial development, and the limited movement from agriculture to industry, a reworking of the numbers by Goldstone shows that while France grew faster and closed in on Britain relatively, the absolute gap widened. The figures as presented in Table 7–1 are rough, since they still omit services (except for trade), as do those of O'Brien and Keyder, and livres have been converted to pounds sterling for convenience at the round rate of 25 livres to the pound.

From this table, British income per capita was £2.9 ahead of French in about 1700, £4.29 ahead at the time of the Revolution, as somewhat larger percentage gains on smaller numbers fell absolutely short of smaller percentage gains on larger bases. Some part of the French gain in industry may have occurred in replacing the thousands of ships lost to enemy and privateering action in the series of wars. The cession of Canada to Britain in the Treaty of Paris of 1763 following the Seven Years' War constituted a capital loss, hurting future French income. French Caribbean trade was badly hurt in 1791 by the slave uprising in San Dominge (later Haiti) as an echo of the French Revolution two years earlier.

Table 7–1 Income per Capita (in Pounds Sterling) in England and France, about 1700 and about 1789

	Overall		Agriculture		Industry and Trade	
	England	*France*	*England*	*France*	*England*	*France*
Circa 1700	7.28	4.38	3.98	3.27	3.28	1.18
Circa 1789	11.95	7.7	5.31	5.29	6.51	2.42
% Increase	65	76	34	61	99	120

Source: Derived from Goldstone, J. *Revolution and Rebellion in the Early Modern World.* Berkeley: University of California Press, 1991. Copyright © The Regents of the University of California.

Productive gains for France in the eighteenth century failed to offset the setback administered by its failures in finance. Successive attempts to reform the fiscal system had been made through the century by three foreigners—John Law, the Scot, and Isaac Panchard and Jacques Necker, both Swiss, the latter on two occasions—and two Frenchmen, Turgot in 1776 and Calonne in 1785. All failed owing to the bitter resistance of the *financiers.* Nobles did not pay taxes. Their contribution to the state was to risk their lives in battle. To the extent that the wars of the eighteenth century were fought at sea rather than on land, a capital-intensive rather than a labor-intensive form of warfare, they might have been held still to owe something to the country after the American War of Independence. Path dependency, however, after centuries of not paying taxes, ensured that they felt no such duty. Fiscal reform was finally achieved in the Revolution when thirty-five *officiers* and *financiers* were arrested and twenty-eight died on the guillotine.

It might be barely possible to squeeze France in the eighteenth century into the model of chapter 2 by emphasizing growth to the 1780s followed by precipitous decline as distributional coalitions—principally the tax-exempt nobles for whom the question barely arose—resisted paying off the burden of taxes accumulated during the wars. The Goldstone analysis is more complex, emphasizing governmental breakdown with more elements. Peasants were strongly hurt, bearing the main burden of taxes on land and that of the bad harvests in the 1780s. Population increase over the period thickened the ranks of those who would normally have expected to rise among the elite. George Rudé supports the Goldstone analysis before the fact in observing that the middle classes had the doors to the purchase of hereditary office closed after 1760, and suffered from a sense of indignity and deep-seated frustration in the face of aristocratic privileges (1972, pp. 246, 248). I choose not to attempt to sort out whether the *causa causans* of the Revolution should be sought among the peasants, the *sans culottes*, the middle classes (who reaped the benefits), or the notables in the Estates General called on to solve the fiscal problem after the failure of Calonne. There reformers were blocked by the *parlementaires*, the higher clergy, aristocratic factions—all the privileged classes that survived the wars of the eighteenth century, but not the Revolution.

One element contributing to the breakdown of the fiscal system under Louis XVI was the mistake of Necker in borrowing on annuities covering several lives without taking their ages into account. Part of the Dutch switch from English to French securities was motivated by overly attractive offerings (Lüthy, 1961, v. 2, pp. 471–518). A classic mistake, it built up the debt.

Without naming Napoleon or Adolph Hitler, near the end of his study Goldstone writes:

> History shows an almost uniform tendency of state breakdown to culminate in populist, usually military dictatorship, terror, disorder, and growing dominance by military men. Rebuilt armies embody energy and ideals, but are impatient of democracy. (1991, p. 479)

The Continental System

There was some economic growth in industry in France during the Revolution, the revolutionary, and the Napoleonic wars, but little compared with that in Britain with its rising industrial revolution. French progress was stimulated by France being cut off from many goods previously purchased from abroad—watches, optical instruments, gunpowder, paints, toilet soap (Chaptal, 1819, pp. 32–3, 76–7, 90, 99, etc.) M. le Comte Chaptal, a chemist, had been minister of the interior, with, naturally, special interests in French progress in chemistry: "France today placed in the first rank of manufacturing nations, and knows no rival for the chemical arts" (ibid., p. xlv), and ". . . blocked everywhere, France had to fall back on its own for goods previously imported. . . . France showed once more an astonished Europe what a great, enlightened nation could do when its independence was attacked" (ibid., p. 37).

French eminence in chemistry continued after the war to about 1830. Paris was a mecca for German chemists, who found its laboratory-centered approach more fruitful than the abstract idealism of the German universities at the time (Hohenberg, 1967, p. 68). A historian of German chemistry makes the point that France lost many chemists in 1871 when Alsace-Lorraine was turned over to Germany, adding that the French were in any case poor at the drudgery that was needed for chemical research, preferring to work for ideas rather than process (Beer, 1959, p. 56).

Chaptal acknowledged that in spite of this progress "we are still far from having as many machines in France as in England" (1819, p. 31). He does exhibit something of a guilty conscience in recounting that William Fox and Lord Cornwallis, going through the Louvre with him after the Treaty of Amiens (1802), marveled at the beauty and richness of products and asked what was available for ordinary people. He defended French industry in showing them cutlery and watches of an inexpensive variety (ibid., p. 92). Later he recurs to the issue in discussing porcelain, claiming that the factory of Messrs. Diehl and Guerard produced a quality worthy of the royal manufactory at Sèvres, not for luxury products so much as for a large body of consumers (ibid., p. 106).

Technical Education in France

In modern times, French reaction to war has frequently been to start a new school of advanced learning, usually scientific, technical, or practical. The Corps des ponts et chaussées with its associated Ecole was founded in 1747, close to the end of the War of the Austrian Succession, to improve French roads. The Ecole des mines came along at the same time. With the revolution and the Revolutionary Wars, the savants began the Ecole polytechnique in 1794 to train scientists and engineers, many for the military, though a sizeable number would upon graduation undertake further study at the Ecole des ponts et chaussées or the Ecole des mines. In 1816 the latter was reorganized into a theoretical branch in Paris and a practical one near the coal mines of St. Etienne. Around these *"grandes écoles"* were a group of smaller ones for military, naval, and other specialized purposes, plus lesser (in prestige) practical schools: the Conservatoire des arts et métiers, established during the Revolution; the Ecole centrale des arts et manufactures, established privately in 1829 by a group of industrialists to increase the supply and quality of engineers available to business, and to train workmen; the Ecole des arts et métiers, transformed on the eve of the Revolution from a school established by the Duc de la Rochefoucauld-Liancourt for the children of his regiment. The Ecole des sciences politiques, for social rather than physical science, came into being at the end of the Franco-Prussian War, the Ecole national d'Administration in 1945, all with the effect, if not the intention, of developing new men and creating a new start.

I have written on technical education in France some years ago and forebear from repeating that discourse (Kindleberger, 1976a). One or two points are worth making here, however. First, emphasis on higher education in France is largely Cartesian and deductive, rather than practical, emphasizing mathematics and pure science, and within the former at the Ecole polytechnique, descriptive geometry. The roots of this emphasis lay, of course, in the Enlightenment of the eighteenth century. Second, prestige was also very much on the minds of the men involved, and the word *"gloire"* runs through the discussion especially of the Ecole polytechnique (ibid., p. 5). The graduates of the *grandes écoles* are referred to in one passage as "that admirable corps of engineers which the world envies us" (Vial, 1967, p. 129). In the twentieth century the Ecole polytechnique, Ecole normale (for academic life), and Ecole nationale d'administration were intense rivals for the most brilliant applicants and for top status in public esteem. Third, while graduates of the Ecole polytechnique would initially be likely to divide between the military and such schools as Ponts et chaussées and Mines, they frequently later entered industry. After the Second World War, alumni of ENA would largely go first to government, preferably by way of the Inspection des finances, the prestigious supervisory and accounting bureau, and then move on into high government position, politics, industry, or banking.

The major point, however, is that French higher education differed sharply from English—though not nearly to the same extent from Scottish—in the nineteenth century, with the French emphasis on science and especially mathematics, as distinct from the humanities. It was more abstract and less practical than the *Hochschulen* in Germany. Comparison among the three countries raises a question about Abramovitz's use of years of education as a proxy for "social capability," a concept useful in estimating the potential for economic growth, when modes of education can differ so widely in emphasis and presumably in their contribution to economic growth. In addition one might note the concern of Rosencrance who observes that more education may not help economic growth if population increase means that trained elites cannot find suitable places of employment (1986, pp. 307–10).

Plant Visits

I return to the end of the Napoleonic wars and the technical relationships between France and Britain. After the wars there was a flood of visitors to Britain at all levels (omitting tourists): scholars, industrialists, engineers, workmen (Ethel Jones, 1930). Among the engineers were deGallois of the Corps de mines, who on his return described the wooden railways for carrying coal from the pithead to the docks on the Tyne, causing fear of unemployment among carters working for such a mine as that at Anzin, which did not adopt railed ways until 1830; Dutens of Ponts et chaussées; and Baron Dupin of Arts et manufactures, who made repeated visits and wrote a six-volume book on British industry.

One French industry especially interested in British method was iron and steel. Two issues dominated French curiosity: puddling to burn off carbon to harden the iron and the substitution of coal for charcoal. Considerable debate continues to this day among historians whether such substitution in France was economic at the time, given the abundance of forests for making charcoal in which the *maîtres des forges* largely operated. France, however, maintained a complex tariff on imported coal—higher at ports near the iron industry than elsewhere—suggesting that the expense of coal was partially man-made and not purely a matter of resource endowment, a conclusion buttressed by the fact that half the forges using coal in 1825 were British owned (Vial, 1967, p. 134, n. 4). Owners of larger plants made trips to Britain to visit iron works, some as late as 1849. One in particular, Benoit, crossed the channel seven times between 1839 and 1849, on one occasion visiting seven establishments on a single visit (Locke, 1978, p. 50). Some brought back workers, but one, after visiting England and Wales, complained that the British workers who stayed home were far more skilled at puddling than the leftovers who came to France (Thuillier, 1959, pp. 224–25).

A significant contrast between French and British industrialists in this period is that successful French ironmasters and machine-builders were in many cases graduates of the *grandes écoles*, and in any case tried to enroll their sons in them, whereas their British counterparts were largely self-taught and sent their sons to Oxford and Cambridge to train for the military, the clergy, or other learned professions. Foreign visits provided a useful complement to the abstract education of the *grandes écoles*. Michel Chevalier's first letter (en route to America) covers the railroad from Paris to London (1836 [1838], 3rd ed., letter 1):

> In Paris they talk about railroads; in London they make them" (p. 1) "England shines by the genius of its business and by the virtues which accompany it, sang-froid, economy, precision, method, perseverance. The lot of France is rather the genius of taste and the arts . . .
>   . . . on one side reason, on the other side imagination, here energy, there intellectual activity without equal. . . . (p. 4)

> At our neighbors, calculating and ambitious pride, pride of the statesman and the merchant which are paid off only in power and wealth. . . . With us, the vain but immaterial pride which savors ideal possessions, thirst for applause, glory for the country, pride which would be content for France if it had the admiration of people. . . . (p. 5)

> . . . in matters of work and production we have much to borrow from the British . . . the instinct for administration . . . credit well founded . . . the spirit of association. . . . (pp. 6–7)

> . . . we come back from England ashamed of our agriculture, our communications, and our schools, humiliated by the narrowness of our commerce. . . . the train from Paris to London will be . . . especially an instrument of education for industries and workers, as *Ponts et chaussées* now sends regularly a small number of engineers. (pp. 8–9)

A prime example of the significance of visits was Ernst Gouin, first in his class at the Ecole polytechnique, then a student at the Ecole des ponts et chaussées, who completed his education by a tour of England, visiting particularly the Sharp locomotive plant in Manchester from which he ordered locomotives for the Paris-Orléans railroad before starting his own locomotive factory in Batignolles (Ecole polytechnique, 1895, vol. 1, p. 578).

Invention was not all one way. Philippe de Girard invented a machine for softening and combing flax to prepare it for weaving into linen, but the French failed to exploit it until it had been taken up successfully by John Marshall in Leeds. Vaucansson invented a loom for weaving silk in intricate patterns, which again was not put to use and was largely forgotten. In 1800 Joseph-Marie Jacquard invented a similar machine, uncovered the Vaucansson model among those stored in the Conservatoire, and combined the best features of the two (Dunham, 1955, p. 253).

Thimmonier, a poor working tailor, invented a sewing machine, of which eighty had been installed by 1831 when other tailor workers smashed them. He also sent a machine to the Great Exhibition in London, but it arrived too late to make the deadline for inclusion. Shortly thereafter the invention passed to Howe and Singer in the United States (Boudet, 1952,

p. 558). Successful inventions of course occurred in chemicals (Kuhlmann, Chardonnet), glass, plate glass, and mirrors (St. Gobain), automobiles (Bollée, Panhard, Levassor, Berliet), and so on. Most of these came later.

Machinery was still being smuggled into France from England as late as 1843, when the British prohibition of export of machines and plans was lifted, a measure that hurt the French machine industry competitively (Dunham, 1955, pp. 248–49). A similar blow to the textile industry of Normandy, but not that of Alsace protected by the distance from England, had been administered by the Anglo-French Eden treaty of 1786 which lowered textile tariffs in France until the French Revolution.

Saint-Simonists

A movement in the United States in the 1930s called "technocracy" was interested in applying technical solutions to economic and social problems. It had only limited popularity before being lost to public view. Technocracy had a predecessor, more or less, in Saint-Simonism in France a century earlier. Claude Henri de Vouvray, Comte de Saint-Simon (great-nephew of the eighteenth-century Duc de Saint-Simon of the celebrated *Mémoires*), visited Spain in 1778 at the age of 18 where he became interested in economic development through public works, banking, education, and the "spirit of association." During the Revolution he speculated in *biens nationaux* (properties seized from the church and nobility), made a fortune and lost it in social experiments, and proselytized a number of leading intellectuals before his death in 1825. His work was taken up by Prosper Enfantin, who formed a sort of cult but who fantasized, well in advance of reality, about a Suez canal, a Panama canal, a trans-Siberian railway, and a tunnel under the English Channel. Interest of the movement's followers in economic development survived the inevitable breakdown of personal relationships. Among those infected were Michel Chevalier, who went to America by way of London to study public works in 1833 and 1834, and Emile and Isaac Pereire, who pushed the Saint-Simonien interest in banks as both stimulus and controller of industry (Vergeot, 1918). The Pereires became friendly with Napoleon III, who had also caught the bug, and obtained from him permission to make long-term investments, the well-known Crédit mobilier. Rondo Cameron ascribes much of the boom in France in the 1850s, following Napoleon's coup d'état of December 1851, to this bank, which also served, in his view, as a pattern for what became known as "universal banks" throughout Europe (1961). It is true that competition from the Crédit mobilier stimulated lending by other banks such as the Rothschilds for railroad-building. This had started slowly in the 1830s following the centralized plan of Le Grand of Ponts et chaussées of 1832 because of bankers' quarrels. Further stimulation came from the Bank of France, which, after serious debate among the regents, made advances to banking enterprises against the collateral of railroad bonds (Plessis, 1985, pp. 89–108, 287). In addition to thus assisting railroad construction, the

Bank of France made advances on the debt of the city of Paris, which was being reconstructed by the cutting of great boulevards by Baron Haussmann, but refused to undertake similar loans for Marseilles or Bordeaux (ibid., pp. 105–6).

The boom of the early 1850s turned the balance of payments of France adverse, led to losses of specie, and a possibility, seriously contemplated by the officials of the Bank of France, that it would have to suspend gold payments and resort to what was called "forced circulation." The Bank raised its discount rate to 6 percent. Panic in Paris and lines of depositors seeking to draw their deposits out in gold in early October 1856 produced a meeting of the emperor and high officials of the Treasury and the Bank. Also present were Pierre Magne, minister of public works, Achille Fould, the president of the Crédit mobilier until 1854, and Emile Pereire, all of whom advised the emperor against suspension on the ground, among others, that it would spoil France's chance of becoming the center for international financial transactions (ibid., pp. 176–78).

I choose not to follow the path of economic growth through the nineteenth century, the boom of the 1850s and 1860s, the deflation of the 1870s to pay off the indemnity, the Great Depression of the 1880s, and the like, to World War I. I devoted considerable enterprise to that purpose on another occasion, attempting to indicate periods of growth and stagnation and within each the forces that made for growth, the forces that together with friction resisted it, and other forces of potential significance in either direction (Table 7–2) (Kindleberger, 1964, pp. 328–29). An example of the last, mentioned earlier in this book, is the guild, useful for growth at the start of an industry through training and setting of standards, harmful later as it pushed for monopolistic restriction and resisted technical change. Guilds happen not to have been cited in the earlier book, which covered only 1851 to 1950, but an apposite example from that period would be increased exports, stimulating growth in new industries and diverting energy into blind alleys when it involved expansion in old and obsolete products.

A parallel exercise focused on French brilliant growth after World War II, *les trentes années glorieuses* (the thirty glorious years) from 1945 to 1975, which attributed it not to planning and a resurgence of Saint-Simonism so much as to a change in mentality or social values that occurred during the war as a result of German occupation, and the emergence of "new men" after the war (Kindleberger, 1963).

Before I address these matters, however, some attention is owed to agriculture in the nineteenth century. O'Brien and Keyder believe that the deliberate pace of French agricultural development and the slowness of the movement off the farm into trade and industry were more or less intentional, based on the choice of a different path to economic development than Britain's industrialization, and that one could be justified on social, if perhaps not on economic, grounds (1978). Earlier analysts like W. Arthur Lewis, Alexander Gerschenkron, William Nichols, and W. W. Rostow regarded the slow release of labor from farms as the consequence of partible inheritance on the one hand and the cause of overall retardation of French growth, on the other (see Kindleberger, 1964, chap. 10, esp. pp. 225ff.). Agricultural regions close to large cities, such as Paris, were forced to rationalize farming because of labor shortages and high wages as the city drew off neighboring young people. Other areas that made considerable progress were Normandy, which specialized in dairying, and the North adjacent to the efficient farming of the Low Countries. On the whole, however, growth in agricultural productivity in France was slowed down by the "disguised unemployment" of young people, staying on the farm, waiting to inherit land. They produced less than they consumed, but as family members they had to be fed anyhow, so their modest marginal product added to total income. Agricultural productivity had risen sharply in the eighteenth century with the introduction of new crops, the potato between 1740 and 1770, which ended periodic famines; clover, other forage crops and Indian corn (maize) between 1770 and 1790, sugar beets during the Continental system, not enough, however, given the bad weather of the 1780s, to forestall peasant unrest. But change slowed down in the nineteenth century, and the peasant remained backward, largely outside modern French society until the Franco-Prussian War and the spread of education after the 1870s. Eugen Weber discusses the process of converting "peasants into Frenchmen," which took from 1800 or so to the last quarter of the century (1976). In contrast with the optimistic picture of O'Brien and Keyder, Weber, using police, prefect, and other archives, shows that despite the adoption of the metric system during the French Revolution, and of the franc germinal in 1804, the peasant before 1870 was still reckoning in *pieds* (feet) and *livres* three quarters of a century later (ibid., esp. chap. 4, entitled "The King's Foot").

Farming suffered in the second half of the century from the diseases of *pébrine*, in silk cocoons, and phylloxera, which attacked vineyards, and from the fall in the worldwide price of wheat, a major French peasant cash crop. Love of land, however, and the need to leave it to one's limited family seems to have held back the rural exodus to the city, however widely it was complained of as early as the 1880s. Some analysts blame the lack of demand for labor in the city for the slowness of the movement off the farm, but farm folk in other countries do not wait for demand to materialize before they crowd into *bidonvilles, favellas*, shantytowns in exurbs, making it clear that the supply need not wait for the demand.

Mentalités

Despite the Revolution, French attitudes toward the world have long been conditioned by the aristocratic values of the ancien régime. This spirit is characterized as pride in individual distinction–the unreproducible act; prowess on the field of battle, in sport, in the arts; talk in the salon; elegance in the consumption of dress and food, even in the boudoir (Pitts, 1957).

Table 7–2 Forces Making For and Resisting Growth in France, 1851–1950

Period	Forces Making for Growth	Forces and Frictions Resisting Growth	Potentially Significant Forces of Negligible Effect
1851–1875 Vigorous expansion	Government spending on cities, communication (1)[a] Railroad investment (1) Industrial banks (1) Expansion of national market (1) *Expanding exports (2) *Import competition (2)	[b]Resource limitations in coal, natural communications (2) Immobility of agricultural labor (3) Diversion of government attention from economy to adventure (1) Banker's quarrels (3)	Aristocratic values Family enterprises Social division Technological aptitude Slow population growth
1875–1896 Stagnation (esp. 1882–1894)	Technological advances (3) Wheat tariff of 1881 (2)	*Fall in wheat price communicated from abroad (1) Phylloxera (3) *Social fissures (3) Overspeculation in 1881 (3) *Resource limitations (3) *Slow population growth (3)	Loss of Alsace-Lorraine Freycinet Plan
1896–1913 Moderate growth	*Loss of Alsace-Lorraine (3) Discovery of iron ore (2) New industries (2) Regional banks (3) *Booming exports due to capital exports (3) *Méline tariff of 1892 (3)	Family enterprises (3) *Resource limitations—coal (3) *Social fissures (3)	Capital exports Slow population growth Government lack of interest in economy
1919–1930 Vigorous disorderly expansion	Government reconstruction (1) Rising exports due to capital flight and later undervaluation (2)	Capital flight to 1926 (3) Foreign-exchange policy (3)	Social fissures Inflation War manpower losses Aristocratic values Family enterprises Technical capacity
1930–1939 Economic decline	*Rising wage costs (3)	Government policies for defense of franc value and deflation (3) World depression (1) *Social fissures (1) *Monopoly (3) Family firms (2)	

Table 7–2 (continued)

Period	Forces Making for Growth	Forces and Frictions Resisting Growth	Potentially Significant Forces of Negligible Effect
1945–1950+ Economic resurgence	Wartime consensus on value of economic growth (1) Government size and initiative (1) *Income redistribution (2) Technical brilliance (1) *Population expansion (2) Expanded productivity in agriculture (3) Elimination of small firms by competition (2)	Inflation (2) Social conflict, especially on Algiers (2) *Limited resources (3) *Wartime destruction (3)	Diversion of resources overseas, partly compensated by aid

Source: Reprinted by permission of the publishers from *Economic Growth in France and Britain, 1851–1950* by Charles Kindleberger, Cambridge, Mass.: Harvard University Press, Copyright © 1964 by the President and Fellows of Harvard College.

[a](1) strong factor, (2) moderate factor, (3) weak factor.

[b]Asterisk indicates a factor that might have operated oppositely under different circumstances.

The nobles think that commerce is not noble, and so think the country gentlemen and the bourgeois (Mathorez, 1919, pp. 95–96). In production, distinction is the goal, as illustrated by the royal manufactories, Sèvres for porcelain for example, Gobelins for tapestries. Aristocrats seldom played a major role in the world of affairs (Boudet, 1952, pp. 554–57). The bourgeoisie aspired to fortunes so as to ascend into the ranks of chateaux owners and the nobility. Graduates of the *grandes écoles* combined intelligence and training with a degree of superiority and even arrogance. A Japanese psychiatrist who had taught in Paris once told me that French intellectuals are trained to make remarks in conversation that are brilliant and final.

In bourgeois circles before World War II, interest in business was said to be focused on the vertically extended family and the creation of dynasties. There is a large literature on the subject, not without considerable contradiction and debate. The indictment alleges that the average businessman was less interested in growth and profit than in continuity of family ownership from generation to generation. Bank loans, public share offerings, mergers, top-level officers from outside the family, were avoided; liquidity was maintained; and bankruptcy, a stain on the family reputation, was avoided at all costs. I have summarized the literature earlier, and rendered a Scotch verdict—not proven

(Kindleberger, 1964, pp. 115–23). But there seems little doubt that positive cooperation was a rare ingredient of French economic life.

The lack of the "spirit of association," as compared with Britain or the United States, has been mentioned earlier in connection with Saint-Simonien doctrine. Charles Boudet asserts that the French were superior in inventiveness, presumably to the rest of the world, but team spirit was lacking (1952, p. 558). Jesse Pitts put it that the French lacked "school spirit" (1957, p. 322), Lawrence Wylie that French farmers in the Vaucluse were weak at cooperation (1957, chap. 14).

There is one exception to this inability or unwillingness to cooperate. Pitts has put forward the concept of the "delinquent peer group" or community, in which pals (*copains*) unite to rebel against the authority of parents, teachers, customers, competitors, and especially government in such a matter as paying taxes (1964, pp. 254–62). Sports and games are minor in French schools and fail to produce peer solidarity (ibid., p. 255); there are or were no "playing fields of Eton" in France. The graduates of the *grandes écoles* were perhaps an exception to this notion, as they maintained a network in which one graduate recruited others until they "enclosed a great part of the economic activities of France" (Bouch, 1952, p. 567). A prominent example of French delinquent behavior, though one shared by wealth holders in many other countries, is to transfer one's liquid funds abroad at times of government crisis, notable in France in 1924, 1936 (under the Popular Front), and 1982 in response to the Mitterand socialist program of 1981.

The Interwar Breakdown

The interwar period conforms to the Mancur Olson model of struggle among distributional coalitions, leading to a Jack Goldstone breakdown of government though without explicit rebellion and revolution. Industry, agriculture, labor, the middle class, and capitalists resisted taxes and refused to share the burdens of reconstruction and repayment of war debts. Part of the difficulty was the fantasy belief that the damages would be paid by the Germans who had lost the war. Government after government would propose taxes, be defeated, resign, and give way to new governments that would repeat the deadly prescription. Left-wing Socialists pushed for a capital levy; labor would sit down; capitalists refused to convert short-term into long-term government obligations, and from time to time sent their capital abroad. Short-term recoveries were never taken advantage of to consolidate the position. In one description by a financial historian, it was a

> . . . grey and dreary picture of the France of the thirties, a country whose economy did not succeed in leaving "the great crisis," whose social fabric seemed frozen in its structures, and whose political leaders let themselves be carried along by the waves instead of seeking to subdue them. The spirit of innovation and the capacity of rapid adaptation seemed to be paralyzed. . . . The leading circles of the banking profession seemed to be devoid of the capacity of inventing and proposing. (Bouvier, 1984, p. 60)

When the German attack came in May 1940, neither the army nor the populace was ready.

Occupation from 1940 to 1944 or 1945 produced a deep-seated change in French attitudes to their lifestyle; along with, in 1945 and 1946, "new men" (Postan, 1967, chap. 12). The change is most readily exemplified by the abrupt discontinuity in demography. The strong peasant sense that led to family limitation in France ahead of most of the world, and well before the laws of equal inheritance of Napoleonic times, suddenly gave way under the boots of the Wehrmacht. The net reproduction rate, measured by the number of female children born per 100 women of childbearing age, moved as shown in Table 7–3. Alfred Sauvy, a French demographic expert, attributes the change to the Code de la Famille, passed in 1939, that provided subsidies to families that rose as the number of their children increased (1960). There is other expert opinion, tying the change explicitly to defeat in 1940 and to a brusque change in the French outlook on life that began during the darkest days of the German occupation (Centre de Diffusion Française, 1959, p. 3; Henry, 1955, p. 67). More children were sought for current enjoyment, rather than fewer so as not to divide land or wealth and thus handicap the extension of the family in time. The explanation is supported by the sudden large postwar movement off the farm into trade and industry, and out of small artisan shops into larger firms. The agricultural population of France went from 7.5 million in 1949 to 5.2 million in 1954, or from 36.6 percent of the active population to 27.4 percent. Another 1.3 million left the farm from 1954 to 1962, although these cannot be subtracted from the 1954 number because the populations were counted on different bases (Kindleberger, 1967, p. 58, note 1). Still another mark of change is the sharp reduction in the age of middle-level executives (*cadres*). The Ministry of Labor in 1951 reported that the top hiring age for this group had declined from 60 years in 1898 to 50 in 1945, 45 in 1950, and 40 in 1951 (Jacquin, 1955, p. 19). A better measure would have been the average age, but government officials evidently attached significance to the decline of the upper limit.

Table 7–3   Prewar, War, and Postwar Net Reproduction Rate in France: 1935–1955

Years	Rate
1935–1939	89.7
1940–1941	79.5
1942–1945	90.5
1946–1950	131.0
1951–1955	124.8
1956–1959	126.25

Source: Averaged from annual figures from INSEE, *Annuaire Statistique Rétrospectif,* 1961, p. 51, table 8.

The Thirty Glorious Years

The change in outlook, the entry into positions of authority of new men who replaced those idled during the war or repudiated by their attachment to the Pétain regime, led to a sustained period of growth. At the start there was an inflationary push as industry, agriculture, and labor each resisted the burdens of reconstruction, as they had after World War I: Farmers raised food prices, leading to strikes for higher wages, leading to industry raising prices, leading to government running deficits when it faced difficulty raising taxes (Aujac, 1950 [1954]). The game of leapfrog was broken by the bumper harvest of 1950, which destroyed the monopoly power of farmers. Planning perhaps helped, although it was more an evangelical exhortation to expansion than a contribution to scientifically decided resource allocation, and gradually disappeared bit by bit, like the Cheshire cat, leaving only the grin of *planification*. New men in nationalized industries, returning to the technocratic or Saint-Simonien tradition, pushed for innovations in chemicals, aircraft, railroading, automobiles, electricity transmission, machine-tool production. While France had not exactly been defeated in the Second World War, she can hardly be said to have won it, and there were aspects of it she chose not to dwell upon. Focus on economic expansion in the Phoenix model mentioned in chapter 3 and the positive side of the Olson model diverted attention from those unhappy days. Soon after the war France, which had played second fiddle to England for two or more centuries (pace O'Brien and Keyder), was outstripping Britain led by old men.

The glorious years were limited to a generation. By the 1970s with their oil shocks, leading to world slowdown, rates of growth tapered off, old divisions opened wider, and new ones sprang into view. Students and labor revolted in the events of May and June 1968. Petty commerce took to politics to form the Poujade movement to resist supermarkets. Farmers rioted against imports of cheap foodstuffs, and labor against the competition of Algerian and south-of-the-Sahara immigrants from French colonies. Preoccupation with glory led to deGaulle (with the help of Jacques Rueff) attacking the dollar as the world currency. French resistance to the spread of English (or perhaps American) as world language was costly in expensive support of its former colonies to help maintain the number of French-speaking members in such organizations as the United Nations.

In 1981 the Socialists elected a new government and started to put a program of nationalization into effect immediately, to correct the mistake thought to have been made when the Cartel du Gauche (left-wing groups) dithered until they were defeated on financial issues in 1926 (Jeanneney, 1977). A middle-class strike in the form of capital flight brought about a change of course. France found itself in a short time in the (relative) decline phase of the national cycle. Looking over the years to the seventeenth century, there was not one long rise followed by a long decline, as in other cases, but a connected series of rises and declines, interspersed from time to time by revolution and breakdown.

8

Britain, the Classic Case

The Classic Case

Great Britain furnishes the classic example of the national life cycle of rapid growth in trade, industry, and finance, reaching a peak and world economic primacy, then slowly declining. The usual formulation starts with the industrial revolution of 1760 to 1830, with varying dates given by different analysts. Some regard the peak as the Great Exhibition in London's Crystal Palace in 1851; others regard it as being later, perhaps 1870 or in the 1890s. Decline was accelerated by the two World Wars of 1914–1918 and 1939–1945, sometimes telescoped into one. The industrial phase was preceded by a rise in trade in the seventeenth and eighteenth centuries, followed by one in finance.

Such is the canonical formulation. Each aspect, except for the early rise of trade, is disputed by revisionist historians. A burst of literature in the 1980s denied the revolutionary character of industrial growth in the last third of the eighteenth century and first third of the nineteenth. Primacy in the middle of the nineteenth century has been said, as noted in an earlier chapter, to have been preceded by a stage of world economic dominance in the seventeenth. Until recently a school of economic historians with econometric techniques denied not perhaps the fact of decline in the late nineteenth and early twentieth century, but the generally held view that it was the result of a loss of entrepreneurial energy or vitality. With mathematical models and contemporary data it was "proven" that entrepreneurs were maximizing profits.

This chapter on the whole supports the traditional view of Britain as conforming to the model set out in chapter 2. I have written on British growth before (Kindleberger, 1964; 1975 [1978]; 1976b; 1992a), and in the interest of saving time, use much of the earlier material. I proceed first to dispose of the notion that there was a British cycle of world leadership from 1688 to 1780, as illustrated in Figure III-2, and then deal with trade, the industrial revolution, British financial leadership in the nineteenth century from 1815 to 1914, the start of decline, and finally the contemporary position.

The Seventeenth Century

In *The Stages of Economic Growth*, W. W. Rostow has a preliminary stretch before "take-off" called "preconditions," in which there is a breakout from traditional society, changes in social attitudes, putting in place of social overhead capital, and in the British case, development of science, within the general Enlightenment that paved the way for the inventions of the industrial revolution (1960, chap. 2). Something, but not much, is made of trade, associated with the discoveries that opened up new continents. In earlier chapters here, the emphasis on trade started with the Mediterranean, then the Baltic to the north coast of Europe, then north-south trade in Europe, before overseas trade in the sixteenth century. Britain had a role to play in all but the strictly Mediterranean trade, but it stretches belief to regard that fact as world leadership.

The British were challengers. They contested the Portuguese, the French, and especially the Dutch for dominance in the Far East, to be sure; interloped in Portuguese and Spanish trade with the West Indies, Brazil, and the west coast of South America; achieved victory over the Spanish Armada in 1588; and raided Cadiz. They were among the pioneers in voyages of discovery, acquiring colonies in North America and the whole of Australia and New Zealand. They chartered trading companies to the Levant, Africa, India, and Hudson Bay, and collected colonies in the East, by conquest of natives, and in the West Indies, New Amsterdam, and Canada, by victories over their European masters. From 1688 to 1720, London achieved a financial revolution that substituted an efficient system of government credit for one that had been jerry-built and subject to royal whim (Dickson, 1967).

Despite these gains it is difficult to overlook the leadership in trade and associated industry (such as shipbuilding) of the Dutch. The British themselves were conscious of their role as challenger rather than the challenged. Their population was greater, but the pivot of world trade and finance was Amsterdam and remained so until the middle of the eighteenth century (Israel, 1989, p. 379). In his book entitled *Dutch Primacy in World Trade, 1585–1740*, Jonathan Israel argues against the view that the Dutch were still ahead in 1780 at the time of the Fourth Anglo-Dutch War. Dutch trade held up in the Baltic in the bulk trades longer than in the more profitable eastern and colonial goods, still longer in international lending. In *The*

Wealth of Nations, written over a decade from 1766 to 1776, Adam Smith made a number of remarks comparing Holland and England, not all of which were congruent: Holland was richer than England in proportion to the number of its people and the extent of its territory (1776 [1937], p. 91); while Dutch trade in particular branches might be decaying, there was no general decay (ibid.); Holland was "by far the richest country in Europe" with "the greatest share of the carrying trade of Europe" and "England, [was] perhaps the second richest country of Europe" (ibid., p. 354); England ". . . is perhaps as well fitted by nature to be the seat of foreign commerce, and manufactures for distant sale . . ." with "no country in Europe, Holland itself not being excepted, of which the law is, upon the whole, more favourable to this sort of industry" (ibid., p. 393). Smith discussed the ruin of manufactures in Holland because of high wages, caused by high taxes on consumption to pay the service on great debts contracted in expensive wars (ibid., pp. 826–27, 857). At the same time, the government of Holland borrowed at 2 percent, and private people of good credit at 3 (ibid., p. 91). Dr. Smith may have lacked the detailed data to demonstrate that Holland, not Britain, was economically dominant in at least the first quarter, third, or half of the eighteenth century, but his perception that such was the case must be taken into account.

Trade

As Dutch trade slipped from 1672 or 1700 or 1740, English overseas trade was growing impressively in the seventeenth and eighteenth centuries (Minchenton, 1969, editor's introduction). With growth came changes in its composition and direction. England had exported first wool, and then woolen textiles, and within the latter initially the "old draperies," largely broadcloth and kerseys—a coarse, woolen, ribbed cloth, sold to Germany and Eastern Europe—and then the "new draperies"—bays, says, and fustians, which were lighter and were bought especially in southern Europe and the Levant beginning after the Thirty Years' War (ibid., p. 7). (A Venetian document is quoted by Braudel as saying as early as 1514 that English kerseys formed "one of the most important foundations of trade in the world" [Braudel, 1949 (1972), vol. 1, p. 213].) The process was the usual one of shifting from raw material to unfinished manufacture; upgrading it; then fulling, finishing, and dyeing; taking over the end processes from Leiden in the Netherlands; and finally marketing the finished product directly. The shift of trade went also from the export of raw materials—tin and copper in addition to wool—and import of finished European manufactures, to import of raw materials—iron, timber, silk, and colonial goods such as sugar, tobacco, and indigo—and to export of manufactures. Europe as a dominant source of imports and market for exports gave way to colonies, later independent countries such as the United States and the Union of South Africa, and semi-independent dominions, as sources of foodstuffs and raw materials and outlets for manufactures.

In the early stages, exports were assisted by governmental extension of rights to export wool to Merchant Adventurers and the eviction of the Hanseatic League from the London Steelyard in 1598. Distant trade required the formation of corporations to raise the large amounts of capital needed for the big ships and substantial inventories involved: the Muscovy Company in 1555, the Spanish Company in 1577, the crucial East India Company in 1601, the Levant Company in 1605, the Hudson Bay Company in 1670, and the Royal African Company in 1672. Shortly thereafter in 1689 the monopoly of the Eastland (Muscovy) Company was withdrawn and the monopoly of the Merchant Adventurers, now in broadcloth rather than wool, was canceled (Minchenton, 1969, pp. 7–12). Trade was turned over to private merchants; government control and assistance were confined to the navigation acts, the first in 1651 leading to what Clapham calls the "Great Navigation Act of 1660" (1910 [1962], p. 144), ship money (a tax levied on towns beginning in 1634 to provide funds to defend merchant ships from "thieves, pirates, and robbers of the sea," including privateers), and subsidies to fishing and the Newcastle-to-London coal trade, the nursery of seamen for merchant service and, of course, for the Royal Navy. Along with the French commerce, British trade boomed in the eighteenth century, but British primacy cannot be said to have begun until the industrial revolution.

Rostow dates "take-off" in Britain somewhat too precisely at 1783, when, after the Treaty of Paris had ratified the independence of the American colonies from George III, exports to the former colonies grew in a sudden spurt. Adam Smith, in a prescient passage, had suggested just this possibility:

> To propose that Great Britain should voluntarily give up all authority over its colonies . . . would be to propose such a measure as never was, and never will be adopted, by any nation in the world. . . . If it was adopted, however, Great Britain would not only be immediately freed from the whole annual expense of the peace establishment of the colonies, but might settle with them in such a treaty of commerce as would eventually secure her to a free trade, more advantageous to the great body of the people, though less so to the merchants, than the monopoly which she at present enjoys. (Smith, 1776 [1937], pp. 581–82).

The spurt in British exports was originally less in cotton goods of the industrial revolution—they came later with heavy imports of raw cotton from the American south—but in woolens from such an area as Leeds in Yorkshire and in nails, buckles, metal buttons, pens, and hardware from Birmingham. America took a fifth of English woolens and worsteds in 1772, two-fifths by 1800 (R. G. Wilson, 1971, p. 111). The shift from exporting to Europe to exporting to the American colonies required new merchant houses to cope with change to new conditions: credit evaluations and longer credits. Many old firms were bankrupted, or their owners retired; by 1830 only 21 of the surviving firms had links to the 135 merchant houses that had existed in 1782 (ibid., pp. 115–16). Birmingham's trade with the

United States kept growing and changing (Allen, 1929). Adam Smith attributed this to the fact that its products were goods of "fashion and fancy," as contrasted with goods of "use or necessity" produced in such a center as Sheffield (1776 [1937], pp. 114–15), but the distinction is overdrawn. And Smith failed to anticipate the changes that the industrial revolution would produce (Kindleberger, 1976b).

The Industrial Revolution

Whether there was or was not an industrial revolution is on the whole a semantic issue of little real economic interest, a point made almost half a century ago (Ashton, 1948, p. 2). Historians have questioned the use of most blanket designations: Dark Ages, Renaissance, Mercantilism, Enlightenment, ancient régíme, and the like. In one view, "finding flaws in labels is much easier than finding patently superior substitutes" (Judge, 1939 [1969], p. 59). One economic historian, who entitled a book *Industrial Evolution*, wrote that there was one break in evolutionary development, the Industrial Revolution (with initial capitals), which belongs beside the Fall of Rome, the Reformation, and the French Revolution as producing a discontinuous alteration in the world's history (Gras, 1930, p. 90)-—this despite Alfred Marshall's epigraph in *Principles of Economics* (1920): "*Natura non fecit saltum*" (there are no discontinuities in nature).

The debate over the issue waxed heated in the 1980s, with many distinguished economic historians on each side. Rondo Cameron and N. F. R. Crafts in articles too numerous to mention, and the former in his *Concise Economic History of the World* (1989), attack the believers in the industrial revolution; Joel Mokyr, R. M. Hartwell, and earlier proponents such as W. W. Rostow uphold it. At a meeting of the Social Science History Association in New Orleans in October 1987, organized by Cameron to debate the issue, many auditors chipped in. Paul David for one remarked that much depended on whether there was "perceptible change" or "imperceptible change." But some are better at perceiving what is going on than others, and one has to choose whom to believe. As stated earlier, Adam Smith was largely unaware of the industrial revolution (Kindleberger, 1976b). My paper with that conclusion was attacked especially by R. M. Hartwell. That others were aware of it, despite Smith, cannot be gainsaid. Samuel Johnson wrote that the world was running mad after innovations: "all the business of the world is to be done in a new way." Men like Watt were fascinated by the Duke of Bridgewater canal of 1761, which initiated a surge of canal building that ended in the canal mania of 1793. Personages from all walks of life visited not only the canal but the Boulton and Watt steam-engine plant at Soho, near Birmingham, and the neighboring Wedgwood factory at Etruria: the king of Denmark, Baron vom Stein of Prussia who incurred Wedgwood's animosity by trying to wheedle secrets out of his workers, Benjamin Franklin, Samuel Johnson, the duke of Buccleugh. Thomas Bently, who marketed Wedgwood's pottery from London, "participated

in the new spirit. Canal navigation, moss draining, new materials for manufacturers, improved processes for industry, new inventions of all kinds
arrested and retained his attention" (Wedgwood, 1915, p. 29). Edmund
Burke in 1769 collected instances of the energies displayed in British manufacture (cited by Koebner, 1959, p. 386). ". . . [A] vast change came over
the general mind; the objects of knowledge, study and pursuit were seen
in altered perspective and acquired altered values" (Wedgwood, 1915,
pp. 28–29).

If one disregards the weight of contemporary opinion, whether there
was a revolution depends largely on whether one measures savings, income
per capita, exports, or invention and innovation. W. Arthur Lewis and
W. W. Rostow were overenthusiastic in believing that the rate of private
savings jumped in the last third of the eighteenth century from 5 percent
to 10 or 15 percent. In this they were probably following T. S. Ashton,
who wrote:

> If we seek—it would be wrong to do so—for a single reason why the pace of
> economic development quickened about the middle of the eighteenth century
> it is to this [the lowering of the rate of interest in the half-century earlier, which
> has never been properly stressed by historians] we must look. (1948, p. 11)

One can agree that it is wrong to seek a single reason for the industrial
revolution, but if one were to do so the reduction of the rate of interest or
a leap in the rate of savings would not be it. More recent research has made
clear that the rate of savings rose but slowly, from 5 to 6 or 7 percent of
national income (Deane and Cole, 1962, chap. 8, esp. pp. 260–63). Crafts's
initial unwillingness to accept the reality of an industrial revolution rested
on his estimates of relatively low rates of macroeconomic growth between
1700 and 1831 in some sectors of the economy for most portions of the
period, and of modest growth in others, as shown in Table 8.1. Growth in
industry picked up continuously through the century and a quarter, but not
at a discontinuous rate.

When it comes to innovation, however, there is more of a case. Ashton
notes that before the 1760s, the number of patents issued in Britain in a
single year rarely exceeded a dozen; in 1766 the number rose "*abruptly*"
(my emphasis) to thirty-one and in 1769 to thirty-six. In the immediately
following years it declined somewhat, but in 1783 there was a "*sudden*"

Table 8–1 British Growth Estimates, 1700–1830 (in percent annum)

Period	Agriculture	Industry and Commerce	Services	Per Capita
1700–1760	0.6	0.7	0.8	0.3
1760–1780	0.1	1.0	0.8	0.0
1780–1801	0.8	1.8	1.3	0.8
1801–1831	1.2	2.7	1.4	0.5

Source: Harley, 1986, p. 683 (a review of Crafts, 1985). Reprinted with permission from the American Economic Association.

(again, my emphasis) jump to sixty-four. This was followed by a slight decline until 1792 when the number leapt to eighty-seven. Down thence to an average of sixty-seven, but from 1798 a slow rise to 107 in 1802. In 1824 it "shot up" once more to 180, and in the following year to 250, a rise of 2,000 percent in the sixty years from 1766 to 1825 (Ashton, 1948, pp. 90–91). Even Cameron, in the book that includes a denial of the existence of an industrial revolution, refers to the "remarkable series of innovations in the last third of the eighteenth century" (1989, p. 197). In his splendid introduction to one of the best books on the subject, Joel Mokyr makes clear that the industrial revolution survives the skepticism that the new economic history has used against it (1985). A revision of annual estimates by Craft and Harley in response to criticism, especially that of Maxine Berg and Pat Hudson (1992) and P. K. O'Brien (1991), gave them an opportunity to correct a general impression that they had been denying— the fact of a fundamental transformation of the British economy from 1750 to 1850. On the contrary, they now say they are happy to agree that in the 101 years in question, "the growth of the British economy was historically unique and internationally remarkable" (Crafts and Harley, 1992, p. 704). While industrial innovations had a more modest impact on output than previously believed, "they did create a genuine industrial revolution. . . ."

Not all patents were of equal importance, to be sure, and breakthrough inventions occurred before the spurt of the century's end: Abraham Darby's substitution of coal for charcoal in 1709, the Newcomen steam engine of the same year, John Kay's flying shuttle of 1733, Hargreaves's spinning jenny about 1764. Then came the burst of inventions too familiar to bear repeating, not only in cotton textiles, steam engines, and iron but in pottery and metal wares (in Birmingham). Of crucial importance for the story of decline is that one success led to another through what Albert Hirschman called "linkages" (1958). Improvements in weaving like the flying shuttle created a bottleneck in spinning, which was solved by Richard Arkwright with the water frame for warp, by Hargreaves with the spinning jenny for weft, and later by Crompton's mule for both. Watt's steam engine increased the demand for coal and helped fulfill it by its use in pumps for draining the water encountered as coal mines went deeper. Wilkinson's boring machine was applied to drilling pistons for Watt's steam engines. So it went in a sort of leapfrog in cotton (woolens productivity improved more slowly) and in iron and steam engines, leading in the nineteenth century to the railroad. "Revolutions" in demography, agriculture, commerce, and transport increased the market in width and depth to stimulate industrial output still more (Deane, 1965 [1979], chaps. 2–4).

Something is made of the fact that in the industrial revolution the inventors came from many walks of life and were, apart from a few scientists, amateurs, often called tinkerers. The contrast runs, of course, with French technical education. Much is made, too, of the fact that many were dissenters—Quakers, Methodists, Baptists, and the like—that is, nonmembers of the Church of England and therefore excluded from government service, high rank in the military, access to Oxford and Cambridge universities, and the learned professions (though not medicine). Men of ambition and drive blocked from success in one direction will often seek it in another. David McClelland, a psychologist, has stressed the psychoanalytical conditions under which men with stronger mothers than fathers seek to make a success, having what he calls a need for achievement (1961), and Everett Hagen has found that this "N-achievement" (for short) is present in many groups excluded from elite status (1962). It is not obvious, however, that the number of such groups rises and falls through economic cycles. To the extent that British society was open and allowed successful entrepreneurs to move into the established church, to acquire country houses, to become justices of the peace and members of Parliament, and to educate their sons in the schools of the elite, the number of energetic outsiders anxious to make their way is likely to have been higher earlier than later.

In his *Afterthoughts on Material Life and Capitalism*, Fernand Braudel remarks that it was "astonishing that the boom of the British industrial revolution was able to develop at the end of the eighteenth, beginning of the nineteenth century without bottlenecks" (1977, p. 108). In my judgment this altogether misunderstands the position. Bottlenecks were there as always in growth, for growth is almost always unbalanced. What accounted for the industrial revolution was the availability of men of vitality and energy, plus requisite mechanical skill, to tackle the bottlenecks and break through them.

At the end of the nineteenth century, bottlenecks were still reached when a process had gone a certain distance, but British entrepreneurs on the whole waited for them to be solved by someone else.

The Nineteenth Century

The stretch from the Congress of Vienna to the Great Exhibition of 1851 was notable in Britain for economic growth in trade and industry and for the beginnings of international long-term lending, beyond the financing of exports and imports. There were backward spots—of hand-loom weavers and hand-nailers as most textiles and the metals industry were becoming mechanized. Spectacular growth took place in cotton textiles, with the demand for cotton igniting the rapid spread of cotton-growing from the sea islands of Georgia to the hills and thence to Alabama and Mississippi, later Texas and California. Machinery for spinning and weaving textile fibers grew rapidly. When domestic orders slowed down, textile-machinery manufacturers fought for removal of the prohibition on machinery exports, on the equitable ground that if the textile manufacturers were allowed to export, so should they be (Musson, 1972). The restrictions were loosened in 1828 by the free-trader William Huskisson, president of the Board of Trade, and were eliminated in 1843. The improved Watt steam engine was mounted on wheels and shifted from roads to iron rails, and a railroad boom started on the line from Stockton to Darlington in 1825. The boom spread all over the world, leading to a stock-market mania in 1847. Locomotive builders, engineers, and financiers took the railroad abroad. By 1850, Britain was "The Workshop of the World" (Chambers, 1961 [1968]).

There were some visitors to the Great Exhibition who were concerned by the appearance of new American machinery, such as the Colt revolver and the McCormick reaper. By the 1867 exhibition in Paris, doubts about British industrial supremacy were growing (1867 report of Lyon Playfair, a juror in the exhibitions of 1851, 1862, and 1867, in Court, 1965, doc. 63, pp. 167–69). R. A. Church affirms that there was a "Great Victorian Boom" from 1850 to 1873, but observes signs of weakness in this industry and that, and suggests the possibility that business euphoria in the 1850s and 1860s might have led the "workshop of the world" to become the cradle of late Victorian complacency (1975, passim and pp. 47–48).

In trade, as opposed to industry, the middle of the century produced a major change—the movement to free trade. William Huskisson was a free-trader to such an extent that he thought increased imports stimulated domestic production, rather than hurt it. Indeed this was the case when increased silk imports from France after 1815 pushed Macclesfield and Spitalfield to lower costs to compete, a result that required industrial vitality. The corn laws had been imposed after Waterloo to hold up the price of corn (wheat in American parlance). With the Reform Bill of 1832, which shifted the weight of voting in the House of Commons to cities from agricultural districts with their "rotten boroughs" (districts where the member was nominated by an individual aristocrat rather than elected by democratic procedures), the manufacturing interest, seeking export markets, became impatient. The corn laws repeal had two proximate causes—the devastating harvest of 1845 along with the potato blight over much of northern Europe and Ireland, on the one hand, and understanding by Sir Robert Peel, the prime minister, that lower food prices would help labor, not profits in manufacturing, and hurt landlords, not farm laborers in agriculture. A long step to free trade had been taken between 1841 and 1846, when more than six hundred duties were eliminated and those on over one thousand other items were reduced under the slogan of "fiscal reform"—getting rid of those duties that raised little revenue but had high collection costs. The Board of Trade especially had been converted to the manufacturers' case, ably pled by Richard Cobden and John Bright. Believing strongly in Hume's law that increased imports gave rise almost automatically to increased exports, the government was little interested in reciprocal lowering of duties abroad in exchange for its concessions (Brown, 1958). The movement to free trade was extended almost immediately after repeal of the corn laws in 1846 by repeal of the timber duties and the navigation acts, the latter of which had become almost infinitely complex through bilateral negotiations with a number of countries (Clapham, 1910 [1962]), and in more leisurely fashion by the Cobden-Chevalier treaty with France in 1860, exchanging removal of discrimination against French wines (in favor of Spanish and Portuguese) for wider markets for British manufactures. Ultimately under Gladstone in the 1860s came the gradual elimination or sharp reduction of remaining duties on goods produced in Britain, particularly meat, eggs, and dairy products, leaving a "tariff for revenue only" on items like wine, brandy, sugar, and tobacco, on which tariffs had no protective effect.

The removal of the navigation laws and timber duties, along with removal of the tariff on grain, especially oats for British horses, produced a surge in Scandinavian exports carried in Norwegian ships, which induced a rapid stimulus to growth in that part of Europe. Despite the repeal of the corn laws, the 1850s were a period of "high farming" in England with rapid technical progress. Transformation in Britain from the growing of wheat to production of meat and dairy products, as rising levels of economic well-being went in considerable part into hearty breakfasts, was minimal, leaving Denmark and Holland to take advantage of the new market opportunity.

The British have been accused of "free-trade imperialism," opening their market to grain and other agricultural products so as to slow down the transformation on the European continent from agriculture to competitive manufactures (Semmel, 1970). The British lead in tariff reduction, as it happened, was followed for a quarter century by France, Germany, Italy, and others lowering tariffs directly and through bilateral agreements. Whether the British free-trade movement was entirely selfish or had an element of the provision of a public good, along with peace (with only an occasional outbreak like the Crimean War of 1856) and the gold standard, is still debated. Relevant to the outcome is that free-trade policies remained in place until World War I, and opposition to tariffs was even the weapon used by the Labor party in bringing down the Tory government in 1923. Except for Switzerland, Belgium, Denmark, and Holland, Europe lost faith in free trade with the fall of the price of wheat in the 1880s, as fast and economical steamships, and railroads from plains to ports, brought cheap grain to Europe from Canada, Australia, Argentina, the Ukraine, and the United States. With its new Reich of 1871, the Germans were a little ahead of the movement and raised tariffs in 1879 with Bismarck's famous tariff of rye and iron. Britain nevertheless clung to free trade, whether from path dependency, collective memory of the glories of high farming in the 1850s, or conviction by the dominant manufacturing interest that free trade benefited it and the country, even when other countries were beginning to impose duties against British goods. An Empire-preference movement of Joseph Chamberlain in the 1890s, which would have involved imposing a general tariff, to be reduced or eliminated against imports from the dominions and colonies, proved premature and was not realized until the meeting on trade at Ottawa in 1932. The persistence of free trade, less and less in Britain's short-term interest, is a classic example of the dominance of collective memory, or institutional lag, in counterexample to the Coase theorem.

Finance

British foreign lending may be said to have begun after the Congress of Vienna in 1815 with Baring Brothers financing of the French government's 700-million franc indemnity to the allies. This loan was a great success, and like many financial successes before and later, proved to be a turning point. A few loans were made to European borrowers, but the next great financial movement came with the independence of the Latin American colonies from Spain and Portugal in the 1820s and a surge of South American government borrowing from London, which ended in a crash in 1825. Boom and crash in foreign securities were paralleled by similar movements in insurance. The 1830s brought boom in domestic railway loans. In the 1840s, Baring Brothers financed a loan to the French Rothschild railroad, the Chemin du Fer du Nord. The bonds were issued in pounds sterling in London and were bought largely by French investors as the London house intermediated, for a commission, between French borrowers and French lenders. It was a learning experience for the French: thereafter investors and railroad borrowers traded with one another directly in French francs (Platt, 1984, chap. 2). The French Revolution of 1848 that resulted in many British railway workers being assaulted, and one or two killed, led to a drastic change in British interest in Continental securities. In 1830, 66 percent of British foreign investment went to Europe; in 1854, 55 percent; in 1870, 25 percent; and in 1900, 5 percent (Pollard, 1974, p. 71). The percentage of cotton-piece goods exported to Europe followed a parallel pattern, starting earlier. In 1820 Europe took half of such exports; in 1850, 16 percent; in 1880, 8 percent; and in 1900, 6 percent. In contrast, in the Far East, including especially India but also China and Java, the proportion went from 6 percent in 1820 to 31 percent in 1850, 54 percent in 1880, and 58 percent in 1900 (Kindleberger, 1964, table 23, p. 273).

Foreign investment has been blamed by a few analysts for the difficulties of British industries in the last third of the nineteenth century (e.g., Burn, 1940, pp. 250–54, 262). For the most part, however, the flow of capital abroad and the gentle decline of domestic industry were both evidence of the same movement, away from risk-taking (as it was thought at the time) to the financing of foreign governments and railroads, just as government and railroads had been financed at home. The enlargement of cotton-spinning mills in the 1870s to 70,000 spindles and more, and of shipping companies converting from sail to steam, had added new industries that needed and attained finance in the London capital market rather than through local capitalists and plowed-back profits. A number of private companies went public, and the monies received by original owners or their heirs may have been invested abroad, especially during depression at home. There were from time to time flurries of domestic investment, as in breweries following the successful public flotation of the private Guiness company in October 1886, running parallel to a boom in Argentine securities that ended in the crash of 1890. The boom in foreign securities from 1904 to 1913 took abroad close to half of British savings and 5 percent of national income (Cairncross, 1953, p. 2). In primacy, Britain produced an enormous flow of capital to the world outside Europe but especially to the Empire, the United States, and Argentina. Lance Davis and Robert Huttenback, a cliometrician and a political historian respectively, try to demonstrate that the costs of defense of the Empire fell on the British middle-class taxpayer while the benefits accrued to business interests in the dominions and colonies and the British elite at home. In public-goods theory, the leader pays for prestige, and free riders-—in this case colonies and dominions—escape any substantial share of the cost. The authors suggest that some of the basis for this was the unfortunate experience of George III and Lord North in trying to tax the American colonies in the 1770s to share the defense burden of the mother country (1986). A recent paper questions the Davis and Huttenback conclusion, partly on statistical grounds and partly in the belief that they underestimate the contribution made by the Empire in defending Britain in World War I (Offer, 1993). A deeper question, raised by Patrick O'Brien, is whether defense of the Empire—a showy and prestigious project—diverted attention from the real concern, containing the aggressive push of Germany in Europe, and on this account proved dysfunctional (1990).

Attempts have been made to demonstrate that the London capital market funneled capital abroad that could have been helpful to domestic industry, particularly on a risk-return basis. Risky industries had difficulty in borrowing at home, even when experience with foreign investments into companies like Siemens in electricity and Mond in chemicals had excellent track records (W. P. Kennedy, 1987, pp. 153ff). Kennedy's book hits hard on the failure of British capital to flow smoothly back and forth between foreign and domestic uses, based on a judicious calculation of risk and return. A contrary view had been put forward earlier by Michael Edelstein who could detect no bias in the market (1982). With enormous amounts of smoke, the question whether there is fire is perhaps still open.

A major financial aspect of British primacy was use of the international gold standard, occasionally interpreted as the sterling standard, in contrast to a later dollar standard. London and Paris were financial rivals for much of the nineteenth century, though the French view that early in the century Paris was the international clearing house for settling payments among Britain, the United States, and the European continent (Bouvier, 1973, p. 238; Braudel, 1979 [1984], p. 608; Lévy-Leboyer, 1964, pp. 437–44) stretches belief. The French rise to prominence as an international financial center came rather in the 1850s, but was lost in 1870 when the Bank of France suspended gold convertibility in the Franco-Prussian War. Bagehot stated that before 1870 there were two stores of ready cash in Europe, the Bank of England and the Bank of France, but since the French suspension "the whole liability for . . . payments in cash is thrown on the Bank of England" (1873 [1938], pp. 63, 141). The Bank of England turned for help in crisis to other central banks, including the Bank of France, both before and after 1870. From that date on until World War I, however, Britain ran the world's monetary system that financed trade largely in sterling. This financial role was taken up as the role of leading the world toward freer trade was coming to an end.

The Boer War in 1900 marked a stage in British primacy in two senses. First, its protracted character and intermediate setbacks hurt British self-confidence as the Vietnam War was to do for the United States in the 1960s. Second, with a tight money market in London and need to borrow to finance the war, the British Exchequer placed part of a £30-million loan in New York, to the distress of London (Burk, 1992, pp. 359–60). "The assertion began to be heard in the United States that New York was destined to oust London as the central market of the world" (quoted in ibid., from Noyes, 1938, p. 178). As noted in chapter 3, a similar sentiment had been expressed, rather more prematurely, in 1857. The New York loan occurred during a cutoff of South Africa gold from its normal shipment to London; with its resumption after the war, and the enormous boom in British foreign lending, the anxiety died down.

Industrial Decline

Questions regarding Britain's industrial decline are whether it occurred, and if so, when and why. If decline is established, the "why" goes to the root of the national life-cycle model set out in chapter 2. Narrowly pinpointing the "when" is a rather secondary question.

"Whether" can be answered, like the question about the industrial revolution, with detailed analysis of particular industries. Proponents of decline are likely to cite horrendous cases like Marshall of Leeds, which went from being the world's leading flax spinner to liquidation in a generation and a half—the classic clogs-to-clogs pattern (Rimmer, 1960), or Welsh tinplate, in which a phenomenal increase in exports as canned food and gasoline came into widespread use after the 1870s, especially in the United States, failed to produce a change in the production technique of dipping sheets one at a time by small-scale, local, satisfied producers, leaving them vulnerable to the rapid development in the United States of new processes (strip mills and pulling rolled sheet through tin baths) to which a small increase in the McKinley tariff gave rise (Minchenton, 1957). In old industries like cotton textiles, coal, iron, and steel (including rails and galvanized iron sheet for roofing), plus railroad equipment, technological improvement in product and process was slow. New industries of the period—chemicals, electricity, automobiles—often relied on foreign entrepreneurs. In one industry that did not, the production of caustic soda, an English manufacturer clung to the obsolete Le Blanc process when the profitability of a changeover to the Solvay method was readily apparent (Lindert and Trace, 1971). An innovative manufacturer like William Morris in automobiles had difficulty inducing domestic machine shops to produce components for his assembly, and was forced to produce them himself or turn to the United States (Maxcey and Silberston, 1959, p. 13). The gap seems to have been one not easily closed: according to the Confederation of British Industry, the productivity of foreign companies in Britain in 1988 was 46 percent higher than that of the equivalent British firms (*The Economist*, August 27, 1993, pp. 46–47).

There were exceptions: Pilkinton's in glass, where a new generation took control in 1870 (Barker, 1968, pp. 318ff); new industries such as sewing machines and bicycles, built on the remnants of the Coventry watch and ribbon industries, the former leaving skilled workers redundant, the latter leaving unskilled (Saul, 1968, pp. 212ff); paints, explosives, soap, the Parsons steam turbine, and shipbuilding in its burst of energy on the eve of World War I before succumbing to competition after the war (Pollard and Robertson, 1979; Lorenz, 1991).[1] But the general story in British industry in the period was dreary, in coal, iron and steel, cotton, woolen and worsted, boots and shoes, electrical products, chemicals, and the mercantile marine (Aldcroft, ed., 1968). German competition was particularly unpleasant when, following the Marks of Origin Act of 1887, passed by Parliament in an effort to identify shoddy import goods imitative of British products, "Made in Germany" proved to be a mark of quality (Hoffman, 1933, pp. 45ff; E. E. Williams, 1890 [1896]), a pattern that was to be repeated in the United States slightly more than half a century later when "Made in Japan" changed its image.

The When

Signs of decline, and spots of vitality, were visible from at least 1870. But the when, like the question of whether there was an industrial revolution a century earlier or only a slow evolutionary process, turns on the criterion or criteria chosen, and the counterfactual, the basis of comparison. The growth of income per capita at constant prices did fall, from 1.5 percent per annum between 1820 and 1870, to 1 percent between 1870 and 1913, and to 0.9 percent from 1913 to 1950, but it rose again to 2.5 percent— the highest since 1700—in 1950 to 1973 (Maddison, 1982, p. 44), the so-called golden age. This last number is large for British history, small compared with levels three times as large in Japan and about twice as large in Germany, Italy, and France (ibid.). As in the industrial revolution, I am not disposed to put much emphasis on slow-moving aggregates, as contrasted with national competitivity in world export markets and performance in invention and especially innovation. Some decline in the world share of exports is inevitable when a country's economic primacy draws a reaction abroad. Technology diffuses. Competitive industry starts up abroad, beginning with low-quality products and moving slowly or quickly up the quality scale. A country may be said to have fallen in the league tables when,

---

[1]For a discussion of the Lorenz book with its denial of entrepreneurial failure, see *International Journal of Maritime History*, vol. 5, no. 1 (June 1993), pp. 221–48.

instead of other countries imitating its leading products, it starts to copy those originating abroad, as Britain did in the 1880s and 1890s, especially in many, but not all, chemicals, in electrical products, and in automobiles.

One industry about which much controversy has swirled is shipbuilding, which may or may not have declined in the Victorian and Edwardian ages, depending on the basis of comparison. On the whole it was an exception to the story of decline. Britain produced 60 to 80 percent of the world tonnage before World War I, aided by naval contracts and by the ability of those replacing old ships to sell them secondhand on world markets (Pollard and Robertson, 1979; Musson, 1978, pp. 308–11). Skilled craftsmen who worked to their own standards and were trusted in the building of specialized ships to order more than made up for the more highly organized methods of the competition in Europe and ultimately in the United States and Japan. The advantage was a dwindling one. Success with steam and coal-burning did not translate readily into oil and diesel, although the Royal Navy was interested in improved design in the nineteenth century. Diesels, oil, and M. V. (motor vessels in which oil was converted to electricity to drive the propulsion) were being developed in Scandinavia before the war, and assembly-line methods were replacing craft methods outside Britain. In addition, British shipwrights were resisting encroachment on their monopoly of work as wooden ships gave way to iron and steel and boilermakers took over; boilermakers in turn resisted the introduction of pneumatic machine tools (after 1900) capable of being handled by less skilled apprentices (Lorenz, 1993, p. 247). After World War II there was no doubt. British shipbuilding was uncompetitive. There were, however, differences by regions, with the south of England losing out to the Clyde, Tyne, and Belfast regions, which achieved a degree of vertical integration among metallurgy, engineering, and shipbuilding (Ville, ed., 1993, p. xii).

Perhaps the most significant measure, symmetrical with the inventions, innovations, and patents on the upside, would be failures to solve technical problems that in due course were solved elsewhere. I collected a number of such instances in writing about Germany overtaking England (Kindleberger, 1975 [1978], pp. 266ff), and merely summarize without citing sources a second time: the delay in adopting the Gilchrist Thomas process, developed in Britain in 1878 and eagerly applied in France and Germany, to the East Midland basic ores until Americans solved the technical problem in 1915; the problem of coking fines in steel-making that did not find full solution for thirty years; the fact that it took the pottery tunnel kiln, developed in 1912, forty years to come into general use; the seventeen-year development period for 100-inch twin grinders and continuous twin polishers at Pilkington's plate-glass plant; the failure of English electrical engineers to respond to the demonstration of long-distance transmission of three-phase current; decade-long efforts by James Marshall to change from mechanical retting of flax for linen to use of the Schlumberger combing machine, only to be given up in 1874; experiments undertaken by the Brush company with a Swedish turbine, which proved "expensive" and were abandoned; the endless "teething troubles" encountered by companies in electric lighting, who gave up. One could doubtless find similar failures alongside the successes of the industrial revolution. Bottlenecks produced responses in many industries in the last third of the eighteenth century; a century later they seemed to have to wait for others to find solutions. The fact that successes are pointed to in the industrial revolution and failures are highlighted at the end of the nineteenth century may by itself be taken as an indicator of fundamental change.

Many explanations have been given, especially by econometricians, for these delays and failures, particularly in iron and steel: the given state of technology, nature of demand, location of the ores in relation to markets (McClosky, 1973; Temin, 1966). These exercises are based on the use of a static model of maximization, rather than one with dynamic features, as illustrated in purely theoretical terms by W. H. Phillips (1989). Whether bottlenecks help or hurt is a function of the response to them.

Additional light on the British position after World War I is provided by the second volume of Lord Skidelsky's magisterial biography of Keynes (1994). Keynes regarded British capitalism as dominated by "third-generation men," by reason of the hereditary principle (ibid., pp. 232, 259, 262). Despite the 1930s' depression in the United States, he saw that country as having nineteenth-century "fluidity," the equivalent, I judge, of vitality or capacity to transform, this in contrast with the sclerotic British economy (ibid., pp. 271, 440).

Moreover, Keynes was distressed at the passing of financial leadership from London to New York, hoping in the 1920s that Britain would cooperate with Germany in resisting the Americanization of the world (ibid., pp. xxvi). He shared the usual cultural prejudices of his class against American materialism, and resented the slipping of British power and prestige to the United States (ibid., 489). On occasion in his voluminous writings, he held that Britain must steer clear of cooperation with the United States, managing its monetary standard independently (ibid., p. 158). He cheered when the pound left gold in September 1931, "regaining at one stroke, the financial hegemony of the world" (ibid., p. 379). Later, of course, he switched back to cooperation.

Sidelsky himself supports the view of Britain as a third-generation country, describing Keynes as "perhaps the first flower of an autumnal civilization" (ibid., p. xviii).

One analysis of British decline that goes beyond the economic to include the imperial role is *The Weary Titan* (1988) by Aaron Friedberg, recommended to me by Patrick O'Brien. Friedberg's analysis concentrates on the years from 1895 to 1905 when critical questions of trade, finance, the Royal Navy, and military defense of India plagued the British government. The trade issue, raised by Joseph Chamberlain, was whether to impose tariffs with preference for the Empire. Finance turned on the national budget, strained by the expenses of the Boer War, and whether the limits of taxation had been reached. Britannia's rule of the waves, threatened by constructions of battleships by France, Russia, Germany, the United States, and Japan, posed the question whether Britain should or could continue to protect its world empire or should give up the defense of Canada (against the United States) in the Atlantic and make an alliance with Japan in the Pacific. After the Boer War had been won, protecting the water route to India, the military question focused on the need to defend India against Russian moves on land. Decision-making in all areas was handicapped by inadequate information, especially before the availability of estimates of national income.

The two military questions were drastically transformed by Japan's defeat of the Russian navy at Tsushima in May 1905. In Europe the rise of a German military threat was thought to be met by the alliance with France and Russia. But Friedberg emphasizes that there was no coherent overall plan, and that especially in the economic sphere, won by the free-traders against imperial preference on the ground that it would raise the cost of food, tariffs were in any case not the answer (ibid., p. 295). The free-traders themselves had only one positive proposal, to the extent that decline was recognized: education. Alfred Balfour, the prime minister, ridiculed this as an inadequate answer to foreign tariffs on British exports.

The Why?

With different timing, one could have blamed British decline on the horrendous slaughter of its bright young men on the fields of Flanders in World War I. Satisfying as that would be—blaming decline on the external or exogenous impact of an accidental war, and the military stupidity that prolonged it—the earlier start of decline forecloses this solution. Lists of reasons found by one analyst and another, for the most part not mutually exclusive, are the penalty of the head start; the amateur tradition of British society; the British system of education; openness of British society, which drew off successful entrepreneurs and their heirs from industry into public life and finance; the particular organization of British industry with institutional rigidities that slowed down needed transformation to large firms of efficient scale; the resistant character of the labor union; and many more.

The penalty of the head start has been derided by some economists on the ground that if a plant or a technique or an institution is obsolete and inefficient it can always be scrapped in favor of something more modern (Jervis, 1947). This overlooks the power of path dependency. British railroads retained an inefficient size of railroad cars for coal until nationalization after World War II because there was separation of ownership of the roadbed and motive power on the one hand (the rail companies), and the coal cars, owned by the mines. Vertical integration that would put the cars under ownership of the railroads would have brought the cars up from 10-ton size to 20- or 40-ton size as in other countries (Kindleberger, 1964, pp. 141ff). It should be added, however, that in this, as in so many instances, there is a revisionist view that holds that British railroad history produced an efficient solution: small cars, even in coal, were useful because of the short hauls from mines to retail distributors with little storage space (van Vleeck, 1993). Standardization can be imposed on an industry by government— though the Great Western railroad refused to adopt the standard of the Gauge Act of 1846 until the 1890s—or by a large firm. Industry in Britain in the nineteenth century received little guidance from government, except from military and admiralty orders concerned with exact specifications.

Small industry on the whole grew up on its own. Diversity of specifications was worsened by the fact that each railroad and municipality had its own engineer, who ordered equipment to his ideas. The result was two-hundred types of axle boxes, forty different types of hand brakes for rolling stock, and many different types of automatic brakes when these were belatedly adopted. It was alleged, with no authority cited, that two-hundred sizes and designs of manhole covers were produced because local authorities and boards insisted on their own standards. In electricity, companies in different regions with their own engineering consultants brought it about that by World War I there were seventy different generating stations, fifty systems of supply, twenty-four voltages, and ten frequencies (Plummer, 1937, p. 21). In Britain, 122 channel and angle sections in steel compared with German industry's 34 (Landes, 1965, p. 495). In agricultural machinery, "an almost unbelievable lack of standardization on the part of British makers lost to German, American and Canadian firms most of the world's trade in ploughs" (Saul, 1968, pp. 211–12). In some industries merchants were so thick on the ground, standing between producers and consumers, that they inhibited technical improvements. This was especially true in cotton textiles and machine tools. Merchants in Manchester ordering from manufacturers for their foreign customers specified thirty types of low-grade poplin when a user could at best distinguish three (Robson, 1957, pp. 92–95). Machine-tool manufacturers dealt with single agents to sell their products, with the agent little interested in solving user problems or finding uses for new tools (Beesley and Throup, 1958, pp. 380–84). Vertical integration of manufacturing and marketing would have advanced technical improvements, with the machine-tool user indicating what he wanted for his purposes and the maker seeing the extent to which the need could be satisfied at reasonable cost. The merchant system in effect imposed a barrier between consumer and producer, the merchant telling the producer, "they don't want them like that," and telling the consumer, "they don't make them like that." This early view of the inefficiency of British industry based on size and firm and a lack of vertical integration have found corroboration in recent work by Bernard Elbaum and William Lazonick and collaborators, who hold that rigidities in British economic and social institutions prevented firms from acquiring control over markets, as well as over labor and management (Elbaum and Lazonick, 1984; Elbaum and Lazonick, eds., 1986; Lazonick, 1991).

The Elbaum–Lazonick approach is a particular variant of the institutional model relying on path dependency and on the difficulty of adapting economic organisms that have become set in their ways to changed conditions. This, again, runs contrary to the Coase theorem, which holds that institutions readily change to conform to the new conditions in demand and supply—with the crucial exception in the case that transaction costs of the change are high. The exception comes close to reducing the theorem to an empty truism: institutions will adapt when adaptation is cheap and easy, not when it is expensive and difficult. M. W. Kirby criticizes Elbaum and Lazonick for focusing too tightly on a single form of business organization, which, in their view, the British economy missed out on (1992). In a more general formulation, the decline is explained by a variety of rigidities or habits inherited from the successful past that, without an infusion of new men, posed transaction costs that proved too high. It can be called "economic arteriosclerosis."

Note that this discussion of rigidities differs from that of Olson, which is focused on distributional coalitions, that is, vested interests, rather than different ways of thinking and difficulties of changing directions after an initial start. Being set in one's ways is different from forming alliances with like-minded people with the same interests to work against (or for) certain changes. Rigidity in industry is doing the same thing in much the same way. For the country as a whole, it blames the slowdown of economic growth on the failure of old markets to keep on expanding, as in cotton textiles (Meyer, 1955), steel rails, galvanized iron roofing, and the like. With growth in world income, a given good is income elastic on its introduction, becomes income inelastic as it is incorporated into everyday standards of living, and may in due course become an inferior good—like galvanized iron sheets for roofing—one for which demand decreases as income rises. Some years ago Sir Donald MacDougall suggested that automobiles may become the cotton textiles of tomorrow (1954, p. 196). Engel's law requires that with economic growth a country must transform out of old into new lines of industry and services. With old firms and old industrial traditions, this is difficult to do.

A précis of the forces working for and against economic growth from 1851 to 1950, comparable to that given for France in Table 7-2, is furnished for Britain in Table 8-2, from an earlier exercise (Kindleberger, 1964, pp. 330–31). For a fuller treatment of this complex subject the reader is referred to the work of thirty years back.

Gentlemen vs. Players

The amateur tradition in the inventions of the industrial revolution was mentioned earlier. Then it proved highly successful. As time went on, however, increasing complexity of process, and in many cases product, made amateurism less helpful. "Gentlemen and Players," the title of a paper on entrepreneurial failure in Britain, is patterned after occasional cricket matches between amateurs and professionals, between whom was a wide social divide (Coleman, 1973). Gentlemen assumed leadership in the coun-

Table 8–2 Forces Making For and Resisting Growth in England, 1851–1950

Period	Forces Making for Growth	Forces and Frictions Resisting Growth	Potentially Significant Forces of Negligible Effect
1851–1875 Vigorous expansion	Technological innovation (1)[a] [b]*Bouyant exports due to foreign demand, gold mining, capital exports (1) *War (2) High farming (3) *Amateur spirit (2)	Goverment regulation (3) *Speculation in securities, cotton spinning (2)	Lack of technical training
1873–1896 Great Depression	Capital exports from 1885–1890 (3) Rising real wages from terms of trade (2)	Slowdown of gold output (3) Monetary disorder (3) *Expansion of overseas supplies, agricultural products (2) Initial excess capacity and high financial costs (2)	Family enterprises Amateur spirit
1896–1913 Moderate expansion	*Firm export demand due to capital exports, gold output (2) *Domestic investment in traditional industries (2)	Aging entrepreneurship (3) Specialized small units joined through merchants, markets (2) Continued lack of technical capacity (2) *Amateur spirit (2)	
1919–1931 Stagnation	Accumulated depreciation (3) Wartime inventions (2)	Speculation of 1919–1920 (2) Overvaluation of sterling (1) *Decline in overseas demand for British textiles, coal, ships (2) Technological backwardness (2)	Wartime manpower losses
1931–1939 Moderate expansion	Devaluation (2) *Improved terms of trade (2) Rearmament (2) Abandonment of hope in prewar structure (1)	*Stagnant exports (3) Weak technology (2)	

Table 8–2 (continued)

Period	Forces Making for Growth	Forces and Frictions Resisting Growth	Potentially Significant Forces of Negligible Effect
1945–1950+ Slow growth	Foreign assistance (2) Investment in new industries, engineering, electrical (1)	Leadership exhaustion by war (1) Doctrine of fair shares and continuation of class divisions (2) Loss of assets, increase of liabilities during war (3) Limited technical capacity (2)	Nationalization of coal, steel, railways, Bank of England, etc.

Source: Reprinted by permission of the publishers from *Economic Growth in France and Britain, 1851–1950* by Charles Kindleberger, Cambridge, Mass.: Harvard University Press, Copyright © 1964 by the President and Fellows of Harvard College.
[a](1) strong factor, (2) moderate factor, (3) weak factor.
[b]Asterisk indicates a factor that might have operated oppositely under different circumstances.

tryside and in public life; bit by bit leadership in industry was taken over in the second and third generation by managers and family retainers from the shop floor. It was difficult for able subordinates to rise to the top of a family firm unless they came from the same social circle as the heirs of the founder, which heirs had been to public school and Oxford or Cambridge (Florence, 1953, pp. 304ff). The inheritor-owners were interested in maintaining dividends, at the expense of plowed-back profits to enlarge investment or research in new lines, and sometimes in having the firm go public so as to invest in trustee securities, but gave no assurance of vigorous management such as had been present at the start. Martin Wiener identifies "a decline in the industrial spirit" in England, associated with English culture, and quotes C. P. Snow and Marxist Tom Nairn who compared the country to the Venetian republic (1981, p. 161), in one instance citing "lack of will to break the pattern which had crystallized," in another, a Venetian twilight in which the country had little interest in catching up, but wanted primarily to defend the tribe's customs and weathered documents.

Education

Blaming the culture comes down in most instances to criticism of the public schools and Oxford and Cambridge. British leaders were not unaware of the need for technical education. At the time of the Great Exhibition, Prince Albert, Queen Victoria's consort, native of Germany, urged steps toward technical education. Earlier, science had been advanced in a series of provincial societies such as the Birmingham Lunar Society and the Manchester Philosophical and Literary Society, but on an amateur rather than a purposeful basis, though purposefully at Edinburgh University, and largely by outsiders (Thackray, 1973). Beginning in the middle of the nineteenth century, however, the government appointed a series of select committees and royal commissions on scientific instruction, including a Royal Commission on Technical Instruction in 1883, and passed the Technical Instruction Act of 1889—financed with "whiskey money" in 1891 (Cotgrove, 1958; Musgrave, 1967). Technology was accepted as a subject of change at Cambridge in 1895, along with the expansion of examinations in mathematics, theoretical and practical chemistry, and metallurgy (Musgrave, 1967, p. 89). Somewhat like France reacting after defeat in wars, Britain established practical provincial ("red-brick") universities in the 1860s and "plate-glass" universities after World War II. But there is doubt as to whether industry's or the nation's hearts were in it. Technical education was for "them," not "us." In France successful fathers sent their sons to the *Ecole polytechnique*, in England to Eton or Harrow, then Oxford or Cambridge. The disinterest extended beyond the end of the nineteenth century. Cotgrove writes:

> The apathy of the industry toward technical education in the interwar years and the small demand for scientific manpower are not surprising in view of the apathy of industry in general towards both research and the application of science to production. (1958, p. 99)

Finance Again

A recent book has strongly attacked the view that the British decline was caused by cultural deficiencies having part of their origin in the system of education. W. D. Rubenstein, who has studied wealth and wealthy individuals in Britain, is scornful of the view expressed, say by Martin Wiener, especially that the British educational system is antibusiness (1993). In a review of Rubenstein's book in *The Economist* (July 17, 1993, p. 85), which is all that I have seen as I write, the author claims that Britain has "proved itself a humane, rational, and successful society" that has "readily adjusted to social and economic change." The criticism that Rubenstein attacks rests on a concentration on manufacturing, which is mistaken in what Daniel Bell calls a "post-industrial state." Youth is educated successfully for the City, which is prosperous. *The Economist* is not prepared to swallow this entirely, pointing out in a later unrelated article that while the British are getting better at making things, they have a considerable distance to go to catch up with the leaders in productivity, creativity, and the social status accorded to the ordinary worker, who is undertrained and poorly skilled (*The Economist*, August 21, 1993, p. 46). The British do better in the service industries, but are at no more than half the world standard in finance, publishing or television, and are happily not too chummy with government (ibid., pp. 46–47).

The Rubenstein critique cannot be evaluated without study, to be sure, but it appears to neglect that only recently has the country undertaken business and management studies; that the Big Bang of October 1986, when finance was deregulated and Britain was thought likely to take over the financial leadership of Europe and probably the world, was a fiasco—with the fading of euphoria, London fell to a rank behind Tokyo and New York (Walter, 1990, p. 149); that Lloyds has fallen on evil days with horrendous insurance losses (Barnes, 1993); and that British banks are on the whole small relative to Japanese and American banks, although size is partly a question of choosing the appropriate exchange rate for converting assets and liabilities.

More significantly, the value of the pound has declined from $4.86 plus—the nineteenth-century rate against the dollar—in successive devaluations to $1.60, at a time when the dollar itself had been devalued to an extent that is hard to measure, as one gets different answers in measuring against gold ($21.67 against $400), or against Japanese yen (360 yen to the dollar shortly after World War II to 110 in 1993 before falling below 90 in early 1995) or other currency. Cairncross and Eichengreen call their study of the devaluations of 1931, 1949, and 1967 *Sterling in Decline* (1983). The 1976 exchange crisis involved borrowing from the International Monetary Fund, subject to its conditionality. It has been written up by Kathleen Burk and Sir Alec Cairncross in a book with a title borrowed from a 1975 *Wall Street Journal* editorial, "Goodbye, Great Britain" (1992).[2] It is hard to know whether the choice of title was ironic or sardonic. Still another sterling crisis took place in the fall of 1992, not yet the subject of a book, in which one short speculator admits to, or boasts of, having made a profit of $1 billion.

The British government had high hopes when it finally was admitted to the European Community in 1973 that it would emerge as the balancer between German and French claims for European ascendancy, and, with luck, with London as the financial center of the European monetary system. London did well in the Eurodollar system starting about 1960, which gradually evolved into one of Euromonies and Eurobonds. With the prospective formation of the European Monetary System it found itself in competition, so far as ambitions were concerned, with Brussels, the headquarters of the Community; Paris, always ambitious; and Frankfurt-am-Main. London's advantage lies in its experience in Eurodollar and Eurobond markets. One liability is that the participants in the market in London (and Paris) lack the foreign languages that Frankfurt and the smaller Brussels can boast. The real weakness of London as a financial center, in my judgment, is that it is missing the steady accumulation of savings that gave it its high place in the years from 1870 to 1914. It is one thing to make a market in other people's monies. As earlier accounts have shown, there is an irresistible urge to save transaction costs through direct dealing.

---

[2]Such pessimistic notes have been struck continuously, even in the midst of "the golden age." A special issue of *The Encounter* (July 1963) was entitled "Suicide of a Nation?" It contained one slashing defense of the country by Henry Fairlie, but a series of pessimistic forecasts by Malcom Muggridge, Michael Shanks, Andrew Shonfield, and others.

Policy

It was indicated earlier that British growth from 1950 to 1973 at 2.5 percent per capita per annum was better than any of the numbers over long stretches from 1700, but drastically below growth in other European countries and Japan, though not the United States. In one view the blame attaches to the socialist policies followed after the war, "out of intellectual error"; and a new beginning was made in 1979 with the election of a Conservative government under the prime ministership of Margaret (now Lady) Thatcher (Minford, 1993, p. 116). If the proof of the pudding is in the numbers, they were worse after 1979, although somewhat better than during the 1970s. Moreover, British ideological commitment to monetarism and privatization have ended in a rejection of monetarism, and with inflation and foreign-exchange crises. Matthews was originally skeptical that policy contributed to the British "golden age" from 1950 to 1973 (1968), but later backed away from that judgment to an extent (Matthews, Feinstein, and Odling-Smee, 1982, p. 313). But whether British policy was responsible for the good times after World War II, or the bad times, such policy in general has tended to be pragmatic rather than ideological (Checkland, 1983). Checkland says that British government policy tended to laissez faire to the middle of the nineteenth century, and then less so, but in general it was one of drift—unsystematic, inadvertent, improvised, piecemeal, undefined, and lacking governing principle.

The aging process in individuals and nations reminds me of a time long ago when I saw friends laughing and asked what the joke was. One of the pair had said, "President Eisenhower is not a father figure; he is a grandfather figure. It's not what he can do for us, but what we can do for him that counts." A third auditor added, "And he is so little trouble." Britain may have moved into the grandparental stage, bereft of the Empire and the special relation with the United States, uncertain as to its relations with Europe, surely not the European leader, but finding it awkward after its glorious history to be just another one of the countries in the group. The gloomiest assessment I have seen was included in *The Economist*'s audit of manufacturing: "By one measure of wealth—GDP per head—Britain is in danger of falling out of the world's top 20" (August 27, 1993, p. 46).

I conclude that Britain's rise to world economic primacy, and subsequent fall, fit well the notion of a national life cycle, guided for the most part by an intrinsic pattern of great vitality gradually eroding into rigidity and resistance to change.

9

Germany, the Latecomer

Overtaking England

In World War II I had occasion to study German industry from the viewpoint of military bombing target selection, and after the war found myself caught up briefly in German economic reconstruction. German economic history, however, I first studied with any intensity in several months at the Institute for World Economy in Kiel in the autumn of 1971, which, following some seminars at the University of Edinburgh in January 1974, resulted in a two-part paper on "Germany's Overtaking England, 1806–1914" (1975 [1978]). Since those days my exposure to German historiography, apart from European financial history in general, has been limited. Hence I am conscious that what follows in this chapter misses out on the discoveries and controversies in German economic history of recent decades, and on that account, should be read with caution.

The 1975 paper's passages on Germany were divided into:

Germany as Apprentice, 1806 to 1848
Germany as Journeyman, 1850 to 1871
Germany as Master, 1873 to 1913

The metaphor is taken of course from the guild system, as mastery has nothing to do with the economic rivalry of Germany with respect to Britain. The dates are arbitrary and chosen largely on political grounds: 1806, Prussia's defeat by Napoleon at Jena, which produced a surge of aristocratic interest in economic development rather along Mancur Olson lines that

149

defeat produces new men and new economic resolve; 1848, the aborted bourgeois revolution, with the emasculated constitution written in Frankfurt that failed to limit the powers of the Prussian monarchy; 1871, the victory over France and the formation of the Reich under the leadership of Prussia: 1913, the last year before World War I. In this chapter, the narrative runs through the fateful interwar period with the fateful inflation, depression, and assumption of power by Adolph Hitler; through World War II and the *Wirtschaftswunder* (economic miracle) that followed; with finally the role of the new Germany in European integration, in which primacy was perhaps not sought, hardly even accepted, within a western European framework rather than in global terms.

The potted history to follow—for I do not propose to repeat the exercise of the early 1970s—places considerable emphasis on the German challenge to British world economic primacy from 1890 or so to 1913, and seeks to make clear that the country's trajectory does not closely follow the model of the national life cycle of chapter 2 illustrated in the chapter on Britain. There was an earlier echo of that cycle. In a wide-ranging historical review, Wilhelm Kaltenstadler wrote:

> . . . up to the 13th century, the members of the Hanseatic League were very active and dynamic men who did not wish to be forced into guilds and therefore succeeded in setting up capital-intensive enterprises. In the 14th century this attitude was replaced by a preference for the security provided by wealth and an attachment to anti-liberal tendencies. (1972, p. 209)

At the other end of the period, a *Washington Post* 2-inch story repeated in the *Boston Globe* under the headline "Kohl Seeks to Aid Competitiveness" refers to a German 110-page plan for the overhaul of the country's social, economic, and educational systems to sharpen the country's competitive edge. Action was needed, the authors held, because Germany is in danger of forfeiting "its top place in the world economy" because of rising unemployment, high taxes, a short work week, and an aging work force (*Boston Globe*, September 3, 1993, p. 8). "The top place in the world's economy" was one among a number of such places, not a place occupied alone.

German practice is often to combine "social" and economic history in the titles of books and designations of academic departments. Social movements and attributes such as mentalities have come to the surface often in the national life cycles described earlier, but nowhere is the importance of social development as crucial to the path of the economy as in Germany. It runs through industrial, tariff, monetary, and economic as well as political history. Foreign and German historians fault the country for its historic inability to achieve peaceful and democratic accommodation of regions and economic classes until after World War II. Otto von Bismarck, who is universally recognized as a consummate politician, is praised for his skill in obtaining passage of the 1879 tariff of "rye and iron," since the agriculturist Junkers detested both cities and industry. Less than a generation later, the Junkers were led to support the naval building programs sought by the steel industry of the Ruhr, as they substituted their hatred of England for that of cities and industry (Kehr, 1965, p. 152). Hatred is a word little found in most economic discourse but frequently in German history (Kahler, 1974, p. 31; Felix, 1971, pp. 166–67; Kehr, 1965, pp. 155–57; Feldman, 1993, pp. 245, 284, 360, 560, 799, 858. Note that Gerald Feldman's account of inflation under the Weimar Republic also includes words like "rage," "fury," and "contempt"). After World War I there was an outbreak of political homicides—376 in four years according to one count—including such prominent persons as Karl Liebknecht, Rosa Luxembourg, Kurt Eisner (head of the Bavarian government) Karl Gareis (a deputy in the Bavarian legislature), and, distinguished at the national level, Walther Rathenau and Matthias Erzberger (Felix, 1971, pp. 125, 163). As a new man, feared for his energy and vigor in pursuing Republican policies, Erzberger was hated by the groups associated with the empire of Wilhelm II—"bureaucrats, officer, junkers, clergymen and industrialists" (Epstein, 1959, p. 367).

Mosaic Germany

Before the Napoleonic wars, Germany consisted of 355 separate states and 1,476 autonomous knightships (Dumke, 1976, p. 32), Napoleon's conquest added the left bank of the Rhine (as one faces north) to France in 1801. In 1803 Napoleon imposed the Treaty of Luneville that eliminated 112 principalities, all religious principalities except two that were secularized, and destroyed the political independence of most smaller cities and towns (Bechtel, 1967, p. 313). Napoleon also wiped out guilds and built some roads. The Congress of Vienna in 1815 validated much of this change, but telescoped the political units of the ancient régime into thirty-nine new independent states, organized loosely into a federation (Bund). Slowly during the rest of the century to 1871 the various states were formed into the German Reich (Empire), largely on Prussian initiative. In 1818, Prussia consolidated tariffs within its borders, which included, after eighteenth-century conquests, Silesia and Saxony and stretched from the east to the Rhineland. A further consolidation occurred in 1834 with the formation of the Zollverein and southern and northern monetary agreements, followed by their joining into a single money. A common law for bills of exchange was agreed on in 1851, weights and measures in 1856–1858, and a commercial code in 1857–1861 (Benaerts, 1933a, p. 628). With the victory of Prussia over France in 1871 the unification of Germany—ex Austria which had been a challenger of Prussia for leadership in the greater Germany until its 1866 defeat by Prussia—was complete, even enlarged by the acquisition of Alsace and Lorraine. The Prussian taler, renamed the mark, was made the empire's monetary unit of account. The Reichsbank was established in 1875. With their interest in world trade, the Hanseatic cities held aloof from the Zollverein as long as politically possible, but the last, Hamburg, finally succumbed in 1881 after the 1879 tariff.

Trade

Chopped up into small units, German principalities failed to develop a rich merchant class except in a few cities. Augsburg and Nuremberg dealt intensively with Venice, as we have seen; south German bankers such as the Fuggers dealt with Antwerp, Lyons, and Seville. The principal Hanseatic cities developed differently: Lübeck went into gentle decline as described by Thomas Mann in *Buddenbrooks* (1901 [1924]). Exports of grain, timber, and naval stores from East Prussia and Danzig had early been dominated by Dutch traders (Braudel, 1979 [1982], p. 215; idem, 1979 [1984], p. 255). Hamburg traded principally with Britain; Bremen developed a trans-Atlantic business in cotton and coffee. Away from the coast, the trade and financial city of Frankfurt-am-Main grew differently from Hamburg, as described by Helmut Böhme, the former populated by court bankers like the Rothschilds, the latter by merchant-bankers especially interested in foreign trade (1968a). In Hamburg the merchant class was cohesive, republican, oligarchic, and ruled the city. Such was not the case in Frankfurt, where merchants divided into two groups—bankers and wholesale merchants forming the "English party" who wanted to stay out of the Zollverein and cling to international commerce, and 300 smaller merchants focused on domestic trade, the fair, freight forwarding, and close cooperation with local industry. The latter group won and Frankfurt joined their Zollverein early (Böhme, 1968a, pp. 36, 107, chap. 5). In the Rhineland, proto- or cottage industry began by relying on Dutch merchants, but gradually took over its own international business.

Within Germany, as opposed to the periphery, there were shopkeepers, but limited numbers of merchants engaged in distant trade. Part of the reason for the absence was the poor state of communication, roads, and rivers and the many tolls on rivers levied by towns. Part was the destruction in the Thirty Years' War (Braudel, 1979 [1982], p. 159; Kahler, 1974, p. 233). Braudel suggests that the place of German merchants was taken by Jewish merchants who came into prominence in the seventeenth century at the Frankfurt fair (loc. cit.). David Landes extends the list to include outsiders in general: Huguenots, English, Greeks, and "above all, Jews" (1960, p. 203). Nobles and bourgeoisie looked down on commerce, and the latter began to change from a merchant class to one of bureaucrats dependent on princes (Kahler, 1974). At the center of Germany were the "home towns," run by guilds, taxing goods that crossed their border, thoroughly regulated, suspicious of outsiders. After a *Wanderjahr*, a journeyman would return to work for his mastership. Permission was needed to marry. It was a sign of failure to work in a factory or to produce goods in large quantities to be sold for export to people the maker did not know (Walker, 1971, passim and pp. 25, 82, 85, 105). Home towns in the west and south were surrounded by peasants who were described in 1786 as marked by "mental and physical laziness, empty-headedness, stupidity, coarseness and drunkenness, slavish subservience mixed with malice, spite, hatred, bitterness, hostility toward authority" and "unthriftiness, no thought for the future, ruled by sensuality" (ibid., p. 119). These peasants worked plots rented from nobles who did not work their own land and the church, a system of *Grundherrschaft*, as contrasted with the Junker *Gutherrschaft*, east of the Elbe river, where a noble worked his own land with peasants as serfs. Along with guilds, both systems were broken up by the Napoleonic wars. The change went deeper in the Rhineland, which was ruled by France for almost twenty years. Elsewhere in the west and south, Napoleonic decrees had considerable effect in changing Germany from feudalism. A major attempt at reform in Prussia, after the defeat at Jena and the crushing Treaty of Tilsit (1807), was made by Baron vom Stein, Prince Hardenberg, and others. It consisted of abolishing feudal restrictions on peasants, but only after payment or after giving up one-third of the land they had been cultivating. By 1819 the reforms had virtually collapsed as far as agriculture was concerned.

Gewerbefoerderung (*Industrial Policy*)

There was movement on other fronts. New universities were created in Berlin, Breslau, and Bonn, and others were enlarged. The gymnasiums were reformed, and existing universities such as Halle and Göttingen moved from such subjects as theology and philosophy to mathematics and science, with a trend led by William von Humboldt to research (Ritter, 1961, pp. 25–30). At the same time there began what one would call today industrial policy: *Gewerbefoerderung* ("craft promotion"). Peter Beuth had become interested in industry when he was billeted near the Cockerill plant in Liège during the Napoleonic war. In 1816 he became head of the Department of Trade and Industry of the Prussian Ministry of Finance in Berlin and began a program of industrial promotion, consisting of subsidizing trips abroad, especially to Britain; training young men in a *Gewerbeinstitut*; funding engineers; starting businesses; collecting foreign machinery for copying and giving the original to entrepreneurs. He himself traveled to England, Belgium, and Holland. A salon was organized in Berlin on a continuous basis, which discussed and published papers on industrial and economic subjects. Among the leading German industrialists whom Beuth helped start were the Cockerill brothers, sons of the English machine-builder in Belgium, F. J. Egells in steam engines and machinery, and August Borsig, who moved from steam engines to locomotives. In 1841 there were twenty locomotives in service in Germany, all imported from abroad. That was the year Borsig produced his first. By 1844 he was up to 44, by the end of 1847, 187. There were other German producers in Aix-La-Chapelle, Storkade, and Magdeburg. By 1854 no foreign locomotives were imported, Borzig produced sixty-seven of the sixty-nine bought in Germany, and additionally exported six to Poland and four to Denmark, a classic example of effective import substitution leading to exports (Benaerts, 1933b, chap. 4).

The visits of Kekulé and Liebig to France in the 1830s for study of chemistry under Gay-Lussac and Berthollet have been mentioned earlier, along with the interest of German bankers in French practice (chap. 7).

Gewerbefoerderung meant more than institutes, exhibitions, and subsidies to students and entrepreneurs. In Baden it involved the award of patents and monopolies, help in the supply of raw materials by forbidding the export of ashes (for soap) and rags (for paper), import tariffs to protect local markets, and requirement of permission to start a factory, which was often refused (Fischer, 1962). The transition from *Gewerbefoerderung* to *Gewerbefreiheit* (freedom of establishment) took two generations from the Napoleonic wars to 1862, though it was spreading elsewhere in Germany at a rapid rate and was assisted by the Zollverein, which with the loss of Alsace to France in 1815 turned the economic attention of Baden from Switzerland and France to the north. In the end, industrial policy became so complex as different interests competed and gained overlapping concessions that it proved easiest to abolish the system altogether and start over again—a policy that eliminated the English navigation laws at roughly the same time, and has been recommended for U.S. income taxes by the late Joseph Pechman of the Brookings Institution and others such as Senator Bill Bradley of New Jersey.

The Zollverein

Integrative steps in Germany before the industrial spurt of the 1850s were numerous and varied. Canals, standardized weights and measures, and gradual unification of money have been mentioned along with the 1818 removal of internal tariffs in Prussia and the wider Zollverein. A widely held view is that the Zollverein's purpose was political: to begin building the greater Germany under Prussian leadership. There was, of course, the commercial purpose, to broaden the trading area. Rolf Dumke, however, has demonstrated that the reason the lesser principalities joined with Prussia was fiscal: elimination of internal borders of those states joining by 1836 saved the costs of patrolling 780 "Meilen" of customs border, with a cost per mile estimated at 2,000 thaler in an age of rampant smuggling (Dumke, 1976, pp. 41–43). By dividing the customs revenues among the states by population, rather than collections (which would have favored Prussia, with its ports of entry), princes and dukes were assured an income that did not have to depend on parliamentary voting.

The Constitution of 1848

Considerable competition reigns in German history as to the timing of fateful steps that were to lead to the disasters of the twentieth century. Friederich Meinike is quoted as designating 1819—the year when the Stein-Hardenberg reforms were reversed—as the "year of the misfortune of the nineteenth century" (Craig, 1970, p. 76). Others may choose the missed opportunity by the Prussian bourgeoisie to rein in the monarch in the writing of a new constitution in Frankfurt in 1848. Frederick William IV was under pressure from liberals as calls for occupational and business freedom spread with the rise of the railroad system and the growth of intercommunication. Revolutions in Paris and Vienna threatened to infect the German states. The potato blight of 1846, plus the crop failure in grain the next year, gave impetus to riots in Cologne and Berlin, including a three-day riot called the "potato rebellion" in 1847. There were also several clashes between the army and workers affected by industrial depression in 1848, as the elected Constitutional Assembly was meeting in Frankfurt (ibid., p. 91ff). The king refused to agree to a constitution that yielded authority over the army to the Assembly. Terrified by the threat of the rising proletariat, the middle class conceded. Craig states that the conflict is rightly called the central event of the domestic history of Germany in "the last hundred years." Failure on the part of the bourgeoisie and middle classes was reinforced in 1866 when Bismarck pushed through the Prussian diet an indemnity act retroactively approving military reform that had been instituted without parliamentary consent. The liberal cave-in was owed partly to fear of the mob, partly to divided aims, but also to a middle-class tendency "to subordinate domestic objectives to a desire for national greatness" (ibid., p. 139).

After the middle of the century, the Germans gradually overcame their inferiority complex against the French, the Belgians, and especially the English. The middle class in the Rhineland sought social prestige by a route that included the gymnasium, technical education, credit, mercantile success, and a good marriage (Aycoberry, 1968, pp. 513, 525). Businessmen in the Ruhr took full part in the movement to Gross Deutschland and expansionism, and even workers found interest in Germany's world-power role (Brepohl, 1948, p. 209). Rheinische-Westfalian resistance to enoblement weakened, and a number of successful businessmen bought estates, gave up industrial activity, and devoted themselves entirely to noble activity (Zunkel, 1962, chap. 4, esp. pp. 121ff).

The 1850s

Gewerbefoerderung, the Zollverein, and the leg-up on the German railway system paved the way for a burst of economic vitality from 1850 to 1857. There were other factors: the repeal of the corn laws in Britain, which produced a boom in grain exports; an inflow of capital especially from Belgium and France to the Ruhr, and especially in nonferrous metals; the establishment of a series of banks in Darmstadt, Berlin, and Hamburg, with others organized or reorganized in Cologne, Leipzig, and Berlin. Hamburg and Bremen, which had overtaken the small Hanseatic cities in shipping in the 1840s, received stimulus from the shift from sailing to steam and from a rapid rise in emigration, primarily to the United States, which on the basis of rather unreliable figures rose from 470,000 in the decade of the 1840s to 1,075,000 in the 1850s (Borchardt, 1972, p. 123). There were three streams: one direct from Bremen, one indirect via Holland and Cherbourg on the continent, and one by way of Hamburg to Liverpool, where some were stranded running out of money (Walker, 1964). Mack Walker makes a number of corrective points to the conventional wisdom: the movement was not driven by intellectuals, nor did it consist of peasants. One needed some money to pay the fare; much of the movement from western and southern Germany was of craftsmen, who had lost faith in Germany's future after the 1840s and were feeling "a sense of impotence, malaise and discontent" (ibid., pp. 65, 104, 130). With the spurt in economic growth the rate dropped off sharply, from one quarter of a million in 1854 to 100,000 in 1855 (Walker, 1964, p. 153).

Rising industrial employment in the Rhineland and Westphalia, Berlin, Saxony, and Silesia provided an opportunity for shorter and cheaper moves to improve one's lot. The Prussian urban population (inhabitants of towns of more than 2,000) went from 27 percent of the populace in 1849 to 32 percent in 1861, though the latter figure is judged to be an underestimate because of the manner and timing of the calculation (Becker, 1960, p. 218, 237). In Rhineland-Westphalia, Gelsenkirchen, Schalke, and Hüllen, among others, grew in the 1850s from villages to great cities (ibid., p. 219). Essen went from 8,800 in 1850 to 52,000 in 1870 as Krupp expanded steel production with local coking coal and responded to the strong demand for steel for railroads, ships, heavy machinery, and armament (Barkhausen, 1963, pp. 226–27). Most of the movement to the cities in the 1850s and 1860s and even the 1870s was local; the massive long-distance migration from east of the Elbe to the Ruhr came later after the fall of the price of wheat and expansion of steel production in the 1880s and 1890s (Brepohl, 1948). Inward movement was experienced to a lesser extent by the textile towns of the Rhineland, as Köllmann shows in a comparison of the origins of the peoples of Barmen (textiles) and Gelsenkirchen (coal for steel) (1965).

Three winning wars of the 1860s gave rise to a euphoria that produced a boom in housing and security prices in the *Gründerzeit*, financed in part by the 5 billion-franc indemnity that brought the country millions of specie and in due course funds to enable state and municipal debts to be paid off (Kindleberger, 1984 [1993], pp. 235–45). The crash that followed in 1873 slowed the economy down, but the "great depression," so-called, was milder in Germany than in the rest of Europe.

The Tariff of Rye and Iron

Prussian tariffs had been low after the consolidation in 1818, and it was the low Prussian tariff that the Zollverein adopted in 1834. There were slight upward adjustments in a few items in the 1840s to accommodate the other states, but with the British repeal of the corn laws in 1846 and the Cobden–Chevalier treaty of 1860 came a move to freer trade throughout Europe in which the Zollverein joined, entering into bilateral treaties with

France and Italy. Bismarck had little interest in economic matters, but approved the low level of the Zollverein tariff insofar as it embarrassed Austria. That country needed protection for a number of its industries, and on that account was unable to join the Zollverein and contest Prussia for its leadership. With the military victory over Austria in 1866 and the triumph of the thaler over the gulden, Bismarck had less interest in low tariffs. Industry, which had favored low tariffs to obtain its intermediate goods cheaply, was producing more of them itself.

As European grain prices weakened with the completion of railroad systems in the plains of the world, so that steamers could carry it cheaply to Europe, Germany lost out in the British market. From 1856 to 1860 Germany provided 25 percent of British grain imports, the United States 18 percent; from 1871 to 1875 the proportions changed to 8.2 and 40.9 percent, respectively. By 1879 the United States share rose to 68.2 percent (Lambi, 1963, pp. 20, 133). Increasing flexibility in the organization of the Zollverein in 1867 made change easier to achieve. In 1876 Rudolph von Delbruck, a strong free-trader and the president of Bismarck's chancellery, retired, in all probability pushed out rather than leaving of his own accord. Lambi ascribes the economic downturn after 1873 as the basic cause of the 1879 tariff (ibid., p. 73). A failed attempt to assassinate the emperor in June 1878 galvanized nationalist sentiment. In 1879, despite a mass meeting of 1,000 merchants in Hamburg and representatives of seventy-five cities in Berlin, duties were raised on iron and grain. Bismarck had forged his union of rye and iron, or "*Rittergut und Hochofen*" (knights' estates and blast furnaces). The Junker opposition to cities and industry had been undermined by national exuberance and because the caste had dwindled in wealth and power. At the end of the century only one-third of the landowners in six eastern provinces were noble, as the agricultural depressions of the 1820s and the 1880s forced the Junkers to sell to the rising middle class despite *fideikommis*, which forbade such sales (Craig, 1970, p. 234).

In the 1880s Bismarck turned to two issues outside of the relations between industry and agriculture. One was worker insurance against sickness (1883), accidents (1884), and old age (1889). Böhme maintains that this step failed to assuage worker sentiment, which continued to reach out for the protection of unions, limits on hours of work for women and children, as well as minimum wages and the right to speak out on company policy (1968b, pp. 89–90). The second was an interest in colonies, on which Germany had missed out because of its slow unification. Belgian King Leopold's conquest of the rich Congo led to the Berlin conference of 1885 in which German unhappiness was expressed. It was to last a long time, with Hjalmar Schacht recurring to the issue time and again in the 1920s and 1930s.

There were economic quarrels with czarist Russia, to which German financial circles stopped lending after the 1887 *Lombardverbot* (the forbidding of orphans funds being invested in Russian bonds), leading to a substitution of French for German lenders from the 1890s to 1913. Problems of east Elbian agriculture led to the massive movement of peasants both to the Ruhr and abroad, peaking at 1,300,000 in the decade of the 1880s, but falling to 530,000 in the new boom in the 1890s to 280,000 in 1901–1910 (Borchardt, 1972, p. 123). The anticyclical movement in migration was matched in capital flows: as investment demand picked up at home, German markets stopped lending not only to Russia but to much of Latin America, cutting down on loans to Argentina, for example, as British lending there was building up to the 1890 Baring crisis.

Attitude toward Britain

Germany emerged as a strong competitor of Britain at the beginning of the 1890s. There is a tradition that rivalry between the two countries goes back to 1780, but Richard Tilly insists that for most of the nineteenth century German industry benefited from its economic relations with England, as it bought yarns for spinning, learned quality control, acquired technological knowledge, and borrowed capital (1968). "In the 1840s every conception of England's had been hailed" (Kehr, 1930 [1970], p. 293). This sentence is followed, however, by "but since the reaction and the establishment of the Reich every concept of England viewed it as a demoniacal director of the puppet theater of Europe which had dominated the world since the sixteenth and seventeenth centuries" (ibid.). In one view, as noted earlier, the economic spurt of the 1850s put an end to the sense of inferiority that the German world of business felt toward the French, the Belgians, and especially the English (Aycoberry, 1968, p. 513). Another detects a national inferiority complex as far back as the Thirty Years' War (Kahler, 1974, p. 234); two and a half centuries later Kahler notes that as the Germans watched England's huge colonial and commercial empire, this inferiority complex grew. The Germans felt they had been cheated and duped. Prussia had built a state with the ethic of hard work and possessed the most efficient government in Europe (ibid., p. 261). Its lowly status was wrong.

In all accounts resentment started or restarted in the 1890s, after the fall of Bismarck. That was also the time in which the British became disturbed by rising German commercial and naval competition, as E. E. Williams's book *Made in Germany* (1890 [1896]) testified. The German emotional upset was heightened by the Boer War, in which Germans sympathized with the Boers and were indignant against the British. Without the British victory at Transvaal, Kehr writes, the Conservatives (Junkers) would never have been reconciled to the expansion of the fleet, which was regarded by the Junkers as the war instrument of industry, as contrasted with the army which they favored (1965, p. 154).

Detestation of Britain continued. Rudolph von Havenstein, president of the Reichsbank, is quoted as saying in a speech of September 25, 1914, presumably to the Reichsbank board, that their enemy was England, whose "jealousy and ill-will toward our economic flowering, our growing world trade and growing power at sea is (sic) in the final analysis the basic cause of the world war" (Feldman, 1993, p. 32).

The Overtaking

A favorite pastime of public figures is to pronounce who is first, and sometimes by how much. In his brilliant thesis on German industrialization, Pierre Benaerts sets out three such pronouncements. About 1820, Germany had a lag of at least half a century on the way to machinism. There was some progress in Prussia, but it was rare and rudimentary (1933a, p. 119). At the end of 1856, Gustav Mevissen, the Cologne banker, stated that Germany had been a hundred years behind France and England, but now had surpassed them thanks to the Darmstädter Bank (that he founded in 1853) (ibid., p. 277). In his chapter on foreign influences on German economic growth in the nineteenth century, Benaerts observes that German contributions were great too. Foreign capital and equipment led the way, but Germany in twenty years had made up a gap of more than fifty years. It is not clear from the context exactly when the twenty years ended, but it would appear to be in the 1850s (ibid., p. 368). Another source quotes Friedrich Engels saying that Germany was not yet up to the English standard in 1860, but altogether changed from the past (Böhme, 1968b, p. 54).

A generation later, relative positions were changing rapidly, especially in new industries: electricity, chemicals, automobiles, machinery, and even some branches of textiles. German steel had risen from 15 percent of the world's output in 1880 to 24 percent in 1913, while England's share was declining from 31 to 10 percent. (The U.S. share in 1913 was 42 percent [ibid., p. 97].) In contrast to independent and small firms in England— apart from a few prominent exceptions like Lever, Lipton, Courtaulds— leading German firms were large, organized in cartels or by vertical integration, in the fashion that Bernard Elbaum and William Lazonick have found missing in British business (see previous chapter). A study of British consular reports for the period 1875 to 1914 revealed many deficiencies in British marketing efforts: lack of languages, failure to study the market and to adapt goods to what was wanted, limited credit terms, reluctance to sell at all unless the order was large, failure to adapt to foreign measure, or foreign currency in quoting prices, and so on (Hoffman, 1933, chap. 3). German remittance men were disdained by the British as pushy and unmindful of the dignity of commerce: "shopkeepers, always; merchants never" (ibid., p. 177). German marketing techniques failed, however, to make much of a dent in British colonies and dominions, or to overcome the leading place of Britain in the major markets of Latin America, despite faster percentage gains (ibid., pp. 198, 201).

British shipping and banking held off German rivalry better than industry and trade. In shipping there were substantial German gains. Britain briefly lost the Atlantic blue ribbon for the fastest crossing first to the Kaiser Wilhelm der Grosse, built in 1897, and then to the Deutschland of 1900, before winning it back in 1906 with Mauretania. An international shipping conference including Germany and England was formed and broken up over deciding fair shares. By 1914, Hoffman states, Britain's monopoly had been lost but she still retained leadership on the seas (1933, pp. 213–21). The same sentiment was expressed in slightly different terms over a wider area by the *Daily Telegraph* in 1901 with regard to British finance and merchant shipping: "What is gone is our monopoly. What is not gone is our supremacy" (ibid., p. 93). In a related passage, Hoffman quotes the Hamburg shipping magnate, Albert Ballin, of the Hamburg-American line (Hapag): "The English saturated and conservative habits would make them negligible were it not for the large sums they have invested" (ibid., p. 97).

German rivalry with Britain in finance went back to the establishment of the Deutsche Bank in Berlin in 1872 specifically to finance German trade directly, rather than through London as the Hamburg banks had done. Plans to fill the gap in foreign trade finance went back at least to 1869 before the formation of the Reich. Georg von Siemens, a cousin of the electrical equipment manufacturer, was chosen to run the bank and wrote that his "goal was to make German export and import trade independent of Britain, the accomplishment of which would constitute a national deed as great as the conquest of any province" (Helfferich, 1923–25 [1956], p. 38). The Deutsche Bank initially set up branches in Hamburg and Bremen because of the difference in foreign-exchange practice between coastal and inland towns, and in addition a joint subsidiary with two other German banks in London. The last was abandoned for a direct London affiliate of its own in the fall of 1872, the only such branch of a German bank for ten years. In its 1871 annual report, the Deutsche Bank complained of the difficulties of direct relationships between Germany and overseas markets because of the preponderance of London, and the existence in Germany of the several German currencies—this before their consolidation into the mark. For prestige purposes the Deutsche Bank sold foreign exchange to the German navy at some cost to itself (ibid., pp. 38–53).

The early intention to move into direct foreign-exchange dealing got sidetracked by the boom of the *Gründerzeit*, and the Deutsche Bank for a time shifted its focus to domestic industry. In due course it returned to the foreign scene in a variety of ways, helping in the start of new banks in Italy, establishing overseas branches, making loans in the Middle East in competition with the British and French, floating foreign bonds. Success was not overwhelming, and the Bank withdrew its early subsidiaries in China and Japan, allowing some of its partners to manage overseas joint ventures. In due course von Siemens gave up the idea of bringing all foreign operations together in a Berlin unit, opting instead for decentralization and specialization (ibid., chap. 4, esp. pp. 111–20). In finance, as in merchant shipping and naval armament but not in electricity, chemicals, or machinery, the German effort fell short of overtaking Britain. Germany gained a place in the sun, but by no means a dominant place.

The effort had consequences at home and abroad. At home the social inferiority to England of conservatives, agrarians, bureaucrats, and academics,[1] partly felt openly, partly subconsciously was decisive for their rejection of the overbearing and economically superior enemy (Kehr, 1965, pp. 156–57). But Kehr goes on: while foreign policy was proclaimed as the major issue of the country, hatred of England was needed by these groups to hold down the proletariat, which was still dominated but in increasing social and spiritual rebellion. Abroad, the drive of Germany to reach her "due share" of world domination worried neighboring countries, which banded together to encircle the country (Böhme, 1968b, p. 102). The accidental spark at Sarajevo touched off the conflagration of World War I.

The Interwar Period

I see no need to go over events of the First World War, the Schlieffen plan that violated the German treaty with Belgium, or the unrestricted U-boat campaign that Admiral Tirpitz thought would win the war against Britain by starving it out—much like Air Chief Marshall Arthur Harris's belief in World War II that mass bombing of German cities would defeat Germany without necessity for invasion, or the belief that Germany would not have lost the war had it not been for the "stab in the back" by the home front, largely its Jewish members. War interrupted the normal life cycle of the country, distorted in any case by the sharp antagonism among social classes. The life-cycle model was rather displaced by one akin to Goldstone's pattern of revolution and breakdown. As the French Revolution produced the populist Napoleon, so the breakdown of the Weimar Republic gave rise to Hitler. Responsibility for Adolph Hitler's takeover of the chancellorship of the Reich in February 1933 can be divided among the Treaty of Versailles with its war-guilt and reparation clauses, the postwar inflation of 1919–1923, and the depression of 1928–1932, which produced unemployment of as many as 1.5 million in May and June 1932, or 15 percent of the working population. Versailles falls outside the scope of this study, but I cannot forebear saying that John Maynard Keynes's polemic, *The Economic Consequences of the Peace* (1919), however brilliantly written, overstated its deficiencies.

German inflation is of more economic interest because it raises a question whether it came about from simple errors of monetary policy or lay deep in the wood of German class antagonism. The contrast runs with the monetary reconstruction after World War II in Germany, discussed below. Thousands of pages have been written on the inflation, with deep insights and great subtlety, but the issue, to my mind, turns on whether German

---

[1]The conservative academic economist, Adolph Wagner, was strongly conscious of the feeling of insecurity in the Germany of the end of the nineteenth century, and urged Germans to develop a healthy sense of egotism like those of the French and British (Barkin, 1970, p. 140).

society in the immediate postwar period was capable of bearing the substantial burdens of reconstruction and reparations, bearing them possibly only if it were to develop enough cohesion to share them. Reparations fixed after Versailles were high, and Keynes's estimate that a figure of $10 billion was bearable, as opposed to the $40 billion he calculated was implicit in the Versailles treaty, or the $33 billion plus export taxes (to be paid over forty-two years) agreed on by a Reparations Commission in April 1921, was far more reasonable (Kindleberger, 1984 [1993], pp. 289ff). The question, however, was whether there was the will to pay.

The monetarist school on the German inflation holds that it came from overissue of marks by the Reichsbank, whereas the structural school believes that it lay in the inability of various segments of the economy to share burdens. There are many refinements to both broad theories, including within the monetary the international flow of capital that enabled reparations to be paid without too much stress when foreign capital came from abroad, largely the United States, but accelerated the rise of prices when foreign and German funds were repatriated or expatriated. In the structural theory, the question turns on what groups gain or lose from inflation and deflation— large and small industry; commerce; large and small farmers; professionals, including civil servants, lawyers, and teachers; and skilled and unskilled workers. The main political groups had survived the war more or less intact, as had their mutual antagonisms. The outflow of capital picked up in the spring of 1921, with the assassination of Erzberger in August 1921, and again more seriously with that of the finance minister, Walther Rathenau, in June 1922. No person was strong enough to rise above the contesting interests and work out a budget. An attempt to form a nonpartisan government under Wilhelm Cuno, an official of the Hamburg-American Line who had successfully negotiated with the Allies on behalf of his company, was a miserable failure. Admittedly Cuno was not a striking figure: Moritz Bohn called him a charming man who would have made an excellent reception clerk in a luxury hotel (Rupieper, 1979, p. 18). Cuno served from November 1922 to August 1923:

> When it came to financing resistance and preparing Germany for the long struggle with France [which with Belgium occupied the Ruhr in January 1923] Cuno clearly failed. This was due to a large extent to the attitude of the bourgeois parties in the Reichstag and industrial interest groups who were not prepared to base the government's policy on a real policy. These groups prevented the balancing of the budget and the modification of the tax system until the moment when the Reich's fiscal system broke down completely. (Ibid., p. 297)

I am not disposed to rehearse the arguments on various sides of the German inflation after World War I except for two that are critical to the thesis of this book: (1) the no-compromise attitudes of trade unions on the one hand and industry on the other on such issues as the eight-hour day, won by workers in the revolution of November 9, 1918, and blamed by industry, especially Hugo Stinnes in iron and steel, along with the strength of the particular unions in the civil service, the nationalized railroad, and coal mines, for the inflation; and (2) the decentralized character of German finance, which went back to the founding of the Reich in 1871 and was barely altered by Karl Helfferich, who was finance minister for most of the war.

Hugo Stinnes thought that lengthening the hours of work was more important to German stabilization than monetary reform, and that the restoration of the prewar ten and one-half-hour day would enable Germany once again to capture world markets (Feldman, 1993, p. 793). The decentralization-centralization issue in German finance was finally tackled in the summer of 1919 by Matthias Erzberger, who levied an income tax for the central government. The division of revenue in Germany was altered from 42 percent for the Reich, 22 percent for the states, and 36 percent for municipalities to 70, 10, and 22 percent respectively. Decentralization is valuable in times of peace, a handicap in emergencies such as war. Change back and forth, as in the case of Holland during the Napoleonic wars, is not readily done.

From the Dawes Plan to 1931

I choose not to go through the miniboom of the late 1920s that followed the end of inflation with the Rentenmark, the Dawes Plan, the establishment of the Reichsmark, and the considerable spurt in German economic output based on imported capital. Success of the Dawes loan, the New York tranche of which was oversubscribed, led to a burst of foreign bond flotation in New York, as unexpected financial successes have done from time to time. Much of the money going to Germany was spent on local improvements as well as industry, to the dismay of Schacht, then head of the Reichbank. The start of the New York boom in equities about March 1928 diverted American investor interest from foreign bonds to domestic stocks, and cut the capital flows to Germany, to countries in Latin America, and to Australia, which had all relied on foreign loans. German and Austrian banks turned as long as possible to short-term borrowing and such a dangerous practice as supporting the prices of their own shares, depleting their cash.

More fundamentally for the background of the depression of the 1930s, European recovery after 1925 took place in a world that had expanded output in many products purchased from Europe before 1914. International commodity prices began to slip from 1925 and were poised for further decline when the New York stock market crashed at the end of October 1929. The view has been widely held, on Keynesian analysis in which price levels do not play a significant role, that the great depression from 1929 to the outbreak of war in 1939, or at least the precedent armament effort, was primarily the fault of deflationary fiscal and monetary policies by President Hoover in the United States, Chancellor of the Exchequer Philip Snowden in Britain, Premier Pierre Laval in France, and Chancellor Heinrich Brüning in Germany, because of slavish adherence to the gold standard. Such a view slights the power of debt deflation, as world prices fell, slowly from 1925 and brutally when New York banks reacted to the crash by rationing credit to commodity brokers who depended on it. A further blow to world prices came with the appreciation of the dollar, franc, and Reichsmark by 40 percent in 1931, as the counterpart of the 30-percent depreciation of the pound sterling (Kindleberger, 1973 [1986]). In a refined analysis, deflationary policies can produce effects on both spending and prices, particularly if the prices are flexible and a policy produces expectations of further price declines (Temin, 1989; Eichengreen, 1992). But to ignore price movements on the ground of money illusion is to commit a gross error. Falling prices damage banks, making them restrict lending, regardless of government policy.

Be all that as it may, interest for this account of the German national cycle, with its differences from the standard pattern, lies in an issue lately raised in German historiography: whether Brüning had alternatives to his pursuit of deflation with the primary purpose of showing that it was impossible for Germany to pay reparations. A strong case has been made that he was constrained by the bylaws of the Reichsbank, by the commitments under the Dawes Plan more generally, and by the Standstill Agreement reached in July 1931 with foreign bankers. This granted a six-month grace period in which Germany would not have to repay short-term credits and made exchange depreciation awkward as it would raise the Reichmark value of foreign debts. Most important of all Brüning had no alternative (Luther, 1964, pp. 131ff), and this view has been supported in a series of article by a distinguished German economic historian, Knut Borchardt, mostly in German (but see 1979 [1991]; 1990; and for an author with an opposite viewpoint, Holtfrerich, 1982; 1990). The debate has lasted more than a decade.

New light was thrown on this question by the recent discovery of a transcript of a debate in September 1931, a week before Britain went off gold, over a memorandum by Wilhelm Lautenbach of the German Economics Ministry, arguing for a program of public works by the government to be financed by special credits from the Reichsbank. Present were distinguished economists such as Eucken, Colm, Neisser, Röpke, and Salin, and representatives of the government, present and past, including the former Socialist finance minister Hilferding. The discussion was lively, heated, and even dramatic, with interruptions from time to time by the Reichsbank president, Hans Luther, who thought his institution was in danger of violation, and by a number of others, often unidentified (Borchardt and Schötz, eds., 1991). There is in fact a Shakespearean quality to the debate over an issue fateful for Germany and the world. Brüning was not present, as also several high government officials, for the most part absent because of their duties. But Lautenbach, who in retrospect has been called "the German Keynes before Keynes," presented a plan almost exactly like that undertaken by von Papen in 1932 after Brüning's resignation "100 meters from the finish"—the Lausanne conference of the summer of 1932 which killed off reparations.

There is controversy whether Brüning's policies were guided in any degree by the east Elbian (Junker) agrarian interest, which also had a hand in persuading President von Hindenberg to not oppose Hitler as chancellor in 1933. I lack knowledge needed to evaluate such suggestions. According to Alexander Gerschenkron (1943), the Junkers led blessed lives over centuries, surviving war, peace, prosperity, depression, inflation, free trade, and tariffs by one or another device, such as governmental assistance in borrowing in hard times, paying off debt during inflationary periods. This pays perhaps too little attention to the losses of *Güter* (estates) by Junkers in the agricultural depressions of the 1820s and the 1880s. It does underline that fixing the eastern border of Germany on the Oder-Neisse line after World War II, and putting Junker territory left in Germany in the Soviet zone of occupation, was what finally finished off a dominant class, as the guillotine had done to French *financiers* and *officiers*.

As indicated earlier, the rise of Hitler is ascribed to many causes—Versailles, inflation, unemployment, German character, making it over determined—like an equation with more explanatory variables than unknowns. Hitler's policy of overstretch bears a strong resemblance to the policies of Napoleon, Louis XIV, and Philip II, part of the human condition that becomes manifest in less earth-shaking forms in the bubbles encountered in financial markets. It is difficult, however, to find it a response to the upswing in German output from 1933 to 1939, on some basis such as the Goldstein model of chapter 3 which has war following boom in a regular fashion.

Space is lacking to discuss the war, the latent hate that burst out in the treatment of Jews in concentration camps, and the working to death in factories on insufficient food of political prisoners and displaced persons from occupied territories.[2]

The Immediate Postwar Period

Defeat of Germany by the Allies, including an enormous contribution by the ground troops of the Soviet Union, introduced a new phase in German history. It started off curiously in the United States with a Joint Chiefs of Staff instruction to the American occupation forces, JCS 1067, that called for denazification, disarmament, democratization, and the like but added

---

[2]In his *Theory of Economic History*, Sir John Hicks notes that slaves are cared for when they are expensive; when cheap or if manumission has been promised they are not maintained but used up (1969, p. 127). In a visit to a concentration camp near Nordhausen in April 1945, I was told that in the nearby underground factory at Kohnstein, a strong man could work a twelve-hour schedule on minimal rations for six months, a thin or weak one for three, before dying. Twenty-thousand men and women worked at the plant at its peak. By the time the place was overtaken, 120,000 had worked there, of which 100,000 were dead (Kindleberger, 1945 [1989], p. 203).

that no steps should be taken to raise the level of living of the German people except insofar as was necessary "to prevent disease and unrest that might endanger occupation forces." This was a reflection of the Morgenthau Plan, named for the American secretary of the treasury under President Roosevelt, who was himself (Morgenthau), as were many of his staff, of Jewish origin. In essence the Morgenthau plan called for a return of Germany to an agricultural state, as opposed to an industrial one, to be specialized in Black Forest cuckoo clocks and Harz mountain canaries. In the surge of anti-German sentiment that arose with the revelation of the concentration camps and the deaths of 6-million Jews, Poles, and Russians at the hands of Nazi bestiality, such an attitude is readily explained. It did not last, nor did the French view that Germany should revert to its pre-1871 mosaic form with the Saar, the Ruhr, and other resource-rich areas occupied by the Allies for an unspecified period. Neither line of action was proof against the dependence of the rest of Europe on the German economy, both as an outlet for their goods and services and a source of capital goods.

I pass over the Potsdam agreement with its unsatisfactory zonal treatment of the reparations question, which ended in splitting off the Soviet zone of occupation from the three western zones: the insistence of the Soviet Union, first on removals of capital equipment as reparations, and when their widespread looting produced little that could be used, a demand for reparations out of current production; the inability to treat the four zones of occupation of Germany—Soviet, British, United States, and French—as a single unit and the need to fall back on the three western zones, especially in trade and monetary affairs; the progressive deterioration of the western zones and much of the rest of western Europe in the disastrous year 1946–1947 with its freezing that tied up transport, followed by flooding that ruined the spring wheat crop. Aid to Europe was provided by the U.N. Relief and Rehabilitation Agency (UNRRA), the $3,750 million British loan (Anglo-American Financial Agreement of 1946), military assistance to allied liberated territory, Government Aid and Relief in Occupied Areas (GARIOA) of Germany. In the spring of 1947 came a breakdown of trade between countryside and city in Germany, plus the inefficient substitution of cigarettes and private barter for money. In addition, a meeting of the western powers with the Soviet Union at the Council of Foreign Ministers in Moscow failed to resolve the questions of reparations and the treatment of the four zones of occupation as a single unit.

On his return to the United States in April 1947, Secretary of State George C. Marshall proposed that the countries of Europe including the socialist countries put forward a new plan for cooperation in economic recovery, with the United States to assist in a reasonable cooperative arrangement. The Economic Recovery Act was passed by the Congress in April 1948 and $14.1 billion of aid was furnished to the participating countries over the years to June 1952. The group did not include the eastern bloc, which regarded U.S. supervision of the use of its commodities as intrusive. At the same time as the Marshall Plan slowly got under way, German monetary reform was put into effect in three western zones. This had been planned in outline by the Colm–Dodge–Goldsmith report of May 1946 but had been held up awaiting agreement on its application to the four zones of occupation.

Again the details of monetary reform and the capital levy that followed it, to adjust the uneven distributional effects of the reduction of money and debt in all forms by one new deutsche mark for ten Reichsmarks, need not concern us. The dramatic recovery that followed passage of the Marshall Plan and monetary reform raises a number of questions interesting to economists and to policymakers more generally. Was the monetary reform a technical question that could have been pursued, for example in the early 1920s, eliminating the inflation of those years? Did it succeed only because the various interest groups that had created deadlock in the twenties had lost power—the Junkers dispossessed by the westward movement of the boundary; labor and peasant agriculture by Nazi measures in the 1930s; the army, industry, and the civil service in disrepute because of the loss of the war and subservience to Hitler? Was it possible only because of the occupation of Germany by foreign powers? Was Marshall Plan aid to German derisory, as some thought (Abelshauser, 1991) on the ground that economic recovery was well under way before American aid under this program began to arrive in volume? Or did the fact that aid was promised and would arrive to fill the pipelines mean that German manufacturers could begin to draw on supplies of materials and components because of assurance that they would be replaced (Borchardt and Buchheim, 1991)? The immediate spurt in output, reported and visible when monetary reform took place, was illusory to a considerable extent. Firms had been underreporting and hiding output for barter purposes when such output could be sold only at fixed prices for worthless money. With the introduction of good money, stocks emerged into the light, and output figures were corrected upward. But there is no doubt that monetary reform and the restoration of market-clearing prices for the arbitrary prices inherited from the Preisstop of October 1939 at the outbreak of the war, plus to at least a limited degree Marshall Plan aid, produced in the years from 1950 an economic miracle. The outbreak of the Korean War in June 1950 gave rise to a setback in the German balance of payments, occurring as it did simultaneously with banking deregulation. Firms borrowed heavily and bought heavily of foreign materials as their prices rose. The German credit in the European Payments Union was increased (Kaplan and Schleiminger, 1989, chap 6). In due course prices stabilized and German precipitous purchasing paid off. The West German economy was off to an economic miracle.

The Wirtschaftswunder (*Economic Miracle*)

German economic recovery was the work of new men. Denazification through questionnaires turned out to be a difficult if not impossible problem, but both in politics and in industry those strongly identified with Nazi aggression were retired. Chancellor Konrad Adenhauer reached out to welcome détente with France in such initiatives as the European Coal and Steel Community (ECSC) of 1950 and the European Economic Community (EEC) agreed to in the 1957 Treaty of Rome. German business turned outward. After years of autarky, rising men in firms sought positions in export in order to travel abroad. Part of the burst of energy came from the efforts of those at home to rebuild their sharply reduced level of living. Part was the drive of refugees and expellees from the eastern provinces, those driven out of former German territories in Poland and Czechoslovakia, and refugees who chose to move west from the Soviet zone of occupation. This stream grew in volume until the Soviet occupation authorities in August 1961 erected the wall that came down with dramatic effect in November 1989. The inflow of middle-class, skilled, impoverished Germans anxious to rebuild their fortunes provided a unique source of vitality. In addition, it and a mass movement of some skilled but largely unskilled workers from first Italy and Greece, then Yugoslavia and Turkey—the so-called guest workers—held down German wages. This had the result that increased sales resulted in increased profits which could be used for increased investment and still greater productivity, a positive feedback process that kept going until the social limits to absorption of foreign guests began to be reached. Old cartels and monopolies like I.G. Farben were broken up.

When the British devalued the pound in 1949, the German government adjusted the *Deutschemark* downward. At that level it proved to be undervalued against the dollar, and the trade surplus built up. The gain in foreign exchange reserves was used in part to clear up old debts from the Standstill period. Germany also acceded to requests of the American government to help support American troops stationed in the country, since German defense expenditure was limited and German security from Soviet attack was provided to a great extent by the United States. Reparations were paid to Israel, largely in kind in the form of prefabricated housing. A striking example of the resilience of the economy is furnished by an attempt in 1956 to dampen the export surplus by reducing tariffs on imports. It failed: while imports rose, exports rose more, an example of Hume's law that imports beget exports and of the British faith in the 1840s that there was no need for reciprocity in tariff reductions as added imports created added exports. Germany rapidly overtook Britain in its standard of living, as did other countries in Europe. After its two previous failures, however, it seemed not to strive for economic and political primacy, content to follow American leadership even as that was seen by many to be slipping.

Germany in Europe

The boom in Germany, as elsewhere in Europe, went on to about 1973 and came to be called a golden age (Cairncross and Cairncross, eds., 1992; Marglin and Schor, eds., 1990). Germany (and on the other side of the world Japan) grew faster than the rest of western Europe and all grew faster than the United States and the United Kingdom. The British nonetheless regarded it as a golden age because their growth rate was greater than over any historical period of similar length for which data are available. The fact that all grew together does not invalidate the notion of a national growth cycle as discussed in chapter 2, perhaps, but the experience does raise a considerable question about whether rising countries inevitably challenge an existing leader for economic primacy. Neither Japan nor Germany challenged the United States for leadership in the west, content to leave it locked in a superpower struggle with the Soviet Union. Slowly, however, West Germany looked to the rest of Europe.

French interest in postwar Europe was in a leadership role. Fear of Britain as a contender led President deGaulle in 1963 to veto Britain's application to join the EEC. Later, when France saw the rising power of Germany in Europe as it gained economic strength and numbers, she was readier to admit Britain and other members of the European Free Trade Area as dilution to German dominance. There were further issues of exchange rates and the formation of a European central bank, in which there was latent disagreement between France and Germany, but the German view seemed likely to prevail.

German policy toward western Europe and indeed to the world economy was complicated by its relationship to East Germany. Germany might well have striven harder to push ahead with European integration if it had not been continuously looking over its shoulder to the east. With the collapse of the wall in 1989, and the joining of East with West Germany, preoccupation with *Ostpolitik* became overwhelming. A mistake was made in converting the East German mark to the deutsche mark at a 1:1 ratio, understandable perhaps politically, but a disastrous error that raised the real income of eastern German workers well above their productivity, which had been undermined in the socialist state by thirty years (since the wall went up) or forty-four years (since Soviet occupation) of little incentive to work and save. Productivity in western Germany had been far higher than that in the east (except for isolated spots like Berlin, Leipzig, and Dresden in the nineteenth century) (Borchardt, 1966 [1991]), but the gradient was much steeper after rapid growth in the west, apathy in the east, and the westward movement of many of the more energetic citizens. The need to support eastern incomes and levels of living unbalanced the Bonn government's budget, leading the Bundesbank to fear inflation and tighten monetary policy, which led to unemployment west as well as east. At the same time, the enlargement of Germany and the collapse of the threat from the Soviet Union, plus the possibility of American economic decline, led the country to be more assertive. One indication of increasing assertiveness was the beginning of a tendency of German diplomats to follow French practice of insisting on speaking one's native language, even when the speaker knew English well as did all others at a meeting (*The New York Times*, February 23, 1992, p. 7). Like Japan, too, it now wants a seat on the Security Council of the United Nations in view of its economic and political power equal or superior to those of the United Kingdom, France, China, and Russia.

The Aging of Germany

In a book I have not had an opportunity to read but have seen reviewed (Tilly, 1993), *The Fading Miracle* (1992), Herbert Giersch, Karl-Heinz Paqué, and Holger Schmieding point to the slowdown in the German economy after about 1973 with shrinking productivity relative to wage increases, insistent union demands for higher wages, "and a consensus that political and economic priorities ought to shift away from mere material progress to raising the quality of life and to achieving more social justice" (1992, p. 160, quoted by Tilly, 1993, p. 943). It is significant that the book was written in 1991 before the difficulties of integrating the East into the West German economy were fully evident, which, the reviewer observes, may cast doubt on their positive view that integration would lead to a second *Wirtschaftswunder* such as that that prevailed from 1948 to 1973 (ibid.). Again it is awkward to have to judge a book by its review, even one by a distinguished economic historian, but I infer that the three authors have an implicit model that is not widely different from the nation cycle of chapter 2.

One further late entry into the historiography is a 1994 issue of *Daedalus* on "Germany in Transition." Many articles are relevant to the notion that Germany is aging, especially that of Kurt Lauk, and most agree that finding the right path to recovery is enormously complicated by the problem of absorbing East Germany with its low productivity, high unemployment rate, and demographic breakdown. Kocka and Lauk both stress the need for Germany to find a new place in a changing world environment (Kocka, 1994, p. 189), which will be possible only when productivity increases to the world competitive level (Lauk, 1994, p. 60). It is suggested that this may require a work week longer than thirty-five hours, and vacations shorter than five weeks (ibid., p. 64), conveying an echo of the Stinnes view mentioned earlier in this chapter.

At the start of this chapter I referred to a report produced by the economics ministry and approved by the Kohl cabinet suggesting that Germany was in danger of "forfeiting its top position in the world economy" because of high unemployment, high taxes, a short work week, stifling bureaucracy and an aging work force" and recommending hard work, punctuality, and community spirits. As if in rebuttal to these views, an interview in the *The New York Times* with Hilmar Kopper, president of the Deutsche Bank, elicited the view that the Germans were looking at the situation too pessimistically (September 13, 1993, pp. D1, D4). Mr. Kopper cited some grounds for pessimism—a decline in output in 1993 and prospects of little or no growth for 1994, rising unemployment, a short work week of 37.5 hours and six weeks of vacation (including public and religious holidays), labor production costs among the highest in the world, and recession abroad that hurt exports, which had always been the driving force of German recoveries. These negative factors, he said, did not mean that Germany was dropping down to the minor league, citing strengths like "the nation's political and social stability, its powerful and stable currency and its highly skilled and well-educated work force." The solution: "We all have to work longer hours. It's that simple" (ibid.).

Perhaps it is that simple. Perhaps, on the other hand, the German economy, like many before it, is becoming somewhat rigidified.

10

The United States

Shortly before 1976 I was asked by *Foreign Affairs* to write an essay on
two centuries of U.S. economic foreign policy to help celebrate the country's
two-hundredth anniversary. The result was published in the January 1977
issue of that periodical, again in a collection of parallel essays in a book of
the Council on Foreign Relations in New York (Bundy, ed., 1977), and a
third time in a collection of my own (1990). I see no need to go over the
ground again except with the broadest possible brush. Thus I start this
chapter after the end of the "golden age," in 1968 or 1971 or 1973 depending on the turning point chosen. I leave the description of the U.S.
nation cycle—from a small country wrapped in isolation to a country claiming world dominance or leadership—to the earlier exercise, and focus, after
the briefest possible summation, on the beginnings of the debated American decline.

The two centuries from 1776 to 1976 marked a movement from a small
country, anxious to stay out of world affairs after throwing off British colonial rule, to slow but sure involvement and then leadership in world affairs.
The major features of that movement are as follows:

- No aristocracy or underclass apart from African slaves in the south
  and some white indentured servants. The country, that is, was mostly
  middle class at the start.
- Vast quantities of land, starting with the thirteen colonies and adding acquisitions from France, Spain, and Mexico to achieve a high
  land/labor ratio; high wages, since a laborer could always quit to

go west and farm; and a strong incentive for labor-saving innovation.

- Massive immigration in the middle of the nineteenth century, Irish in the 1846 potato famine, German a few years later, and southeastern European from the 1880s, all of which converted the country from one developing with unlimited supplies of land to one with unlimited supplies of labor, following the well-known model of Sir Arthur Lewis (1954).
- After initial export-led growth with timber, shipping, tobacco, cotton, and sugar, a move by the north to import substitution, with tariffs to protect industry, adding another north-south disagreement to that over slavery, which led to the disastrous war between the states (Civil War) in the 1860s.
- Beginnings of investment overseas in labor-saving manufactures.
- The spread of railroads and western settlement, which exhausted the frontier of cheap land.
- Trust and trust busting.
- Increasing involvement in international affairs with the Black Ships of Commodore Perry in Japan in 1854, the Spanish-American War of 1898, gaining of independence for Cuba and American protectorates over Puerto Rico and the Philippines, plus the Boxer rebellion in China in 1900.
- Belated (1917) entry into World War I because of the "special relationship" with Britain and unrestricted submarine warfare launched by Germany.
- Institution of mass production techniques before and during World War I.
- Refusal after November 1918 to take a responsible role in world affairs, rejecting the Versailles treaty and membership in the League of Nations and staying aloof from reparations from Germany, while insisting on collecting war debts from the Allies.
- The coming of age of the automobile and electricity in the 1920s, with relocation of housing and industry.
- The stock-market crash of 1929 following a bubble starting in the spring of 1928, sharp pressure on world prices and trade with deep depression, exacerbated by the Hawley–Smoot tariff of June 1930.
- Gradual responsible involvement in international economic affairs and, after World War II, impressive world economic leadership: a generous settlement of Lend-Lease, UNRRA, the British loan, relief for both allies and defeated enemy countries, the Bretton Woods institutions of the International Monetary Fund and World Bank; ending in the European Recovery (Marshall) Plan (and help for Japan), that sought to push European countries into closer cooperation in trade, industry, and finance.
- Signing on to the General Agreement on Tariffs and Trade (GATT), and assistance for development of Third World countries.

• Conducting a policy of containment of the socialist bloc in the "Cold War" until it collapsed in 1989.

In a separate paper on "The United States and the World Economy in the Twentieth Century," I compiled a schematic table showing how U.S. economic foreign policy had evolved along several functional lines deemed important for the attention of a world economic leader: goods markets, the market for foreign exchange, capital flows, coordination of national macroeconomic policies, and serving as a lender of last resort in financial crisis (Kindleberger, 1989b) (Table 10–1). These interest areas had grown out of a study of the world depression of the 1930s that I ascribed, in its length, width, and depth, to the fact that the United Kingdom had been too weak economically to assume the role of lender of last resort in the bank run that ricocheted from country to country after its start in Austria in May 1931, while the United States (and France) were unwilling to do so (Kindleberger, 1973 [1986], chap. 14). After World War II, the American attitude was transformed: The country took strong roles in these functional areas to some such time as 1971, following which its commitments began to erode. To get the information on a single page, I abbreviated heroically, and defined the abbreviations tersely. Most of what the table sets out will be known to students of the economic history of the period; others can obtain a fuller explanation from the original paper. The use of the device, however, together with the earlier parsimonious summary, permits this chapter to begin at the end of the Golden Age, about 1970, when signs of the decline of the United States as the world's leading economic power began to appear.

The Golden Age, from 1945 or 1950 for a quarter of a century, was one of unchallenged American preeminence in economic questions, but with indications of catching up abroad and slippage on the part of the United States. In new industries—aircraft, computers, electronics, pharmaceuticals, inertial guidance that allowed humans to set foot on the moon, medical equipment like the cat scan—the wide gap of the 1950s was beginning to be narrowed in the following decade, especially by Germany, Japan, Sweden, and Switzerland, but also by France and Italy. A large flow of direct investment emerged from the United States over the industrial world, evoking fears of "overforeignization" as decried by Jean-Jacques Servan Schreiber in *The American Challenge* (1968). It gradually slowed down and was followed by foreign direct investment in the United States. More significant were the slowdown in the growth of productivity, the decline in savings, twin deficits in the federal budget and the current account of the balance of payments, the shift from manufacturing to services in what Daniel Bell called the "post-industrial state" (1976), and especially increasing preoccupation with finance, with the buying and selling of assets rather than goods, and the development of new, or revival of old, financial instruments, instead of new products and processes in manufacturing.

Productivity

There is general agreement that the rest of the developed world and much of the underdeveloped has caught up a long way to the United States in productivity since 1950, but there remains a series of questions as to how much, when, and why. In the first place are measurement difficulties, whether to be guided by output per worker (or per worker-hour), especially in services where output is difficult to measure, or by total factor productivity, with allowance for capital, and if so whether only physical capital or also human capital embodied in the training of workers, and how that is measured, and even whether some attention should be paid to "land" or physical resources. In this last category the United States' former abundance is turning to scarcity as more and more resource-based commodities move from the export to the import list (Vanek, 1963).

How much productivity has slowed down absolutely becomes a highly technical matter depending, as just said, on the measure used. Much also depends on the industry under discussion, whether low tech such as textiles, automobiles, and steel or high tech like aircraft, computers, and scientific instruments. One measure comes from trade balances in manufactured goods, although these are affected overall by substantial changes in exchange rates that occurred in the 1980s, first up as the dollar appreciated during the Reagan years of "benign neglect" until the Plaza Accord of September 1985, then down to the end of the decade. Charts show large import surpluses in 1991 compared with 1978, in automobiles, other consumer goods, apparel, and household goods, and increased percentages of the U.S. market for high-tech goods being taken over by foreigners, especially in computers and scientific instruments (Baily, 1993, p. 31, fig. 1). But all seems not to be lost. The automobile industry has achieved substantial gains in efficiency in the last several years, through "downsizing," that is, letting go large numbers of middle-management and supervisory personnel and closing inefficient plants such as the Ford facility at Willow Run, Michigan, built in World War II to produce aircraft. Large integrated steel plants based on iron ore have given way to smaller units, located near consuming centers, using steel scrap in place of iron ore and many of them electricity instead of coal (Acs, 1984). Service industries, especially in finance, spent years adding office machinery such as computers without letting workers go, but since 1987 have increasingly reduced numbers without loss of output. Paul David has suggested that gains in productivity may lag years behind the invention and investment in capital equipment that ultimately make them possible, citing electrical machinery in manufacturing that took more than eighty years to make a major reduction in costs (1990). In particular, firms in molecular biology and genetic engineering are growing rapidly, absorbing much venture capital, without thus far showing profits. Their promise, if real, lies ahead.

Table 10-1 U.S. Foreign Economic Policy and
the World Economy—Twentieth Century[a]

Function	1901–14	1919–29	1930–39	1945–70	1971 to 1990	Notes
Goods markets	Strong protection, moderated 1913	Antidumping tariff, ignore 1927 tariff truce, resist Stevenson rubber plan	Hawley–Smoot irresponsible; begin reversal RTAA, 1934	ITO, GATT, Dillon, Kennedy etc. rounds, sale of commodities out of strategic reserve Combined, Boards, NTBs	Bilateral XR, MFA, soya bean "shocku," AOPEC embargo left to oil companies	Gephardt threat of bilateral retaliation, ambivalence in commodity agreements, GSP
Foreign exchange	"Automatic" under gold standard	FRBNY interest in European cooperation	Thomas amendment, change gold price, torpedo WEC, Tripartite Monetary Agreement, silver price	Bretton Woods, British loan, Marshall Plan, gold pool swaps, G-10, SDR	10% devaluation floating, benign neglect, Louvre to correct 1982–85 appreciation	Gold bugs: Mundell, etc., free fall? Liquidity a nonproblem
Capital flows	Mature debtor repays FDI	Dawes loan, spurt X 1924–28, halted 1928 when NYSE boomed	Widespread default, stop lending to all but Canada	X-M Bank, World Bank, regional DBs, IET, VCRP, MCP	Bank lending to sovereign states after "crime of 1971," Baker and Brady plans on Third-World debt, big inflow,	Baker insistence on banks continued lending, Black Monday 1987

					Treasury bonds, real estate, equities	
Coordination of monetary, fiscal policy	Gold standard, Aldrich Comm., Fed. Res. Act	Sterilize war gold, 1927 Ogden Mills CB meeting	Feeble attempt to coordinate B of E	IMF, OECD, Working Party #3, Chequers	Carter program, locomotives, summit meetings ineffective	Inability of U.S. to persuade Japan to limit export-led growth, FRG to relax about inflation
Lender of last resort	Not needed	Isolationism, insist on repayment of war debts	Too little too late, sabotage World Economic Conference	Marshall Plan etc., swaps, Paris Club, G-10, Basel Agreement	Mexico 1982, Basel protocol 1975	Unclear where responsibility lies today

aSee chapter 12 for discussion of some of these points.

Abbreviations:

AOPEC—Arab Organization of Petroleum Exporting Countries; B of E—Bank of England; CB—central banks; DB—development banks; FDI—foreign direct investment; FRBNY—Federal Reserve Bank of New York; FRG—Federal Republic of Germany; GATT—General Agreement on Tariffs and Trade; GSP—Generalized System of Preferences; G-10—group of 10 leading financial countries; IET—Interest Equalization Tax; IMF—International Monetary Fund; ITO—International Trade Organization; MCP—Mandatory Control Program; MFA—Multi-Fiber Agreement; NTB—Non-Tariff Barrier; NYSE—New York Stock Exchange; OECD—Organisation for Economic Co-operation and Development; RTAA-Reciprocal Trade Agreements Act; SDR—Specialized Drawing Rights; VCRP—Voluntary Credit Restraint Program; WEC—World Economic Conference; WP—Working Party; X—export of capital; X-M—exports minus imports, or trade balance; XR—export restraints.

Source: Kindleberger, 1989, pp. 290–91. Reprinted with permission from Harvester/Wheatsheaf.

I put aside the possibility that the decline in productivity in the United States from perhaps 1964 (Gordon, 1993) to the end of the 1980s is in process of reversal, and focus on the decline that preceded it. First, decline was relative, not absolute, as countries that had been held back in the war caught up and pushed ahead in certain industries, if not overall (Abramovitz, 1986 [1989], chap. 7). Technology, in the view of many, is a public good, freely or almost freely available to all with the capacity to adapt it effectively (Nelson and Wright, 1992). Richard Nelson and Gavin Wright do not dismiss the possibility that the United States may be in process of slipping to "second, third, or fifth rank in productivity and per capita income," but emphasize technology and its improvement through innovation as a world public good. (ibid., p. 1961).

Two major analyses of American productivity are books by William Baumol, Sue Anne Batey, and Edward N. Wolff (1989) and the MIT team of Michael Dertouzos, Richard Lester, and Robert Solow (1989). The former relates the relative decline in technology to other elements in economic slowdown: the fall of savings and investment, surge in capital exports, diversion of scientific and engineering attention to the military, inadequate attention to education, and possibly increased scarcity of natural resources (Williamson, 1991, pp. 52, 67). The MIT study focuses on bad management, an area spotlighted by the troubles experienced by General Motors, International Business Machines, U.S. Steel, LTV, Sears, and a number of other huge companies. Some are making heroic efforts in the 1990s to overcome deficiencies.

One rather bizarre (as it happens French) view is that the United States gave up the fight for technological superiority when the Congress in 1971 refused to allocate funds for building a supersonic transport airplane (Gimpel, 1976, p. 14). In testimony to the Congress in April 1992, W. W. Rostow observed that President J. F. Kennedy, one of the few American leaders interested in technological innovation, had asked James Webb, then head of the space program, NASA, why so few peacetime innovations had been spun off by the exercise as had happened from military invention in World War II (1992, pp. 3–4). More recently since the collapse of the Soviet bloc, the military unit in the Pentagon, DARPA (Defense Advanced Research Project Agency), has been exploring the extent to which military research and development can be transformed to peacetime purposes.

Explanations for the decline in productivity since the 1960s include, along with bad management (sometimes described as advancing institutional sclerosis), outside shocks such as the rise in oil prices in 1973 and 1979 at the hands of the Organization for Petroleum Exporting Countries (OPEC); the inflationary explosion of the 1970s, which led business to economize on its own R&D; and especially the shift of American attention to finance with its preoccupation with the short rather than the long run, and buying and selling of assets rather than goods and services.

Saving

One explanation for the decline in productivity is the slowdown in domestic capital investment in the United States. Part of this comes from U.S. corporate enterprise investing abroad, although this should be offset to a degree by foreign investment—often with new techniques—coming here. Corporate saving available for investment in the United States may have declined slightly. More significant, especially as an indication of American values, is the downward movement of household savings from 9 or 10 percent in the 1960s, already well below Japanese and German rates of close to 20 and 15 percent respectively, to 3 or 4 percent in the 1980s, and much of that in contractual rather than voluntary form, that is, in insurance policies and pensions. Household debt—negative saving—has risen from $359 billion in 1965 to nearly $3.3 trillion in 1988, with a small acceleration in the rate of increase in 1985 (Pollin, 1990). The figures are in nominal terms; after correction for inflation, which encouraged borrowing, the rate of increase was lower. In one jeremiad about the American economy, J. Irwin Miller, a successful retired businessman, stated that the country that used to put the future ahead of the present no longer does so (Miller, 1991, p. 43). Some of the decline in savings at lower income levels is the result of the difficulties of getting along in inflationary times, especially with rising costs for education in college and medical care. Increased skewness in income distribution should raise savings in the upper income quintiles, but seems not to have done so. President Reagan's program for tax reduction in 1981 was intended to increase savings and hence investment. It failed. As the marginal tax rate was reduced from 70 to 28 percent (before rising slightly under President Bush), retained income seems to have been spent on consumption: second and third houses, travel, luxury apparel, cars, jewelry, yachts, and the like, rather than being saved and invested. Some savings were held in liquid form to take advantage of "investment" opportunities in funds for mergers and acquisitions, takeovers, or arbitrage in securities of companies possibly subject to takeovers; in other words, held liquid for trading in assets rather than being invested in capital equipment for production.

There is a powerful theory in consumption, the life-cycle hypothesis, that families save in youth and spend in old age, as income first rises and then falls (Modigliani, 1980, vol. 2). Such a pattern applies well to the national life cycle of chapter 2, as illustrated by the post-1971 decline of U.S. household savings. But there are difficulties in applying it to families, as exemplified by econometric testing. On a theoretical level, if the pattern were valid one would expect substantial demand for wasting life annuities, which would be paid out over an individual's or a married couple's retired life. Interest in this sort of investment is limited, suggesting a bequest motive for leaving monies to children. Second, there are problems with the pattern in both youth and age. In youth today, people borrow rather than save, for education, housing (through mortgages), and household goods and consumption—with credit cards, installment loans, charge accounts. Some of this is paid down in the individual case in middle age and beyond, which constitutes saving. Incomes of the elderly are supported by Social Security transfers, indexed for increases in the cost of living, from the working to the retired population. Less significant, the appetite of older people, for goods at least, if not perhaps for services such as medical expense, travel, and dining out, tends to decline.

But if the life-cycle hypothesis encounters difficulty in application to the individual American family, it does well for the United States as a whole. The country saved at high levels during mature robust growth, and has now slowed down in aging.

A third source of decline in savings was the explosion of the federal budget deficit. This occurred in spite of, or owing to, the massive tax reduction of 1981 that was intended to increase savings and investment, raise national income, and thereby increase total tax returns despite lower rates, as predicted by the U-shaped Laffer curve. Expenditure for entitlements such as Social Security transfers and health care kept rising; military or defense spending did not decline, but even expanded with the beginning of the Strategic Defense Initiative (SDI) ("Star Wars" program). In the eyes of many, the federal government was neglecting maintenance of roads, bridges, waterways, dams, sewerage systems, the cleaning up of sites damaged by toxic waste, and investment in new infrastructure such as airports. A certain amount of deferred maintenance accumulated at the state and local level as well.

A case could be made that the defense expenditure evoked a competitive response in the Soviet Union, which lacked the administrative capacity to handle it and broke down, thereby justifying the American effort. On this showing, a substantial "peace dividend" might be said to be available for tackling deferred maintenance. The collapse of the Soviet Union, however, has destabilized the world in various regions such as the former Yugoslavia and Somalia, and for a time in the Middle East, tempering the willingness of the U.S. government to cut military spending drastically. In addition, resistance to reduced military procurement came from affected localities, concerned with employment. President Clinton's major program of deficit reduction was passed in the Senate in 1993 by the single vote of the president of the Senate, Vice President Albert Gore, after the Senate as a whole produced a tie. Republicans voted against the tax bill en bloc in a partisan exercise, and a significant number of Democrats did so as well, even after concessions had been offered them by the administration. It proved easy to vote for tax reduction in 1981, hard to reverse course even modestly a dozen years later, despite the demonstration that the earlier action had been mistaken. A second crisis occurred with the defeat in Congress of President Clinton's health plan providing for universal coverage requiring tax money to care for those not qualified for employer contributions or membership in health maintenance organizations (HMOs).

In one view of a competent economist, Robert Eisner, too much is made of the federal deficit. He would subtract from official figures capital assets accumulated by the federal government, surpluses run by state and local governments, and the inflation tax (inflation times the national income). In so doing he converts a $155-billion 1988 fiscal year federal deficit into a $44-billion surplus (Eisner, 1992, Table 13.2, p. 257). When it comes to balance of international indebtedness—the value of U.S. claims and assets held abroad measured against those held by foreigners against the United States—he finds other measurement difficulties—investments valued at cost instead of market or replacement, gold at $41 an ounce instead of a market value closer to $400—and manages to transform a negative balance of indebtedness for 1987 of $368 billion into a surplus of $59 billion based on market value, or $116 billion based on replacement cost. The balance of international indebtedness is a most unsatisfactory concept, but the rise in the unadjusted position from plus $141 billion in 1981 to minus $368 billion in 1987, a change for the worse of $509 billion, is not drastically altered by a shift to Eisner's measures, which show a deterioration from a surplus of $390 billion 1980 on market-value calculation to $59 billion in 1987 (a worsening of $331 billion), or from plus $527 billion in 1980 to plus $116 billion (off by $410 billion) using replacement cost (ibid., Table 13.8, p. 266). The levels are unsatisfactory as measures, but the change measured on a consistent basis tells a story of slippage.

The Balance-of-Payments Deficit

It is a tyro economic error to connect any two items in the balance of payments, or a single domestic item in national income accounts with an international one, such as any one item in the balance of payments. In general equilibrium, all items determine all items, like the location of balls in a bowl, to use the simile of Alfred Marshall. If the federal deficit were reduced, the reduction might not improve the deficit in the balance of payments by an equal amount—in fact would be most unlikely to do so—as some reduction in federal expenditure or increases in taxes would be offset in part by reductions in other savings. Nevertheless it is a truism that increases in domestic savings, without offsetting increases in spending, would improve the balance of payments on current account.

It is also accepted by economists that a reduction in imports or an increase in exports of a given amount will not improve the balance of payments to the same extent, since expenditure diverted from imports or added by exports raises domestic income and spending and spills again into incremental imports. An economist hesitates, therefore, to identify change in any item in international payments with a change in the balance, since other things will not remain equal.

Having said as much, there is a dynamic case for associating continuous improvements in productivity and continuous innovations that lead to expanded exports with improvement in the balance of payments. A new export improves the balance of payments on the instant, and while it alone would be reversed at least in part when its repercussions work their way through the national income accounts, in a highly progressive economy it may be that a new innovation comes along with a new transitory export surplus, and with a third innovation, a third ephemeral surplus. The integral of all results in an improvement in the balance. Per contra, in an economy that is losing comparative advantage in one item after another, the transitory deficits, cumulated, add up to a worsening of the balance on current account. It is difficult to determine the weight to be attached to this model, given the many other factors affecting the current account: exchange-rate appreciation from 1981 to 1985, depreciation that followed, inflation in the United States and unemployment in Europe, and the dynamic series of innovations coming from Japan.

The value attached to the exchange rate as a determinant of the balance has been a matter of considerable controversy among economists. Some hold that the rate is never undervalued or overvalued but adheres rigorously to purchasing-power parity (McCloskey and Zecher, 1976), a view that commands little acceptance, while others insist that the U.S. deficit has been produced in the early 1980s primarily by overvaluation, working with a two-year lag, and is in process of moving into surplus—or at least in that direction, from the depreciation that followed the Louvre agreement of 1987 (Krugman, 1990a). In my judgment, the absorption model that ties the current account to the difference between savings overall and business investment is the principal operator, but I would make some allowance for the effects of the dynamic model where a succession of transitory effects for relative innovation at home, or abroad, play a role.

Finance

Along with the decline in the rate of productivity increase went a strong movement into finance. The phenomenon is not new: Italian city-states moved from trade and industry to finance (Florence and Genoa to a greater extent than Venice perhaps); Bruges, Antwerp, Amsterdam, and London did so as well. American interest in banking was early: Michel Chevalier noted in 1834 that in settling a new town, Americans built first an inn with a bar, next a post office, several houses, a church, a school, a print shop, and then a bank, this in communities that were still populated by bears and rattlesnakes (1836, vol. 1, pp. 262–63). He also mentions Port Carbon, Pennsylvania, three times in various writings, with thirty houses, burned tree stumps in unpaved streets, but a sign saying "Office of Deposit and Discount, Schuykill Bank" (e.g., ibid., p. 264). Thomas Jefferson described the period as one of Bancomania, according to Chevalier, and gambling was endemic. Thus behavior along the lines of the 1980s is not altogether new. It was, however, a considerable departure from the American behavior of 1945 to 1975, with successive financed innovation in conglomerates; leveraged buyouts; mergers and acquisitions; contracts for futures and options; and bundling up and selling of mortgage, credit card, installment, and other forms of debt as new types of securities. Speculative fads came and went in real estate investment trusts (Reits), Third World debt, mutual funds, junk bonds.

Commenting on the Netherlands, P. W. Klein has been quoted as saying that finance is not the worst occupation (I assume the measure is moral) but that it is divisive of society (Schama, 1977 [1992], p. 35). It is difficult for merchants and entrepreneurs to make fortunes on the scale of bankers and security dealers. Adam Smith contrasts speculation with regular, established, and well-known branches of business, saying that "it seldom happens that great fortunes are made in the latter but in consequence of a long life of industry, frugality and attention," whereas "sudden fortunes" are sometimes made in speculation (1976 [1987], pp. 113–14). In nineteenth-century England, the richest men were nobles who inherited large amounts of land and urban property, but next came those engaged in business and financial occupations (which are not distinguished from one another), with infrequent fortunes built up in manufacturing and industry (Rubenstein, 1980, p. 59). In a world permeated by the spirit of envy and emulation, seeing financial experts become rich by handling paper rather than producing tangible objects may incite others to push for higher rewards when, on the basis of "satisficing," quitting while one is ahead, there might have been little incentive to demand more.

The difficulties compound when there are large rents involved. Television frequencies were originally awarded gratis to applicants, who made large sums from the profitability of television advertising. In due course, owners of sports teams raised the prices at which they would allow television stations to show their games. A considerable portion of the profits of stations and advertisers went to them. Athletes and their agents moved in, and bargained for a substantial share of the excess profit or rent. Team play lost ground to individual performance in popular sports, and the system by which players signed lifetime contracts gave way to a "free agent" system, whereby an individual was able to auction his services after a probationary period. When one baseball pitcher negotiated a higher contract than another, the latter sulked and wanted more, even though he was already earning millions of dollars a year, enough to finance early retirement unless an unscrupulous financial adviser took advantage of his possible financial innocence. Team play decayed not only in sports but in professional business. In law offices, for example, it had been customary to be underpaid, not only as an associate but also in the first years of partnership, and overpaid as an old partner whose capacity to attract clients had slipped. In the 1980s in the United States, young partners fought for all they could command, and if frustrated would split off and form a new firm. Similar loss of lasting partnerships occurred in accounting, architecture, finance, advertising. The "star system" crept into academic life as well, with competition for the leading researchers (rather more than leading teachers) being bid for not only with salary but with reductions in duties, such as teaching and administrative work, less highly valued by the individual. Widening difference in emoluments between stars and journeymen in frequent instances in a game of winner-take-all was hard on morale and subversive of more stable systems, such as promotion from within and promotion by seniority.

In manufacturing, the returns to finance and to stars in sports and the professions led to a push for higher salaries, perquisites, benefits such as stock options, and large payments on retirement and even on discharge. To the extent that salary or options depended on the price of a company's stock, focus turned to short-run income statement, away from long-term growth. The tax system distorted resource allocation, since for the most part capital gains were taxed at lower rates than income, and many financial people pushed hard for exempting capital gains from taxation altogether.

Preoccupation with income and wealth, moreover, encouraged gambling on the one hand, and swindles or malfeasance on the other. Reuven Brenner developed a theory that gambling on long odds as in lotteries is a tactic of lower income groups who find it their only opportunity, if a poor one mathematically, to escape upward from the lower middle or lowest class in a single bound (1983). Swindles, as I have observed before, come in two forms: one when the temptation to take risks spreads widely in an inflationary time or bubble—with more people anxious to get rich, the temptation to exploit them becomes irresistible. In the other instance, those who have taken risks and are in danger of being caught may swindle to make good their losses and hide their misdeed (Kindleberger, 1978 [1989], chap 5). The late Fred Hirsch, in a reference that I have misplaced, raised the question whether the world, including the United States (though he was British), had begun to consume its moral capital. One can understand the force behind the remark as applied to the 1980s in the United States, but at the same time doubt that the world has ever had much. Possibly the stock of moral capital moves in cycles. One German economic historian ventured the idea that the East India Company of the eighteenth century was the most corrupt organization in world history (van Klaveren, 1957). If there are cycles in financial crimes, the 1980s with Ivan Boesky, Martin Siegel, Michael Milken, Charles Keating, and colleagues stand out. It is possible that the establishment of courses on ethics in business schools will reduce the numbers in finance tempted to cut corners. Many ethicists, however, would think that late in the individual life cycle.

Polarization

The decline of team play and possibility of weakening moral scruples raises the question whether the United States has become more polarized as a society, with less readiness to compromise among different classes, races, income groups, sexes, Americans of different national origin, management, and labor. The widening gap between rich and poor and the thinning of the middle class, which affords a step for those on the way up and a cushion for those coming down from the upper levels, diminishes social cohesion. The resistance of the white poor to steps like school busing, affirmative action, and efforts at racial integration in general is part and parcel of the antipathy between black and Irish in Boston, black and Koreans in Los Angeles, blacks and Hasidic Jews in the Crown Heights district of New York. Faith in the melting pot, which followed the wave of immigration into the country before World War I, except for Asians, has waned. There are substantial gains. The inflation of World War I brought black men into northern factories for the first time; that of World War II gave opportunities for black women to escape the trap of domestic service and move into white-collar jobs in offices and stores. Discrimination against professionals of Jewish origin is almost completely gone, as student bodies, faculties, college presidencies, law firms, and especially suburbs that used to discriminate against Jews have shown. Ambitious and hard-working Asians move ahead on the basis of merit. The problem in lower-income ranks persists. And the ideological antipathy over fundamentalism, politics in general, religion, abortion, feminism, shows little sign of disappearing. Rights are demanded, rather than duties cheerfully performed. Lawsuits to make someone pay for an accident, or malpractice suits for medical procedures known to involve high risk, suggest the country has forgotten that much of the world is chaotic with outcomes based on luck, good and bad, and that practice is needed before one becomes a master.

To the extent that groups organize and dig in to achieve their goals, becoming "distributional coalitions" in Olson's phrase, or vested interests unwilling to compromise, the political and social agenda becomes blocked. The 1993 tax act came within an eyelash of failure. But the Rush Limbaughs, Pat Buchanans, Pat Robertsons, Ross Perots in political life, and their myriad followers, plus the Republican "revolution" in the November 1994 election suggest that the social cohesion that operated at the time, say, of the Marshall Plan, has evaporated, at least temporarily. Attitudes are rigid, uncompromising, sclerotic.

One should add, of course, that many "thinking" people on the liberal wing of the political spectrum are somewhat ideological and intolerant. Criticism of them has resulted in name calling in which they are attacked for being "politically correct."

Capital Flows

In the usual definition, "basic balance" in the balance of payments meant that the current account covering exports of goods and services was exactly offset by the long-term capital flow, a surplus by an outflow, a deficit by an inflow, leaving transactions in short-term capital and gold equal to zero. Short-term capital was thought to be the equivalent of money, as was gold, and if an outflow of gold was matched by a reduction in foreign balances in a country, or an increase in the country's net short-term claims on residents of foreign countries, matters were judged to be basically in balance. In the 1950s there was a change in this attitude, and first the U.S. government and then the world began to distinguish between U.S. claims on the rest of the world, and the world's claims on the United States. The former were thought to be like long-term capital—an investment, not necessarily a balancing item—whereas foreign claims on the United States were like bank deposits that might readily be withdrawn, moving in far more volatile fashion than U.S. short-term claims on the rest of the world. With the change in definition to "liquidity balance" came a change in the historical record. Instead of being in equilibrium or having a surplus on basic balance account, the United States was judged in the late 1950s as having had a continuous deficit of $2 to $4 billion, as foreigners used some of their long-term borrowing and aid from the United States to add to their dollar balances. This conclusion was questioned by a minority of economists on the ground that the United States had been acting as a bank for the rest of the world, investing abroad monies part of which were used to buy goods and services, but part left to add to the borrowing countries' liquidity, the need for which grew with the growth of foreign trade (Despres, Kindleberger, and Salant, 1966). As a "bank" the United States was not in deficit, just as banks were not in deficit when loans and investments grew along with deposits.

U.S. authorities disagreed entirely with this minority view and undertook a series of measures to tie foreign aid to exports of U.S. products and to restrain the capital outflow each undertaken when the preceding one failed: the Interest Equalization Tax (IET); the Gore amendment applying the IET to bank loans as well as security issues; the Voluntary Credit Restraint Program for foreign investment by nonfinancial corporations; the Mandatory Control Program (MCP), ordering these corporations to restrict investment abroad; and issue of Roosa bonds to foreign central banks, which guaranteed the exchange rate on the dollar holdings. None proved successful: world capital markets were joined by multiple conduits; to plug one put pressure on others to flow faster.

In the mid-1960s the U.S. Treasury finally agreed to a scheme to add to the potential of the International Monetary Fund (IMF) by creating Special Drawing Rights (SDRs), sometimes called "paper gold," which could be used to settle international balances. Countries were given quotas, patterned primarily on their quotas at the IMF. The purpose of the United States was to have its international reserves grow in step with its international liabilities, since new gold production no longer flowed to New York and Fort Knox, but was increasingly sought by other central banks along with their rising dollars. New reserves for the country which acted as a bank for the world made some sort of sense, but in the political world, paper gold for one had to be accompanied by paper gold for all. It was soon recognized that the world was not short of reserves; this was true only of the United States relative to its large dollar liabilities. The panacea was accordingly allowed to lapse.

One further change in the position occurred in the 1960s with the evolution of the Eurodollar market that came into being as a result of easy transatlantic communication on the one hand and a couple of accidents on the other: first, the fact that foreign time deposits in the United States were allowed a slightly higher rate of interest than domestic time deposits, making it advantageous to shift the latter abroad to the foreign branch of an American bank to be returned to New York as a foreign, not domestic deposit; and second, the fear of the Soviet Union that dollars in New York were more exposed to confiscation than dollars deposited in London. Some added incentive was the time difference between Europe and the eastern United States.

With Europe and the United States tightly joined through the Eurodollar market, it was a serious error on the part of the Federal Reserve System in 1970 to undertake lowering interest rates to speed up the economy— allegedly to assist in the 1972 reelection of Richard Nixon as president—at a time when the Federal Republic of Germany was tightening its money market to restrain inflation. Funds flowed from New York to the Eurodollar market, lowering interest rates there; first international corporations in Germany, then German corporations, borrowed from the Eurodollar market to pay off higher interest loans at home. The Bundesbank was forced to buy the dollars sold for Deutschemarks, redepositing them in the Eurodollar market. Interest rates declined worldwide, setting off a wave of lending to Third World countries, largely in Latin America, such as had occurred earlier in the 1920s. The mania went on for ten years, with the realization that it had been excessive not dawning on American bankers until Mexico threatened default in August 1982. First James Baker, secretary of the treasury under President Reagan, then Secretary Nicholas Brady under President Bush pushed the banks to renegotiate the loans and to continue lending. This last was a distinct advance on historical experience when a lending boom, suddenly cut off, produced a sharp decline in borrower spending, leading to recession.

The Dollar

The surprise in this history is that with the exception of the limited issue of Roosa bonds to central banks, there was no general revulsion against lending in depreciating dollars in favor of some other currency. A number of attempts were made to transact in synthetic currencies, like the Unit of Account in Europe, the SDR mentioned earlier, and in the 1980s and 1990s the European Currency Unit or ECU. None recorded much success. Synthetic currencies have the awkward feature that they have to be converted to a national money before they can be spent. This militates against loans denominated in them, despite the protection afforded against depreciation.

In addition, neither Germany nor Japan encouraged international use of the Deutschemark and the yen by foreigners, in fact taking early steps to discourage it, later somewhat relaxed (Tavlas, 1991; Tavlas and Ozeki, 1992). The French attempt to return to gold, exemplified in speeches by President deGaulle, papers by Jacques Rueff, and the action of the Bank of France in converting $1 billion into gold in 1965 and $500 million in 1966, lost credibility when a heavy capital outflow at the time of the events of May and June 1968—student and worker riots—induced the French to borrow dollars rather than spend gold to meet the drain. Some Japanese investors switched from investing in dollar debt to buying real assets in the United States, only to get caught in a bubble in commercial real estate from which losses followed. At a meeting in Washington in 1985, David Hale cogently observed the absurdity of the Japanese, whose housing was tight, investing large sums of money in U.S. apartments and condominia which were long unoccupied. After the closing of the gold window in 1968, the 10-percent import tax, the modest rise in the price of gold of 1971, and the abandonment of a fixed parity in 1973, the U.S. dollar became a poor vehicle to serve as international money. It continued nevertheless in use for lack of an adequate substitute. Commodities such as oil were priced in dollars, as was gold, which not only ceased to be money but became an expensive commodity that rose in a bubble as high as $850 an ounce before declining to as low as $330. The world stayed with the dollar as a limping standard faute de mieux. A case has been made that the United States' provision of the dollar as a world money, and push for tariff reductions in GATT, plus capital outflows, produced the resurgence of the world economy from 1945 to 1970 or so—the Golden Age (Meltzer, 1991). Uncertainty over the value of the dollar after 1973 removed one prop from that support.

Part of the reason for continued foreign lending to and investment in the United States was the unsettled political and military position in Europe with the collapse of the socialist bloc, the breakup of the Soviet Union, and civil strife in Yugoslavia. The United States may have been losing productivity and capacity to solve problems of deficits, worsening income distribution and the like, but it was not threatened by revolution or attack.

Policy

In apologizing for passing his begging bowl to the European countries and Japan to help finance the 1992 Gulf War to counter the Iraqi attack on Kuwait, President Bush said the United States had the will but not the wallet. This remark is reversed by Joseph Nye, who claims that the United States has the wallet but not the will and is in fact rich, is not overtaxed compared with other countries but acts poor (1990, p. 259). A number of analysts lay out almost identical recommendations as to what should be done in the fields of budget balance; increasing productivity, savings, and investment; and stimulating productive entrepreneurship, saying that all that is needed is the will. Henry Nau distinguishes between the structural model, in which decline is inexorable, and the choice-oriented model, in which he asserts that choice is available to the United States but that it needs a clear and self-confident purpose to avoid decline and maintain its leadership (1990, esp. pp. 370–71). Richard Rosencrance states that the United States has the economic strength and potential to hold world economic primacy but needs to be galvanized into action by a crisis. This would enable it to harness its latent social energy and forge new social cooperation. For the crisis, he suggests something on the order of a collapse of the stock market, a collapse of the dollar, or a depression like that of the 1930s (1990, pp. 201–18). The notion evokes Simon Schama's remark (see chapter 6) that the Dutch lacked a great dramatic event such as the French 1789 attack on the Bastille to help them dissolve fiscal federalism and produce centralized unity.

Most recommendations for improving the position of the United States involve the provision of incentives to savers, entrepreneurs and researchers, largely by way of lower taxes, what fiscal economists call "tax expenditures." The experiment of President Reagan in 1981 is thought by some not to have gone far enough. For entrepreneurs the clamor is for a reduction or abolition of the capital-gains tax, although not everyone who recommends this limits it to future investments, as contrasted with those made earlier. If all capital gains went untaxed from a given date, there might be massive asset sales to reorder portfolios, sharp declines in securities, and even depression.

Education is one field thought to hold the potential for improving economic performance, especially correcting the low level of literacy in general and mathematics capacity in particular. The contrast is drawn between U.S. practices and the long hours in school and high achievement of the Japanese at the secondary level, with intense competition to get into the elite universities. Not always noted, however, is the sharp letdown in scholarly ambition in Japan once the entry to a leading university has been achieved. In the American system, the urban school with children from poor families without traditions of learning—and with violence, guns, and drugs—receives the most attention, although successful remedies, apart from busing to the suburbs, remain elusive. One recommendation is to begin early with Head Start, that instills an interest in education into children at the prekindergarten level. Others are to involve college and universities, and especially their students, in tutoring and inspiring inner-urban children. The need to improve elementary and secondary schooling is widely evident. The prospect for producing early change in the country's performance is remote.

At the college and university level there is much more satisfaction. In an issue of *Daedalus* devoted to research universities, Kenneth Prewitt notes that the American public expressed "great confidence" in medicine (50% of those in the sample), in the scientific community (40%) and in education (34%), as contrasted with more limited votes for the executive branch of government (19%, the Congress (16%), and labor organizations (16%) (1993, p. 90). In the same issue, however, Eugene Skolnikoff notes that technical universities today emphasize engineering design and disciplinary accomplishment, while relegating manufacturing design and accomplishment to second-class status (1993, p. 234). Whole departments like sanitary engineering, textile technology, geography, and (animal and plant) biology are dropped from curricula, and within existing departments such as civil engineering or materials science, practice is more or less abandoned in favor of theory. A recent effort at the Massachusetts Institute of Technology has been made to train students in the Sloan School of Management for work in manufacturing instead of finance or consulting. It responds to a belief in the need for more effective entrepreneurship perhaps more than to a broad market for its graduates.

America in Decline?

Half full or half empty? The answer, of course, depends on the counter-factual—what theoretical alternative one is comparing a given situation with. Optimists look about them and see other countries doing less well; they may even take comfort from the slipping that some detect in German growth, the economic miracle of which is said to be fading (Giersch, Paqué, and Schmieding, 1992), or the bursting of the Japanese stock-market bubble in 1990. Others lose heart when they compare the 1990s with the 1950s and 1960s (until the war with Vietnam shattered American confidence in its uniqueness).

As I add the symptoms of aging: the demands for tariff protection and subsidies; intensive lobbying by contending interests for government favor; decline in productivity growth; low rates of saving and high levels of national, corporate, and household debt; rising incomes of stars in finance, industry, sports, and entertainment and slippage of real income in the lower ranks; spread of gambling and probably, though data are shaky, white-collar crime; and a weakening of responsibility in the international economic area, from rising debt to the United Nations for peacekeeping, increasing demands for contributions to such American-led efforts as the Gulf War, plus many others, I side with the pessimists. A special issue of *The Economist* is entitled "A Survey of America: The Old Country" (1991). An article entitled "The Great European Sea Change" by Diana Pinto states: "For those living in Europe there is a palpable feeling that the United States is becoming less crucial and relevant, that it will be even less so in the years to come . . ." (1992, p. 130).

The returns are not all in. At the time of President Clinton's January 1994 trip to Europe, *The New York Times* quoted Dominique Moisi, deputy director of the French Institute of International Relations, in "nostalgia for American leadership":

> . . . we're looking for impetus and reassurance from the United States. . . . Impetus because we've sadly realized that without the United States to kick us, we don't move. Reassurance because Europe is again becoming a danger-ous place. And we don't feel safe alone with ourselves. (January 9, 1994, p. E5)

Within the United States, moreover, strong leadership in opposing antitax interest and fighting such a fearsome lobby as the National Rifle Association has been exhibited by eastern governors in New Jersey and Connecticut. Payoffs of some innovations with long lags may come on-stream and produce resilience. As not a gambler but one who has some appreciation of odds, I think the changes are in favor of sclerosis and decline, and as promised in the title of a book by Paul Krugman, *The Age of Diminished Expectations* (1990).

11

Japan in the Queue?

My knowledge of the Japanese economy is even more superficial than that of European countries outside of Britain, France, and Germany, and my library on the subject in the study at home is limited. Nevertheless the question must be asked whether Japan is in line to take over world economic primacy in the twenty-first century—asked but by necessity left less than fully answered. Japan grew fastest among the leading industrial countries in the quarter century after 1950. It seems nonetheless in the 1990s to be sharing the troubles of others, not the same troubles—unemployment in Europe; deficit, low savings, and declining productivity increase in the United States—but troubles of its own which put any prospect of primacy it might entertain in jeopardy.

Japan resembles Great Britain in many physical respects: a string of islands off a massive continent, with few natural resources except for coal and in its early history copper, silver, and gold. It benefited from access to rich fishing waters and from the necessity to trade, building a merchant class that learned how to maximize and gained wealth, but remained at some risk in the necessity to import a high proportion of its food. National defense was assisted by the barrier of the sea against invasion. Its cultural identity was preserved by continuously fending off foreigners.

Pre-World War I

The Portuguese in 1542 were the first Europeans to break into Japanese isolation, but were expelled because of attempts by the Jesuits who accompanied them, among them Saint Francis Xavier, to convert the population to Christianity. The Dutch, who had been limited to the single port of Nagasaki, were driven out about 1600 in the Tokugawa era. Economic growth ensued with a rising merchant class, but indebted noble *daimyo* and *samurai*, plus oppressed peasants, weakened the social structure. This structure seemed to be beginning to break down about the time of the arrival of Commodore Perry's Black Ships in 1854. Attempts to push out the foreigners in the following years were met with bombardment and defeated. The shogunate, attacked from within and without, collapsed in 1867, to be followed by the "restoration" of the boy emperor Meiji in 1868. From then on the Japanese held to resolves to catch up with the West, to enrich the country, promote enterprise, and strengthen the army (Komiya, 1990, p. 7).

Economic growth picked up from about 1885. In the years from 1870 to 1913, while not growing as rapidly as the United States or Germany, Japan outstripped the United Kingdom and France, as shown in Table 11–1. During the years leading to World War I, Japan constructed a single currency in 1881, established a central bank in 1882, and adopted the gold standard in 1897. Foreign policies, both political and economic, were aggressive. The country forced a commercial treaty on Korea in 1876, attacked China in the first Sino-Japanese War in 1894–1895, and attacked Russia in 1904–1905. Korea became a virtual protectorate in 1905 after the naval victory over Russia, and was annexed in 1910. Formosa (Taiwan) was acquired in the treaty that followed the war on China.

The 1920s

While it had only limited naval involvement in World War I, Japan did not escape the early stock-market and commodity crash of March 1920, with sharp falls particularly in the prices of silk (hurt by the innovation of rayon) and cotton textiles, its prime exports (Hamada, 1994). By July of 1920, 230 firms had gone bankrupt. The Bank of Japan served as lender of last resort, making ¥240 million ($120 million at two yen to the dollar) available to restore order.

Next came the devastating earthquake of September 1, 1923, that killed 140,000 people and did damage estimated at ¥515 billion, equivalent to

Table 11–1   Indexes of Gross National Product,
1900, 1913

(1870 = 100)	1900	1913
United States	349	585
Germany	225	330
Japan	206	281
United Kingdom	184	224
France	160	200

Source: Calculated from Maddison, 1989, Table B-1, p. 119.

42 percent of a year's national income (ibid.). Again the Bank of Japan came to the rescue, discounting a special issue of "earthquake bills," issued in substitution for existing commercial bills coming due for payment and to supply credit to damaged areas. Various banks acquired large numbers of these bills, on the basis of which they extravagantly expanded lending, leading to a financial crisis in 1927 when the bills were not renewed. One bank, the Watanabe, closed its doors for a few hours, but long enough to start runs on a series of other banks. Thirty-two banks failed in April and May of 1927, and forty-five more by the end of the year. The damage to the economy strengthened the military party, which gradually moved in and took over the government.

A near-fatal mistake was made, to go back on the gold standard in January 1930, short weeks after the October 1929 crash of the New York stock market. The appreciation of the yen and the rationing of credit for commodity brokers put heavy pressure on Japanese commodity prices, and in particular on silk, which fell from $5.20 a pound in September 1929 to $3.56 in June 1930 and $2.69 by December. Silk accounted for 36 percent of Japan's exports by value in 1929, almost one-fifth of farm income and a sizeable portion of farmers' cash flow. Exports of silk fell almost in half between 1929 and 1930, from ¥781 million to ¥417 million. The resulting gold losses at the Bank of Japan increased deflationary pressure and produced a new strengthening of the military forces. The country was led into attacks on Manchuria and Shanghai in 1931. The intuitively Keynesian finance minister, Korekiyo Takahashi, who tried to restrain inflation by reducing military expenditure, was assassinated in 1936.

A second Sino-Japan war erupted in July 1937. When war broke out in Europe in 1939, Japan entered the Axis pact of Germany and Italy, announced a "Greater East Asia Co-Prosperity Sphere," and sent troops to Indo-China. In April 1941, a mutual nonaggression pact was concluded with the Soviet Union. The military took over the government entirely in a coup in October 1941; and bombardment of the U.S. naval base at Pearl Harbor took place from aircraft-carrier-based airplanes on December 7, 1941, along with attacks on American military installations in the Philippines and British naval forces in Singapore. The claim was made that the American policy of limiting exports of crude oil and scrap steel that resource-poor Japan needed for its armament program was a hostile act, to which the Pearl Harbor attack was a reply.

In the early stages of the war, Japan made rapid advances in Asia and in capturing Pacific islands. Gradually, however, battle lines stabilized, and with the conclusion of the war in Europe in May 1945, the fire-bombing of Tokyo and other major Japanese cities, and the atomic devastation of Hiroshima and Nagasaki in August 1945, Japan surrendered. Military casualties numbered 1,550,000 at a minimum, not counting those missing. The official estimate of civilian casualties came to 300,000 dead, 25,000 missing, and 145,000 seriously wounded, for a total of 470,000, without including civilian deaths in Okinawa (Tsuru, 1993, p. 9).

1945 to the Korean War (June 1950)

Allied occupation of Japan was carried through almost entirely by U.S. forces under the Supreme Commander of the Pacific (SCAP), General Douglas MacArthur. The initial directive opposed trying to rebuild the country, in fact followed the formula applied in Joint Chiefs of Staff (JCS) directive 1067 for Germany, to aid the Japanese only to the extent necessary to prevent disease and unrest that might interfere with the operations of the occupying forces (Hara, 1993, p. 608). In September 1945 the Japanese government pleaded for food and gasoline to alleviate hunger. The situation became serious in the spring of 1946, at which time the American government loosened up and provided the Japanese with food, largely from U.S. farm surpluses. In due course, revival of the economy became an objective of the American government, along with demilitarization and democratization—revival believed to be necessary for economic stability in East Asia after the Communists had won in China. Cotton was shipped from Commodity Credit Corporation surpluses; a loan provided by the Export-Import Bank, along with Government and Relief in Occupied Areas (GARIOA); and a new program, not applied in Germany, Economic Rehabilitation in Occupied Areas (EROA), which was enacted to parallel the Marshall Plan for Europe (ibid., pp. 609–10).

SCAP went beyond reform to revival. A new constitution was drawn up for Japanese adoption, including a prohibition against the maintenance of armed forces. Land reform was imposed on the countryside, education reform on Japanese schools. The *zaibatsu*, powerful cartels among the leaders of which were the Mitsui and the Mitsubishi, were ordered dissolved, although the restrictions were later relaxed in the peace treaty of April 1952. New firms entered new industries and grew rapidly, especially during the Korean War—Sony in radio and television, Hitachi in electronics, Toyota and Nissan in automobiles.

Hamada and Kasuya ascribe the readiness of the Japanese economy to rise in meteoric fashion in the 1950s to the monetary reforms of, first, Ralph Young, and when this proved insufficient, of Joseph Dodge, as leader of a team of monetary economists who in 1949 produced a monetary conversion that shrank the money supply, and fixed a low exchange rate of 360 yen to the dollar (1993).

The outbreak of war in Korea in June 1950 when U.N. forces, largely from the United States, came to the rescue of South Korea, attacked by North Korea, brought about sea change in U.S. policy toward Japan. General MacArthur was shifted from his duties as SCAP to a role as commanding general of troops in the field. United States quasi-indifference to the state of the Japanese economy gave way to strong enthusiam for economic recovery to furnish logistic support to U.S. forces in Korea from Japan's strategic location across the Sea of Japan. Japanese balance-of-payments data show a ten-fold increase in an item for "Government," that represents largely military procurement (Table 11–2).

Japan's capacity to respond to this exigent pressure rested on the latent vitality of the economy in general after defeat, the early control of inflation, cheap capital from high savings and government subsidies, and cheap and skilled labor. I come to the rate of savings later. Cheap labor came from two sources: movement off the farm, and the return of not only military personnel from the armed forces, but the forcible repatriation of the many Japanese who had worked in East Asia, especially railroad labor from Manchuria. Tsuru comments that Japan was favored by "an unusually flexible labor supply": more than 10-million workers released from war-connected activities, made up of 7.1 million from demobilization; 2.6 million repatriated, mainly from Asian countries; and 1.6 million from drafted work in the armament industry (1993, p. 68). He comments that the majority were able-bodied and had some skill. Those who could not be employed immediately returned to the countryside and were fed into the industrial labor supply over time. Hamada and Kasuya add that this labor force was well educated and that its availability enabled the economy to conform to the Arthur Lewis model of growth with unlimited supplies of labor (1993, pp. 177–78). After encouraging trade unions and collective bargaining in the initial stages, moreover, and recognizing the right to strike in the Trade Union Law of December 1945, MacArthur forbade a general strike threatened in January 1947 when government workers demanded wage increases comparable with those in private industry. An American civil servant asserted that prevention of this general strike represented a turning point in the occupation as the Japanese people became conscious of the need for limits (Tsuru, 1993, pp. 23–25). They were to forget limits in the stock-market and real estate bubble of the late 1980s.

Trade and Industry

Japanese foreign-trade experience after the outbreak of the Korean War is divided by Ryutaro Komiya into three distinct periods, with different bases of comparative advantage, balance-of-payments outcomes, and, in the usual Japanese view, trade policy, although many analysts in the United States and Europe believe that the Japanese government and industry pushed exports and hindered imports throughout the three periods (1990, chap. 1).

Table 11–2 "Government" in the Japanese Balance of Payments (in millions of dollars)

1947	0	1952	788
1948	19	1953	803
1949	49	1954	602
1950	63	1955	511
1951	624	1956	505

Source: Hamada and Kasuya, 1993, Table 7.9, p. 171.

In the first period, from 1950 to 1967, Japanese exports were labor intensive, dominated by textiles, apparel, chinaware, toys, and household articles. This was much the line of comparative advantage that the country followed, along with silk, in the period between the World Wars, with some technology pirated or stolen from abroad. A sewing machine company tried to camouflage its product as Singer by marking it "Seager," selling it for ¥25,000 in the domestic market, ¥10,000 abroad (Tsuru, 1993, pp. 78–79). It was rumored that some manufacturers of gimcrack articles created a town of "Usa" so that they could stamp articles "Made in Usa" and confound American mark-of-origin rules. Although savings were high, capital in this period was scarce because of the demands of reconstruction. At 360 yen to the dollar, the exchange rate was undervalued. Trade showed an import surplus, to which was added a negative balance in shipping, but U.S. procurement for the Korean War effort offset this in most years in the 1950s. Japan pushed exports and held back all but the most vital imports, adopting the attitude "export or die" (Komiya, 1990, p. 7). Loans at low interest and preferential tax treatment were available for exports. Japan joined GATT in the period but without enthusiasm, insisting on many exceptions to the linear tariff reductions called for in the Kennedy round that was finished in 1965. Ryutaro Komiya makes the point that U.S. enthusiasm for GATT was also limited, basing the argument on the ground that the United States joined only by agreement, whereas the participation of Japan and many other countries was by treaty (ibid., p. 11). My recollection has a different explanation. The draft charter of the International Trade Organization agreed to in Havana in 1948 was riddled with so many exceptions insisted on by countries other than the Unted States—for balance-of-payments deficits, pockets of hard-core unemployment, and the like—that the Congress refused to ratify the treaty on the ground that the United States would be held to the rules while the rest of the world would take advantage of the exceptions. Inability to get the treaty through the Congress led the Department of State to shift from the ITO to GATT, which was not technically a treaty and did not require congressional approval.

Komiya does acknowledge that the United States opened its markets to Japanese exports until the pressure of cotton textile imports led to the negotiation of so-called Voluntary Export Restraints, basically forced first on Japan in 1955 and then on other exporters. European countries fended off Japanese exports far longer. All this time Japan applied administrative guidance to exporters and importers, regulated prices, and restrained internal competition, objecting to changes in market shares among domestic companies. Japan joined GATT, Komiya asserts, not because it believed in the principle of free markets, but because it wanted to be accepted as a full member of the world community and to play a major role in it. Liberalization was careful, slow, and only in response to external pressure. Some steps at liberalization were reversed later (ibid., pp. 15–16). Many ostensible steps in liberalization were purely window dressing, such as 100-percent permission for foreign firms to invest in lines in which no firm would contemplate an investment—sake bars and billiard parlors—or in industries in which Japanese exports revealed a strong comparative advantage—steel, cement, motorcycles, cotton, and synthetic-fiber spinning (Kindleberger, 1969, pp. 88–103). All the while Japan was acquiring technology from abroad, largely by license, and starting to produce it at home. Foreign investment was admitted in a few cases when an important branch of technology could not be acquired under license. In the usual case a joint venture was mandated and was broken up when the foreign techniques had been absorbed.

The second phase, which Komiya places at 1968 to 1975, involved a shift from products using cheap labor to those that were capital intensive and/or embodied high technology and quality control: steel and ships, using abundant capital; cameras, radio and televisions sets, household appliances, watches, along with automobiles, where quality counted.

Steel and shipping were closely connected. Before World War II there was relatively little transoceanic trade in steel because of the high costs of transporting iron ore, coal, and steel in freighters of 20,000 tons or less. Heavy industry was largely confined to its own continents. After the war, with the building of the first supertankers for oil of up to 250,000 and 300,000 tons dead weight, and ore carriers of 200,000 tons or so, steel became almost a footloose industry, like cotton and wool textiles, that could be located anywhere ports could accommodate ships of deep draught. Japanese mills could produce steel readily with U.S. scrap, or Brazilian or Australian iron ore, and market the resultant product in the United States, landing it at New Orleans and shipping it up the Mississippi and Ohio rivers almost to Pittsburgh. Japan pioneered in building these supercarriers from its steel, as well as in other innovations in marine transport—container ships, roll-on–roll-off ships for transporting trucks and automobiles (rather than lowering and raising them one at a time down and up from a hatch). World trade exploded partly as a result of reductions in tariff barriers under successive rounds of GATT negotiations, but also because of the cheapening of transport, which extended the trading range of heavy goods. In due course Japan invested in newly discovered iron-ore deposits in northwestern Australia. Tsuru is by no means a chauvinist but calls attention to the fact that the modernization of Japanese steel mills, begun in 1950, led the Ministry of International Trade and Industry (MITI) to plan a tenfold increase in steel output from 1951 to 1955, following which there was a rise of production from 9.4 million tons in 1955 to 117.1 million in 1974. Of the twenty largest blast furnaces in 1975, thirteen were in Japan, which also topped all others in continuous casting. MITI and the banks financing the industry worried about excessive competition. The two largest companies, Yawata and Fuji, were merged in 1965 under administrative guidance to create the largest steel company in the world, at 32,500,000 tons, almost 10 million tons larger than US Steel (Tsuru, 1993, pp. 58–59, 98–100).

Along with the reduced cost of transport of bulk cargo by sea, of course, were the cheapening and increased speed of time-sensitive goods, and of people who could more readily reach agreements with face-to-face contact, by air.

The end of the 1960s and the early 1970s were a period of upheaval in world trade. Official support for the London gold market was stopped in 1968. In August 1971 President Nixon closed the gold window in the United States and imposed a 10-percent import surcharge on U.S. imports; he devalued the dollar by the same amount in December of that year. The Japanese refer to this as the Nixon "*shocku.*" A second shock, more directly aimed at Japan, came in 1973 when the U.S. government halted the export of soybeans, a leading Japanese import, to hold down the price at home. The dollar moved to floating in the spring of 1973, breaking up the rationale of the International Monetary Fund (IMF).

The world was next hit by the Organization of Petroleum Exporting Countries (OPEC) embargo on oil exports, which raised the price of crude oil from $3 to $12 a barrel. Since Japan depended heavily on imported oil, its immediate reaction was one of quasi-panic, following which it settled down to find its way around the difficulty, expanding coal production and hydroelectricity, investing in nuclear power and in an Arabian oil company. Dollar depreciation raised the rate for the yen from 360 to the dollar to 265. This and the spike on the price of oil raised the percentage of oil in total imports from 21 in 1970 to 44 in 1975. The later 1979 price shock brought the level to 51 percent in 1981 (Komiya, 1990, p. 30). Despite this, the Japanese current account in the balance of payments went into deficit only briefly in 1974 (and again in 1980), recovering promptly in both cases in a remarkable demonstration of economic resilience.

After 1975 comparative advantage moved from capital-intensive products to those embodying "organizational and managerial skills, intelligent and cooperative labor, efficient use of information, and flexibility in shifting resources from one item to another (ibid., p. 46). Komiya goes on to make an uncharacteristically expansive remark: "It appears that Japan will lead other countries in this kind of technology and hence in a fairly wide range of manufacturing industries for some time to come" (ibid.).

All this time friction with the United States was building over trade. U.S. negotiators blamed the large and growing trade deficit of the country on Japan's pushing exports and limiting imports. Japan's officials and scholars admitted to having pursued such a policy in the early postwar period, but contested its relevance thereafter on two scores: first, deregulation and tariff reductions had gone a long distance. The accusation was no longer valid except in a few politically critical lines such as rice. Second, they made the valid economic point that balance-of-payments deficits are rooted in macroeconomic, not microeconomic, variables such as protection, subsidies, inefficient distribution, and the like. (This neglects the possibility that continually changing comparative advantage with transitional surges, up in exports, down in imports, may aggregate to an export surplus as each innovation leading to a transitory surplus is followed by another). A high-level economic meeting in 1990 to discuss strategic initiatives and the Japanese current-account surplus ended with the United States blaming subsidies and protection, including the practices of *keiretsu* trading companies, the Japanese pointing to low household savings in the United States and the large and unmanageable governmental deficit. The protagonists on the Japanese side also occasionally indulged in a moderate amount of *tu quoque* argumentation. Komiya points to the fact that nontariff barriers (NTBs) have been raised in the United States and lowered in Japan, and cites the cumbersome import procedures found in the United States by Japanese exporters of such products as Japanese noodles (1990, p. 60, fn. 32). The main causes of the Japanese export and U.S. import surplus were macroeconomic, not microeconomic—the high rate of savings in Japan in excess of domestic investment, the low rate of saving in the United States compared with business investment and the government budget deficit.

The issue at the microeconomic level divides American economists. The *Journal of Economic Perspectives* ran a debate between Robert Lawrence and Gary Saxonhouse in which the former stressed especially the trading companies of the *keiretsu*, which favored their manufacturing affiliates over potential importers without great regard to price (and pushed exports), while Saxonhouse dismissed the anecdotes of frustrated American exporters to Japan as the tail of a normal curve—a considerable distance from the mean—and thought it likely that a similar distribution of stories of American obstacles could be found on the Japanese side (Lawrence, 1993; Saxonhouse, 1993). Saxonhouse further claimed that the *keiretsu*, like the preceding *zaibatsu*, had been built up into a bogeyman, and that there was no clear meaning to the category or definitive list of companies that belonged within it.

A particular charge against Japan is that it engages in very little intrasectoral trade, as do other developed countries while buying and selling differentiated manufactures. Japan exports a great many manufactured goods, imports few. The question is whether this is the result of strong public and private policy or simply a reflection of comparative advantage in a country with limited natural resources. Econometric tests have been applied to the issues without persuasive results. Another troubling question is whether Japanese exporters raise prices in foreign currencies when the yen appreciates, that is, pass through a fixed domestic price at the new exchange rate, or leave the foreign price unchanged in order to hold on to market share and accept a spread between a higher domestic and lower foreign price.

Similar disparate views appear in a single 1991 international periodical. A Japanese economist dwells on MITI's "International Cooperation Program," under which administrative guidance is pushing companies to reduce their exports by one-third by 1993 and one-half by the year 2000, substituting direct investment for exports in the national interest (Yamazawa, 1991). An Italian student of the Japanese economy, on the other hand, believes that import substitution in Japan came not from administrative guidance but from the spontaneous action of the market. Japanese trading companies were slow in marketing foreign beer, whiskey, and pasta because they believed the local product (Suntory and Kirin in the first two instances) superior. Japan's success, in this opinion, lies in promoting promising industries and closing down declining ones (or moving them to the Asian mainland), while the United States remains preoccupied with saving declining ones (Fodella, 1991, pp. 660–63).

But the striking contrast in Japanese trade has been with Britain. After World War II, Japan kept changing its product mix, more on the export side than importing to be sure. In contradistinction, Britain, in the late Victorian and early Edwardian periods, kept the export product mix but shifted from competitive to less competitive markets.

One further indication of Japanese industrial vitality is provided by its insouciance in the late 1970s and again in the mid-1980s as the yen appreciated. In the early period the yen rose from 291 to the dollar to 241, an appreciation of 25 percent, and later in 1980 to 218, despite efforts of the Bank of Japan to hold it down. American observers faulted Japanese industry for not passing through the appreciation to prices in dollars, keeping them at their old level. A Japanese view by Toyoo Gyohten, a high official of the Ministry of Finance, was that the rise of the yen pushed Japanese industry to greater rationalization of costs and lower yen prices (Volcker and Gyohten, 1992, p. 175). Five years later, after the Plaza Agreement of September 1985, with the yen rising to 171 in May 1986, 165 in June, and 154 in July, Gyohten expressed amazement that Japanese industry and the public were not worried. The public benefited, of course, from lower prices of traded goods, but industry took the change as an incentive to invest abroad and to push still harder for industrial rationalization (ibid., pp. 257–58). The dynamic response echoes the German reaction to lower tariffs in 1956, when imports rose but exports rose still more, to leave the trade balance still strongly positive.

Direct Foreign Investment

Friction has developed too over the difficulties faced by American firms trying to build or acquire plants in Japan. The slow and somewhat disingenuous dismantling of restrictions has been mentioned earlier, along with the dissolution of joint ventures after the foreign technology has been absorbed. The surge of Japanese direct investment abroad in the 1970s and 1980s has been a response to foreign limitations on imports and to the appreciation of the yen. Many of the companies could have preferred to operate so-called "screw-driver factories," plants that assembled parts produced in Japan with economies of scale. Local-content laws, some requiring as much as 45 percent of the value of the finished good to be manufactured locally, made that option impossible (Yamazawa, 1991, p. 643). Japanese techniques for organizing production included keeping initiative coming from the lowest levels, rather than down from top management; productivity and quality circles; and just-in-time component delivery that saves capital tied up in inventory. These are said to be difficult to transfer to foreign cultures that do not rely as heavily as the Japanese on social inter-action and group bonding (Clark, 1993a, p. 19).

Japan lost its foreign investments as a result of defeat in World War II. Immediately afterward, with government participation, it began investment in raw materials—Alaskan pulp, iron ore in Brazil, Arabian and Indonesian oil—followed by investments in nonferrous mines. The largest investment category in the decade of the 1960s was mining, which was the second-highest class after manufacturing in the 1970s (Komiya, 1990, p. 118 and Table 3, p. 119). Data for April 1981 to March 1993 (twelve years) show manufacturing investment at $104 billion, well ahead of finance and insur-ance at $75 billion, commerce $40 billion, transportation $22 billion, and mining only $19 billion (Keizai Koho Center, 1993, p. 55). Shigeto Tsuru draws a comparison of Japanese investors after 1975 when "the position of leadership in the Pacific passed from the United States to Japan, with Japa-nese captains of industry now residing in Australia far from resembling the erstwhile British remittance men of the nineteenth century" (1993, p. 201). Japan's investment in Australia went well beyond raw materials such as iron mines and wood chipping and pulp mills into real estate, including hotels and golf courses for the relaxation of Japanese tourists. The government has joined with private investors in proposing a "High Technology City," with a residential community for 100,000 people, and ultimately an invest-ment of 5-trillion yen. "Japanese investment extends into every phase of the Australian economy" (ibid., pp. 201–4). Komiya observes that Japa-nese direct investment has not been especially profitable because of its "im-mature state" (1990, pp. 137–39, p. 150). Particularly disappointing was the failure of Japanese banks to do well when responding to London's "Big Bang" of deregulation in October 1986.

The move of Japanese banking abroad was in part an attempt to es-cape regulation at home. It was also helped by its ability to raise cheap capital at home, which led Masahiko Takeda and Phillip Turner to call the move-ment "artificial" (1992, p. 93).

However driven, Japanese banks grew in size to dominate world lists in terms of assets. The 1992 *Fortune* ranking of the world's largest banks lists eight Japanese banks before coming to one of any other country, with five more Japanese banks among the second ten. Comparison is somewhat difficult because of the problem of choosing the appropriate exchange rate, but the Dai-ichi Kangyo bank with $476 billion of assets was more than twice the size of the largest American bank, Citicorp, with its $217 billion. Japanese banks are not notably profitable at home or abroad because of the narrow spread between interest rates charged on loans and paid on deposits, compared with the spreads in banks in other countries (Takeda and Turner, 1992, p. 41, Table 17). The narrowness of the spread is a ben-efit for bank borrowers and depositors. The rate of profit, such as it was in 1984–1989, declined abruptly in the following years, doubtless to nega-tive numbers, as the bubble in real estate and stock prices burst.

Education and "Salarymen"

One of the themes of those who see Japan pulling up rapidly and going ahead of the United States or threatening to do so in the race for ascendancy in the world economy, if there be such a race, is education. Japanese students, it is held, study longer hours in school, learn more mathematics, and are in general better equipped for their life vocations than the average youth in the United States. Japanese schooling is highly competitive, with private cram schools at the secondary level to supplement the regular public system, as parents push their children in an effort to get them to do well and gain admission to a prestigious university. Many observe that life is hell for students 14 to 18 years old, who arrive at the university so exhausted that they relax for four years before going on into business, chosen for a major company, largely on the basis of having been admitted to such a university. In one opinion,

> . . . at senior high school, an experience rightly called "examination hell." It damages their eyesight, does little for their health, and nothing for their minds. But before they descend into other forms of hell—mainly Japanese company life—students are provided with four years of licensed holiday. (Lowe, 1993, p. 596)

Hired by a large corporation, as the successful university graduate aspires, he or she becomes a "salaryman," who "will work like a robot until retirement." (Hironaka, 1993). Working in Tokyo, a city that is "hellish" with

> roads, parks, homes, offices, trains, movie theatres, restaurants and hospitals . . . contend[ing] with two or three times the numbers they were designed for, the salaryman lives two or more hours from his work, leaves home at seven o'clock in the morning, gets back at 11 at night every day. There is no family dinner during the week, including Saturday. In Japan, family life has been supplanted by the race to get ahead. (ibid.)

Much of the reason for returning so late is that among the men at least, bonding requires a certain amount of partying after office hours. The life is not one of relaxation, and occasionally results in *karoshi*, the Japanese word for working oneself to death, said to have "a high incidence among Japan's international business people" (Shimada, 1992, p. 29). Juliet Schor claims that Americans overwork, with long hours and sometimes two jobs, and in the case of women, additional hours of home-making (1992). The educational path to that unhappy position, if the judgment is correct, seems far more relaxed than that in Japan, perhaps too relaxed for optimal efficiency.

Keiretsu

The theme of the *keiretsu* has already found its way into these pages, first as a replacement for the prewar *zaibatsu*, and second in the debate between Robert Lawrence and Gary Saxonhouse over their importance in shaping the Japanese trade structure and balance of payments. The reach stretches further into the provision of cheap capital. Most of the horizontal *keiretsu* have, along with a trading company and producing companies, banks and insurance companies that collect savings from the public and make them available to other members of the combination. A defensive motive is involved. Vertical integration, combining finance with commerce and production, is used to ensure that the latter cannot be cut off from finance in times of trouble, just as steel companies feel more secure in the possession of iron and coal mines. At the same time, Ryutaro Komiya insists that the insurance companies of the *keiretsu*, which he discusses in detail, respond to external market forces and would not be allowed by their owners to subsidize other members of the combine, as contrasted with charging competitive prices (1990, chap. 6). Nonfinancial members of the combine are financed through shares and bonds held by the insurance company and short-term loans provided by the bank, but are free to go outside if they can do better. All commentators agree, however, that it is difficult to determine whether the trading company of a *keiretsu* favors its partner member over others, especially foreign suppliers, when it comes to purchases.

"Orgware"

An Italian scholar of Japan, Gianni Fodella, has coined the unattractive expression "orgware" representing organizational practices, on the analogue with hardware and software. The term includes the *keiretsu*, but more importantly the organization practices of firms in general. In definition, orgware consists of the institutions, rules, and behavior of companies, and includes the narrow spread between borrowing and lending rates of the lending units, just-in-time component delivery, lifetime employment, circles for quality control and other production methods, and especially the bottom-up *ringi* method for introducing changes in product and process, rather than management direction from the top (1991, p. 664). This sort of decision-making is sometimes thought unduly slow, as polling wide numbers takes time. An American journalist who writes for *Japan Update*, Tanya Clark, thinks not. She observes that a paper on a change is prepared by the bureaucratic staff and then signed off on by the various individuals concerned, if they agree, or debated if they do not (1993a). As described, the system reminds me of policy formation for the general run of affairs in the Department of State in the United States: a telegram or memorandum to the field is initiated at the lowest possible concerned level, then "cleared" with parallel and higher units that have an interest in the problem, before dispatch. Authority to sign for the secretary of state goes far down the line of authority; neglect to get concurrences from concerned officers is revealed the next day when copies of outgoing communications are circulated. Clark insists that the system in Japan is fluid and interactive, working well be-

cause of the smooth flow of information, widespread acceptance of authority, and to some extent trust.

The system is in some danger of breaking down since the collapse in
1990 of real-estate and stock prices. Shigeto Tsuru's *Japan's Capitalism*
discusses the "double price revolution" in the 1973 and 1979 increases in
the price of oil on the one hand, and the 1980s boom in real-estate prices,
followed by collapse, on the other, (1993, chap. 6). The former reinforced
what Clark calls "Japan's basic guiding light": its view of itself at that time
as a small country with limited natural resources, threatened by isolation,
poverty, and hunger, which fear keeps the country on a treadmill "unable
to look up and take pleasure in its success" (1993b, p. 19). My sources are
largely limited to *The New York Times* and Japanese periodicals in English
distributed free to scholars in the United States, which may convey a public-
relations bias. In both sources, in the summer of 1993 it is reported that
the Japanese are thinking of curbing their bureaucracy (and administrative
guidance), starting to link pay to performance rather than seniority in lifetime employment, worrying about pollution, congestion, housing, and
overwork. Japan, many say, should shift the emphasis from global economic
expansion to the welfare of its citizens.

Japanese Savings

The surplus in the Japanese balance of payments on current account is the
result of a high rate of national saving relative to the rest of the world and
relative, especially, to that of the United States. The role of *keiretsu* insurance companies and banks in collecting savings has been noted. The Japanese government has run budget surpluses for most of the postwar years—
in contrast to the deficits in the United States—in considerable part because
it was forbidden by its constitution to spend money for defense. Household savings reach levels close to 15 percent of gross domestic product
compared with 3 or 4 percent in the United States.

Many reasons are adduced for this high rate. One is the seventeen-
month annual salary system, paying bonuses in both summer and winter.
The permanent-income hypothesis of Milton Friedman holds that while
permanent income is spent, windfalls are saved. It may be that the extra-
months' salaries are windfalls, though with rational expectations and regular receipt they would seem to belong in permanent income. Another incentive has been tax exemption for one private savings account and an
account in the Post Office. The Post Office offers high rates of interest for
ten-year deposits, but in practice allows savings to be withdrawn from an
account after six months. Funds accumulated by the Post Office are made
available to the government, and to enterprise only indirectly. They thus
enjoy not only a high return but a governmental guarantee (Okina 1993).
Other factors may be early retirement, first at age 55, then 60, and a primitive system of social security that makes the Japanese save for their own
retirement, the late introduction of credit cards, high down payments on

house purchases, and the lack of deductability of mortgage interest on income taxes, which discourages borrowing.

Despite these explanations, the high rate of personal savings in Japan remains a puzzle. Tsuru notes "the high propensity to save" of households, provides figures for it for the 1970s when that chapter of his book seems to have been written (1993, p. 71), but does not explain its origin. Earlier detailed figures by Koichi Hamada and Monehisa Kasuya show that the Japanese were saving in double-digit percentages of GNP as far back as 1950 (1993, tables 7.6 and 7.7, pp. 166–67). Tsuru hints that the high rate of savings arises from the high price of land in Tokyo and in Japan in general, which makes personal purchases of houses difficult, and, in the boom of the late 1980s, virtually out of the question. Young people may have saved intensively to acquire a house, and older people in part to assist their children in so doing.

Change in the rate of savings seems now under way. Bill Emmott calls the Japanese now a nation of "consumers, pleasure seekers, pensioners, investors and speculators" (1989, titles of chapters 2–6 with a reprise, p. 239). He states that saving out of disposable income could fall from 16 percent (18 percent in 1980) to 8 percent as workers continue to work beyond the retirement age of 55, and the social security system is improved (1989, chap. 4). The increase of life expectancy from 71.73 years for males and 76.89 years for females in 1975 to 75.86 and 81.81 respectively in 1990 is also likely to play a role. But more than demography is involved. Tsuru suggests that since even inherited wealth does not suffice to buy a house in the ordinary case, the younger generation is now turning to "perverted" conspicuous consumption, buying expensive imported cars and spending freely on foreign travel (1993, p. 169).

The high cost of housing is not due solely to the price of land. Construction costs are also high, running as much as ¥80,000 per square meter, compared with one-third that level (equivalent to $45) in the United States (Sakuta, 1993, p. 89). The explanation, according to an expert, lies not entirely in the inefficiency of carpenters, plasterers, and other workers but deep in the structure of the industry and of Japanese society. A house takes ten times the number of man-hours for a building of a given size than it would in the United States, owing to a change in construction types, regulation—for earthquake-proof standards inter alia, lack of standardization, and irregularly shaped and small house plots. The price of land has been the main stumbling block, however, a price held high by subsidies to rice farmers and especially by the speculation of the 1980s. Tsuru observes that the Japanese government was beginning to take steps in 1989 and 1990 against such speculation through increased capital-gains taxation, taxes on undeveloped land held, requirements that land be developed, and the like, as well as creating new land by extensive land fills on shallow portions of the shore and moving functions to them from the city. Whether the collapse of real-estate prices slows down these steps in the Henry George direction is not now evident.

The Bubble

The real-estate and stock-market bubble at the end of the 1980s, which burst in 1990, was the result of liberalization of Japanese financial regulations and of the tension between the Ministry of Finance (MoF) and the Bank of Japan (BoJ) (Wood, 1992). The liberalization was not the result of a dash for escape from financial repression as recommended from time to time for heavily regulated financial systems (McKinnon, 1963). The pace of liberalization had been deliberate, which should have allowed time for the market to adjust to each step. In McKinnon's later explanation why deregulation in South Korea was followed by financial uproar, the order of procedure counted a great deal, with deregulation within a country thought best to precede that in trade and foreign-exchange control (McKinnon and Mathieson, 1981). This issue seems not to have arisen in Japan.

Liberalization in Japan has been slow, under way since at least 1970, as a result primarily of foreign (especially U.S.) pressure (for a chronology, see Takeda and Turner, 1992, appendix 1). Following the Louvre Agreement of February 1987 to stabilize the dollar, which had been declining since the Plaza Accord of September 1985, the Bank of Japan reduced its discount rate to 2½ percent, an all-time low, and allowed the money supply to grow at the rate of 10 to 12 percent a year at a time when real income was growing at 4.4 to 6.6 percent. The Bank was not concerned about asset prices, says Hamada, because goods prices were steady (1994). The Ministry of Finance had been party to the Louvre Agreement but was reluctant to use fiscal policy in aid of the dollar, leaving the burden to the Bank of Japan.

The sharp break in the New York stock market on October 19, 1987, further disposed the Bank to follow an easy-money policy. Turnover in the Tokyo stock exchange rose along with the spike in stock-market prices, the Nikkei index rising more than threefold, from roughly 12,000 in 1986 to 27,000 in 1988 and 39,000 in 1989 before crashing to 15,000 in 1992 and recovering to 20,000 (see Figure 11–1). I have no data for real-estate prices but understand that they moved in parallel fashion. Banks and insurance companies lost heavily, not only on direct holdings of land, buildings, and securities, actually and in prospect, but on loans to speculative financial institutions at the periphery of the financial market. The decline also uncovered some dubious financial practices such as making good the losses of large investors, manipulating security prices, and hiding losses through imaginative accounting (Takeda and Turner, 1992, pp. 58–65, esp. p. 64). Simultaneously with this trouble, it was revealed that corruption had infiltrated high political places, even to the extent of officials acquiring strong rooms loaded with gold bars.

In October 1993, with the Nikkei index up from its low of 15,000 to 20,500, a correspondent for The Economist was unsure that the financial troubles of Japan had been laid to rest. Corporate profits were low, so low indeed that the price/earnings ratio of the index was 78, suggesting that

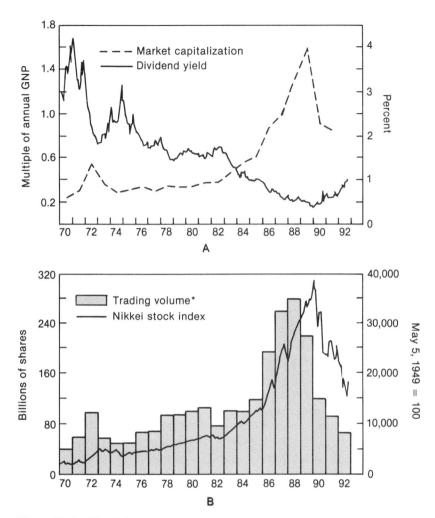

Figure 11–1 The Tokyo stock market. A. Market capitalization and average dividend yield. B. Annual trading volume and the Nikkei index. The 1992 figure is for the first half year, at an annual rate. *Source:* Takedo and Turner, 1992, graph 8, p. 53, from Tokyo Stock Exchange *Fact Book 1991* and national data.

the market was widely overpriced (*The Economist*, September 25, 1993, p. 92). With a 15-percent decline in earnings expected, the ratio would rise to 100. Rents in Tokyo had fallen 20 percent. Foreign enthusiasm for Japanese equities, expressed in the formation of many mutual funds to invest in them in the mid-1980s, evaporated. The banks, the article said, were not handling their bad debt effectively, and 1,000 firms were going bankrupt per month (roughly the rate shown in a chart in Takeda and Turner, 1992, p. 63; *The Economist*, September 25, 1993). These were especially small firms that lacked ready access to capital but supplied four out of five jobs in Japan. Additionally, according to the 1993 *Economist*, "MITI reckons that much of the dynamism Japan needs to escape its economic torpor will have to come from small companies, since big companies have grown staid and bureaucratic."

Japan as Number One?

The burst of the bubble in stock and real-estate prices, and the ensuing (to American eyes) mild recession, have in Japan given rise to questions about a change of direction. Rather than push for world-market share and even primacy, working like robots and becoming an economic giant, perhaps the time has come, some political and business leaders think, to turn to domestic problems:

> Bad air, bad water, contaminated soil, respiratory disease, cadmium and mercury poisoning, and noise, . . . [shifting] emphasis from global economic expansion to the welfare of the citizens, concentrating more on education, welfare, wages, medical services, urban infrastructure, family and community life and the status of foreign guest workers. (Hironaka, 1993)

The agenda reads as though it would suit the United States. Such an industrial leader as Akio Morita, chairman of Sony and vice chairman of the influential business organization Keidanren, thinks it is time that Japanese businessmen move closer to the practice in the rest of the world and focus less on efficiency and competition (1992). In the second half of 1993, *The New York Times* is filled with dispatches from Tokyo to the effect that change is under way in lifetime employment, the seniority system, management of trade, and dominance of the bureaucracy in administrative guidance. A typical article in one of the Japanese periodicals distributed in the United States, but selected from originals written for Japanese eyes, is "Lifting the Heavy Hand of Bureaucratic Guidance" (Sakaiya, 1993), stating that Japan has become an undisputed "assets superpower" with stable prices and much less skewness of income than in a country like the United States, but that there is trouble in paradise, with material affluence offset by a drab way of life.

Not all Japanese think in these ways, to be sure, if one can judge adequately from the Japanese thought exposed in this country. For one who says that Japan should support *Pax Americana* in every way it can (Okazaki, 1993), another, a diplomatic correspondent of Asahi Shimbun who serves on editorial boards of American publications, argues that Japan should stop being a spectator, formulate its own proposals, work to strengthen the United Nations, and presumably insist on a Japanese seat on the Security Council (Funabashi, 1993). Some Japanese energy, indeed, is focused on territorial rather than economic questions, notably the return of the Kurile Islands seized by the Soviet Union in 1945. A significant body of opinion argues that Japan's interests lie not in the declining economies of Europe and the United States but in the less developed countries of the world, perhaps Africa, but certainly South America and the Far East and especially China.

My intuition tells me that Japan's burst of vitality from 1950 to 1985 is tapering off, and that while it looked for a time as if its trajectory was leaping out of the Gompertz-curve track in a spurt of economic growth never before seen in economic history, it is now slowing down to conform to the familiar pattern. Political change coming from corruption that has been exposed suggests uncertainty, loss of confidence, and perhaps something of a return to the earlier inferiority complex that broke out from time to time in assertiveness.

For this reason, I predict that Japan will not succeed to the American role as acknowledged leader of the world economy, with the prestige and responsibilities that go with it. The prediction contains, however, in metaphorically small print, the usual Surgeon General's warning: I have been wrong many times before. In any event, I choose not to dignify by discussion the occasional Cassandra prediction from history that economic competition for pride of place will again lead to major war.

The well-informed Emmott, now editor of *The Economist*, takes the view that aging will limit Japan's potential as a great power, and that the United States can regain its position as "number one" if it succeeds in reducing the deficit, raises savings back to 7.9 percent of disposable income, and clings to free trade without insistence on reciprocity. If the United States is number one, Japan, he thinks, will clearly be number two. What is to be feared is a leaderless world, with three balanced powers—the United States, Japan, and Europe—with no umpire or guide (1989, p. 254 and chap. 12).

12

Conclusion

This conclusion is in two parts. One part covers the national cycle and especially aging, the other the nature of succession of world economic primacy. It reprises, if you will, chapters 2 and 3.

The National Life Cycle

Since starting to write this book at the beginning of 1993, I have learned that another economist is working on a book on the "national life cycle," like mine in an historical dimension, but going back to Greece and Rome, and in cycles of five hundred and two hundred years as the author comes up to modern times, when fifty-year cycles take over (Athanas, forthcoming). Christos Athanas is also interested in the analogy of nations with human beings, postulating an adult productive life cycle of *homo sapiens* of fifty years. He acquainted me with a study by Daniel J. Levinson, *The Seasons of a Man's Life* (1978), which divides the human life span into childhood and adolescence (to age 22), early adulthood (17 to 45), middle adulthood (40 to 65), late adulthood (after 80). Peak biological functioning runs from 20 to 40 years of age. By age 20 a man is close to his full height, strength, sexual capacity, cardiac and respiratory capacity, and general biological vigor, and close to his peak in intelligence, memory, and capacity for abstract thought. These aspects of life are generally stable to age 40, which in his (Levinson's) intuition is a critical time, though some men start to decline at 30. Levinson looked for some attribute like menopause in women which brought about changes in men, but was unable to find it (ibid., pp. 21–24).

Much later he observes that primitive man died at age 40, his work completed (ibid., p. 328), but does not relate that fact to 40 years as a turning point in modern man. While energy is somewhat diminished after age 40, a man's bodily and mental powers are still ample for an active life. Youthful drives such as lust, anger, self-assertiveness, and ambition are not altogether missing in the middle stage, but they are under better control. For many men, however, life in the middle years becomes a process of gradual or rapid stagnation (ibid., pp. 24–26).[1]

These rather evident statements should be qualified of course, by noting wide variance on the one hand and very considerable doubt on the other whether one can extrapolate from the average individual to the average nation. They are nonetheless suggestive. All peoples and all nations are different, but they share traits in common relating to growth and aging.

In their youthful stage at least, each nation, as each individual person, regards itself as unique. The evidence is readily collected:

"While most men combined earth, air, water and fire to make simple goods, the Florentines, according to Pope Boniface VIII in 1300, were a fifth element" (Veseth, 1990, p. 19).

"The Spaniards were *sui generis*" (Brenan, 1950, p. xvii).

"The Portuguese were *sui generis*, different from Europeans and Spaniards, unique . . . the uniqueness of Portuguese character produced a special postcolonial humanity" (Rogers, 1989, pp. 76–77).

"The most extraordinary invention of a country that was to become famous for its ingenuity was its own culture. . . . The Dutch created a fresh identity" (Schama, 1988, p. 67).

"Holland is represented in Huizenga's 1941 book as in all respects a unique case. It is clear that the unique cannot be explained. It is therefore to be admired and described as a gift from God" (Kossmann, 1974, p. 49).

"The French unconsciously inherited from Louis XIV a conviction of superiority to Continental Europe" (Herr, 1958, p. 229).

"The French in the past have been proud of their unique economic 'balance.' This was a significant component of their sense of social distinctiveness" (Hoffmann, 1993, p. 77).

In the 1980s, German economic historians discussed the *Sonderweg*, or special path to German modernization, connecting the German *Zeitgeist*, culture, collective identity and the economy, with some debate as to whether the *Sonderweg* was myth or reality (D'Elia, 1993, passim, but especially p. 382 and footnotes 2, 3).

---

[1]A letter from Thomas Jefferson, age 71, to John Adams, age 76, on July 14, 1818, reads: "But our machines have now been running 70 or 80 years, and we must expect that, worn as they are, here a pivot, there a wheel, now a pinion, next a spring, will be giving way, and however we may tinker them for a while, all will at length surcease motion" (Nuland, 1994, p. 44).

American exceptionalism was the subject of a conference in Britain, at which Seymour Martin Lipset and Daniel Bell (among others) presented papers (Shafer, ed., 1991). Bell maintains that exceptionalism differs from uniqueness, that all nations are unique to some extent, but that America has been described as exceptional as far back as de Tocqueville (ibid., pp. 50–51).

Japan is widely recognized as "a peculiar and abnormal country" (Pyle, 1988, quoted in Rosencrance, 1990, p. 147), and the Japanese themselves raise such questions as, "Is it not possible that Japan might be quite different from other countries: Is it not possible that Japan might be quite superior to other countries?" (Pyle quoting Tsueneo Iida, in Rosencrance, ibid., p. 141).

Among these examples, compiled haphazardly during the course of reading, there are no entries for Bruges, Antwerp, or Britain. This is because I was late in becoming sensitized to the notion, and lacked the time to re-read old sources.

Note that young countries feel unique and look ahead. In later stages they become less confident of their exceptionalism, and tend to look back with nostalgia to one or more golden ages.

Trade, Industry, and Finance

The usual progression in the national cycle is from trade to industry to finance. Each has its own internal line of development. In the first stage, trade is likely to be competitive and aggressive, ready to acquire foreign technology by less than honorable means, and to disguise its product as foreign during the learning process. Growth is frequently export led, occasionally import substituting in competition with the products of other countries. Protection is designed for the incubation of infant industries. In later stages, the pushing of exports may be harmful to growth, for example in the case of Britain and Empire preference, where pressure is exhibited to maintain dying industries when attention should be diverted, if it were possible, to innovative activities. Protection in these circumstances is usually for geriatric industries, although occasionally it is offered on a limited basis to an industry trying to recover from a bad spell.

Similar cycles are followed in industry, imitative but adaptive to emerging conditions in the beginning, then innovative. Gradually the survivors become large, resistant to change, defensive, and sometimes following the innovations of others. Not all industries in a country go through growth and decline phases of a cycle at the same time, but enough are likely to do so as to make the cyclical pattern applicable to the aggregate.

As mentioned more than once in this book, institutions like guilds are positive in early stages as they diffuse productive techniques and set standards of quality, subversive of growth later when they restrict output to maintain prices, cling to obsolete standards, and resist improvements or changed process where the lower-cost somewhat-lower-quality payoff is advantageous for consumer and producer. The same is likely to be true of cartels and monopolies, applauded by Schumpeter for their contribution to innovation and growth (but only in early stages), later resistant.

The cycle in finance starts with promotion of trade and industry through short- and sometimes long-term capital lending, and ultimately moves to trading assets and preoccupation with wealth rather than output. Merchants and industrialists graduate from risk-taker to rentier status, and conserve flagging energy. Consumption out of given incomes rise, savings decline. Various interests push their concerns at the political level, and if enough do, they block effective government action. Income distribution tends to become more skewed, the rich richer, the poor poorer. With greater access to the reins of political power, the wealthy are likely to resist some ethically appropriate sharing of national burdens, such as the costs of defense, reparation, infrastructure, and other public goods.

In the typical case, a country is likely to be more decentralized, or federal, or pluralistic in the earlier stages, though Spain and France in modern times may constitute exceptions. Pluralism is useful for eliciting competitive initiatives, not exclusively in economic endeavors, since the generalization applies equally or more in art, music, literature, but usefully so. As development proceeds, need arises for more central direction to coordinate increasingly powerful and sometimes conflicted local interests. This may be difficult to achieve. The seven Dutch provinces blocked the centralization of taxation that would have allowed the country to face more competently the wars with Britain, France, and Prussia after 1780, and Napoleon's later exactions (Schama, 1977 [1992]). Erzberger's reform of decentralized German finances, needed to address the appalling problems of reconstruction, reparations, and inflation, was sabotaged by state financial offices with their bureaucratic delays and by the wealthy, and ended in his assassination in August 1921 (Feldman, 1993, p. 347), this despite efforts that led Feldman to call him "ebullient, energetic, resourceful, optimistic," with "vigor and skill rarely found, not only in the Weimar Republic, but in governments anywhere through modern history" (ibid., p. 160). Economic growth reaches a stage where men both in business and in government resist change. As Mancur Olson and M. M. Postan have indicated, the resulting sclerosis is arrested in some cases because of traumatic defeat that calls for the dismissal of the old, and takeover by new men.

In chapter 7 it was said that France was an exception to the national life cycle because of the breakdown of the political system in the French Revolution, the defeat of Napoleon, the revolution of 1848, the Commune of 1871, and France's undistinguished role in World War II. Germany and Japan, too, are partial exceptions, as originally pointed out by Mancur Olson (1982) because of defeat in the Second World War. Fifty years later, however, both appear to be slipping into the prototypical arteriosclerotic mode.

I lack a background in political science, which would enable me to hold forth on why some countries have a two-party political system and others a greater number of parties or party splinters. If the operative constitution provides for regular elections in which one party runs the risk of being voted out of office and succeeded by the other, one would think that the retirement of worn-out politicians and their succession by new men in the rival party would institutionally provide the new men needed to arrest economic decline. Such seems not to be the case, for reasons that I am unable to fathom.

The Causes of Decline

Chapter 2 suggested that the human being collapses more or less all at once, and that while newspaper obituaries cite a given condition or organ failure as the cause of death, in all likelihood the person's time had run out, and if the particular cited cause had not intervened, another would have come along shortly. Since that writing I have had the opportunity to talk to a neighbor pathologist who tells me that this idea is not wide of the mark. In many autopsies, he maintains, it is quite impossible to determine an explicit cause of death. Under compulsion to report to the family, and directly or indirectly to the press and the health officials that compile statistics, pathologists often pick a villain from a number of handy candidates. In cases where there is no disease and no trauma, brain, nerves, and muscles all lose cells as time proceeds, especially if they are not exercised. In the case of little or no exercise, people who first ran and walked vigorously, move over time successively to a cane, walker, wheelchair and bed, with no conspicuous cause of debility. In years gone by they would in due course die of pneumonia. Today, with sulfa drugs available, that fate is more or less excluded. Disease and trauma abound, of course, but the natural life cycle ultimately ends as the body wears out, even without such intervention.

My interest in this risky analogy lies in the causes of national decline, whether external like trauma and disease—war, overstretch, acute competition from thrusting upstarts; or internal like the aging process—digging in of distributional coalitions that resist taxation and shared burdens; lower rates of productivity gain and innovative creativity; resistance to change by governments, large corporations, and individuals; the shift of national heros from production to consumption, or to being manipulators of assets who pile up wealth in the process; inflation because of inability to match tax income to government expenditure, or printing money because of inability to acceptably allocate among income groups; perhaps the "Dutch" or "Spanish disease" in which one element in society becomes rich and others push for income beyond the capacity of their sector to produce it.

These contributory causes of decline, by no means mutually exclusive, are found not only in aging economies. Corruption, flagrant today in Japan (and Italy), not to mention the United States (e.g., the Savings and Loan debacle of the 1980s), has an ancient lineage. I have earlier noted that the East India Company was pointed to by a German economic historian as the high (or low) point in this dishonorable business (Van Klavaren, 1957).

Thomas Mun's denunciation of conspicuous consumption in the 1620s in England is sufficiently graphic to merit extended quotation. Mun deplores Britain taking leave of

> ... our honourable exercises and studies, following our pleasure, and of late years besotting ourselves with smoke and pot, in a beastly manner, sucking smoke and drinking healths, until death stares many in the face. ... the sum of all is this, that the general leprosie of our Piping, Potting, Feasting, Fashions and misspending of our time in Idleness and Pleasure (contrary to the Law of God, and the use of other Nations) hath made us effeminate in our bodies, weak in our knowledge, poor in our Treasure, declined in our Valour, unfortunate in our Enterprize and condemned by our Enemies. ...
>
> As plenty and power do make a nation vicious and improvident, so penury and want do make a people wise and industrious. ... (1622 [1664], pp. 179–80)

Although Mun is out of style today about "smoking," which is no longer approved conduct, uses the word "pot" differently than youth use it today, and is unaware of present-day attitudes toward gender in disdaining things effeminate, his diatribe suggests that excessive attention to consumption is not limited to mature economies.

External Causes

The division of causes of national decline into the external, like disease and trauma in the individual, and internal, like the overall aging process in the human body, is arbitrary and ambiguous. War, for example, may be regarded as an external cause par excellence in a country that believes itself attacked from without, but war guilt, as historians have shown time and again, can often not be pinned on a particular participant beyond a reasonable doubt, but is rather shared in various degrees. Moreover, while the Fourth Anglo-Dutch War of 1780–1784, and the French attack on the United Provinces and occupation in the 1790s, administered the coup de grâce in Holland's decline, symptoms of internal decline had long been apparent. I resist Joshua Goldstein's view that war is endogenous in the economic growth cycle (1988), but that it generally speeds up growth of young countries and hastens decline of old is fairly evident.

Other external forces are shocks, notably discoveries and inventions, that broaden horizons or undermine existing activities. Columbus's discovery of the new world in 1492, the discovery of silver at Potosí and gold in California, Australia, and the Rand, are normally regarded as external shocks, although Pierre Vilar observes that the sixty-five entries in Columbus's diary mentioning gold demonstrate that the voyage of discovery was a response to the bullion famine of the fifteenth century (1969 [1976], p. 169). The development of nylon, which replaced silk in women's stockings, was a brutal blow to Japanese economic growth in the 1930s. The OPEC price hikes of 1973 and 1979 also belong in this category.

Whether the external change speeds or slows economic growth, however, depends on the response of the economy to it, such response being a function of its vitality, energy, and resilience at one end of the spectrum or lethargy and torpor at the other. Years ago I wrote that for a country to be preoccupied with its terms of trade—the relative prices of exports and imports—was a sign of debility, like an individual continuously taking his or her temperature, pulse, or blood pressure. Under optimal conditions a country reorders its resources in response to shifts in the prices of exports and imports, away from those with falling prices, unless they come from falling costs, into those with stable or rising prices (Kindleberger, 1956). "Capacity to transform" was the needed ingredient to accommodate changes in the terms of trade, one conditioned by internal factors.

External and internal sources of decline meet again in the concept of "overstretch," which came into prominence in Paul Kennedy's *The Rise and Fall of Great Powers* (1989). The notion, of course is not new. In his *The Army of Flanders and the Spanish Road, 1567–1659* (1972), Geoffrey Parker uses as an epigraph a quotation from a Mr. Wylkes in July 1587: "The matter of the greatest difficulty in the . . . maintenance of this action is in proportioning the charges of the warres and the number of souldiers to be maynteyned with the contributions and means of the countrey" (p. 125). Parker goes on about the Spanish attempt to repress rebellion in the Netherlands:

> On the whole there were few in Spain prepared to admit the possibility that the war in the Netherlands could not go on indefinitely and that its costs would prove too great for the treasury to bear. As Mr. Wylkes observed, the problem of proportioning the expense of a war with the resources available was one which challenged and defeated almost every government in the sixteenth century: politics in those days were seldom weighed in the "Scale of a Tradesman." So the Army of Flanders was under orders to maintain maximum military pressure on the Dutch until all resistance collapsed, whatever the costs . . . the cost of the exercise was ruinous, of course. . . . (Ibid., p. 145)

The statement conveys echoes of Louis XIV's deathbed "Too many palaces, too many wars," of President L. B. Johnson's attitude to the Vietnam War, and of the (Junker) German general staff motto, *Geld spielt keine Rolle* (literally, "money plays no role," more colloquially, "hang the costs"). The "scale of a tradesman" evokes Jesse Pitts, the sociologist on French aristocratic values, with mottos such as "His men adored him," "Never take cover," "Never count your change" (1964, pp. 244–49).

The relevance of overstretch to today's world is found in the widely held criticism that the United States has taken on too much in providing a nuclear umbrella over the rest of the world, maintaining a two- or three-ocean navy, and acting as the world's policeman in the Middle East, Somalia, Haiti, earlier in Guatemala and Panama, and possibly in prospect in Bosnia and the breaking-off constituents of the former Soviet Union. There is a will–wallet problem here of the type referred to in chapter 9. A country that can spend half its national income in World War II can undertake a wide variety of policing actions if it is willing to tax itself sufficiently for the purpose. The criticism arises from those who are not so willing. It is not enough to will the ends; one must will the means. "We cannot afford it" is an indirect way of saying that there are too many other expenditures we prefer to make, or that the country—not just the administration, or the Congress, but the country as a whole, pressure groups and voters—will not give up other things for the purpose.

The foregoing does not deal with willing the ends and expecting or hoping for others to provide the means, as when President Bush passed the hat to Japan, Middle East countries like Saudi Arabia, and others, to pay for U.S.-decided policies which, to be sure, benefited those who were asked to pony up. In the usual case of economic primacy, such as Britain, for example, the leader of the coalition hired others to contribute to the fighting with subsidies. In Operation Desert Storm, the roles were reversed.

Internal Causes

I choose not again to run through internal causes of decline: risk aversion, increased consumption, decreased savings, reduced gains in productivity, decline in innovation, resistance to taxation, mounting debt, rent-seeking, envy leading to the Dutch disease, speculative bubbles, and gambling, corruption, increasing governmental and corporate bureaucracy, unwillingness to adapt to change. I do want to make two points, however: one about Cardwell's law, on which Joel Mokyr has written a series of interesting papers (1992a, 1992b, 1992c, 1994), and the other on the federal/centralized or pluralist/hierarchical organization issue.

D. S. L. Cardwell, it will be recalled from chapter 3, observed that no country remained at the cutting edge of technological innovation for more than two or three generations (1972). He failed to provide a theoretical basis for what was essentially an empirical finding. That task has been taken up by Joel Mokyr, who points out that there are resistances to change exemplified not only by Luddites, Chartists, guilds, trade unions, long-lived cartels, and declining industries but by less organized groups and individuals. Over time these forces tend to block threats to losses from innovation of what he calls "vintage specific skills" and "unmalleable assets" (Mokyr, 1994). The argument leans heavily on Olson's "distributional coalitions," but is widened to vested interests in general, and in the British case includes "nostalgic romantics" (1992c). Mokyr allows for cases of incompatibility of innovations with network technologies, as in the market failure mentioned earlier of coal wagons, inefficiently small, because they were owned by the mines and not by the railroad, an instance where vertical integration was needed to internalize the gains from change in the light of inability of the market to negotiate a sharing of costs and profits (see above, chapter 8, but see also Van Vleeck, 1993). In essence, the argument is that after technological progress in a single country goes a certain distance, resistance builds up to continued change. On a wider scale, such as Europe or the world, overall progress is maintained by new starts in new areas, which threaten the laggards and may force them to adapt.

The federal/central issue covers innovation and its slowdown but goes well beyond it to include organizational problems in business, government, the military, universities—practically any institution that starts small and grows large. Small may or may not be beautiful, but it is either efficient or it dies. Mokyr suggests that the city-state may be the most efficient economic unit—vide not only Venice and Genoa, but today Hong Kong and Singapore (Mokyr, 1993)—but that when it enlarges troubles begin. Loose federal structures may work well, but when substantial growth or agglomeration sets in there is a problem of how to divide powers, duties, and rights between the apex and the lower units. Much depends on the environment being faced, whether it is stable, in which case the federal structure is likely to work well; whereas if the situation is fraught with tension and change or opportunities for creative change, requiring coordination among constituent elements or commands to move one or more off in a different direction, central decision may be needed.

The dilemma is this: stable times favor decentralization to bring out the instinct of workmanship and the innovative capacity of lower levels: crisis or significant change favors central direction. With too much growth at the center, however, bureaucratic sclerosis creeps in, slowing down the capacity of the centralized authority to respond in the next crisis.

General Electric was a brilliant company in the middle of the twentieth century, with a series of profit-making subsidiaries producing generators, airplane engines, and electrical appliances such as refrigerators, washing machines, and toasters, but its spare head office missed out on the opportunity presented by the computer. The success of General Motors long lay not in its centralization under the presidency of Alfred P. Sloan, Jr. but in its decentralization, giving independence to Chevrolet, Buick, Oldsmobile, and Cadillac. When competition suggested that savings could be made by standardizing some engines and some body parts, and the fad of conglomeration led off into diesel locomotives and electronics, not to mention investment in automobile plants in Germany, Britain, Australia, and the Union of South Africa, trouble crept in. As in government and universities, middle management proliferated, giving rise to what Charles Dickens in *Little Dorrit*, describing the Circumlocution Office, called the work of "form filling, corresponding, minuting, memorandum making, signing, counter-signing, backwards and forwards, and referring sideways, crosswise and zigzag" (1857 [1894], p. 92).

Armies have learned that when the number of units above the single soldier—squads, platoons, companies, battalions, regiments, divisions, armies, army groups—rises above three, it is better to split up the lower unit and add an additional higher one to keep matters manageable. There remains potential dissidence between higher and lower units, the higher scanning broader horizons, the lower in more intimate contact with proximate reality. General (later Secretary of State) George C. Marshall worried about what he called "localitis," the preoccupation of the lower unit—in the instant case the American representative on the Control Council in Occupied Germany after the war, General Lucius D. Clay, to focus exclusively on German economic and political problems without sufficient regard to their impact on Europe as a whole.

In universities, the question is whether progress is made and monies should go to the top administration or to lower schools, institutes, departments, laboratories. The question was posed in the famous 1910 battle between Dean Andrew West, and Woodrow Wilson, then president of Princeton University, as to which of them should control $2 million raised by West—whether it should go to the Graduate School for building a new campus or to the University as a whole. Wilson lost, retired to run for governor of New Jersey and in 1912 for president of the United States. The Harvard motto of "every tub on its own bottom" means that schools and departments dispose of the money they raise. This is hard on departments like theology and classics, which lack the fund-raising capacity of, say, the business or law school, and poses a problem whether a university ought to push ahead with its strengths, with danger of distortion among fields of knowledge, or invest to bring weakness up to the level of the whole. President Neal Rudenstine's report for 1992–1993 suggests a step to more central control in the interest of balance, at a time when other universities are killing off departments that have difficulty attracting money and/or students.

Whether one embraces federalism as a general principle or believes that some small or large degree of centralization is needed, especially when new circumstances call for a change of direction, change is difficult. Indeed, as the cases of Holland at the end of the eighteenth century under Isaac Jan Alexander Goguel and Johannes Goldberg (Schama, 1977 [1992]), or Mattias Erzberger, finance minister reforming the German tax system in 1921, it is often impossible (Feldman, 1993). One case with which I had a brief acquaintance was the attempt of a Canadian commission, headed by Rowell and Sirois, in 1939 to reorder the distribution of financial powers laid down in the British North America Act of 1867, which had become obsolete, and in particular to shift some power to raise and spend money from the provinces to the dominion level. It failed.

A move from a hierarchically organized institution to a decentralized or federal one, or vice versa, is probably more readily carried through in relatively small organizations, such as a university or middle-size company, and with far greater difficulty in a giant corporation or a country as a whole. Moreover, any and all systems of organization are subject to entropy, or growing rigidity. Some time ago in the Department of State, it seemed to me that the staff was best kept on its toes by frequent reorganizations—on the order of every decade or thereabouts—from geographic lines to functional, or in the opposite direction. There would always be a need for regional political specialists, and, say, economists who work generally on trade, international finance, petroleum, communications, shipping, and the like—under any system. Too long domination by the regionalists or by the economic specialists tilts the system heavily in the direction of inaction. If one cannot get new faces as through defeat in war, the regular shuffling about of old faces may be a decent second best.

While there are movements to agglomeration and integration of small into larger units in the economic and political world, there is also a move toward disintegration. The most conspicuous cases are those of the former Soviet republics and Yugoslavia, if one does not go back to the postwar dissolution of the British, Dutch, Portuguese, Belgian, to some degree French and Japanese empires. In addition, and not without importance, there are the breakaway movements of the Basques in Spain, Québecois in Canada, Welsh and Scots in the devolution movement in Britain, perhaps even Staten Island, which shows signs of wanting out of its membership in New York City. Centralization and decentralization are movements in continuous tension at the local and national levels, and also worldwide.

The issue is posed in the European Union as one of "subsidiarity"—which functions to elevate to the Union level and which to retain at the level of member countries. The discussion is primarily in terms of governmental functions, and the criteria run in terms of spillovers. Labor, health and safety in one country are unlikely to affect those in another, so that regulation in this field may be safely left to the countries, whereas migration has spillover effects and should be regulated, if at all, by the Union. In cartel or antitrust policies, takeovers within a country may or may not have impacts abroad, depending on the size of the resulting firm, whereas mergers or takeovers of firms within a single industry in different countries presumably do. Making sense of subsidiarity, the Centre for Economic Policy Research holds, must be done on a case-by-case basis (1993, pp. 2, 3).

A separate criterion, emphasized in the preceding pages, is timing: peacetime, with economies moving on trend and when decentralization, federal, pluralistic devolved bases, or subsidiarity should normally be indicated; or time of crisis, when centralization or leadership is called for or coordination is needed. To favor centralization over decentralization, or the reverse, at all times and places is unrealistic.

Policy

The question remains whether the national life cycle can be fundamentally altered by design, and national decline, if that be threatened, averted or pushed off into the future because of a wave of resilience, by appropriate policy. In chapter 2 it was suggested that the human life cycle could be extended on average by good medicine in the case of disease or trauma. Where no external factors intervene, the quality of life in what Levinson calls late, late adulthood, that is, after 80 years of age, can be improved by good medicine, even without extending its length (1978, pp. 36–39). The issue is posed by Henry Nau's analysis of growth and decline in terms of "structural theories" on the one hand, in which change is inexorable, and "choice-oriented models," in which a society can order policy to resist decline, as he believes possible (1990).

Many economic specialists have therapies for arresting and reversing economic decline. To take a sample from a review of a recent book:

> Rivlin's reform agenda follows directly from . . . the causes of our economic stagnation. To solve the problem of productivity slowdown she favors increased investment in private plant and equipment, in worker skills and in new technological applications of basic research. Narrowing income inequality will require improved worker productivity as well, but a serious effort must be made to bring the economic underclass into the mainstream economy to share in this growth. To this end, Rivlin recommends improved public education with emphasis on basic skills needed to work with new technologies. To improve the nation's saving rate, Rivlin's advice is simple: reduce the federal deficit. To contain health care costs, she favors system wide cost controls which set reimbursement rates for all payers, whether public or private. (Inman, 1993, reviewing Rivlin, 1992, pp. 1455–58)

The review observes that "these measures require a political process—trim, contain, reorient, cut back, and maybe increase taxes. None seems likely when the political process is caught in deadlock." He goes on that Rivlin's way through these difficulties is to

> reinvigorate the American states as independent centers of economic policy-making. Fiscal responsibility between the federal government and the states would be redrawn. The federal government would reduce the deficit and take care of the national health care crisis. With the help of a national tax distributed to the states, the latter would take over the productivity agenda. . . . (Ibid.)

The program sounds formidable.

It is unfair to distill a two-hundred-page book into a couple of paragraphs, relying on a reviewer's summary. The program thus cruelly compressed is a long advance over that of specialists in economics with only one string to their bow: fix the money supply, or go all out for antitrust policy, or apply industrial policy in the way it's done by MITI in Japan, or push incomes policy, or go back to the gold standard, and the like. It nonetheless reminds me of Alice in Wonderland's Red Queen and "six impossible things to do before breakfast." One can wholeheartedly work on improving education; correcting income distribution; increasing productivity, savings, and investment; reducing uneconomic subsidies; balancing the budget; and making affordable health care universally available. In the present state of political power, however, each reform evokes strong resistance from powerful and well-financed lobbies that affect the legislative process through political contributions. One does not want to sound cynical, but realism seems to warrant the conclusion that broad programs of the sort outlined are utopian.

In another book, directed to a discussion of U.S. trade policy for security in a world when the number of superpowers has been reduced from two to one, Theodore Moran starts with a chapter on reversing American decline, which is "at least in principle, eminently reversible" (1993, p. 13).

> The required macro-economic steps (constraining consumption, rewarding savings and investment, reducing the federal government deficit) are relatively straightforward. The difficulty springs from the political task of putting them into place. . . . in the comforting absence of clear and present dangers [after the end of the Cold War] there appears to be less need for uncomfortable solutions that require discipline, sacrifice, and concerted purpose. (Ibid.)

Ascribing the unreadiness of the country to face squarely its economic and political problems to the comfort generated by the end of the Cold War, rather than to more deep-seated malaise (to use a word that President Carter was mocked for using), begs the question. By 1990, discipline and readiness to sacrifice for a concerted purpose had been lost for more than a decade.

There are times when countries gird their loins, so to speak, and accomplish wonders: one thinks of the French payment of the Franco-Prussian indemnity in 1871–1872; the Finnish payment of reparations to the Soviet Union in 1944 and again in 1945–1947; the economic miracles of Germany and Japan after World War II; even the bipartisan effort in the United States to assist war-weakened Allies and defeated enemies after 1945, including but not limited to the Marshall Plan. Those efforts called for political unity that is rare except in wartime and in dire straits.

In general, countries respond better to what medicine calls disease and trauma, crises produced by external events, than they do to slow decline. The external crises are more readily countered when a country is "younger" and imbued with vitality, energy, and vigor, than later when ossification has set in. Whether the internal causes of decline can be successfully overcome in the same way at later stages in the national life cycle is more doubtful. Tariff protection advocated by the late Lord Kaldor for Britain's economic troubles seems especially unlikely to serve as a fountain of youth or set of monkey glands. Experiment in jump-starting a declining economy is worth pursuing. It is hard for this economist to admire President Franklin D. Roosevelt's willingness in the depression to try one nostrum after another, without much in the way of theoretical support for any one of them. Eclecticism may be more appropriate, too, in a world depression than to a gradual decline into low-grade growth intermixed with periods of stagnation, and occasional flush of fever.

In discussing Dutch decline, Simon Schama notes that the country lacked a great *coup de théatre*, like the storming of the Bastille in Paris in 1789 (1977 [1992], p. 216). Rosencrance, a believer in American economic resurgence, says that thus far the spark has been lacking that would ignite the country's social energies and forge a new social cooperation. He counts on a crisis to produce such an impetus, suggesting four possible scenarios: (1) the collapse of the Japanese stock market (at an all-time high when he was writing), spreading to New York; (2) continued need for U.S. borrowing, leading to tighter interest rates; (3) a worsening of the U.S. trade deficit, leading to foreigners dumping dollars in a hard landing for the currency; (4) a slow relapse of the country into depression (1990, chap. 8). In the fall of 1993, the Japanese stock market had fallen without affecting New York, scenarios 2 and 3 had not occurred, and the "contained depression" of 1991–1993—extended recession followed by slow growth, if you will—did not produce a crisis. Rosencrance's optimism is commendable: he believes that the abundant good will of the American public needs to be harnessed in crisis, *and will be* (ibid., p. 214).

Policy formulation is cheap. Putting the right policies into practice takes doing, as observed earlier of the Spanish *arbitristas* whose sound advice was thoroughly ignored. A parallel reflection is made with regard to catatonic France before World War II:

> . . . as one looks at the thirties in retrospect, one cannot but note the striking contrast between the general awareness of reforms that were conceived as necessary and the incapacity of bringing them to maturity. This was, as Monsieur de Lapalisse would have pointed out, because the forces of immobilisme were still dominant. (Bouvier, 1984, p. 74)[2]

Will Decline of a World Economic Leader Be Followed by the Rise of Another?

Before 1973, the decline of one country exercising world economic leadership was followed as a rule by the rise of another, willing and sometimes even anxious to take over. As the cases of France, Germany, and Japan (the latter two before 1939) indicate, there have often been candidates for the succession when the place has not been vacated. A paper focusing on hegemonic shifts over three thousand years, from 1700 B.C. to 1450 A.D. observes that during many of the fifteen periods of ascent (A) and descent (B) there was no hegemon (Frank and Gilles, 1992, p. 157). Between the sixteenth and seventeenth centuries no one was really quite sure as to where the center of gravity lay (Braudel, 1979 [1984], p. 35). I am in no position to pass judgment on the point. I can observe that sometimes the change is made precipitously, as from Bruges to Antwerp about 1440 and from Antwerp to Amsterdam largely in the single year 1585. At other times it is clear which country is rising, which declining, although the exact date of the change in primacy is hard to pin down. An earlier study insisted that there was a long interregnum, so to speak, between the start of British decline, say about 1870, and its gradual loss of primacy in the Edwardian era, and the U.S. readiness to accept responsibility for world economic stability, appearing slowly in 1934 (the Reciprocal Trade Agreements Act),

---

[2] *La Petit Larousse* does not list a M. de Lapalisse, but does include one Captain Jacques de Chabanne La Palice, born about 1470, who was killed in the battle of Pavia in 1525. His soldiers sang of him that one quarter of an hour before he died, he was still alive, meaning that he was still fighting. In time the captain came to represent an obvious and incontestable truth.

1936 (the Tripartite Monetary Agreement), 1941 (the Lend-Lease Act), 1944 (Bretton Woods), 1948 (the Marshall Plan) (Kindleberger, 1973 [1986]).

Ambiguity exists between economic strength on the one hand and readiness to apply it in the production of the public good of world peace, stability, and growth on the other. In 1890, U.S. income per capita was higher than that of Germany or Great Britain, but as it clung to its isolation the United States cannot be said to have occupied the seat of world economic leader. Japan may or may not have had a higher income per capita than the United States in 1993, $33,701 for Japan, $25,009 for the United States, if one accepts the exchange rate chosen by the Keizai Koho Center, but while U.S. economic primacy was slipping, Japan did not challenge for or claim it (1994, p. 11).

In contrast to earlier periods, when one country was growing rapidly as another was slowing down, all industrial countries grew rapidly in the Golden Age from 1945 or 1950 to 1973, and all grew more slowly in the two decades that followed. Not all slowed down at the same time: Britain was first in the early 1970s; the United States followed briefly in 1974 and again in 1980–1981, before entering a period of stagnation at the end of the 1980s and beginning of the 1990s; France slowed in 1982 after President Mitterand's experiment in socialization, undermined by a middle-class strike that took the form of capital flight; Germany and Japan slowed in 1989–1990 for different reasons, Germany because of choosing the wrong exchange rate to convert East German marks to deutsche marks, 1:1 when something like 2:1 would have been less inflationary and would not have required the Bundesbank to apply the brake; Japan because of the bubble described in the previous chapter, which burst in 1990 with effects that threaten to leave lasting trauma. Early chapters have indicated that while Germany and Japan may vie for local preeminence in Europe and the Far East, neither seems likely to seek or hold the position of world economic primacy that Holland in the seventeenth century, Britain from 1770 to 1870, and the United States from 1945 to 1971 enjoyed, or perhaps more accurately, merely held.

With no leader in waiting, ready to take over, what next? The possibility remains, as asserted by Nye, Nau, Peterson, Rosencrance, and others, that the American economy will show new resilience, and that American economic and political leadership will prevail again as in the 1950s and 1960s. Economic growth has picked up in cyclical fashion in the 1990s to such an extent that the Federal Reserve Board in the spring of 1994 began to apply the brake of higher interest rates to forestall a slippage into inflation. U.S. foreign policy has won successes in Haiti and in forcing Saddam Hussein of Iraq back from his renewed threat to Kuwait. These rebounds, however, fall well short of the vitality exhibited by young countries. The mood of the nation is sour, not confident. Counsels are divided. Readiness to compromise in the general interest is scarce. Greater skewness of income distribution is both a product of the loss of social cohesion and a symptom of incipient decline. Creativity slackens, except in the field of finance. While innovation dwindles, productivity increases as corporations with bloated white-collar staffs downsize and reduce employment at well-paid levels, at a cost in anxiety in the employed middle class and among those hoping for good jobs on completing their educations. From a long-run perspective, recovery in the United States starting in 1991 looks more like a cyclical uptick than part of a trend.

A variety of reforms is needed—in the United States, Italy, Japan, not least in the successor states to the Soviet Union—but the likelihood of achieving it in timely and satisfactory fashion is remote. The public everywhere has become cynical, not to say angry, negative with regard to the incumbents in office, but less than optimistic about success in correcting the deficiencies of the system of possible replacements. Conservatives condemn bureaucracies and politicians for government failure, without noticeable attempts to relate to market failures that called for government action.

If the United States does not succeed in making a comeback and resume the role of world economic center or leader, as seems to me the outcome with the shorter odds, what then? It is easy to list a series of alternative scenarios, but virtually impossible in my judgment to say with any confidence that one is more likely than others in the immediate future.

Political scientists such as Stephen Krasner and Robert Keohane believe in "regimes"—institutions, habits, practices that develop during the dominance of a hegemon, which continue through inertia after the persuasive or coercive power of the hegemon has been lost. After World War II the United States built a regime of international organizations, consisting of the United Nations, primarily in military security; the General Agreements on Tariffs and Trade in commerce; the World Bank to foster economic growth and development in the countries that were successively called backward, underdeveloped, less developed, and then developing; and the International Monetary Fund to handle short-term imbalances in international payments. After a slow start, during which the United States itself took over with military relief, aid to occupied areas, the British loan, and the Marshall Plan, this set of institutions began to function more or less effectively. Currencies became convertible; tariffs were reduced; private international investment, which had dried up in the 1930s, came back. It was in effect a Golden Age. In one view, the question is why it came to an end: in another, how it happened to last so long.

It is difficult to pin down exactly when this regime broke down, but the early 1970s is the period usually selected. The system of fixed exchange rates failed. Monetary policies in the larger countries were no longer coordinated, with the result that the world was flooded with dollars. The Organization of Petroleum Exporting Countries (OPEC) raised the price of oil first fourfold at the end of 1973, and nearly triple again in 1979. Syndicated bank loans to developing countries soared, based on real interest rates that approached negative levels. The United Nations, initially handicapped by Soviet vetos in the Security Council, became less representative of reality as Germany and Japan rose in economic, though not military, strength but failed to gain permanent seats on the Security Council. The reduction of trade barriers, which had gone far through various rounds of multilateral negotiation—Geneva, Dillon, Kennedy, and Tokyo—was slowed by the rise of nontariff barriers, Voluntary Export Restrictions forced on exporters by importing nations, largely the United States. The Uruguay Round of trade negotiations, intended to widen the scope of concessions from industrial goods to agricultural products and services, such as banking and insurance, was finally agreed on in 1994 by governments after twice having to extend the five-year limit for reaching agreement. Its successor will be the new World Trade Organization (WTO). International organizations, however, are no cure-all. Many function poorly. It took eighty years to build the World Health Organization (WHO), whose common purpose, the gains to be had from cooperation, and the modesty of shared national costs should have been at their most obvious (Cooper, 1985). They are surely worth encouraging and building on, but their record makes it hard to feel confident that the world economy can be effectively handled in crisis by supranational entities.

International organizations are not limited to those just mentioned. To some, the future of economic order lies in regionalism, with the European Union (formerly the European Economic Community); the North American Free Trade Agreement among Canada, Mexico, and the United States; and a Southeast Asian confederation of some sort, including Japan, the four "tigers" (Hong Kong, Singapore, South Korea, and Taiwan), along with such "emerging markets" as Indonesia, Malaysia, the Philippines, Thailand, and perhaps ultimately China. NAFTA may well grow through the adhesion of states in South and Central America, the leading candidate at this writing being Chile. The three blocs are sometimes thought of in terms of foreign exchange rather than politics or trade, as the area of the European Currency Unit (the ECU), the U.S. dollar, and the Japanese yen, with the local leaders, rather than pluralist organizations, being Germany, the United States, and Japan. While those configurations are possible, to be sure, they would not be completely satisfactory. A world divided in this fashion would isolate the Middle East, South Asia, and Africa, at a minimum, and perhaps the former Soviet Union, unless Russia and some other former members joined the European Union, and Oceania, unless Australia and New Zealand went along with the Southeast Asian bloc. A long process of sorting out relationships beyond those now more or less existing would be called for, and settled not by fiat but by a Darwinian evolutionary process.

Some political forecasters put faith into the division of the world along developmental rather than geographic lines, between, say, the Organization for Economic Cooperation and Development (OECD), on the one hand, and the U.N. Conference on Trade and Development (UNCTAD), on the other. The latter organization would appear currently to be moribund. At the least it has dropped out of the line of sight of the developed world. The OECD is equally or almost equally remote from major decision-making circles.

Less formal organization rests in the Group of Seven (G-7), which started as the G-5—Britain, France, Germany, Japan, and the United States—and was later pressured into adding Canada and Italy. The G-7 meets at "summits" once or twice a year, prepared in advance by finance ministers, central bankers, and staffs, called "sherpas," who prepare decisions to be confirmed by the heads of state (Mulford, 1991). In the absence of less developed countries, any member of the former Soviet bloc, and China, its representativeness is questionable. The managing director of the IMF attends meetings of the G-7, and especially of the deputies, but as an information resource rather than a contributor to policy decisions.

Annual meetings of heads of state are not a useful recipe for international decision-making. Negotiations should be conducted at a lower level, by civil servants and politicians well connected to their home bases. The contrast runs between international political disasters like the reparations meeting at Spa (Belgium) in July 1920 (Feldman, 1993, chap. 7), the World Economic Conference of 1933 (Kindleberger, 1973 [1986], chap. 9), the Potsdam Conference of July–August 1945 on the one hand; and successful operation on the other—Working Party No. 3 of the Organization for Economic Cooperation and Development (while it lasted) and the Managing Board of the European Payments Union (Kaplan and Schleiminger, 1989), where continuous meetings at a medium but expert level produced results.

There is much to be said for frequent interaction at various functional economic levels, especially in macroeconomic policy, trade, and other perhaps lesser areas such as health, pollution, migration, refugees . . . one could go on. The record, despite many successes, is not totally reassuring. When national interests diverge, it is hard to keep cooperation on track without one party arm-twisting and persuading others to agree. West German fear of inflation, French paranoia over eruption of its farmers, lobbies of various strengths in the United States, function parochially rather than in the international public interest. Strong leadership, best when it is disguised, as with the gold standard (in the instance of Britain); the International Monetary Fund and World Bank (United States), at least up to the early 1970s; or the retaliatory threats of GATT, may ride through or over such roadblocks. Absent the requisite strength and purpose of an effective leader, the system transforms into a game of prisoner's dilemma, in which the first to move in the useful direction is at the mercy of the others who function as free riders.

If benevolent despotism is the most efficient system, as I believe, it too, like a pluralist system of cooperation among equals, or the balance of power, is subject to entropy. The despot is unlikely to stay benevolent, working in the overall interest of the totality, and if it succeeded in so doing, it would not be perceived in this way. Small countries may stay in line, unless they defect in a group as sometimes happens, but the larger are likely to go off on their own, as in the case of French missiles for all azimuths (aimed at the United States as well as at the Soviet Union), or the French attempt in 1965 to chastise the United States by converting dollars into gold. Leaders pay a disproportionate share of the costs of stability, and grow weary in so doing, especially when they are accused of reaping exploitive national gains, seignorage for providing international money, or amassing private investments without providing savings, technology, or other valuable considerations, quite apart from the prestige sought.

Next?

Given decline in the United States and the difficulty of reversing it, if these notions be accepted despite the demurrers of Nau, Rosencrance, Peterson, Rivlin, Moran, and others, and a weakening of growth in Germany and Japan on top of reluctance to challenge for world economic primacy, what next? In the early 1990s, governments of all the leading powers are weak, some troubled by corruption, others with only minority support, still others faced with intractable problems.

I happen not to be a prophet or the son of a prophet, but I predict muddle. Many problems will be dealt with one at a time, others will persist and produce conflicts that linger and mildly poison international economic and political relations. Some agreements reached will not be carried out. On occasion irresolvable disagreements will gradually fade into unimportance. There will be some regionalism, some cooperation among great powers, some persistent low-level conflict. In sum, muddle is indicated. In due course a country will emerge from the muddle for a time as the primary world economic power. The United States again? Japan? Germany? the European Community as a whole? Perhaps a dark horse like Australia or Brazil or China? Who knows? Not I.

Bibliography

Abelshauser, Werner. 1991. "American Aid and West German Economic Recovery: A Macro-Economic Perspective." In *The Marshall Plan and Germany*, edited by Charles S. Maier. New York and Oxford: Berg, pp. 367–411.

Abramovitz, Moses. 1986 (1989). "Catching Up, Forging Ahead and Falling Behind." *Journal of Economic History* 46(2) (June). Reprinted in idem, *Thinking About Growth and Other Essays on Economic Growth and Welfare*. Cambridge: Cambridge University Press, pp. 220–42.

Abramovitz, Moses. 1990. "The Catch-Up Factor in Economic Growth." *Economic Inquiry* 28:1–18.

Acs, Zoltan J. 1984. *The Changing Structure of the American Economy: Lessons from the Steel Industry*. New York: Praeger.

Aldcroft, Derek H., ed. 1968. *The Development of British Industry and Foreign Competition, 1875–1914*. London: George Allen & Unwin.

Allen, G. C. 1929. *The Industrial Development of Birmingham and the Black Country, 1860–1927*. London: Allen & Unwin.

Arruba, José Jobson de Andrade. 1991. "Colonies as Mercantile Investments: The Luso-Brazilian Empire, 1500–1800." In *The Political Economy of Merchant Empires*, edited by James D. Tracy. Cambridge: Cambridge University Press, pp. 360–420.

Ashton, T. S. 1948. *The Industrial Revolution, 1760–1830*. London: Oxford University Press.

Athanas, Christos N. (NYP), "The Lifecycles of Nations."

Attman, Artur. 1983. *Dutch Enterprise in the World Bullion Trade, 1550–1800*. Göteborg: Kungl. Vetenskaps-och Viterhets-Samhället.

Attman, Artur. 1986. *American Bullion in the European World Trade, 1600–1800*. Translated by Eve and Allen Green. Göteberg: Kungl. Vetenskaps-och Viterhets-Samhället.

Aujac, Henri. 1950 (1954). "Inflation as the Monetary Consequence of the Behavior of Social Groups: A Working Hypothesis." Translated *Economie appliquée* 3(2) (April–June), in *International Economic Papers*, no. 4, pp. 109–23.

Aycoberry, Pierre. 1968. "Problem der Sozialschichtung in Köln in Zeitalter der Frühindustrialisierung." In *Wirtschafts- und Sozialgeschichte Probleme der früher Industrialisierung*, edited by Wolfram Fischer. Berlin: Colloquium Verlag, pp. 512–28.

Aymard, Maurice. 1956. *Venise, Raguse et la commerce du blé pendant la seconde moitié du XVIᵉ siècle*. Paris: S.E.V.P.E.N.

Bagehot, Walter. 1873 (1938). *Lombard Street*. Reprinted in *The Collected Works of Walter Bagehot*, edited by Norman St. John Stevas. Vol. 9. London: The Economist, pp. 48–233.

Baily, Martin J. 1993. "Made in the U.S.A." *The Brookings Review* (Winter), pp. 34–39.

Ballot, Charles (Claude Gevel). 1923. *Introduction du machinisme dans l'industrie française*. Paris: Rieder.

Barbour, Violet. 1930 (1954). "Dutch and English Merchant Shipping in the Seventeenth Century." In *Essays in Economic History*, edited by E. M. Carus-Wilson. Vol. 1. London: Arnold, pp. 227–53.

Barbour, Violet. 1950 (1966). *Capitalism and Amsterdam in the Seventeenth Century*. Ann Arbor: University of Michigan Press. Paperback, 2nd printing.

Barker, T. C. 1968. "The Glass Industry." In *The Development of British Industry and Foreign Competition, 1875–1914*, edited by Derek H. Aldcroft. London: George Allen & Unwin, pp. 307–25.

Barkhausen, Max. 1963. *Aus Territorial- und Wirtschaftsgeschichte*. Krefeld, Germany: Krefeld Publishers.

Barkin, Kenneth D. 1970. *The Controversy over German Industrialization, 1890–1902*. Chicago: University of Chicago Press.

Barlow, Edward. 1934. *Barlow's Journal of His Life at Sea in King's Ships, East and West Indian and other Merchantmen from 1659 to 1703*. Transcribed from the original manuscript by Basil Lubbock. London: Hurst and Blackett.

Barnes, Julian. 1993. "Letter from London: The Deficit Millionaires." *The New Yorker*, September 20, pp. 74–93.

Baumol, William J., Sue Anne Batey, and Edward N. Wolff. 1989. *Productivity and American Leadership, the Long View*. Cambridge, Mass.: MIT Press.

Bautier, Robert-Henri. 1971. *The Economic Development of Medieval Europe*. New York: Harcourt Brace Jovanovich.

Bechtel, Heinrich. 1967. *Wirtschafts- und Sozialgeschichte Deutschlands: Wirtschaftsstile und Lebensformen von die Vorzeit zur Gegenwart*. Munich: Verlag Georg D. W. Callway.

Becker, Walter. 1960. "Die Bedeutung der nichtagrarischen Wanderungen für die Herausbildung des industrielle Proletariats in Deutschland, unter besonderer Berücksichtigung Preussens von 1850 bis 1870." In *Studien zur Geschichte der industrielle Revolution in Deutschland*, edited by Hans Mottek et al. Berlin: Akademie-Verlag.

Beer, John Joseph. 1959. *The Emergence of the German Dye Industry*. Urbana: University of Illinois Press.

Beesley, M. E. and G. W. Throup. 1958. "The Machine-Tool Industry." In *The Structure of British Industry*, edited by Duncan Burn. Vol. 1. Cambridge: Cambridge University Press, pp. 359–92.

Bell, Daniel. 1976. *The Coming of Post-Industrial Society: A Venture in Social Forecasting.* New York: Basic Books.

Bell, Daniel. 1991. "The 'Hegelian Secret:' Civil Society and American Exceptionalism." In *Is America Different? A New Look at American Exceptionalism,* edited by Byron E. Shafer. Oxford: Clarendon Press, pp. 46–70.

Benaerts, Pierre. 1933a. *Les origines de la grande industrie allemande.* Paris: Turot.

Benaerts, Pierre. 1933b. *Borsig et des débuts de la fabrication des locomotives en Allemagne.* Paris: Turot.

Berengo, Marino. 1963. *L'agricoltura veneta dall caduta dell republica all'unità.* Milan: Banca Commerciale Italiana.

Berg, Maxine and Pat Hudson. 1992. "Rehabilitating the Industrial Revolution." *Economic History Review* 45(1) (February):24–50.

Bergesen, Albert. 1985. "Cycles of War in the Reproduction of the World Economy." In *Rhythms in Politics and Economics,* edited by Paul M. Johnson and William R. Thomson. New York: Praeger, pp. 313–31.

Bergier, Jean. 1963. *Genève et l'économie européene de la Renaissance.* Paris: S.E.V.P.E.N.

Bergier, Jean François. 1979. "From the Fifteenth Century in Italy to the Sixteenth Century in Germany: A New Banking Concept," In *The Dawn of Modern Banking,* Center for Medieval and Renaissance Studies, University of California at Los Angeles. New Haven, Conn.: Yale University Press, pp. 105–30.

Berner, Samuel. 1974. "Italy: Commentary." In *Failed Transitions to Modern Industrial Society: Renaissance Italy and Seventeenth-Century Holland,* edited by Frederick Krantz and Paul M. Hohenberg. Montreal: Interuniversity Center for European Studies, pp. 19–22.

Berry, Brian J. L. 1991). *Long-Wave Rhythms in Economic Development and Political Behavior.* Baltimore: Johns Hopkins University Press.

Blanchard, Olivier. 1974. "Was France Backward Compared to England in 1789?" MIT term paper, unpublished.

Böhme, Helmut. 1966. *Deutschlands Weg zur Grossmacht: Studien zum Verhältnis von Wirtschaft und Staat während der Reichsgründerzeit.* Cologne: Kiepenheuer and Witsch.

Böhme, Helmut. 1968a. *Frankfurt und Hamburg, Des Deutsches Reiches Silber- und Goldloch und die Allerenglischste Stadt des Kontinents.* Frankfurt: Europaische Verlagsanstalt.

Böhme, Helmut. 1968b. *Prolegomena zu einer Sozial- und Wirtschaftsgeschichte Deutschlands in 19. und 20. Jahrhundert.* Frankfurt-am-Main: Suhrkamp Verlag.

Boonstra, O. W. A. 1993. *Die Waadrij van eene Vroege Opleidung,* no. 34. Wageningen: A.A.G. Bidragen.

Borchardt, Knut. 1972. "Germany 1700–1914." In *The Emergence of Industrial Societies.* Vol. 4, part 1 of *The Fontana Economic History of Europe,* translated by George Hammersley, edited by Carlo M. Cipolla. London and Glasgow: Fontana/Collins, pp. 76–180.

Borchardt, Knut. 1966 (1991). "Regional Variations in Growth in Germany in the Nineteenth Century with Particular Reference to the West-East Development Gradient." In idem, *Perspectives on Modern German Economic History and Policy.* Cambridge: Cambridge University Press, pp. 30–47.

Borchardt, Knut. 1979 (1991). "Constraints and Room for Manœuvre in the Great

Depression of the Early Thirties: Towards a Revision of the Received Historical Picture." In idem, *Perspectives on Modern German Economic History
and Policy*. Cambridge: Cambridge University Press, pp. 143–60.

Borchardt, Knut. 1990. "A Decade of Debate about Bruening's Economic Policy."
In *Economic Crisis and Political Collapse: The Weimar Republic, 1924–1933*,
edited by Jürgen Baron von Kruedner. New York: Berg, pp. 99–132.

Borchardt, Knut and Hans Otto Schötz, eds. 1991. *Wirtschaftspolitik in der Krise:
Die (Geheim-) Konferens der Friederich List-Gesellschaft im September 1931
über Möglichkeiten und Folgen einer Kreditausweisung*. Baden-Baden: Nomos.

Borchardt, Knut and Christopher Buchheim. 1991. "The Marshall Plan and Key
Economic Sectors: a Micro-Economic Perspective." In *The Marshall Plan
and Germany*, edited by Charles S. Maier. New York and Oxford: Berg,
pp. 410–51.

Bouch, Antoine. 1952. "Les grandes écoles." In C. Boudet, *Le monde des affaires
en France de 1830 à nos jours*. Paris: Société d'Edition de Dictionnaires et
Encyclopédies, pp. 566–74.

Boudet, Charles. 1952. *Le monde des affaires en France de 1830 à nos jours*. Paris:
Société d'Edition de Dictionnaires et Encyclopédies.

Bouvier, Jean. 1973. *Un siècle de banque française*. Paris: Fayard.

Bouvier, Jean. 1984. "The French Banks: Inflation and the Economic Crisis,
1919–1939." *Journal of European Economic History*, Special Issue on Banks
and Industry in the Interwar Period 12(2):29–80.

Boxer, C. R. 1965. *The Dutch Seaborne Empire*. New York: Knopf.

Boxer, C. R. 1969. *The Portuguese Seaborne Empire*. New York: Knopf.

Boxer, Charles R. 1970. "The Dutch Economic Decline." In *The Economic Decline of Empires*, edited by Carlo M. Cipolla. London: Methuen, pp. 253–63.

Boyer-Xambeau, Marie Thérèse, Ghislain Deleplace, and Lucien Gillard. 1986.
Monnaie privée et pouvoir des princes: L'économie monétaire à la Renaissance.
No place stated: Presse de la Foundation Nationale des Sciences Politiques.

Brachtel, N. E. 1980. "Regulation and Group Consciousness in the Later History of London Italian Merchant Colonies." *Journal of European Economic
History* 9(3) (Winter):585–610.

Braudel, Fernand. 1949 (1972). *The Mediterranean and the Mediterranean World
in the Age of Phillip II*, vol. 1. Translated by Siân Reynolds. New York: Harper
& Row.

Braudel, Fernand. 1966 (1975). *The Mediterranean: and the Mediterranean World
in the Age of Philip II*, vol. 2. Translated Siân Reynolds. New York: Harper
& Row.

Braudel, Fernand. 1977. *Afterthoughts on Material Life and Capitalism*. Baltimore: Johns Hopkins University Press.

Braudel, Fernand. 1979 (1981). *Civilization & Capitalism, 15th–18th Century*,
vol. 1. *The Structures of Everyday Life*. Translated by Siân Reynolds, New York:
Harper & Row.

Braudel, Fernand. 1979 (1982). *Civilization & Capitalism, 15th–18th Century*,
vol. 2, *The Wheels of Commerce*. Translated by Siân Reynolds. New York:
Harper & Row.

Braudel, Fernand. 1979 (1984). *Civilization & Capitalism, 15th–18th Century*, vol.
3, *The Perspective of the World*. Translated by Siân Reynolds. London: Collins.

Braudel, Fernand. 1986 (1988). *The Identity of France*, vol. 1, *History and Environment*. Translated by Siân Reynolds. New York: Harper & Row.

Braudel, Fernand. 1986 (1990). *The Identity of France*, vol. 2, *People and Production*. Translated by Siân Reynolds. New York: Harper Collins.

Braun, Rudolph. 1960. *Industrialisierung und Volksleben: Die Veränderungen der Lebensformen in einen ländlichen Industriegebiet vor 1800 (Zürcher Oberland)*. Erlenbach-Zurich and Stuttgart: Eugen Rentch Verlag.

Braun, Rudolph. 1965. *Sozialer und cultureller Wandel in einem ländlichen Industriegebiet im 19. und 20. Jahrhundert*. Erlenbach-Zurich and Stuttgart: Eugen Rentch Verlag.

Brenan, Gerald. 1950. *The Spanish Labyrinth: An Account of the Social and Political Background of the Civil War*. 2nd ed. Cambridge: Cambridge University Press.

Brenner, Reuven. 1983. *History: The Human Gamble*. Chicago: University of Chicago Press.

Brepohl, Wilhelm. 1948. *Der Aufbau des Ruhrvolkes im Züge der Ost-West Wanderung: Beiträge zur deutschen Sozialgeschichte des 19. und 20. Jahrhunderts*. Rechlingshausen: Verlag Ritter.

Brezis, Elise S., Paul R. Krugman, and Daniel Tsiddon. 1993. "Leapfrogging in International Competition: A Theory of Cycles in National Technological Leadership." *American Economic Review* 83(5) (December):1211–19.

Broeze, Frank. 1991. "Roundtable: Comment on Yrjo Kaukiainin, *Sailing into Twilight: Finnish Shipping in an Age of Technological Revolution*." *International Journal of Maritime History* 3(2) (December):121–69.

Brown, Lucy. 1958. *The Board of Trade and the Free-Trade Movement, 1830–42*. Oxford: Clarendon.

Buist, Marten G. 1974. *At Spes Non Fracta, Hope and Co., 1770–1815: Merchant Bankers and Diplomats at Work*. The Hague: Martinus Nijhoff.

Bulferetti, Luigi and Claudio Costanti. 1966. *Industriale e Commercio in Liguria nell'età del Risorgimento (1700–1862)*. Milan: Banca Commerciale Italiana.

Bundy, William P. 1977. *Two Hundred Years of American Foreign Policy*. New York: New York University Press (Council on Foreign Relations).

Burk, Kathleen. 1992. "Money and Power: The Shift from Great Britain to the United States." In *Finance and Financiers in European History, 1880–1960*, edited by Youssef Cassis. Cambridge: Cambridge University Press, pp. 359–69.

Burk, Kathleen and Alec Cairncross. 1992. *"Goodbye, Great Britain:" The 1976 IMF Crisis*. New Haven: Yale University Press.

Burke, Peter. 1974. *Venice and Amsterdam, A Study of Seventeenth Century Elites*. London: Temple Smith.

Burn, Duncan. 1940. *Economic History of Steel-Making*. Cambridge: Cambridge University Press.

Butter, Irene Hasenberg. 1969. *Academic Economics in Holland, 1800–1870*. The Hague: Martinus Nijhoff.

Cairncross, A. K. 1953. *Home and Foreign Investment: 1870–1913: Studies in Capital Accumulation*. Cambridge: Cambridge University Press.

Cairncross, Alec and Barry Eichengreen. 1983. *Sterling in Decline: The Devaluations of 1931, 1949 and 1967*. Oxford: Blackwell.

Cairncross, Frances and Alec Cairncross, eds. 1992. *The Legacy of the Golden Age: The 1960s and Their Economic Consequences*. London and New York: Routledge.

Cameron, Rondo. 1961. *France and the Economic Development of Europe (1800–1914)*. Princeton, NJ: Princeton University Press.

Cameron, Rondo. 1983. "A New View of European Industrialization." *Economic History Review* (second series) 38(1) (February):1–23.

Cameron, Rondo. 1989. *A Concise Economic History of the World, from Paleolithic Times to the Present.* New York: Oxford University Press.

Cardwell, D. S. L. 1972. *Turning Points in Western Technology: A Study of Technology, Science and History.* New York: Neale Watson Academic Publications.

Carswell, John. 1960. *The South Sea Bubble.* London: Cresset Press.

Carter, Alice Clare. 1975. *Getting, Spending and Investing in Early Modern Times: Essays on Dutch, English and Huguenot Economic History.* Assen, Netherlands: Van Gorcum & Co.

Central Planning Bureau (the Netherlands). 1992. *Scanning the Future: A Long-Term Scenario of the World Economy, 1990–2015.* The Hague: Sdu Publishers.

Centre de Diffusion Française. 1959. *The Young Face of France.* Paris.

Centre for Economic Policy Research. 1993. "Institutions and Markets: Balance of Power." *European Economic Perspectives,* no. 2 (December), pp. 2–3.

Cervantes, Miguel de. 1606 (1950). *The Ingenious Gentleman, Don Quixote de la Mancha.* New York: Modern Library.

Chambers, J. D. 1961 (1968). *The Workshop of the World: British Economic History from 1820–1880.* 2nd ed. London: Oxford University Press.

Chaptal, M. le Comte (Jean Antoine Claude de). 1819. *De l'industrie française,* 2 vols. Paris: Renouard.

Chatelaine, Abel. 1956. "Dans les campagnes française du XIX siècle: La lente progression de la faux." *Annales: Economies, Sociétés, Civilisations* 11(3) (October–December):495–99.

Checkland, Sydney. 1983. *British Public Policy, 1776–1939: An Economic, Social and Political Perspective.* Cambridge: Cambridge University Press.

Chevalier, Michel. 1836 (1838). *Lettres sur l'Amerique du Nord,* 2 vols. 3rd ed. Paris: Gosselin.

Church, R. A. 1975. *The Great Victorian Boom, 1850–1873.* London: Macmillan.

Churchill, Winston S. 1925 (1974). *Winston S. Churchill, His Complete Speeches, 1897–1963,* vol. 4, *1922–38,* edited by R. R. James. London: Chelsea House.

Cipolla, Carlo M. 1968. "The Economic Decline of Italy." In *Crisis and Change in the Venetian Economy in the Sixteenth and Seventeenth Centuries,* edited by Brian Pullan. London: Methuen, pp. 127–45.

Cipolla, Carlo M., ed. 1970. *The Economic Decline of Empires.* London: Methuen.

Cipolla, Carlo M. 1974. "The Italian 'Failure'." In *Failed Transitions to Modern Industrial Society: Renaissance Italy and Seventeenth-Century Holland,* edited by Frederick Kranz and Paul M. Hohenberg. Montreal: Interuniversity Center for European Studies, pp. 8–10.

Cipolla, Carlo. M. 1976. *Before the Industrial Revolution: European Society and its Economy, 1000–1700.* New York: W. W. Norton.

Clapham, J. H. 1910 (1962). "The Last Years of the Navigation Acts." Vol. 3 in *Essays in Economic History,* edited by E. M. Carus-Wilson. London: Edward Arnold, pp. 144–78.

Clark, Colin. 1945. "Public Finance and the Value of Money." *Economic Journal* 50(4) (December):371–81.

Clark, Tanya. 1993a. "Decisions? Decisions: Japanese Decision Making Is Clearer and More Familiar Than the West Thinks." *Japan Update* 23 (August):18–19.

Clark, Tanya. 1993b. "The Twain Imitate: Japan and the United States Learn from Each Other's Strengths." *Japan Update* 24 (September):18–19.

Cole, W. A. and Phyllis Deane. 1965. "The Growth of National Income." In *The Industrial Revolution and After: Incomes, Population and Technological Change*, edited by H. J. Habakkuk and M. Postan. Vol. 6 of *The Cambridge Economic History of Europe*. Cambridge: Cambridge University Press, pp. 1–55.

Coleman, D. C. 1973. "Gentlemen and Players." *Economic History Review*, 2nd series, 26(1) (February):92–116.

Comité pour l'Histoire Economique et Financière de la France. 1989. *Etudes et documents, I*. Paris: Imprimerie Nationale.

Commerce, Ministère du, Direction des Etudes Techniques. 1919. *Rapport général sur l'industrie française*. 3 vols. Paris: Imprimerie Nationale.

Cooper, Richard N. 1985. "International Economic Cooperation: Is It Desirable? Is It Likely?" *Bulletin of the American Academy of Arts and Sciences* 39 (November).

Coste, Pierre. 1932. *La lutte pour la suprématie: les grandes marches financiers: Paris, London, New York*. Paris: Payot.

Cotgrove, Stephen E. 1958. *Technical Education and Social Change*. London: Allen & Unwin.

Court, W. H. B. 1965. *British Economic History, 1870–1914: Commentary and Documents*. Cambridge: Cambridge University Press.

Crafts, N. F. R. 1985. *British Economic Growth during the Industrial Revolution*. Oxford: Clarendon.

Crafts, N. F. R. and C. K. Harley. 1992. "Output Growth and the British Industrial Revolution: A Restatement of the Crafts-Harley View." *Economic History Review* 45(4):703–30.

Craig, Gordon A. 1970. *The Politics of the Prussian Army, 1640–1945*. London: Oxford University Press.

Crouzet, François. 1968. "Economie et société (1715–1789)." In *Bordeaux au XVIIIème siècle*, edited by François-George Pariset. Bordeaux: Fédération historique du Sud-ouest., pp. 193–286.

Dahrendorf, Ralf. 1965 (1969). *Society and Democracy in Germany*. Garden City, N.Y.: Anchor Books.

Da Silva, Jose-Gentil. 1969. *Banque et crédit en Italie au XVII siècle*. Vol. 1, *Les foires de change et la dépréciation monétaire*. Vol. 2, *Sources et cours des changes*. Paris: Editions Klincksieck.

David, Paul A. 1985. "Clio and the Economics of QWERTY." *American Economic Review* 75(2) (May):322–37.

David, Paul A. 1990. "The Dynamo and the Computer: An Historical Perspective in the Modern Productivity Paradox." *American Economic Review* 80(1) (March):335–61.

David, Paul A. 1994. "Why Are Institutions the 'Carriers of History'?: Notes on Path-Dependency and the Evolution of Conventions, Organizations and Institutions." In *Structural Change and Economic Dynamics*, 5(2):205–20.

Davis, Lance E. and Robert A. Huttenback. 1986. *Mammon and the Pursuit of Empire: The Political Economy of British Imperialism, 1880–1913*. Cambridge: Cambridge University Press.

Davis, Ralph. 1973. *The Rise of the Atlantic Economies*. Ithaca, N.Y.: Cornell University Press.

Day, John. 1978 (1987). "The Great Bullion Famine of the Fifteenth Century." In idem, *The Medieval Market Economy*. Oxford: Blackwell, pp. 1–54.

Deane, Phyllis. 1965 (1979). *The First Industrial Revolution.* 2nd ed. Cambridge: Cambridge University Press.

Deane, Phyllis and W. A. Cole. 1962. *British Economic Growth, 1689–1959.* Cambridge: Cambridge University Press.

D'Elia, Costanza. 1993. "Miracles and Mirages in the West German Economy: A Survey of the Literature of the 1980s." *Journal of European Economic History* 22(2) (Fall):381–401.

de Roover, Raymond. 1942 (1953). "The Commercial Revolution of the Thirteenth Century." *Bulletin of the Business Historical Society,* reprinted in *Enterprise and Secular Change: Readings in Economic History,* edited by F. C. Lane and J. C. Riemersma. Homewood, Ill.: Richard D. Irwin, pp. 80–85.

de Roover, Raymond. 1948. *Money, Banking and Credit in Medieval Bruges: Italian Merchant Bankers, Lombards and Money Changers: A Study in the Origins of Banking.* Cambridge, Mass. Medieval Academy of America.

de Roover, Raymond. 1949. *Gresham on Foreign Exchange, An Essay on Early English Mercantilism, with the Text of Sir Thomas Gresham's Memorandum for the Understanding of the Exchange.* Cambridge, Mass.: Harvard University Press.

de Roover, Raymond. 1949. "Thomas Mun in Italy." *Bulletin of the Institute of Historical Research.* 30(81):80–85.

de Roover, Raymond. 1966. *The Rise and Fall of the Medici Bank.* New York: W. W. Norton.

Dertouzos, Michael, Richard K. Lester, and Robert M. Solow. 1989. *Made in America.* Cambridge, Mass.: MIT Press.

Despres, Emile, C. P. Kindleberger, and W. S. Salant. 1966 (1981). "The Dollar and World Liquidity: A Minority View." *The Economist.* Reprinted in C. P. Kindleberger, *International Money.* London: George Allen & Unwin, pp. 42–52.

de Vries, Jan. (1974). *The Dutch Rural Economy in the Golden Age, 1500–1700,* New Haven, Conn.: Yale University Press.

de Vries, Jan. (1976). *The Economy of Europe in the Age of Crisis, 1600–1750.* Cambridge: Cambridge University Press.

de Vries, Jan. 1978. *Barges and Capitalism: Passenger Traffic in the Dutch Economy.* Wageningen: A.A.G. Bijdragen 21.

de Vries, Jan. 1984a. *European Urbanization, 1500–1800.* Cambridge, Mass.: Harvard University Press.

de Vries, Jan. 1984b. "The Decline and Rise of the Dutch Economy, 1675–1900." In *Technique, Spirit and Form in the Making of the Modern Economies: Essays in Honor of William N. Parker, Research in Economic History,* suppl. 3, pp. 149–89.

de Zeeuw, J. W. 1978. *Peat and the Dutch Golden Age: The Historical Meaning of Energy-Sustainability.* Wageningen: A.A.G. Bijdragen 21.

Dhondt, J. 1955 (1969). "The Cotton Industry at Ghent during the French Regime." In *Essays in European Economic History, 1789–1914,* edited by F. Crouzet, W. H. Chaloner, and W. M. Stern. New York: St. Martin's Press, pp. 15–52.

Dickens, Charles. 1857 (1894). *Little Dorrit.* 2 vols. Boston: Houghton Mifflin.

Dickson, P. G. M. 1967. *The Financial Revolution in England: A Study in the Development of Public Credit, 1688–1756.* New York: St. Martins Press.

Dollinger, Philippe. 1964 (1970). *The German Hansa.* Translated and edited by D. S. Ault and S. H. Steinberg. Stanford, Calif.: Stanford University Press.

Doran, Charles F. 1985. "Power Cycle Theory and Systems Stability." In *Rhythms in Politics and Economics*, edited by Paul M. Johnson and William R. Thompson. New York: Praeger, pp. 292–312.

Dornic, François. 1955. *L'industrie textile dans le Maine et ses débouches internationaux, 1650–1815.* Le Mans: Editions Pierre-Belon.

Dufraise, Roger. 1992. "Flottes et flotteurs de bois du Rhin a l'époque napoléonienne." In idem, *L'Allemagne à l'époque napoléonienne, Questions d'histoire politique, économique et sociale.* Bonn and Berlin: Verlag Bouvier, pp. 217–43.

Dumke, Rolf H. 1976. "The Political Economy of German Economic Unification: Tariffs, Trade and Politics of the Zollverein." Doctoral dissertation in economic history, University of Wisconsin, Madison.

Dunham, Arthur Louis. 1955. *The Industrial Revolution in France, 1815–1848.* New York: Exposition Press.

Ecole polytechnique. 1895. *Livre de centenaire, 1794–1894.* 3 vols. Paris: Gauthier-Vilas et Fils.

The Economist. 1991. "A Survey of America: The Old Country." Vol. 321, no. 7730 (October 26), survey pp. 1–26.

The Economist. 1993. "The British Audit: Manufacturing." Vol. 328, no. 7825 (August 21), pp. 46–47.

The Economist. 1993. "Tokyo's Inflating Shares." Vol. 328, no. 7830 (September 25), p. 92.

The Economist. 1993. "When Other Nations Play Leap Frog." Vol. 329, no. 7833 (October 16), p. 84.

Edelstein, Michael. 1982. *Overseas Investment in the Age of High Imperialism: The United Kingdom, 1850–1914.* New York: Columbia University Press.

Ehrenberg, Richard. 1896 (1928). *Capital and Finance in the Age of the Renaissance: A Study of the Fuggers.* New York: Harcourt Brace.

Eichengreen, Barry. 1992. *Golden Fetters: The Gold Standard and the Great Depression, 1919–1939.* New York and London: Oxford University Press.

Eisner, Robert. 1992. "The Twin Deficits." In *Profits, Deficits and Instability*, edited by Dimitri B. Papadimitriou. London: Macmillan, pp. 255–67.

Elbaum, Bernard and William Lazonick. 1984. "The Decline of the British Economy: An Institutional Perspective." *Journal of Economic History* 44(2) (June):567–83.

Elbaum, Bernard and William Lazonick. 1986. *The Decline of the British Economy: An Institutional Perspective.* Oxford: Oxford University Press.

Elliot, J. H. 1961 (1970). "The Decline of Spain." In *The Economic Decline of Empires*, edited by Carlo M. Cipolla. London: Methuen, pp. 168–95.

Elliot, J. H. 1968 (1982). *Europe Divided, 1559–1598.* Ithaca, N.Y.: Cornell University Press (paperback).

Emmott, Bill. 1989. *The Sun Also Sets: The Limits to Japan's Economic Power.* New York: Time Books.

Encounter. 1963. "Suicide of a Nation?" Special issue, no. 118 (July).

Epstein, Klaus. 1959. *Matthias Erzberger and the Dilemma of German Democracy.* Princeton, N.J.: Princeton University Press.

Evans, D. Morier. 1859 (1969). *The History of the Commercial Crisis, 1857–1858, and the Stock Exchange Panic of 1859.* Reprint ed. New York: A. M. Kelley.

Faure, Edgar. 1977. *La banqueroûte de Law, 17 juillet 1720.* Paris: Gallimard.

Feldman, Gerald D. 1993. *The Great Disorder: Politics, Economics and Society in the German Inflation, 1914–1924.* New York and Oxford: Oxford University Press.

Felix, David. 1971. *Walther Rathenau and the Weimar Republic: The Politics of Reparations.* Baltimore: Johns Hopkins University Press.

Fischer, Wolfram. 1962. *Der Staat und die Anfänge der Industrialisierung in Baden, 1800–1850.* Berlin: Duncker und Humblot.

Florence, P. Sargent. 1953. *The Logic of British and American Industry.* London: Routledge and Kegan Paul.

Flynn, Michael W. 1953 (1965). "Sir Ambrose Crowley, Ironmonger, 1658–1713." In *Explorations in Enterprise,* edited by Hugh G. J. Aitken. Cambridge, Mass.: Harvard University Press, pp. 241–58.

Fodella, Gianni. 1991. "Can New Europe Compete with Japan and the United States?" *Rivista di Politica Economica* 81(3) (May):653–73.

Forster, Robert. 1975. "Review" of Charles Carrière, *Négociants Marseillais au XVIIIᵉ siècle: Contribution à l'étude des économies maritimes,* 1973, 2 vols. *Journal of Modern History* 47(1) (March):162–65.

Forsyth, Peter L. and Stephen J. Nicholas. 1983. "The Decline of Spain: Industry and the Price Revolution: A Neoclassical Analysis." *Journal of European Economic History* 12(3) (Winter):601–10.

Frank, Andre Gunder and Barry K. Gilles. 1993. "World System Economic Cycles and Hegemonial Shift to Europe, 100 BC to 1500 AD." *Journal of European Economic History* 22(1) (Spring):155–83.

Friedberg, Aaron L. 1988. *The Weary Titan: Britain and the Experience of Relative Decline, 1895–1905.* Princeton, N.J.: Princeton University Press.

Froelich, Norman and Joe A. Oppenheimer. 1970. "I Get Along with a Little Help from My Friends." *World Politics* 23(1) (October):104–20.

Frye, Northrop. 1974. "*The Decline of the West,* by Oswald Spengler." *Daedalus* 103(1) (Winter), "Twentieth Century Classics Revisited":1–13.

Funabashi, Yoichi. 1993. "Structural Defects in Tokyo's Foreign Policy" *Economic Eye* 14(2) (Summer):25–28.

Garber, Peter M. 1990. "The Dollar as a Bubble." In *The Economics of the Dollar Cycle,* edited by Stefan Gerlach and Peter A. Petri. Cambridge, Mass.: MIT Press, pp. 129–47.

Gerschenkron, Alexander. 1943. *Bread and Democracy in Germany.* Berkeley: University of California Press.

Gerschenkron, Alexander. 1962. *Economic Backwardness in Historical Perspective: A Book of Essays.* Cambridge, Mass.: Belknap Press of Harvard University Press.

Gerschenkron, Alexander. 1968. *Continuity in History and Other Essays.* Cambridge, Mass.: Belknap Press of Harvard University Press.

Gerschenkron, Alexander. 1977. *An Economic Spurt That Failed: Four Lectures in Austrian History.* Princeton, N.J.: Princeton University Press.

Geyl, Peter. 1961. *The Netherlands in the Seventeenth Century, Part One, 1600–1648.* Rev. and enlarged. New York: Barnes and Noble.

Giersch, Herbert, Karl-Heinz Paqué, and Holger Schmieding. 1992. *The Fading Miracle: Four Decades of Market Economy in Germany.* Cambridge: Cambridge University Press.

Gimpel, Jean. 1976. "How to Help the United States Age Gracefully." Unpublished memorandum.

Girard, L. 1965. "Transport." In *The Industrial Revolution and After: Incomes, Population and Technological Change,* edited by H. J. Habbakkuk and M.

Postan. Vol. 6 of *The Cambridge Economic History of Europe*. Cambridge: Cambridge University Press, pp. 213–73.

Glick, Thomas P. 1970. *Irrigation and Society in Medieval Valencia*. Cambridge, Mass.: Belknap Press of Harvard University Press.

Goldstein, Joshua S. 1988. *Long Cycles, Prosperity and War in the Modern Age*. New Haven, Conn., and London: Yale University Press.

Goldstone, Jack A. 1991. *Revolution and Rebellion in the Early Modern World*. Berkeley: University of California Press.

Goodwin, Richard M. 1991. Comment on Joshua S. Goldstein, "A War-Economy Theory of the Long Wave." In *Business Cycles: Theories, Evidence and Analysis*, edited by Niels Thygesen, Kumaraswamy Velupillai, and Stefano Zambelli. London: Macmillan, p. 326.

Gordon, Robert J. 1993. "American Economic Growth: One Big Wave." National Bureau of Economic Research paper.

Grantham, G. W. 1993. "Division of Labour: Agricultural Productivity and Occupational Specialization in Pre-Industrial France." *Economic History Review* 46(3) (August):478–502.

Gras, N. S. B. 1930. *Industrial Evolution*. Cambridge, Mass.: Harvard University Press.

Greenfield, Kent Roberts. 1965. *Economics and Liberalism in the Risorgimento, A Study in Nationalism in Lombardy, 1814–1848*. Rev. ed. Baltimore: Johns Hopkins University Press.

Greif, Avner. 1989. "Reputation and Coalitions in Medieval Trade: Evidence on the Maghribi Traders." *Journal of Economic History* 49(4) (December): 857–82.

Habakkuk, H. J. 1952. *American and British Technology in the Nineteenth Century*. Cambridge: Cambridge University Press.

Hagen, Everett E. 1962. *On the Theory of Social Change: How Economic Growth Begins*. Homewood, Ill.: Dorsey Press.

Hamada, Koichi. 1995. "Bubbles, Bursts and Bail-Outs: Comparison of Three Episodes of Financial Crisis in Japan." In *The Structure of the Japanese Economy*. New York: Macmillan. Paper presented March 11, 1993, at a conference at National Taiwan University.

Hamada, Koichi and Munehisa Kasuya. 1993. "The Reconstruction and Stabilization of the Postwar Japanese Economy: Possible Lessons for Eastern Europe?" In *Postwar Economic Reconstruction and Lessons for the East Today*, edited by Rudiger Dornbusch, Wilhelm Rölling, and Richard Layard. Cambridge, Mass.: MIT Press, pp. 155–87.

Hamilton, Earl J. 1934 (1965). *American Treasure and the Price Revolution in Spain, 1501–1650*. Cambridge, Mass.: Harvard University Press. Repr. New York: Octagon Books.

Hamilton, Earl J. 1938 (1954). "The Decline of Spain." In *Essays in Economic History*, vol. 1, edited by E. M. Carus-Wilson. London: Edward Arnold, pp. 215–26.

Hamilton, Earl J. 1969. "The Political Economy of France at the Time of John Law." *History of Political Economy* 1(1) (Spring):123–49.

Hara, Akira. 1993. "American Aid and the Reconstruction of the Japanese Economy." In Comité pour L'Histoire Economique et Financière de la France, *Le Plan Marshall et le relèvement économique de l'Europe*. Paris: Imprimerie Nationale, pp. 607–19.

Haring, Clarence Henry. 1918. *Trade and Navigation between Spain and the Indies in the Time of the Hapsburgs.* Cambridge, Mass.: Harvard University Press.

Harley, C. Knick. 1986. Review of N. F. R. Crafts, *British Economic Growth during the Industrial Revolution* (1985). *Journal of Economic Literature* 24(2) (June):683–84.

Harris, Robert D. 1979. *Necker, Reform Statesman of the Ancien Regime.* Berkeley: University of California Press.

Heckscher, Eli F. 1935 (1983). *Mercantilism.* 2 vols. Translated by Mendel Shapiro. New York: Macmillan. Repr. Garland Publishing.

Heckscher, Eli F. 1954. *An Economic History of Sweden.* Translated by Göran Ohlin. Cambridge, Mass.: Harvard University Press.

Heers, Jacques. 1964. "Gênes." In *Città mercanti dottrine nell'economia Europea dal IV al XVIII secolo, Saggi in memoria di Gino Luzzato,* edited by Amintore Fanfani. Milan: A Giuffre, pp. 85–103.

Helfferich, Karl. 1921–23 (1956). *Georg von Siemens: Ein Lebensbild aus Deutchlands grosser Zeit.* 1 vol., rev. and abr. ed. of 3 vols. Krefeld: Richard Serpe.

Henderson, W. O. 1954. *Britain and Industrial Europe, 1750–1870, Studies in British Influence on the Industrial Revolution in Western Europe.* Liverpool, Liverpool University Press.

Henry, M. L. 1955. Discussion in Colloques Internationaux de la Recherche Scientifique, *Sociologie comparée de la famille contemporaine.* Paris: Editions du Centre National de la Recherche Scientifique.

Herr, Richard. 1958. *The Eighteenth Century Revolution in Spain.* Princeton, N.J.: Princeton University Press.

Herr, Richard and John H. R. Pont. 1989. *Iberian Identity: Essays on the Nature of Identity of Portugal and Spain.* Berkeley: University of California Press.

Hicks, Sir John. 1969. *A Theory of Economic History.* London: Oxford University Press.

Hironaka, Wakako. 1993. "Through Rosy Glasses: Darkly." *The New York Times,* op. ed. communication, June 5, p. 21.

Hirsch, Fred. 1976. *Social Limits to Growth.* Cambridge, Mass.: Harvard University Press.

Hirschman, Albert O. 1958. *The Strategy of Economic Development.* New Haven, Conn.: Yale University Press.

Hoffman, Ross J. S. 1933. *Great Britain and the German Trade Rivalry, 1875–1914.* Philadelphia: University of Pennsylvania Press.

Hoffmann, Stanley. 1993. "Thoughts on the French Nation." *Daedalus* 122(3) (Summer):63–79.

Hohenberg, Paul M. 1967. *Chemicals in Western Europe, 1850–1914: An Economic Study of Technical Change.* Chicago: Rand McNally & Co.

Holtfrerich, Carl-Ludwig. 1982. "Alternativen zu Brüning's Wirtschaftspolitik in der Weltwirtschaftskrise." *Historische Zeitschrift* 235:605–31.

Holtfrerich, Carl-Ludwig. 1990. "Was the Policy of Deflation in Germany Unavoidable?" In *Economic Crisis and Collapse: The Weimar Republic, 1924–1933,* edited by Jürgen Baron von Kruedner. New York, Oxford, and Munich: Berg, pp. 63–81.

Hopkins, Terrence K., Immanuel Wallerstein, et al. 1982. "Cyclical Rhythms and Trends of the Capitalist World Economy." In idem, *World-System Analysis: Theory and Methodology.* Beverly Hills, Calif.: Sage Publications.

Hulen, Sherwin B. 1994. *How We Die.* New York: Knopf.

Huntington, Ellsworth. 1915. *Civilization and Climate*. New Haven, Conn.: Yale University Press.

Ilie, Paul. 1989. "Self-Images in the Mirror of Otherness." In *Iberian Identity: Essays on the Nature of Identity of Portugal and Spain*, edited by Richard Herr and John H. R. Pont. Berkeley: University of California Press, pp. 156–80.

Ingesias, Maria Carmen. 1989. "Montesquieu and Spain: Iberian Identity as Seen Through the Eyes of a Non-Spaniard in the Eighteenth Century." In *Iberian Identity: Essays on the Nature of Identity of Portugal and Spain*, edited by Richard Herr and John H. R. Pont. Berkeley: University of California Press, pp. 145–55.

Inman, Robert P. 1993. Review of Alice M. Rivlin, *Reviving the American Dream* (1992). *Journal of Economic Literature* 31(3) (September):1466–68.

INSEE (Institut National de la Statistique et des Etudes Economiques). *Annuaire Statistique de la France*. Paris: Imprimerie Nationale, various years.

Isard, Caroline and Walter Isard. 1945. "Economic Implications of Aircraft." *Quarterly Journal of Economics* 59(1) (February):145–69.

Israel, Jonathan I. 1989. *Dutch Primacy in World Trade, 1585–1740*. Oxford: Clarendon Press.

Jackson, Gordon. 1991. "Roundtable: Comment on Yjro Kaukiainin, *Sailing into Twilight: Finnish Shipping in an Age of Technological Revolution*." *International Journal of Maritime History* 3(2) (December):121–69.

Jacquin, François. 1955. *Les cadres de l'industrie et du commerce en France*. Paris: Colin.

Jeanneney, Jean-Noël. 1977. *Leçon d'histoire pour une gauche au pouvoir, 1914–1940*. Paris: Seuil.

Jensen, Michael C. and W. H. Meckling. 1976. "Theory of the Firm: Managerial Economics, Agency Costs and Ownership Structure." *Journal of Financial Economics* 3(4) (October):305–30.

Jervis, F. R. J. 1947. "The Handicap of Britain's Early Start." *Manchester School*, 15(1):112–22.

Jones, E. L. 1978. "Disaster Management and Resource Saving in Europe, 1400–1800." In *Natural Resources in European History*, edited by Antoni Maczak and William N. Parker. Washington, D.C.: Resources for the Future, pp. 113–36.

Jones, E. L. 1987. *The European Miracle, Environments, Economies and Geopolitics in the History of Europe and Asia*. 2nd ed. Cambridge: Cambridge University Press.

Jones, E. L. 1988. *Growth Recurring: Economic Change in World History*. Oxford: Clarendon Press.

Jones, Ethel. 1930. *Les voyageurs français en Angleterre de 1815 à 1830*. Paris: Boccard.

Judge, A. V. 1939 (1969). "The Idea of a Mercantile State." In *Revisions in Mercantilism*, edited by D. C. Coleman. London: Methuen, pp. 35–60.

Kahler, Erich. 1974. *The Germans*. Edited by Robert and Rita Kimber. Princeton, N.J.: Princeton University Press.

Kaltenstadler, Wilhelm. 1972. "European Economic History in the Recent German Historiography." *Journal of European Economic History* 1(1) (Spring): 193–218.

Kamen, Henry. 1969. *The War of Succession in Spain, 1700–1715*. London: Weidenfield and Nicholson.

Kaplan, Jacob J. and Günter Schleiminger. 1989. *The European Payments Union: Financial Diplomacy in the 1950s.* Oxford: Clarendon Press.

Kehr, Eckart. 1930 (1970). "Imperialismus und deutscher Schlachtflottenbau." In *Imperialismus,* edited by Hans-Ulrich Wehler. Cologne and Berlin: Kiepenheuer & Witsch, pp. 289–308.

Kehr, Eckart. 1965. *Der Primat der Innenpolitik: Gesammelte Aufsätze zur preussische-deutschen Sozialgeschichte im 19. und 20. Jahrhundert.* Edited and introduced by Hans-Ulrich Wehler. Berlin: Walter de Gruyter.

Keizai Koho Center. 1994. *Japan, 1995: An International Comparison.* Tokyo: Keizai Koho Center.

Kellenbenz, Hermann. 1963. Editor's foreword to Ludwig Beutin, *Gesammelte Schriften zur Wirtschafts- und Sozialgeschichte.* Cologne: Böhllau Verlag.

Kellenbenz, Hermann. 1963 (1974). "Rural Industries in the West from the End of the Middle Ages to the Eighteenth Century." In *Essays in European Economic History, 1500–1800,* edited by Peter Earle. Oxford: Clarendon, pp. 45–88.

Kennedy, Paul. 1987. *The Rise and Fall of Great Powers: Economic Change and Military Conflict.* New York: Random House.

Kennedy, William P. 1987. *Industrial Structure, Capital Markets and the Origins of British Decline.* Cambridge: Cambridge University Press.

Keynes, John Maynard. 1919. *The Economic Consequences of the Peace.* London: Macmillan.

Keynes, John Maynard. 1930. *The Applied Theory of Money.* Vol. 2 of *A Treatise on Money.* New York: Harcourt Brace & Co.

Kindleberger, Charles P. 1945, 1946 (1989). *The German Economy, 1945–1947: Charles P. Kindleberger's Letters from the Field.* Westport, Conn.: Meckler.

Kindleberger, Charles P. 1956. *The Terms of Trade: A European Case Study.* New York: The Technology Press of MIT and John Wiley & Sons.

Kindleberger, Charles P. 1958 (1965). *Economic Development.* New York: McGraw-Hill.

Kindleberger, Charles P. 1964. *Economic Growth in France and Britain, 1851–1950.* Cambridge, Mass.: Harvard University Press.

Kindleberger, Charles P. 1967. *Europe's Postwar Growth: The Role of the Labor Supply.* Cambridge, Mass.: Harvard University Press.

Kindleberger, Charles P. 1969. *American Business Abroad: Six Lectures on Direct Investment.* New Haven, Conn.: Yale University Press.

Kindleberger, Charles P. 1973 (1986). *The World in Depression, 1929–1939.* 2nd ed. Berkeley: University of California Press.

Kindleberger, Charles P. 1974. "An American Climacteric?" *Challenge* 17(1): 35–45.

Kindleberger, Charles P. 1974 (1978). "The Formation of Financial Centers," in idem., *Economic Response: Comparative Studies in Trade, Finance, and Growth.* Cambridge, Mass.: Harvard University Press, pp. 66–133.

Kindleberger, Charles P. 1975 (1978). "Germany's Overtaking England, 1806–1914." In idem., *Economic Response: Comparative Studies in Trade, Finance and Growth.* Cambridge, Mass.: Harvard University Press, pp. 185–236.

Kindleberger, Charles P. 1976a. "Technical Education and the French Entrepreneur." In *Enterprise and Entrepreneurship in Nineteenth- and Twentieth-Century France,* edited by Edward C. Carter, Robert Forster, and Joseph N. Moody. Baltimore: Johns Hopkins University Press, pp. 3–39.

Kindleberger, Charles P. 1976b. "The Historical Background: Adam Smith and the Industrial Revolution." In *The Market and the State: Essays in Honour of Adam Smith*, edited by Thomas Wilson and Andrew S. Skinner. Oxford: Clarendon Press, pp. 3–25.

Kindleberger, Charles P. 1978 (1989). *Manias, Panics and Crashes: A History of Financial Crises*. New ed. New York: Basic Books.

Kindleberger, Charles P. 1978 (1990). "The Aging Economy," in *Weltwirtschaftliches Archiv*, reprinted in idem, *Historical Economics*. New York: Harvester/Wheatsheaf, pp. 235–45.

Kindleberger, Charles P. 1984 (1993). *A Financial History of Western Europe*. Rev. ed. New York: Oxford University Press.

Kindleberger, Charles P. 1989. "The United States and the World Economy in the Twentieth Century." In *Interactions in the World Economy: Perspectives from International History*, edited by Carl-Ludwig Holtfrerich. New York, London: Harvester/Wheatsheaf, pp. 287–313.

Kindleberger, Charles P. 1990. "The Panic of 1873." In *Crashes and Panics: the Lessons from History*, edited by Eugene N. White. Homewood, Ill.: Dow Jones-Irwin, pp. 69–84.

Kindleberger, Charles P. 1992a. "Why Did the Golden Age Last So Long?" In *The Legacy of the Golden Age: The 1960s and their Economic Consequences*, edited by Frances Cairncross and Alec Cairncross. London: Routledge, pp. 15–44.

Kindleberger, Charles P. 1992b. *Mariners and Markets*. New York: Harvester/Wheatsheaf.

Kirby, M. W. 1992. "Institutional Rigidities and Economic Decline: Reflections on British Experience." *Economic History Review* 45(4) (November):637–60.

Klein, Julius. 1920. *The Mesta*. Cambridge, Mass.: Harvard University Press.

Klein, Peter W. 1970a. "Entrepreneurial Behaviour and the Economic Rise and Decline of the Netherlands in the 17th and 18th Centuries." *Annales Cisalpines d'Histoire Sociale*, no. 1, pp. 7–19.

Klein, P. W. 1970b. "Stagnation économique et emploi du capital dans le Hollande des XVIIIᵉ et XIXᵉ siècles." *Revue du Nord* 52(204) (January–March):33–41.

Klein, Peter Wolfgang. 1982. "Dutch Capitalism and the World Economy." In *Dutch Capitalism and World Capitalism*, edited by Maurice Aymard. Cambridge: Cambridge University Press, pp. 75–91.

Kocka, Jürgen. 1978. "Entrepreneurs and Managers in German Industrialization." In *The Industrial Economies: Capital, Labour and Enterprise*. Part I: Britain, France, Germany and Scandinavia. Vol. 7. *The Cambridge Economic History of Europe*, edited by Peter Mathias and M. M. Postan. Cambridge: Cambridge University Press, pp. 492–589.

Kocka, Jürgen. 1994. "Crisis of Unification: How Germany Changes." *Daedalus* 123(1) (Winter):173–92.

Koebner, R. 1959. "Adam Smith and the Industrial Revolution." *Economic History Review* (2nd ser.) 11(3) (August):281–91.

Köllman, Wolfgang. 1965. "The Population of Barmen before and during the Period of Industrialization." In *Population in History: Essays in Historical Demography*, edited by D. C. Glass and D. E. C. Eversley. London: Edward Arnold, pp. 588–607.

Komiya, Ryutaro. 1990. *The Japanese Economy: Trade, Industry and Government*. Tokyo: University of Tokyo Press.

Konvitz, Josef W. 1978. *Cities & the Sea: Port City Planning in Early Modern Europe*. Baltimore: Johns Hopkins University Press.

Kossmann, E. H. 1974. "Some Meditations on Dutch Eighteenth-Century Decline." In *Failed Transitions to Modern Industrial Society: Renaissance Italy and Seventeenth-Century Holland*, edited by F. Krantz and P. M. Hohenberg. Montreal: Interuniversity Center for European Studies, pp. 49–54.

Krantz, Frederick and P. M. Hohenberg, eds. 1974. *Failed Transitions to Modern Industrial Society: Renaissance Italy and Seventeenth-Century Holland*. Montreal: Interuniversity Center for European Studies.

Krasner, Stephen D. 1983. "Structural Causes and Regime Consequences: Regimes as Intervening Variables." In *International Regimes*, edited by Stephen D. Krasner. Ithaca, N.Y.: Cornell University Press.

Krugman, Paul R. 1990a. "Hindsight on the Strong Dollar." In *The Economics of the Dollar Cycle*, edited by Stefan Gerlach and Peter A. Petri. Cambridge, Mass.: MIT Press, pp. 92–118.

Krugman, Paul R. 1990b. *The Age of Diminished Expectations: U.S. Economic Policy in the 1990s*. Cambridge, Mass.: MIT Press.

Kuznets, Simon. 1930. *Secular Movements in Prices and Production*. Boston: Houghton Mifflin.

Lambert, Audrey M. 1971. *The Making of the Dutch Landscape: An Historical Geography of the Netherlands*. London: Seminar Press.

Lambi, Ivo Nicolai. 1963. *Free Trade and Protection in Germany, 1868–1879*. Wiesbaden: Fritz Steiner Verlag.

Landes, David S. 1960. "The Bleichröder Bank: An Interim Report." In publications of the Leo Baeck Institute, *Yearbook V*. London: East and West Library, pp. 201–20.

Landes, David S. 1965. "Technological Change and Development in Western Europe, 1750–1914." In *The Industrial Revolution and After: Incomes, Population and Technological Change*, edited by H. J. Habakkuk and M. Postan. Vol. 6 of *The Cambridge Economic History of Europe*. Cambridge: Cambridge University Press, pp. 274–601.

Landes, David S. 1989. "Some Thoughts on Economic Hegemony: Europe in the Nineteenth Century World Economy." In *Interactions in the World Economy: Perspective from International Economic History*, edited by Carl-Ludwig Holtfrerich. New York and London: Harvester/Wheatsheaf, pp. 153–67.

Lane, Frederic C. 1944. *Andrea Barbarigo, Merchants of Venice, 1418–1449*. Baltimore: Johns Hopkins University Press.

Lane, Frederic C. 1965. "Gino Luzzato's Contributions to the History of Venice: An Appraisal and Tribute." In *Studi e Testimonianze su Gino Luzzato*. Milan: Società Editrice Dante Aligheri, pp. 49–80.

Lane, Frederic C. 1968. "Venetian Shipping during the Commercial Revolution." In *Crisis and Change in the Venetian Economy in the Sixteenth and Seventeenth Centuries*, edited by Brian Pullan. London: Methuen, pp. 22–46.

Lane, Frederic C. 1973. *Venice: A Maritime Republic*. Baltimore: Johns Hopkins University Press.

Lapeyre, Henri. 1953. *Simon Ruiz et les "asientos" de Phillipe II*. Paris: Colin.

Lapeyre, Henri. 1955. *Une famille des marchands, Les Ruiz: Contribution à l'étude du commerce entre la France et l'Espagne au temps du Philippe II*. Paris: Colin.

Lauk, Kurt J. 1994. "Germany at the Crossroads: On the Efficiency of the German Economy." *Daedalus* 123(1) (Winter):57–83.

Lawrence, Robert Z. 1993. "Japan's Different Trade Regime: An Analysis with Particular Reference to *Keiretsu.*" *Journal of Economic Perspectives* 7(3) (Summer):3–20.

Lazonick, William. 1991. *Business Organization and the Myth of the Market Economy.* Cambridge: Cambridge University Press.

Letwin, William. 1969. *Sir Josiah Child, Merchant Economist.* Boston: Baker Library, Harvard Graduate School of Business Administration.

Levinson, Daniel J. 1978. *The Seasons of a Man's Life.* New York: Knopf.

Lévy-Leboyer, Maurice. 1964. *Les banques européenes et l'industrialization internationale dans la première moitié du XIXe siècle.* Paris: Presses Universitaires de France.

Lewis, W. Arthur. 1954. "Development with Unlimited Supplies of Labour." *The Manchester School* 22(2) (May):139–91.

Lindert, Peter H. and Keith Trace. 1971. "Yardsticks for British Entrepreneurs." In *Essays on a Mature Economy,* edited by Donald N. McCloskey. Princeton, N.J.: Princeton University Press, pp. 239–74.

Locke, Robert R. 1978. *Les fonderies et forges d'Alais à l'époque des premiers chemins de fer: La création d'une enterprise moderne.* Paris: Marcel Rivière et Cie.

Lodge, Eleanor C. 1931 (1970). *Sully, Colbert and Turgot: A Chapter in French Economic History.* Repr. Port Washington, Wis.: Kennikat Press.

Lopez, Robert S. 1951. "The Dollar of the Middle Ages." *Journal of Economic History* 11(3) (September):209–34.

Lorenz, Edward H. 1991. *Economic Decline in Britain: The Shipbuilding Industry, 1890–1970.* Oxford: Oxford University Press.

Lorenz, Edward H. 1993. "Crafting a Reply: British Shipbuilding Decline Revisited." *International Journal of Maritime History* 5(1) (June):239–48.

Lowe, John. 1993. "Letter from Kyoto." *The American Scholar* 62 (Autumn):571–79.

Lo Romer, David G. 1987. *Merchants and Reform in Leghorn, 1814–1868.* Berkeley: University of California Press.

Lucassen, Jan. 1984 (1987). *Migrant Labour in Europe, 1600–1900: The Drift to the North Sea.* Translated by Donald A. Bloch. London: Croom Helm.

Luther, Hans. 1964. *Vor dem Abgrund, 1930–1933: Reichsbankpräsident in Krisenzeiten.* Berlin: Propyläen.

Lüthy, Herbert. 1961. *De la banque aux finances (1730–1794).* Vol. 2 of *La Banque protestante en France de la révocation de l'édit de Nantes à la révolution.* Paris: S.E.V.P.E.N.

Lynch, John. 1964. *Empire and Absolutism, 1516–1598.* Vol. 1 of *Spain under the Habsburgs.* New York: Oxford University Press.

MacDougall, Sir Donald. 1954. "A Lecture on the Dollar Problem." *Economica* 21(203) (August):185–200.

Maddison, Angus. 1982. *Phases of Capitalist Development.* Oxford: Oxford University Press.

Maddison, Angus. 1989. *The World Economy in the 20th Century.* Paris: Organization for Economic Cooperation and Development.

Mann, Thomas. 1901 (1924). *Buddenbrooks.* New York: Knopf.

Marglin, Stephen A. 1974. "What Do Bosses Do?," part 1. *Review of Radical Political Economy* 6(2) (Summer):60–112.

Marglin, Stephen A. and Judith B. Schor, eds. 1990. *The Golden Age and Capitalism: Reinterpreting the Postwar Experience.* Oxford: Clarendon Press.

Marshall, Alfred. 1920. *Industry and Trade: A Study of Industrial Technique and Business Organization and of Their Influence on Various Classes and Nations*. London: Macmillan.

Marshall, Alfred. 1920. *Principles of Economics*. London: Macmillan.

Mathorez, J. 1919. *Les étrangers en France sous l'Ancien Régime: Histoire de la population française*. Vol. 1. Paris: Edouard Chapinon.

Matthews, R. C. O. 1968. "Why Has Britain Had Full Employment since the War?" *Economic Journal* 77(311) (September):558–69.

Matthews, R. C. O., C. H. Feinstein, and J. C. Odling-Smee. 1982. *British Economic Growth, 1856–1973*. Oxford: Clarendon Press.

Mauro, Frédéric. 1990. "Merchant Communities, 1350–1750." In *The Rise of Merchant Empires: Long Distance Trade in the Early Modern World, 1350–1750*, edited by James D. Tracey. Cambridge: Cambridge University Press, pp. 255–86.

Maxcy, George and A. Silberston. 1959. *The Motor Industry*. London: Allen & Unwin.

McClelland, David C. 1961. *The Achieving Society*. Princeton, N.J.: Van Nostrand.

McCloskey, Donald N. 1973. *Economic Maturity and Entrepreneurial Decline: British Iron and Steel, 1870–1913*. Cambridge, Mass.: Harvard University Press.

McCloskey, Donald N. and J. Richard Zecher. 1976. "How the Gold Standard Worked, 1880–1913." In *The Monetary Approach to the Balance of Payments*, edited by J. A. Frenkel and H. G. Johnson. Toronto: Toronto University Press.

McKinnon, Ronald I. 1963. *Money and Capital in Economic Development*. Washington, D.C.: Brookings Institution.

McKinnon, Ronald I. and Donald J. Mathieson. 1981. *How to Manage a Repressed Economy*. Princeton Essays in International Finance, no. 145 (December).

McNeill, William H. 1974a. *Venice: The Hinge of Europe, 1081–1797*. Chicago: University of Chicago Press.

McNeill, William H. 1974b. *The Shape of European History*. New York: Oxford University Press.

McNeill, William H. 1976. *Plagues and Peoples*. Garden City, N.Y.: Anchor Books.

McNeill, William H. 1982 [pb. 1984]. *The Pursuit of Power: Technology, Armed Force and Society since A.D. 1000*. Chicago: University of Chicago Press.

McNeill, William H. 1983. *The Great Frontier: Freedom and Hierarchy in Modern Times*. Princeton, N.J: Princeton University Press.

McNeill, William H. 1992. "History Over, World Goes On," a review of Francis Fukuyama, *The End of History and the Last Man. New York Times Book Review*, January 26, pp. 14–5.

Meilink-Roeloesz, M. A. P. 1962. *Asian Trade and European Influence in the Indonesian Archipelago between 1500 and about 1630*. The Hague: Martinus Nijhoff.

Meltzer, Allan H. 1991. "U.S. Leadership and Postwar Progress," unpublished paper.

Menéndez Pidal, Gonzalo. 1941. *Atlas historico Español*. Barcelona: Editora Nacional.

Meyer, J. R. 1955. "An Input-Output Approach to Evaluating the Influence of Exports in British Industrial Production in the Late 19th Century." *Explorations in Entrepreneurial History* 8:12–34.

Miller, J. Irwin. 1991. "Competing with our Ancestors." *Bulletin of the American Academy of Arts and Sciences* 44(7) (April):36–50.

Minchenton, W. E. 1957. *The British Tinplate Industry*. Oxford: Clarendon Press.

Minchenton, W. E. 1969. "Introduction." In *The Growth of Overseas Trade in the 17th and 18th Centuries*, edited by W. E. Minchenton. London: Metheun, pp. 1–51.

Minford, Patrick. 1993. "Reconstruction and the U.K. Postwar Welfare State: False Start and New Beginning." In *Postwar Economic Reconstruction and Lessons for the East Today*, edited by Rudiger Dornbusch, Wilhelm Rölling, and Richard Layard. Cambridge, Mass.: MIT Press, pp. 115–38.

Ministère du Commerce. 1919. *Rapport générale sur l'industrie française*. 3 vols. Paris: Imprimerie Nationale.

Ministère des Finances et Ministère de l'Agriculture du Commerce et des Travaux Publiques. 1867. *Enquête sur les principles et les faits généraux qui régissent la circulation monétaire et fiduciaire*. 6 vols. Paris: Imprimerie Impériale.

Miskimin, Harry. 1977. *The Economy of Late Renaissance Europe, 1450–1600*. Cambridge: Cambridge University Press.

Modelski, George. 1983. "Long Cycles of World Leadership." In *Contending Approaches to World Systems Analysis*, edited by William R. Thompson. Beverly Hills, Calif.: Sage Publications, pp. 15–139.

Modigliani, Franco. 1980. *The Life Cycle Hypothesis of Saving*. Vol. 2 of *The Collected Papers of Franco Modigliani*. Cambridge, Mass.: MIT Press.

Mokyr, Joel. 1977. *Industrial Growth and Stagnation in the Low Countries, 1800–1850*. New Haven, Conn.: Yale University Press.

Mokyr, Joel. 1985. "The Industrial Revolution and the New Economic History." In *The Economics of the Industrial Revolution*, edited by Joel Mokyr. No place stated: Rowman & Littlefield, pp. 1–51.

Mokyr, Joel. 1990. *The Lever of Riches: Technological Creativity and Economic Progress*. New York: Oxford University Press.

Mokyr, Joel. 1991. "Dear Labor, Cheap Labor and the Industrial Revolution." In *Favorites of Fortune: Technology, Growth and Economic Development since the Industrial Revolution*, edited by Patrice Higonnet, David S. Landes, and Henry Rosovsky. Cambridge, Mass.: Harvard University Press, pp. 177–200.

Mokyr, Joel. 1992a. "Technological Inertia in Economic History." *Journal of Economic History* 52(2) (June):325–38.

Mokyr, Joel. 1992b."Is Economic Change Optimal?" *Australian Economic History Review* 32(1):3–23.

Mokyr, Joel. 1992c. "Progress and Inertia in Technological Change." In *The Contest of Capitalism: Essays in Honor of R. M. Hartwell*, edited by John James and Mark Thomas. Chicago: University of Chicago Press.

Mokyr, Joel. 1994. "Cardwell's Law and the Political Economy of Technological Progress." *Research Policy* 23(5):561–74.

Mollat du Jourdain, Michel. 1993. *Europe and the Sea*. Translated by Teresa Lavander Faga. Oxford: Blackwell.

Moran, Theodore H. 1993. *America's Economic Policy and National Security*. New York: Council on Foreign Relations Press.

Morita, Akio. 1992. "A Critical Moment for Japanese Management." *Economic Eye* 13(3) (Autumn):4–9.

Mueller, Dennis C. 1988. "Anarchy, the Market and the State," *Southern Economic Journal* 54(4) (April):821–30.

Mulford, David. 1991. "The G-7 Strikes Back." *The International Economy* 5(4) (July–August):15–23.

Mun, Thomas. ca. (1662, 1664). *England's Treasure by Forraign Trade or, The Ballance of our Forraign Trade Is the Rule of our Treasure.* London: Thomas Clark.

Musgrave, P. M. 1967. *Technical Change, the Labour Force and Education: A Study of the British and German Iron and Steel Industries, 1860–1964.* Oxford: Pergamon Press.

Musson, A. E. 1972. "The Manchester School and the Exportation of Machinery." *Business History* 14(1) (January):17–50.

Musson, A. E. 1978. *The Growth of British Industry.* New York: Holmes and Meier.

Myllyntaus, Timo. 1990. *The Gatecrashing Apprentice: Industrializing Finland as an Adopter of New Technology.* Helsinki: Institute of Economic and Social History, University of Helsinki.

Nau, Henry R. 1990. *The Myth of America's Decline: Leading the World Economy into the 1990s.* New York: Oxford University Press.

Nef, John U. 1952. *War and Economic Progress: An Essay on the Rise of Industrial Civilization.* Chicago: University of Chicago Press.

Nelson, Richard R. and Gavin Wright. 1992. "The Rise and Fall of American Technological Leadership: The Postwar Era in Historical Perspective." *Journal of Economic Literature* 30(4) (December):1931–64.

New York Times. 1992. "Thus Sprach Helmut Kohl auf Deutsch," by Stephen Kinzer, February 23, p. 7.

New York Times. 1993. "At Deutsche Bank, View is Good," by Ferdinand Protzman, September 13, pp. D1, D4.

North, Douglass C. and Robert Paul Thomas. 1973. *The Rise and Fall of the Western World: A New Economic History.* Cambridge: Cambridge University Press.

North, Michael. 1990. *Geldumlauf und Wirtschaftskonjunktur im südlichen Osterraum am der Wende zur Neuzeit (1440–1570).* Sigmaringen: Thorbecke.

Noyes, Alexander Dana. 1938. *The Market Place: Reminiscences of a Financial Editor.* Boston: Little, Brown.

Nuland, Sherwin B. 1994. *How We Die: Reflections on Life's Final Chapter.* New York: Knopf.

Nye, Joseph S. Jr. 1990. *Bound to Lead: The Changing Nature of American Power.* New York: Basic Books.

O'Brien, Patrick K. 1990. "The Imperial Component in Decline of the British Economy before 1914." In *The Rise and Decline of the Nation State,* edited by M. Mann. Oxford: Blackwell, pp. 12–46.

O'Brien, P. K. 1991. "The Industrial Revolution: A Historiographical Survey." Mimeographed. Cited in N. F. R. Crafts and C. K. Harley. 1992. "Output Growth and the British Industrial Revolution: A Restatement of the Crafts-Harley View." *Economic History Review* 45(4): 704, note 7.

O'Brien, Patrick and Caglar Keyder. 1978. *Economic Growth in Britain and France, 1780–1914: Two Paths to the Twentieth Century.* London: Allen & Unwin.

Offer, Avner. 1993. "The British Empire, 1870–1914, A Waste of Money?" *Economic History Review* 46(2) (May):213–48.

Okazaki, Hisahiko. 1993. "Security Options for the Coming Age." *Economic Eye* 14(2) (Summer):19–24.

Okina, Yuri. 1993. "Resolution Methods for Bank Failure in Japan." *Japan Research Quarterly* 2(3) (Autumn):78–88.

Olson, Mancur. 1982. *The Rise and Decline of Nations: Economic Growth, Stagflation and Social Rigidities.* New Haven, Conn.: Yale University Press.

Omrod, David. 1974. "Dutch Commercial and Industrial Decline and British Growth in the Late Seventeenth and Early Eighteenth Centuries." In *Failed Transitions to Modern Industrial Society: Renaissance Italy and Seventeenth-Century Holland,* edited by Frederick Krantz and P. M. Hohenberg. Montreal: Interuniversity Center for European Studies, pp. 36–43.

Organzki, A. F. K. and J. Kuglar. 1981. *The War Ledger.* Chicago: University of Chicago Press.

Origo, Iris. 1957. *The Merchant of Prato, Francesco di Marco Datini.* New York: Knopf.

Ortega y Gasset, Jose. 1937. *Invertebrate Spain.* New York: Norton.

Outhwaite, R. B. 1969. *Inflation in Tudor and Early Stuart England.* London: Macmillan.

Parker, Geoffrey. 1972. *The Army of Flanders and the Spanish Road, 1567–1659: The Logistics of Spanish Victory and Defeat in the Low Countries Wars.* Cambridge: Cambridge University Press.

Parker, Geoffrey 1984. *The Thirty Years' War.* London: Routledge and Kegan Paul.

Parker, William N. 1984. *Europe and the World Economy.* Vol. 1 of *Europe, America and the Wider World: Essays on the Economic History of Western Capitalism.* Cambridge: Cambridge University Press.

Parker, William N. 1991. *America and the Wider World.* Vol. 2 of *Europe, America and the Wider World: Essays on the Economic History of Western Capitalism.* Cambridge: Cambridge University Press.

Parry, J. H. 1966. *The Spanish Seaborne Empire.* New York: Knopf.

Partridge, Eric. 1967. *A Dictionary of Slang and Unconventional English.* 6th ed. New York: Macmillan.

Phillips, Carla Rahn. 1986. *Six Galleons for the King of Spain.* Baltimore: Johns Hopkins University Press.

Phillips, Carla Rahn. 1990. "The Growth and Composition of Trade in the Iberian Peninsula." In *The Rise and Fall of Merchant Empires: Long-Distance Trade in the Early Modern World, 1350–1750,* edited by James D. Tracey. Cambridge: Cambridge University Press, pp. 34–101.

Phillips, W. H. 1989. "The Economic Performance of Late Victorian Britain: Traditional Historians and Growth." *Journal of European Economic History* 18(2) (Fall):393–414.

Pike, Ruth. 1972. *Aristocrats and Traders: Sevillian Society in the Sixteenth Century.* Ithaca, N.Y.: Cornell University Press.

Pinto, Diana. 1992. "The Great European Sea Change." *Daedalus* 121(4) (Fall):129–50.

Pirenne, Henri. 1933 (1936). *Economic and Social History of Medieval Europe.* Translated by I. E. Clegg. New York: Harcourt Brace and World.

Pitts, Jesse. 1957. "The Bourgeois Family and French Economic Retardation." Unpublished doctoral thesis in sociology, Harvard University, Cambridge, Mass.

Pitts, Jesse. 1964. "Continuity and Change in Bourgeois France." In *In Search of France,* edited by Stanley Hoffmann et al. Cambridge, Mass.: Harvard University Press, pp. 235–304.

Platt, D. C. M. 1984. *Foreign Finance in Europe and the USA, 1815–1870: Quantities, Origins, Functions and Distribution.* London: Allen & Unwin.

Plessis, Alain. 1985. *La politique de la Banque de France de 1851 à 1870.* Geneva: Droz.

Plummer, Alfred. 1937. *New British Industries in the Twentieth Century.* London: Pitman.

Pollard, Sidney. 1974. *European Economic Integration, 1815–1970.* New York: Harcourt Brace Jovanovich.

Pollard, Sidney and Paul Robertson. 1979. *The British Shipbuilding Industry, 1870–1914.* Cambridge, Mass.: Harvard University Press.

Pollin, Robert. 1990. *Deeper in Debt: The Changing Financial Condition of U.S. Households.* Washington, D.C.: Economic Policy Institute.

Poni, Carlo. 1970. "Archeologie de la fabrique: la diffusion des moulin à soie 'alla Bolognese' dans les Etats Venetiens du XVIème siècle." Preprint of paper presented to the Colloque International on "L'industrialization en Europe au XIXème siècle," Lyons, October 7–10.

Postan, M. M. 1967. *An Economic History of Western Europe, 1945–1964.* London: Methuen.

Posthumus, N. W. 1928 (1969). "The Tulip Mania in Holland in the Years 1636 and 1637." Reprinted in *The Economic Development of Western Europe: The Sixteenth and Seventeenth Centuries,* edited by Warren C. Scoville and J. Clayburn La Force. Lexington, Mass.: D. C. Heath, pp. 138–49.

Powelson, John P. 1994. *Centuries of Endeavor: Parallel Paths in Japan and Europe, and their Contrast with the Third World.* Ann Arbor: University of Michigan Press.

Prestwich, Michael. 1979. "Italian Merchants in Late Thirteenth and Early Fourteenth Century England." In the Dawn of Modern Banking, Center for Medieval and Renaissance Studies, University of California at Los Angeles; New Haven, Conn.: Yale University Press.

Prewitt, Kenneth. 1993. "America's Research Universities under Scrutiny." *Daedalus* 122(4) (Fall):85–99.

Pullan, Brian, ed. 1968. *Crisis and Change in the Venetian Economy in the Sixteenth and Seventeenth Centuries.* London: Methuen.

Pyle, Kenneth B. 1988. "Japan, the World and the Twenty-First Century." In *The Changing International Context,* Vol. 2 of *The Political Economy of Japan,* edited by Takashi Inoguchi and Daniel I. Okimoto. Stanford, Calif.: Stanford University Press, pp. 446–86.

Rapp, Richard Tilden. 1976. *Industry and Economic Decline in Seventeenth-Century Venice.* Cambridge, Mass.: Harvard University Press.

Rappard, William. 1914. *La révolution industrielle et les origines de la protection légale du travail en Suisse.* Berne: Stämfli.

Reddy, William M. 1987. *Money and Liberty in Modern Europe: A Critique of Historical Understanding.* Cambridge: Cambridge University Press.

Redlich, Fritz. 1968. "Frühindustrielle Unternehmer und ihre Probleme im Lichte ihrer Selbszeugnisse." In *Wirtschafts- und sozialgeschichtliche Probleme der frühen Industrializierung,* edited by Wolfram Fischer. Berlin: Colloquium Verlag, pp. 339–413.

Riesman, David, Nathan Glazer, and Reuel Denny. 1950. *The Lonely Crowd.* New Haven, Conn.: Yale University Press.

Riley, James C. 1980. *International Government Finance and the Amsterdam Capital Market, 1740–1815*. Cambridge: Cambridge University Press.

Rimmer, W. G. 1960. *Marshall of Leeds, Flax-Spinners*. Cambridge: Cambridge University Press.

Ringrose, David R. 1983. *Madrid and the Spanish Economy, 1560–1850*. Berkeley: University of California Press.

Ritter, Ulrich Peter. 1961. *Die Rolle des Staates in den Frühstadien der Industrialiserung*. Berlin: Duncker und Humblot.

Rivlin, Alice M. 1992. *Reviving the American Dream: The Economy, the States and the Federal Government*. Washington, D.C.: Brookings Institution.

Roberts, J. M. 1953. "Lombardy." In *The European Nobility in the Eighteenth Century: Studies of the Major European States in the Pre-Reform Era*, edited by A. Goodwin. London: Adam and Charles Black, pp. 60–82.

Robson, R. 1957. *The Cotton Industry in Britain*. London: Macmillan.

Rogers, Francis M. 1989. "Portugal: European, Hispanic or Sui Generis?" In *Iberian Identity: Essays on the Nature and Identity of Portugal and Spain*, edited by Richard Herr and John H. R. Pont. Berkeley: University of California Press, pp. 71–78.

Romano, Ruggiero. 1968. "Economic Aspects of the Construction of Warships in the Sixteenth Century." In *Crisis and Change in the Venetian Economy in the Sixteenth and Seventeenth Centuries*, edited by Brian Pullan. London: Methuen, pp. 59–87.

Rosenberg, Nathan and L. E. Birdzell, Jr. 1986. *How the West Grew Rich: The Economic Transformation of the Industrial World*. New York: Basic Books.

Rosencrance, Richard. 1990. *America's Economic Resurgence: A Bold New Strategy*. New York: Harper and Row.

Rostow, W. W. 1960. *The Stages of Economic Growth: A Non-Communist Manifesto*. Cambridge: Cambridge University Press.

Rostow, W. W. 1990. *Theorists of Economic Growth from David Hume to the Present, with a Perspective on the Next Century*. New York: Oxford University Press.

Rostow, W. W. 1991. "Technology and the Economic Theorists: Past, Present, Future." In *Favorites of Fortune: Technology, Growth and Economic Development since the Industrial Revolution*, edited by Patrice Higonnet, David S. Landes, and Henry Rosovsky. Cambridge, Mass.: Harvard University Press, pp. 395–431.

Rostow, W. W. 1992. "Policy for a Viable American Economy." Paper submitted to the Senate Committee on Banking, Housing and Urban Affairs, April 7.

Rubenstein, W. D. 1980. "Modern Britain." In *Wealth and the Wealthy in the Modern World*, edited by W. D. Rubenstein. New York: St. Martin's Press, pp. 46–89.

Rubenstein, W. D. 1993. *Capitalism, Culture and Decline in Britain, 1750–1990*. London: Routledge.

Rudé, George. 1972. *Europe in the Eighteenth Century: Aristocracy and the Bourgeois Challenge*. Cambridge, Mass.: Harvard University Press.

Rupieper, Hermann J. 1979. *The Cuno Government and Reparations, 1922–23: Politics and Economics*. The Hague: Martinius Nijhoff.

Sakaiya, Taichi. 1993. "Lifting the Heavy Hand of Bureaucratic Guidance." *Economic Eye* 14(2) (Summer):29–32.

Sakuta, Masaharu. 1993. "Why Is Japanese Housing So Expensive?" *Japan Research Quarterly* 2(3) (Summer):89–98.

Salter, W. E. G. 1960. *Productivity and Technical Change*. Cambridge: Cambridge University Press.

Saul, S. B. 1968. "The Engineering Industry." In *The Development of British Industry and Foreign Competition, 1875–1914*, edited by Derek H. Aldcrost. London: George Allen & Unwin, pp. 186–237.

Sauvy, Alfred. 1954 (1989). "La programme économique et financière de Mendès France." In Comité pour l'Histoire Economique et Financière de la France, *Etudes et Documents, I*. Paris: Imprimerie Nationale, pp. 493–524.

Sauvy, Alfred. 1960. *La montée des jeunes*. Paris: Calman-Lévy.

Saxonhouse, Gary N. 1993. "What Does Japanese Trade Structure Tell Us about Japanese Trade Policy?" *Journal of Economic Perspectives* 7(3) (Summer): 21–43.

Schama, Simon. 1977 (1992). *Patriots and Liberators: Revolution in the Netherlands, 1760–1813*. New York: Vintage Books.

Schama, Simon. 1988. *The Embarrassment of Riches: An Interpretation of the Dutch Culture of the Golden Age*. Berkeley: University of California Press.

Schor, Juliet B. 1992. *The Overworked American: The Unexpected Decline of Leisure*. New York: Basic Books.

Schramm, Percy Ernest. 1969. "Hamburg und die Adelsfrage (bis 1806)." *Zeitschrift des Vereins für Hamburgische Geschichte* 55:81–93.

Schuker, Stephen A. 1976. *The End of French Predominance in Europe: The Financial Crisis of 1924 and the Adoption of the Dawes Plan*. Chapel Hill: University of North Carolina Press.

Schumpeter, Joseph A. 1939. *Business Cycles: A Theoretical, Historical and Statistical Analysis of the Capitalist Process*. 2 vols. New York: McGraw-Hill.

Scoville, Warren C. 1960. *The Persecution of Huguenots and French Economic Development, 1680–1720*. Los Angeles: University of California Press.

Sella, Domenico. 1968a. "Crisis and Transformation in Venetian Trade." In *Crisis and Change in the Venetian Economy in the Sixteenth and Seventeenth Centuries*, edited by Brian Pullan. London: Methuen, pp. 88–105.

Sella, Domenico. 1968b. "The Rise and Fall of the Venetian Woolen Industry." In *Crisis and Change in the Venetian Economy in the Sixteenth and Seventeenth Centuries*, edited by Brian Pullan. London: Methuen, pp. 106–26.

Sella, Domenico. 1970 (1974). "European Industries, 1500–1700." In *The Sixteenth and Seventeenth Centuries*, edited by Carlo M. Cipolla. Vol. 2 of *The Fontana Economic History of Europe*. Glasgow: Collins/Fontana Books, pp. 354–426.

Sella, Domenico. 1974a. "The Two Faces of the Lombardy Economy in the Seventeenth Century." In *Failed Transitions to Modern Industrial Society: Renaissance Italy and Seventeenth-Century Holland*, edited by Frederick Krantz and Paul M. Hohenberg. Montreal: Interuniversity Center for European Studies, pp. 11–18.

Sella, Domenico. 1974b. "Italy." Participants' discussion in *Failed Transitions to Modern Industrial Society: Renaissance Italy and Seventeenth-Century Holland*, edited by Frederick Krantz and Paul M. Hohenberg. Montreal: Interuniversity Center for European Studies, p. 31.

Semmel, Bernard. 1970. *The Rise of Free Trade Imperialism: Classical Political*

Economy, the Empire of Free Trade and Imperialism, 1750–1850. Cambridge: Cambridge University Press.

Servan-Schreiber, Jean-Jacques. 1968. *The American Challenge.* New York: Atheneum Publishers.

Shafer, Byron E., ed. 1991. *Is America Different? A New Look at American Exceptionalism.* Oxford: Clarendon Press.

Shaw, L. M. E. 1989. "The Inquisition and the Portuguese Economy." *Journal of European Economic History* 18(2) (Fall):415–32.

Shell Briefing Service. 1991. *Research and Development in the Oil Industry,* no. 4. London: Royal Dutch/Shell Group.

Shimada, Haruo. 1992. "Japanese Capitalism: The Irony of Success." *Economic Eye* 13(2):28–32.

Sideri, Sandro. 1970. *Trade and Power: Informal Colonialism in Anglo-Portuguese Relations.* Rotterdam: Rotterdam University Press.

Skidelsky, (Lord) Robert. 1994. *John Maynard Keynes: The Economist as Savior, 1920–1937.* Volume 2 of a 3-vol. biography. New York: Viking Penguin.

Skolnikoff, Eugene B. 1993. "Knowledge without Borders: The Internationalization of the Research University." *Daedalus* 122(4) (Fall):225–52.

Slicher van Bath, Bernard Hendrik. 1982. "The Economic Situation in the Dutch Republic during the Seventeenth Century." In *Dutch Capitalism and World Capitalism,* edited by Maurice Aymard. Cambridge: Cambridge University Press, pp. 23–35.

Smith, Adam. 1759 [11th ed. 1808]). *The Theory of Moral Sentiments, or an Essay toward an Analysis of the Principles by which Men Naturally Judge Concerning the Conduct and Character, First of the Neighbors, and Afterward of Themselves.* Edinburgh: Bell and Bradfute.

Smith, Adam. 1776 (1937). *The Wealth of Nations.* New York: Modern Library.

Smith, Cyril Stanley. 1970. "Art, Technology and Science: Notes on their Historical Interaction." *Technology and Culture* 2(4) (October):494–549.

Smith, Cyril Stanley. 1975. "Metallurgy and Human Experience," the 1974 Distinguished Lectureship in Materials and Society. *Metallurgical Transactions, A.,* 6A(4) (April).

Spooner, Frank C. 1983. *Risks at Sea: Amsterdam Insurance and Maritime Europe, 1766–1780.* Cambridge: Cambridge University Press.

Starr, Chester G. 1989. *The Influence of Sea Power on Ancient History.* New York and Oxford: Oxford University Press.

Steensgaard, Niels. 1973. *Carracks, Caravans and Companies: Crisis of the European-Asian Trade in the Early 17th Century.* Copenhagen: Scandinavian Institute of Asian Studies, Monograph Series No. 17.

Steinberg, Siegfried Henry. 1968. "The Thirty Years' War: Economic Life." *Encyclopedia Britannica,* 14th ed., vol. 21, p. 1060.

Stendhal, Henri Beyle. 1835 (1960). *Lucien Leuwen.* Paris: Gallimard.

Strange, Susan. 1971. *Sterling and British Policy: A Political Study of an International Currency in Decline.* London: Oxford University Press.

Subrahmanyam, Sanjay and Louis Filipe R. R. Thomas. 1991. "Evolution of Empire: The Portuguese in the Indian Ocean During the Sixteenth Century." In *The Political Economy of Merchant Empires: State Power and Trade, 1350–1750,* edited by James D. Tracy. Cambridge: Cambridge University Press, pp. 298–331.

Sutch, Richard. 1991. "All Things Reconsidered: The Life-Cycle Perspective and the Third Task of Economic History." *Journal of Economic History* 51(2) (June):271–88.

Swart, K. W. 1975. "Holland's Bourgeoisie and the Retarded Industrialization of the Netherlands." In *Failed Transitions to Modern Industrial Society: Renaissance Italy and Seventeenth-Century Holland*, edited by Frederick Krantz and Paul M. Hohenberg. Montreal: Interuniversity Center for European Studies, pp. 44–48.

Takeda, Masahiko and Philip Turner. 1992. "The Liberalization of Japanese Financial Markets: Some Major Themes." *BIS Economic Papers*, no. 34 (November).

Tavlas, George S. 1991. "On the International Use of Currencies: The Case of the Deutsche Mark." *Essays in International Finance*, no. 181 (March). Princeton, N.J.: International Finance Section.

Tavlas, George S. and Yuzura Ozeki. 1992. "The Internationalization of Currencies: An Appraisal of the Japanese Yen." International Monetary Fund. Occasional Paper no. 90 (January).

Temin, Peter. 1966. "The Relative Decline of the British Steel Industry, 1880–1913." In *Industrialization in Two Systems: Essays in Honor of Alexander Gerschenkron*, edited by Henry Rosovsky. New York: John Wiley.

Temin, Peter. 1989. *Lessons from the Great Depression*. Cambridge, Mass.: MIT Press.

Thackray, Arnold. 1973. Seminar on "Natural Knowledge and Cultural Context: A Case Study in the Technical, Social and Cultural Background of Scientific Change in the Industrial Revolution." MIT, Cambridge, Mass., May 2.

Thirsk, Joan and J. P. Cooper, eds. 1972. *17th Century Economic Documents*. Oxford: Clarendon Press.

Thompson, E. P. 1963. *The Making of the English Working Class*. New York: Pantheon Book.

Thuillier, Guy. 1959. *Georges Dufaud et les débuts du grand capitalisme dans la métallurgie, en Nivernais, au XIXᵉ siècle*. Paris: S.E.V.P.E.N.

Tilly, Richard H. 1968. "Los von England: Probleme des Nationalismus in der deutschen Wirtschaftsgeschichte." *Zeitschrift für die gesamte Staatswissenschaft* 124(1) (February):179–96.

Tilly, Richard. 1993. "Review" of Giersch, Paqué and Schmieding, *The Fading Miracle* (1992). *Journal of Economic History* 53(4) (December):942–43.

Tracy, James D. 1985. *A Financial Revolution in Habsburg Netherlands: Renten and Rentiers in the County of Holland, 1515–1565*. Berkeley: University of California Press.

Tsuru, Shigeto. 1993. *Japan's Capitalism: Creative Defeat and Beyond*. Cambridge: Cambridge University Press.

van der Wee, Herman. 1963. *The Growth of the Antwerp Market and the European Economy (fourteenth–sixteenth centuries)*. 3 vols. The Hague: Martinus Nijoff.

van der Wee, Herman. 1988. "Industrial Dynamics and the Process of Urbanization and De-Urbanization in the Low Countries from the Late Middle Ages to the Eighteenth Century: A Synthesis." In *The Rise and Decline of Urban Industries in Italy and the Low Countries (Late Middle Ages–Early Modern Times)*, edited by Herman van der Wee. Leuven: Leuven University Press, pp. 307–81.

Vanek, Jaroslav. 1963. *The Natural Resource Content of United States Foreign Trade, 1870–1955.* Cambridge, Mass.: MIT Press.

van Houtte, J. A. 1964. "Anvers." In *Città Mercanti Dottrine nell'Economia Europea dal IV al XVIII Secolo, Saggi in Memoria Gino Luzzato,* edited by Amintore Fanfani. Milan: A Giuffre, pp. 297–319.

van Houtte, J. A. 1967. *Bruges: Essai d'histoire urbaine.* Brussels: La Renaissance du Livre.

van Houtte, Jan A. 1972. "Economic Development of Belgium and the Netherlands from the Beginning of the Modern Era." *Journal of European Economic History* 1(1) (Spring):100–20.

van Klavaren, Jacob. 1957. "Die historische Erscheinungen der Korruption." *Vierteljahrschrift für Sozial- und Wirtschaftsgeschichte* 44 (December): 289–324.

van Vleeck, Va Nee L. 1993. "Re-assessing Technological Backwardness: Absolving the Silly, Little Bobtailed Coal Car." Unpublished Ph.D. dissertation, University of Iowa.

Vergeot, J.-B. 1918. *Le crédit comme stimulant et régulateur de l'industrie: La conception saint-simonienne, ses réalizations, son application au problème bancaire d'après-guerre.* Paris: Jouve.

Vernon, Raymond. 1966. "International Investment and International Trade in the Product Cycle." *Quarterly Journal of Economics* 80(2) (May):190–207.

Veseth, Michael. 1990. *Mountains of Debt: Crisis and Change in Renaissance Florence, Victorian Britain and Postwar America.* New York: Oxford University Press.

Vial, Jean. 1967. *L'industrialization de sidérurgie française, 1814–1864.* Paris: Mouton.

Vicens Vives, Jaime. 1952 (1967). *Approaches to the History of Spain.* Translated and edited by Joan Connally Ullman. Berkeley: University of California Press.

Vicens Vives, Jaime. 1970. "The Decline of Spain." In *The Economic Decline of Empires,* edited by Carlo M. Cipolla. London: Methuen, pp. 121–67.

Vilar, Pierre. 1969 (1976). *A History of Gold and Money, 1450–1920.* London: New Left Books.

Ville, Simon, ed. 1993. *Shipbuilding in the United Kingdom in the Nineteenth Century: A Regional Approach.* Research in Maritime History no. 4. St. Johns, Newfoundland: International Maritime Economic History Association et al.

Volcker, Paul A. and Toyoo Gyohten. 1992. *Changing Fortunes: The World's Money and the Threat to American Leadership.* New York: Times Books.

Wagner, Adolph. 1879. *Allgemeine oder theoretische Volkswirtschaftslehre.* Leipzig and Heidelberg: C. F. Verlagshandlung.

Walker, Mack. 1964. *Germany and the Emigration, 1816–1885.* Cambridge, Mass.: Harvard University Press.

Walker, Mack. 1971. *German Home Towns: Community, State and General Estate, 1648–1871.* Ithaca, N.Y., and London: Cornell University Press.

Wallerstein, Immanuel. 1980. *The Modern World-System II: Mercantilism and the Consolidation of the European World-Economy, 1600–1750.* New York: Academic Press.

Wallerstein, Immanuel. 1982. "Dutch Hegemony in the Seventeenth-Century World-Economy." In *Dutch Capitalism and World Capitalism,* edited by Maurice Aymard. Cambridge: Cambridge University Press, pp. 93–145.

Walter, Norbert. 1990. "Frankfurt Financial Centre Challenged by 1992." In

Financial Institutions in Europe under New Competitive Conditions, edited by Donald E. Fair and Christian de Boisseu. Dordrecht/Boston/Lancaster: Kluwer, pp. 145–57.

Weber, Eugen. 1976. *Peasants into Frenchmen: The Modernization of Rural France, 1870–1914*. Stanford, Calif.: Stanford University Press.

Wedgwood, Julia. 1915. *The Personal Life of Josiah Wedgwood*. London: Macmillan.

Wiener, Martin J. 1981. *English Culture and the Decline of the Industrial Spirit, 1850–1980*. Cambridge: Cambridge University Press.

Wijnberg, Nachoem M. 1992. "The Industrial Revolution and Industrial Economics." *Journal of European Economic History* 21(1) (Spring):153–67.

Williams, E. E. 1890. *Made In Germany*. 2nd ed. London: Heinemann.

Williams, E. N. 1970. *The Ancien Régime in Europe: Government and Society in the Major States, 1648–1789*. New York: Harper & Row.

Williamson, Jeffrey G. 1991. "Productivity and American Leadership." *Journal of Economic Literature* 39(1) (March):51–68.

Wilson, C. H. 1939 (1954). "The Economic Decline of the Netherlands." In *Essays in Economic History*, edited by E. M. Carus-Wilson. Vol. 1. London: Arnold, pp. 254–69.

Wilson, Charles. 1941 *Anglo-Dutch Commerce and Finance in the Eighteenth Century*. Cambridge: Cambridge University Press.

Wilson, R. G. 1971. *Gentlemen Merchants: The Merchant Community of Leeds, 1700–1830*. Manchester: Manchester University Press.

Wojnilower, Albert M. 1992. "Heresies Acquired in Forty Years as an Economics Practioner." Pamphlet, First Boston Asset Management.

Wood, Christopher. 1992. *The Bubble Economy: Japan's Extraordinary Boom in the 1980s and Dramatic Bust in the 1990s*. New York: Atlantic Monthly Press.

Woodham-Smith, Cecil. 1962. *The Great Hunger: Ireland*. New York: Harper & Row.

Woolf, S. J. 1968. "Venice and Terra Ferma: Problems of the Change from Commercial to Landed Activities." In *Crisis and Change in the Venetian Economy in the Sixteenth and Seventeenth Centuries*, edited by Brian Pullan. London: Methuen, pp. 175–203.

Wright, H. R. C. 1955. *Free Trade and Protection in the Netherlands, 1816–1830: A Study of the First Benelux*. Cambridge: Cambridge University Press.

Wylie, Laurence. 1957. *Village in the Vaucluse*. Cambridge, Mass.: Harvard University Press.

Yamazawa, Ippei. 1991. "The New Europe and the Japanese Strategy." *Revista di Politica Economica* 81(3) (May):631–53.

Young, Arthur. 1790 (1969). *Travels in France during the Years 1787, 1788 and 1789*. Garden City, N.Y.: Doubleday Anchor Book.

Zamagni, Vera. 1980. "The Rich in a Late Industrializer: The Case of Italy, 1800–1945." In *Wealth and the Wealthy in the Modern World*, edited by W. D. Rubenstein. New York: St. Martin's Press, pp. 122–66.

Zunkel, Friederich. 1962. *Der Rheinische-Westfälische Unternehmer, 1834–1879: Ein Beitrag zur Geschichte des deutsche Bürgertum im 19. Jahrhundert*. Cologne and Opladen: Westdeutsche Verlag.

Index